Peak Performa...

The authors are all affiliated with the University of Waikato Management School in New Zealand.

Professor Clive Gilson holds the Chair in Human Resource Management at the University of Waikato Management School and is also Editor of the Electronic Journal of Radical Organization Theory. He consults to the chief executives and top teams of some of the world's largest corporations. Professor Mike Pratt is Dean of the Waikato Management School and a specialist in accountability, leadership and organizational transformation. He too consults to the chief executives and top teams of some of the world's largest corporations.

Dr. Kevin Roberts holds a Professorship in Sustainable Enterprise at the University of Waikato Management School and is the Chief Executive of Saatchi & Saatchi Worldwide.

Dr Ed Weymes is Executive Director of International Relations at the University of Waikato Management School.

Website: www.mngt.waikato.ac.nz/ppo/
e-mail: ppo@waikato.ac.nz

Peak Performance

Inspirational Business Lessons
from the World's Top
Sports Organizations

CLIVE GILSON • MIKE PRATT
KEVIN ROBERTS • ED WEYMES

PROFILE BOOKS

This edition published in Great Britain in 2003 by
PROFILE BOOKS LTD
3A Exmouth House
Pine Street
London EC1R 0JH
www.profilebooks.com

First published in Great Britain by HarperCollins*Publishers* in 2001

3 5 7 9 10 8 6 4 2

Printed in the UK by CPI Bookmarque, Croydon, CR0 4TD

The moral right of the authors has been asserted.

A CIP catalogue record for this book is available from the British Library.

ISBN 978 1 86197 503 4

Foreword

A t some stage in our lives many of us are filled with an overwhelming desire or inspirational dream to achieve something
that we know will stretch our abilities to the utmost. But all too
often, sadly, the dream fades and we revert to being very normal
human beings.

I have often been asked the question "When you have spent some
years of your life devoted to achieving some great objective and you
finally succeed—is there a sense of anticlimax and does life become
rather empty for you?" I have known a few successful explorers who
have confessed to me that when their greatest imaginable challenge
has been achieved, they feel a little lost in the pressures of society. I
have tried to reignite their enthusiasm and focus, to seek out other
new challenges, for they are undoubtedly at their peak when they are
attempting the seemingly impossible.

Although a person of modest abilities, I have never experienced
this problem—I have always had half a dozen other adventures
churning around in my mind, so when one is completed I can automatically carry on to the next. I can well remember standing on top
of Mount Everest having reached the top of the world in every sense
of the term and looking east toward the great unclimbed summit of
Makalu. Instinctively my eyes followed up the mighty face of the
mountain and I automatically picked out a route by which Makalu
could be climbed—and was indeed climbed later by a strong French

expedition. I had achieved an ultimate success but I was still looking for new and exciting challenges. Real success is a continuing process—one's objectives may well change but one always has an eye for something new and exciting. The authors of the book you are about to read call this "greatest imaginable challenge."

During the eighty years of my life, my attitudes and purpose modified as my physical ability and experience developed. In my teens I was a reader and a dreamer about adventure. Then mountaineering captured my imagination and I strove with all my effort to be an outstanding member of each expedition. I was highly competitive and determined to be one of the leading climbers, and my fitness and motivation carried me through. In my forties the challenges remained but now they were different. In my organizational life, I was now the leader and planner, selecting the teams, raising the funds, and making the major decisions. They were great days in many ways. In later years I became deeply involved in a new inspirational dream—the welfare of the people of the Himalayas—building schools and medical clinics, mountain airfields and freshwater pipelines. Fund-raising around the world is a major effort and I quickly learned that the old story of my ascent of Mount Everest, many years before, still gave my name rather astonishing prestige.

I learned early to select my companions carefully. Mostly my decisions were based on the previous performance of team members. My own personal experience of them was important too but I sometimes listened to the views of friends whose knowledge I respected. But it was always vitally important to me to search out people with a good sense of humor and community. I have never warmed to those who have an exaggerated sense of their own importance. And the people I remember with respect and affection are those who can laugh when the going gets tough.

I once interviewed a young man who I had never met before but who had a reputation as a powerful and successful climber. He was a very self-effacing person who I automatically liked but he was most reluctant to talk about his achievements. I finally discovered that apart from his climbing successes he had also won a New Zealand canoeing medal. This was more like it! I asked him, "What do you have to do to be invited to participate in a canoeing championship?" He shrugged his shoulders. "The main thing is to have a canoe," he told me calmly. I chose him on the spot and he proved a great success.

There are some people who seem to be born leaders, but most of us have to learn to be inspirational players in organizational life. You need to have a clear picture in your mind about what you plan to do and yet be prepared to make a rapid change if a better proposition is presented to you. You have to be ready to listen without losing executive control. It is advisable to have turned over in your mind all possible alternatives so if an emergency occurs you can act immediately and overcome the problem. And it is enormously important that when total agreement has been reached you hand the task of implementation over to your colleagues, while ensuring that backup support is always available if something goes wrong. So I am a firm believer in both an individual and a team effort, but ultimately someone may have to make a final decision, and that's the leader's responsibility. Naturally, it is important that it is a sound and sensible decision.

My programs in the Himalayas are small yet complex, but over the years I have accumulated some expert assistants—both Sherpa and European. With their help we have worked together for thirty-five years responding to the expressed desires of the Himalayan mountain people. My life has been a busy one but I could have done little without the support of colleagues. We have worked together as a strong and motivated team—as indeed we did on Mount Everest—and it was reaching the summit of Mount Everest that made all the adventures and programs possible.

Big or small projects carried out by the famous sports organizations featured here, or any business, demand a similar philosophy for success. I believe that the theory that is presented by the authors of this book also works rather well for our projects in the remote Himalayas. Peak performance is indeed the challenge.

—Sir Edmund Hillary
Auckland
January 2000

Acknowledgments

O ur special thanks go to all our case study organizations and in
particular to those to whom we spoke and whose names are included within our narrative. Without them we would have had no
book and no Peak Performing Organization (PPO) Theory. We were
honored to be admitted as temporary honorary members of their
PPO families, and the enduring friendships that have developed from
the project are an ongoing privilege. Not all the organizations we interviewed made it through to the finals of this edition. We nonetheless
much appreciate the time and assistance they gave us.

The logistics behind this project were highly complex. Although
every one of our participants enabled us to see and understand
things better, we need to thank additionally those who spent considerable time and effort ensuring that our visits ran smoothly. We were
always well aware that the daily demands placed on these organizations were huge, but our "handlers" nevertheless generously gave up
their valuable time for us. Our special thanks go to Jane Gorard
(Williams), Bill Duffy (San Francisco 49ers), Bob Wolfe (Atlanta
Braves), Steve Schanwald (Chicago Bulls), Carley Baker (Netball
Australia), Pam Tye (Women's Hockey Australia), Gwen Lloyd (FC
Bayern Munich), Kristen Sneyd (Team New Zealand), David Moffet
(New Zealand Rugby Union), Wolfgang Niersbach (German Foot-
ball Association), Ray Philips (Australian Cricket Board), Lonn

9

Trost (New York Yankees), and Aaron Heifitz (U.S. Women's Soccer). Maryanne Schneider, from the University of Western Australia, hosted and helped to prepare our visits to Perth where we met Women's Hockey Australia officials and team members and Australian Cricket Board coaching staff.

We sincerely thank University of Waikato vice-chancellor Professor Bryan Gould for his support for our project and for his belief in its potential importance to the university. Our PPO project began as part of our search for a better way, beyond the MBA, and we continue to drive it to that end. We thank our colleagues at the University of Waikato Management School for stimulating conversations about excellence in organizations, and our students in MBA and Ph.D. programs for their critical and constructive feedback on early versions of PPO Theory.

Sarah Knox, in particular, provided peak performing research assistance, assistance with theory development, and critical commentary on our drafts. Many of our friends and colleagues, who spent considerable time reading early versions of chapters, provided vital feedback throughout the project. The unrelenting critical eyes and sharp reflections of Dorothy Gilson, Helga Pratt, Delwyn Clark, and Carolyn Boell of Saatchi & Saatchi undoubtedly improved the final product. Carolyn Boell also provided superb logistical support and field research assistance with women's teams. Bobbie Wisneski and Sarah Knox manage the treasured memorabilia that we accumulated during our travels, and Bobbie and Claire McIntosh expertly juggled logistics to facilitate our focus on writing. Our project required thousands of pages of transcribing. Lorraine Brown-Simpson, who heads up the transcription services at the University of Waikato, and her staff, helped to bring the project to life by producing the raw data from our many interviews. Nicky Haisman also ably assisted by transcribing some of our interviews.

We are indebted to Kate Pope of College Hill for patiently and engagingly introducing us to the world of global publishing. Our agent, Mark Lucas of Lucas Alexander Whitley, transformed the project by suggesting the idea of organizational storytelling. Until

Mark's intervention we had been proceeding down the path of a traditional business book, with chapters devoted to each element of the theory and examples drawn from all the research.

On a more personal level, we owe the most to our families and partners. They have encouraged us when things went wrong and excused our preoccupation when the project was in flow. They have shared our dream.

CLIVE GILSON
MIKE PRATT
KEVIN ROBERTS
ED WEYMES

Contents

Introduction

Is it possible to achieve sustained peak performance and keep exceeding an organization's best year after year?

Given that people in organizations—even star performers—come and go, can we discover why certain organizations keep on winning?

To seek answers to these questions we chose to study the most competitive domain of all human activities. Elite professional sports provide entertainment and involvement on a global scale. Fifty-five billion television viewers are attracted to Formula One Grand Prix motor races during a season. Nearly two billion people watched the 1998 World Cup Soccer finals, and the cumulative audience throughout the World Cup was thirty-seven billion people. An estimated six billion people watched the America's Cup 2000. One hundred thirty-three million people in the United States and eight billion households worldwide watched the last Super Bowl.[1] Elite sports engender passion, grueling hard work, sacrifice, and dedication to the greatest imaginable challenges in its participants. Riches beyond imagination are certainly available in today's sporting areas for those capable of sustained peak performance. But for the dedicated professional, sports is not just a job—it is a way of life. And this focus that players exhibit is mirrored in the millions of dedicated fans around the globe who seek more than entertainment from their dedication to a particular sport. They experience passion, elation, and heartache and they

---

1 *http://www.nfl.com/sb33/news/981204facts.html*

secure meaning and purpose from their commitment to their chosen sport. An incredible link is forged among individuals—players and fans—who have never met. But this person-to-person connection is temporary; the permanent link is between the fan and the organization itself.

We believe there are general organizational ideas that enable people to work together enjoyably and effectively toward the organization's greatest imaginable challenge. Where better to search for these ideas than in the teams and organizations of elite sports, the icons of the late twentieth century? One of the benefits of choosing sports industries to study peak performing organization relates to outcomes. Sport offers a simple yet effective measure of success, the win record.

Because peak performance derives from sports psychology, it constitutes by far the most rigorously researched domain of elite human endeavor. We reasoned that, if we were ever to discover a coherent theory that explained peak performance, it would probably be found in the sports industry. In this sense, the choice of research domain was almost decided for us. Elite team sports, by their nature, have significant organizations supporting them, and we hoped to observe peak performance within an organizational context rather than on an individual basis. Given that all our chosen organizations have experienced sustained success, and that players come and go, we assumed that organization would have a great deal to do with the winning formula. This proposition proved to be correct.

Our approach is different from that of conventional business books, which are rarely grounded in explicit data and are usually marked by a rapid rush to assert how ideas might be implemented immediately. Even research-based business books often present only the authors' conclusions, which deny readers access to the deeper and richer insights available from directly comparing their own experiences with the stories. In contrast, by telling stories about peak performance we will show you how you can discover your own path to greatness.

We would like to introduce ourselves. We are from the University of Waikato Management School. Clive Gilson is professor of Human Resource Management, Mike Pratt is dean, Kevin Roberts is a senior fellow and chief executive of Saatchi & Saatchi plc, and Ed Weymes is associate dean. We have each lived on several continents. We fly tens of thousands of miles a year in our roles as academics, consultants, and executives. We have all chosen New Zealand as our home base. From this edge-dweller vantage point, we have observed passing trends in organizational theory and attempted to apply them. And we have found them wanting.

We have experienced a parade of military models and metaphors for management over our working lives. We have devised strategies to destroy the competition, launched preemptive strikes, deployed sales forces to capture customers, and fired staff in re-engineering, rightsizing, and restructuring exercises. We think managers and staff would prefer to go to work to have fun than to wage war. This book is about making work both fun and peak performing.

We have used conventional organization theory throughout our professional and academic lives and have observed with great interest the new theories of management superstars such as Peters and Waterman (1982), Senge (1993), and Collins and Porras (1994). Yet we have been troubled both by the frequent appearance of conflicting ideas of effective organizing and their tendency to appear and disappear without trace. The ephemeral nature of many of these ideas led us to examine their origins and to discover new terrain. We were particularly interested in the sustainability of outstanding performance.

The search for effectiveness lies at the center of organization endeavor. Tools from traditional organization theory have proved to be less than useful; in effect they are tainted because they include data from all organizations, excellent or otherwise. In 1982, Tom Peters and Robert Waterman, in their book *In Search of Excellence*, narrowed the data to those organizations that were deemed to be high-performing organizations (HPOs). They conducted anecdotal inquiries in an array of unrelated clients, which were defined as excellent by attribution rather than by reference to objective criteria. However, the concepts used to understand HPOs are still mired in the language and metaphor of organization theory, which distorts the picture. In contrast, our theory of peak performing organizations (PPO) uses a single sharply focused lens.

In *Built to Last*, Collins and Porras (1994) identified the distinguishing characteristics of eighteen "visionary" companies that have maintained high performance and compared these with the practices of a group of good but not outstanding performers. The organizations were selected by explicit criteria (premier institutions in their industry, widely admired by their peers, have made an indelible impact on the world, have experienced multiple generations of chief executives, and were founded prior to 1950). The resulting group has outperformed the stock market by more than fifteen times since 1926. However, they used secondary data to analyze these companies rather than in-depth empirical investigation, and the result lacks the richness of firsthand inquiry, which leads to difficulty in implementation. By contrast, the principles and concepts that constitute PPO Theory are based on firsthand empirical research. They are derived from what we observed and heard in the elite sports organizations that were the domain of our study.

Organization theory provided us with a benchmark for our research. Richard Daft, author of the most popular textbook on organization theory, defines organizations as: "(1) social entities that (2) are goal-directed, (3) are designed as deliberately structured and coordinated activity systems, and (4) are linked to the external environment" (1998, 11). He explains organization theory as "a way of thinking about organizations" (20). He states that "the way to see and think about organizations is based upon patterns and regularities in organizational design and behavior" (21). We sought these patterns in an elite subset of organizations and presumed that while traditional organization theory would provide some guidance, the concepts were unlikely to be directly applicable, or sufficient to explain the peak performance of these organizations.

There is a long-established tradition of generating organization theory through observation of cases in a specific organizational setting. For example, Geert Hofstede developed his theories of organizational culture by studying IBM companies throughout the world (1997), while Burns and Stalker developed their influential ideas of mechanistic and organic organizations by reference to fifteen organizations in the UK electronics industry (1961). We have followed that tradition, but have situated ourselves within the world of elite sports rather than high tech or electronics.

The Research

So how was the research conducted? We spent three years traveling to sports organizations around the world, prompted by a deep dissatisfaction with old-world management ideas and a belief that there had to be a better way. Because we were forced to reject long-cherished academic concepts of what leads to highly effective organizations, the intellectual journey took us much farther than the miles we covered. Our former ideas simply did not sit comfortably alongside everything that we heard and observed.

We studied the world's consistently most successful sports organizations, across different sports codes, countries, and cultures. In this book are U.S. Women's Soccer, FC Bayern Munich, WilliamsF1, Team New Zealand, the Atlanta Braves, the New York Yankees, the New Zealand Rugby Football Union, the San Francisco 49ers, the Chicago Bulls, Netball Australia, Women's Hockey Australia and the Australian Cricket Board. We spent time in their organizations; we observed; we listened.

The sports we chose were team-based and global, with a critical mass of competitors and high participation rates in the general population. The teams we selected were championship contenders at the time of the study, had exhibited continuous championship contention for at least a decade, and were recognized as leaders in the sport. We also ensured that we analyzed as diverse a range of sports organizations as possible.

Such is the passion engendered by sport that we know many readers, having read the criteria for inclusion, will wish to challenge our selection, particularly if their team is not among our chosen elite. We wish to make it clear that these are not the only peak performing sports organizations that exist, and that in some cases we could have made a different choice. We believe that no one will dispute, however, the amazing records of sustained success achieved by these organizations. Their inside organizational stories are fascinating, and many of them are previously untold. Descriptions of the win records upon which our selection was based appear in "The Teams" at the end of the book.

Our focus is on the role played by the organization, rather than on the teams and players themselves. In order to carry out this research, we gained unprecedented inside access to their stories. Our research question was, "How do organizations sustain peak performance?" In our interviews this translated into a more colloquial, "How do you keep on winning?"

Our project methodology was based on building theories from case study research, as explained by Eisenhardt (1989). The sporting organizations we spoke to were businesses, in many cases very large and successful businesses, with a razor-edged competitive spirit. By definition, the search for competitive advantage within each sports code is always relentless and unforgiving. All the organizations exist within the fast-changing entertainment industry, in which competition for disposable cash is fierce. With the advent of each new season and competition, the games begin afresh. To sustain peak performance in such environments requires organizational excellence.

We spoke to more than 500 organizational participants including owners, players, coaches, managers, marketers, finance people, engineers, referees, board members, ushers, cleaners, ticket sellers, fans, and receptionists. In each case we watched games and went behind the scenes. For example, we spent time in the pit garage during the Grand Prix season with WilliamsF1, racing on the Black Magic boats with Team New Zealand, in the locker room with Michael Jordan and the Chicago Bulls, and at spring training with the Atlanta Braves. We listened intently, intrigued by the similarity of the answers, across countries, cultures, and codes, to our research question, "How does your organization keep on winning?" We anticipated that it would be unlikely that a world-class sports team could be continuously in contention without world-class organization. You will see from the subsequent stories that this proved to be the case.

We used multiple data-collection methods including interviews, focus groups, participant observation, and archival material. All interviews were tape-recorded and subsequently transcribed. We amassed a staggering amount of data: 4,000 pages as well as piles of archival material. Key to our research were our field notes of significant observations. These enabled us to focus on the important lessons from each case, as we agreed on these by consensus after each set of interviews or observations. Two or more researchers conducted almost all the interviews. The interviews were considered carefully after each round, and again after the transcriptions of the tapes had been completed. These conversations were pursued until there was a convergence of perceptions within the research team.

During the case study debrief we identified words and ideas or ways of doing things that were commonly repeated or observed. We identified these as "descriptors." As our research proceeded, we were able to aggregate these descriptors into groups that we defined as "concepts." We maintained a relational database of concepts and descriptors across all of the cases, and as time went by we found that a remarkable commonality developed. As we learned more we found it necessary to return to some of the organizations in order to round out our analysis. We learned new insights from each case. Most of the concepts were apparent after the first few cases, but some were subtler and took much longer to understand. Naturally enough, the concepts that were most difficult to define were the ones where the ideas involved were novel. Eisenhardt (1989, 540) explains the difficulties of searching for cross-case patterns. We concur, and note how the work proceeded with endless conversations that seemed to go around in circles, interspersed with flashes of inspiration, which revealed ideas that, with hindsight, appeared obvious.

Each of our concepts was assigned a name that was consistent with a peak performance metaphor. This usage of metaphor is a significant departure from Eisenhardt (1989) but is a common approach in organization theory. Peak performance provides a coherent theme and language for PPO Theory. The concepts were realigned many times as we struggled to understand their interrelationships.

As the concepts became more robust, we compared the emergent theoretical framework with the cases to determine whether this framework actually did fit with the reality of what we had observed, and in so doing we confirmed the empirical validity of our emergent theory with growing confidence. Not all the cases exhibited all of the concepts to the same extent, but significant evidence of each one was revealed in all of the organizations included in this book.

We became intimately familiar with each case by writing it as a story. We agree with Dyer and Wilkins's approach to case study research in which they call for "an exemplar, that is, a story against which researchers can compare their experiences and gain rich theoretical insights" (1991, 613). People within the case study organizations read all our stories in order to ensure the accuracy of our facts. This feedback prompted further commentary and insights in many cases. PPO Theory cannot be properly understood without the rich insights from these stories.

Finally, we compared PPO Theory to organization theory and to the theory of high-performing organizations. The comparison enabled us to be confident that there were no areas within our data that we had overlooked. By comparing our theory in this way we were able to test its robustness.

We closed the research project once we believed we had reached theoretical saturation (once further cases were adding nothing significantly new to our theoretical insights), and when description and explanation of our theoretical framework was complete. From our research we developed a set of concepts that pursued in combination, lead toward sustained peak performance. We describe this as our theory of peak performance organization, or PPO Theory.

How To Read the PPO Stories

A chapter is devoted to the stories of each of the sports organizations that we studied. The stories are told in a way that tries to capture the spirit of the organizations and their atmosphere of success. We share the insights and incidents recounted to us, together with our observations.

All the PPOs have characteristics in common. They all have a long history of successful championship contention. They are part of the entertainment industry and the fitness industry—both great areas to be in so far as current social trends are concerned. Yet each PPO story is different. The teams are separated by geography, gender, and game rules. The All Blacks (chapter 9) have a 72 percent win record for the last hundred years. By contrast, some of our teams have been top performers for only about a decade. Through these differences, broader knowledge arises.

These contrasts mean that each story starts in a different place, and therefore reads quite differently. We determined our starting points after deciding the key concept from each organization. Wherever possible we tell the story in the words of those to whom we spoke. In reading through the chapters it becomes clear just how similar their words are, despite the varying stories.

This book can be enjoyed on many levels, by managers, organizational participants, and, of course, sports enthusiasts. The first nine chapters tell the stories of the sports organizations, while the final chapter offers a theoretical framework for peak performance derived from the preceding stories, which we hope will be transformational for the management practitioner or organizational scholar.

When we began our research, we had no idea whether we would

gain access to the elite organizations that we wished to study. However, persistence paid off, and one organization led to the next. For example, the marketing vice president of the Chicago Bulls flew to Atlanta to meet his counterpart at the Braves to see if we were worth talking to. In the end, we were invited into all the organizations that we targeted and discovered that many of their organizational stories had never been told. The organizations valued seeing their reflections in the PPO mirror, and this assisted their relentless drive to exceed organizational best. Each of our PPOs was generous in the extreme with their time and in providing us with opportunities to watch the organizations in action. The sports odyssey was a unique privilege for each of us. The intellectual journey will last a lifetime.

Although our research is now complete, and we have described the transformational organization concepts that sustain peak performance, our inspirational dream of contributing to the creation of fun-filled, peak performing organizations lives on. We are imagining new challenges, and we are sharing our dream as widely as possible through books, videos, and seminars and by acting as consultants to organizations that want to implement PPO Theory. Thank you for sharing our dream by reading this book. Please see our Web site at http://www.mngt.waikato.ac.nz/ppo/ for the latest on the PPO project. To contact the authors, e-mail ppo@waikato.ac.nz.

The U.S. Soccer Federation: World Cup Women

"We want to leave a legacy, a mark in history, to show people what kind of passion we have for this sport. We've won World Cups and Olympic gold medals, but the dream of everyone on this team is that even when we take our leave, as we must do, we have left such a great legacy that future players and fans will always know that this didn't happen by accident. This was something that was carefully calculated and it worked because of love and passion. We wanted to play. We want people to know that we did it for the right reasons."

—JULIE FOUDY, COCAPTAIN OF
THE U.S. NATIONAL WOMEN'S SOCCER TEAM

For several minutes that stretched into an eternity, Carla Overbeck, Joy Fawcett, Christine Lilly, Mia Hamm, and Brandi Chastain carry the nascent passion and hopes of ninety thousand spectators and forty million television viewers. With them is Lauren Gregg, assistant coach of the U.S. National Women's Soccer team, the person responsible for choosing these five players who each must score a sudden-death penalty-kick goal to defeat China and win the soccer World Cup for the United States. Despite appearances, they do not stand alone. As each player is destined to place the ball on the penalty spot, linking arms, the remaining ten players behind them are physically and emotionally connected with them. When Carla Overbeck paces forward to strike the ball, she takes with her every player from the first-ever national team squad of 1985. Anson Dorrance, the coach of the women's team who won the World Cup in 1991, shadows Overbeck and all five penalty-takers, as does every player who has proudly pulled on the U.S. national team jersey.

In this cauldron of unspeakable tension, along with all others the president of the United States admits to facing pressure and suspense he has never been equipped to handle. Yet for these five supremely prepared players, this moment represents the culmination of fifteen years' toil. It is an authentication of their life's work before the largest audience for a women's sporting event the world has ever witnessed. Amid this incredible backdrop, Lauren Gregg reveals the almost clinical approach that clinched the World Cup trophy. "I knew that the first three would get on the board because of their mental sharpness." Gregg's choice of Mia Hamm for the fourth penalty kick came as a shock to the superstar who, in a few fleeting moments, anxiously inquired as to why Shannon MacMillan was not taking the kick in her place. Lauren Gregg:

> Two days before the final I was watching Mia taking penalty shots by herself and she went from missing, missing, and then all of a sudden she found this groove. Instinct is very important to me so I went with Mia. I had the pulse. I told Mia, "You will be fine today." I also thought, my God, if we lose because Mia doesn't make the kick—that will be the end of my coaching career.

The stakes could go no higher, but Gregg's instincts proved trustworthy, as both Mia Hamm and Brandi Chastain made their penalty kicks, enabling the team to reap the benefit of Briana Scurry's earlier magnificent game-winning save from China's Liu Ying. Once more, the women's soccer World Cup belongs to the United States.

First Mover

It is December 1998 and Aaron Heifetz, the ubiquitous, globe-trotting press officer for the U.S. Women's National Team (WNT), finds himself, along with the then National Women's coach, Tony DiCicco, invited to a Union of European Football Associations (UEFA) women's soccer conference in London. The gathering includes women's national team coaches, frontline program administrators, and progressive policy makers. Aaron Heifetz:

> I felt like I couldn't even contribute, we were so far ahead of them. The problems they were discussing were like from the 70s for us. We don't, for example, play mixed soccer competitively, because we've got tons of girls who play soccer now. We are so far ahead of the rest of these countries as far as development of our women's game and how we treat women. Now the actual top national teams are all very good, but the fact of the matter is that we're just far ahead of the rest of the world.

A spectacular World Cup victory lies several months away from this December meeting, yet the foundations for success are already in place, and have been for several years. The victory achieved by the U.S. national team was no flash-in-the-pan surprise built on the advantages that come with being the host nation. This victory was hard earned and meticulously planned. Heifetz and a sprinkling of others are privy to how and why it happened. For much of the 1990s, there are in fact two stories that run in sometimes stormy parallel, converging with explosive resonance in July of 1999. These histories reflect first, at core, a commitment from the U.S. Soccer Federation to the women's game and second, and more important, a remarkable and truly inspirational women's story of athletic ability and highly personal yet team endeavor. Although the WNT comes under the auspices of the Federation's infrastructure, team logistics and their management have historically operated independently. In the early days, the dedication and commitment of players and coaches was the mainstay of the WNT's success. During the 1980s, the Federation's interest in women's soccer mirrored the attitude of other soccer associations around the world. In a male-dominated sport, it was at best seen as a novelty, and at worst an irritant. Inevitably, this encouraged an antagonistic atmosphere between the WNT and their Federation, with reverberations continuing throughout the 1990s.

Director of event operations Thom Meredith and secretary general Hank Steinbrecher are the only surviving Federation employees who in December 1991 moved from Colorado Springs to Soccer House in Chicago. Meredith actually began working for the Federation in 1986.

> When I first started, I think we had seven or eight employees. We now have over 100 people working here. I was one of the people lucky enough to meet the women's team when they came home in 1991 from China, as the world champions. The women in that team will tell you that there was almost nobody at JFK airport to meet them. But I was one of those people that met them and there is no doubt that following the scale of their success in 1999, that's probably the one thing that's changed the most.

The role of the Federation is to oversee the development of the game of soccer in the United States. This involves overseeing the national teams for both men and women. In addition to the senior national sides, there are eight youth squads that fall under the Federation umbrella. The hundred or so employees are located in Soccer House according to their functional contribution. With the men's and women's national teams are the various services and functions necessary to maintain their operations. Event management occupies a critical place in the structure of the organization, which in turn is closely allied to marketing and communications. Membership services, refereeing, coaching, and finance and administration are the remaining departments that make up the structure of the Federation. Other than a general manager who oversees the logistics associated with specific tournaments, the Federation has resisted since inception administrative separation between the men's and women's national teams. Nevertheless, each department makes its own special contribution toward the overall purpose of the organization. Bill Sage, recently hired by the Federation as chief administrative officer, has no doubt what that purpose is in relation to the WNT:

> The dream is twofold. First, to raise the level of women's soccer throughout the world. Second, through the game of soccer, we want to be part of the worldwide social revolution which sees women filling a different role in society. We see our women as ambassadors to do that. That is a global dream.

While creating and developing this wide-ranging purpose—or global dream—the Federation has also set a startling challenge to the women's team in the shape of Project Goal. According to Bill Sage, it is simply "to continue winning World Cups forever." Putting both the inspirational dream and greatest challenge into action requires an explicit focus on the relentless maintenance of the women's program. This important lesson was learned the hard way, when early successes were not sustained.

Chief operating officer Tom King argues that there is no formal distinction between men and women, in that their respective programs are administered centrally. However, there is little doubt that the early successes throughout the 1980s, driven by a dedicated women's team, pushed the Federation into making commitments to the women's program at a level not actively considered by other soccer associations around the world. Social and political advancements for women during the 1980s and 1990s undoubtedly played a part, but without due diligence in establishing the necessary infrastructure for women's soccer, little or no progress was going to be made. Tom King:

> We saw that in 1991, by winning the first women's World Cup, we had found a niche within women's sport where we were arguably the best in the world. By winning that tournament we proved that we were, but we noticed also that by 1995, many teams had

caught up and they had closed the gap. The wake-up call was not even making it to the final in Sweden. Unfortunately, the commitment that was made by the Federation, which had started just before the 1995 World Cup, was much too late—even though we'd invested just shy of three million dollars by putting the team into residency with full-time salaries. The real fruits weren't realized until we won the gold medal at the Atlanta Olympics. We found that in order to compete with the rest of the world we would have to have full-time athletes in an all-professional environment. We would also have to create a staff whose number one job was to create that environment that would allow the players to focus only on playing soccer and learning to be the best in the world. So it was really a mind-set—how can we make sure that it really makes U.S. Soccer stand apart, how can we win the World Cup again that we lost to Norway in 1995?

The infrastructure necessary to maintain peak performance vests in the under-twenty-one, under-eighteen, and under-sixteen teams that are run by the director of national teams administration, Jim Froslid. Froslid is also responsible for an under-fourteens camp in San Diego that takes place during a one-week period. The women's under-eighteens and under-sixteens programs were established after the Atlanta Olympics, further deepening the decade-old, state-run Olympic Development Program (ODP), which was one of the first programs established by the Federation. The annual budget for these twenty-ones, eighteens, and sixteens programs offers little change from a quarter of a million dollars. However, even this extensive youth development initiative presents Froslid with a range of frustrations.

The biggest challenge is the size of our country in that it's very hard to mobilize teams and bring them together for long periods of time. Another obstacle is facilities. We just don't have enough real soccer facilities in this country. More important still, it's very difficult to set up games for this age level, whether it's the twenty-ones, the eighteens, or the sixteens, because there's only a handful of teams in the world that can compete at a very high level at that age group. The teams that we watch in the World Cup are the only teams from that nation. They've got one team that they deal with, pretty much, and they put all their money into it. We have more time, more resources to develop our youth games, but the problem is, I'll put our under-twenty-one team into a college tournament to play the top college team and the closest game will be 3–0. And the most lopsided game was 8–0. So how do you prepare them to take penalty kicks in front of 90,000 fans? It's very hard to duplicate that pressure-filled situation with our youth games right now.

One of the ways this problem has been addressed relates to the way in which the national teams are vertically integrated. Lauren Gregg, one of the most important figures in U.S. women's soccer, worked for many years with the senior national team and was a key figure in the World Cup victory in 1999 before joining the women's professional soccer league. Gregg was instrumental in putting in place the system whereby the assistant coach of the national team is the head coach of the under-twenty-one team. Likewise, the assistant coach of the under-twenty-one team is the head coach of the under-eighteens and so on. Along with former head coach Tony DiCicco, Gregg also astutely ensured that the twenty-ones camp coincided with the World Cup final in Pasadena, to which they were then invited, enabling them to share the magic of the occasion. Prior to the tournament, five of the twenty-ones had spent six months in residency with the senior team. This level of integration has helped the twenty-ones to amass a startling record. Gregg's charges have maintained a lock on the unofficial World Cup for under-twenty-ones, the annual Nordic Cup. A loss in the 1998 final, alongside two losses to the senior team, are the only blemishes on a near-perfect record. Encouraging association ensures that the hunger for success remains powerful. Dana Schoenwetter, national teams coordinator, explains the impact of the World Cup victory:

When we won the [1999] Nordic Cup in Iceland, they got in the locker room afterwards and got to pass the cup around. Just watching the players celebrate—of course it was not close to what the full women's team experienced, but they definitely wanted their own celebration. You could see that they were following the ritual they had witnessed at the World Cup final a few weeks earlier.

It wasn't always this way. Gregg reminded us of the humble beginnings.

What people don't realize is that we have only had a U.S. team since 1985. Between 1985 and 1989 we only had one or maybe two events each year. We did have a miniresidency in 1991 for six weeks prior to the World Cup, and during the spring we went to the Soccer Cup in Haiti. Now that was a whole different story—showering by candlelight because there was no electricity. It was just crazy! By 1992 we were almost dormant, with only one event a year later, and only two of our World Cup players were there. Basically the program was almost dropped for 1992.

Gregg is a tenacious, passionate advocate for women's soccer who credits both past presidents of the Federation, Allan Rothenberg and Hank Steinbrecher, for their support for women's soccer. Since the Atlanta Olympics, more frequent residency programs and an expansion of youth development infrastructure are among the critical factors that have enabled the Federation to create the future.

The Road to Pasadena and Brand Recognition
The commitment evidenced by the Federation post-Atlanta reflects the constant pressure from both coaches and players for sustained development of the women's game. In the lead-up to the 1999 World Cup, the Federation invested more than twelve million dollars to ensure that the team was provided with the opportunity to perform at the highest level. This included a series of high-profile games billed as "The Road to Pasadena," an investment that was critical to

the buildup and resulting marketing mania that gripped the U.S. for the summer of 1999. Tom King, however, saw this in a broader context:

> The Road to Pasadena was just like a tiny segment of the overall preparation. It was eleven games that were used for two reasons. Number one, maximize the promotional benefit for our number one sponsor, Nike, and then also to try and recoup some of that investment in the technical preparation of the residency program, which included salaries and expenses. This was a three-million-dollar commitment each year for four years. In the World Cup year, we probably brought in about 1 to 1.1 million dollars, so we said, Okay, we are going to make a 1.9 million–dollar investment in this team knowing that, initially, revenues are not going to match expenses. But that didn't matter because we were willing to pay 1.9 million dollars in 1999 to win a World Cup. We simply had to give our team the best possible technical preparation going into the tournament.

Although many of the core Women's National Team (WNT) players have, across the years, expended considerable energy in cajoling Federation administrators to increase their commitment to women's soccer, they are very much aware of the strides that the Federation has made: in particular, the opportunity to play a significant number of games. With the Federation able to resource, sponsor, and support women's soccer tournaments domestically and abroad, several members of the team can boast more than one hundred appearances. This has enabled a core group of players to establish a disciplined rhythm born out of a steady stream of competitive international events. Brandi Chastain, defender and scorer of the famous penalty kick against China, places that remarkable moment in its true context:

> It's the Federation who have given us an opportunity to play more games, and that is the most critical aspect. There's no denying that

fact. They've put money in so that we can go overseas and bring teams in. The only way you can truly improve is if you play more games. To play other countries is very important for the growth of our sport.

At a more visceral level, Tiffeny Milbrett, a WNT forward who made her debut in 1991, emphasizes the critical nature of establishing an intuitive understanding between team members, which can be reached only by constantly playing together.

We have been playing soccer and athletics a lot longer than other countries. Other teams might be skilled, good soccer players, but they're not as athletic, not as strong as our team. Our power comes from being together for ten years, and you can see the difference in results. I've been playing with Mia for a long time now, and being more familiar with each other naturally makes things happen. We can almost play together blindly sometimes. In an intuitive way you can anticipate and communicate without eye contact or words.

Milbrett's direct line of sight between games played and games won is strongly echoed by Christine Lilly, currently the most capped soccer player in the world. Although Lilly is acutely aware of the important role the Federation has played, she also provides an astute interpretation of the wider issues involved.

We've had a women's side in the Federation, which is perhaps not what everyone there wanted, but U.S. soccer has been fighting another battle and that is to get soccer out there—and that is not an easy thing to do. At the same time, we're asking for a women's side when women athletes aren't highly recognized either. But they continually gave us the opportunity. Along the way, they have had to change their set of views to grow in line with what is happening in women's sports. It has been difficult, but they have been supportive.

Federal legislation in the form of Title Nine, which ensures equal college scholarships for men's and women's sports, is often credited as the prime reason for the success of the WNT. Yet Bill Sage believes that it is Federation policies, from the Olympic Development program (ODP) to the sophisticated running of the youth development programs, that effectively creates long-term support for the WNT. Moreover, the fact that the infrastructure was already in place means that it made sense to resource specific WNT activity. Long-standing cocaptain Carla Overbeck, who is at the very heart of the WNT, occupies a prime position to assess the value of the Federation toward sustained peak performance on the field of play. "The Federation has supported us throughout our careers by enabling us to move into residency. To get us the necessary money, the Federation had to go to their board and fight the battle there too. They are a great support."

With membership fees to U.S. Soccer seemingly stuck forever at 50 cents, the Federation faced, and continues to face, the dilemma of how to raise the necessary funds to ensure the long-term viability of both the youth and WNT programs. Sponsorship by leveraging off brands values is the traditional way for organizations like U.S. Soccer to raise much-needed cash. However, even the multimillion-dollar arrangement with title sponsor Nike alone is insufficient to cover the breadth and depth of Federation activities. Chief Marketing Officer Mark Noonan carries the burden of raising sufficient interest and revenues from sponsors. Noonan, like several other employees, found favor with the Federation via a previous encounter with Secretary General Hank Steinbrecher. Noonan joined the organization in the summer of 1998, and proceeded to reenergized the brand image by spending four months on the road talking and listening to players, media, consumers, and, of course, sponsors.

Working alongside the International Management Group (IMG), Noonan now has a suite of sponsorship programs that account for more than 40 percent of Federation revenues. Interestingly, and in keeping with the centralized policy structure, Noonan concentrates upon building a "branded house" rather than a "house of brands." What this means is that neither the men's nor women's teams are separately branded. The dream that is shared is of U.S. Soccer as a whole. Mark Noonan:

> We want a consistent image. We don't want our brand to live and die by what happens to one team on the field. We want the U.S. Soccer brand to be reflective of taking on the world. That is our greatest challenge. We want to take on the world by winning world championships with the right attitude and with the right spirit. We want to be representative of the American dream. So we have tried very hard to have a very consistent and simple brand message, but we have a long way to go because it is a new process. Our women's team has been a great reflection of our brand because they took on the world, they did it with class, they did it with style, they did it with emotion, and with personality.

The Nike Road to Pasadena was one of the main tools used to build the momentum toward the World Cup. For the WNT, it consisted of a sixteen-game television package, nine of which were pre–World Cup games. The aim was simply to create demand for the product and the values associated with the WNT property. Although members of the team had worked tirelessly for many years, doing charity work, interviews on demand, and autograph signings, the critical breakthrough had not quite been achieved. Federation officials still speak angrily of NBC's decision not provide adequate coverage of women's soccer at the 1996 Atlanta Olympics. The suspicion was that even though some of the players had established name recognition through their exploits, the level of knowledge about them as a very special team appeared parsimonious at best. The steady diet of sporting individual superheroes that had dominated the latter years of the 1990s, it was argued, might be vulnerable to the simple yet powerful message of "team." This theme was picked up by carefully crafted television commercials emphasizing that from dating to dentistry, the players do things together. By the time of the World Cup, the "two fillings for all" commercial, in particular, had all but achieved iconlike status with fans. Jim Froslid, director of national teams administration running the under-twenty-one, under-eighteen, and under-sixteen teams, confirms that his national teams program was substantially lifted by the reaction of the media and the general public.

> The team is a slice of American pie. It is a slice of suburbia which large masses of people can easily relate to. Women's and girl's soccer began with moms and dads taking their kids to soccer games in minivans—the whole thing. The WNT look, talk, and act in a way which resonates with them. It was interesting to see this happen, although you could see it coming a year ago.

In terms of pure planning, the Nike Road to Pasadena carefully selected playing venues that equated with the World Cup market, thus helping to build general interest as well as ticket sales. Given the size of the upcoming competition and the likelihood of an American victory, the opportunity to brand the WNT in the image of the nation became a real possibility. The final game on the road tour against Canada featured the first-ever live telecast on ABC, creating further significant national awareness. The road tour was clearly a critical part of the Federation's strategy to obtain maximum impact from sharing the dream. Mark Noonan:

> The people that executed the road tour knew exactly what was being done, yet all the public knows is that the World Cup was a phenomenal success. We first started with the strategy of a special theme. The whole purpose was to build demand and create an awareness of this team and the mission that they were on. Over the course of six months we created an incredible amount of demand for the WNT as well as for the World Cup. Yes, Pasadena was demand creation, it was marketing, but at the same time, I'm not so sure that we could have predicted the phenomenon that they became.

That phenomenal success is directly handled by the manager of marketing and sponsor services, Greg Drozda, yet another Hank Steinbrecher recruit, who dryly notes that nowadays, "everybody wants to be associated with the women's team." At the start of the 1990s, the Federation was lucky to have three sponsors on board, whereas Drozda's department now handles twelve, which in addition to Nike, includes such household names as Chevrolet, Allstate, Quaker Oats, Anheuser Busch, Pepsi, Motrin, and Gatorade. These partnerships are carefully selected according to the brand values of U.S. Soccer. Drozda knows that he has a hot commodity, but resists the temptation to open the floodgates.

> We've had a lot of inquires from different organizations, different agencies representing organizations that want to be sponsors of just the women's team, but that is something we steer away from. We have ten national teams and U.S. Soccer is a family here. We treat all of our sponsors as members of this family.

The theme of family and friends lies at the heart of these sponsorship arrangements. Drozda has to struggle with a never-ending stream of contingencies that have the potential to undermine a carefully constructed relationship with a sponsor. For instance, when the WNT plays at Soldier Field in Chicago they are "walking into a Coke stadium." This means that it is not possible to provide Pepsi with the opportunities they would like. To keep the partnership on track, Drozda has to "make it good later on down the road." This requires constant open dialogue designed to encourage sponsors to come up with their own initiatives that extend their brand identity into the markets offered by their association with the WNT. Coordination of a plethora of initiatives is a fine balancing act that aims to keep the family of sponsors in harmony.

In simple terms, the ongoing success of marketing and sponsorship activity keeps the national team's program intact and quite literally on the road to success. However, without consumer interest in the product, sponsor interest is apt to wane. Filling each stadium for each and every game played by the WNT is therefore essential. Choice of venue and the operational running of each game falls under the preserve of the director of event operations, Thom Meredith. Certainly, members of the WNT were acutely aware of the important decisions that had been taken regarding the scale of their endeavors. Tiffeny Milbrett:

> Do you think we made the decisions to make the World Cup as big as it was? No way. It was the people behind the scenes. We just showed up and got behind the people who were fighting for us. Those working for us behind the scenes are equally as important as us getting out there on the field.

Many naysayers had, for some time, been unwilling to argue in favor of using larger venues for the women's World Cup. In the crowded sports market, low television ratings and games with fewer than two or three thousand spectators made a compelling argument for locating the tournament in smaller stadiums. In addition, the culture of the sport is that families spend many hours ferrying their kith and kin to participate in tournament after tournament, rather than actually kicking back and going to games just for idle pleasure. Put simply, before the World Cup, the habit of watching soccer had not been established. The Federation bid to FIFA to hold the World Cup in the U.S. actually included a business plan to use small stadiums. However, the success of the Atlanta Olympics, where the gold-medal game attracted a crowd of more than 76,000, persuaded the Women's World Cup Organizing Committee, under President Marla Messing, to recalibrate their planning with larger venues in mind.

Professionalism at Every Level

Thom Meredith, who was seconded from the Federation by the organizing committee to work the various World Cup sites, brought with him the necessary experience and consummate operational expertise that fortuitously benefited the WNT. The detail, complexity, and special cadence of orchestrating a large sporting event requires planning and fortitude. Done well, the impact can be breathtaking. The rhythm of ceremony and celebration can however unnerve and buckle even the hardened professional athlete. For this precise reason, Meredith had long put into place a policy of gender equity in terms of prematch fanfare.

> We made a conscious decision to treat our women's team the same as we do our men's team, which would be culturally, economically, and socially a heretical statement in other parts of the world. But I give them the same attention when we operate each game, no matter what the size of the stadium might be. They get the same bells and whistles in terms of pregame music, marching out, and for the anthem. I made a conscious decision to do that and I think it helped them. We had some women's games that drew 1,200 to 1,500 and we did the same things as we would for a men's game of 60,000. This means that when it gets to big events, with 90,000 people, they already have a real feel for what it's like. And of course, Atlanta was a great rehearsal for them.

Seemingly peripheral to matters that are directly settled on the field of play, the Federation has recognized the value of professionalizing all elements that are likely to impact on the team's ability to perform. Thus, event management to the last detail attracts and commands as much attention as any other facet associated with the WNT. Because large sporting events are invariably outsourced to specialized promoters, Meredith sees considerable merit in developing in-house capabilities, since this enables the organization to "have a factor of control over what you do, when and how it is done." While Meredith does not claim that he has a primary influence on winning, he nevertheless believes, along with the players, that his vocation is woven into the tapestry of sustained achievement.

The relationship between the staging of events and team performance is not the only aspect for which the Federation provides contextual support for the WNT. The unsung and often abused role of the match official—the referee—comes within the ambit of Esse Baharmast, who is the director of officials. A 1998 World Cup referee himself, Baharmast stands at the head of a monster operation.

Through his office and the National Referee Program (NRP), the Federation coordinates more than 100,000 referees, 16,000 of whom are women, who are responsible for more than 2,000 matches and the conduct of the game. Aided and abetted by a swiftly operational Power Point presentation, Baharmast is able to illustrate, via a sequence of bar charts, that the Federation organizes the activities of more match officials than England, Scotland, Italy, Spain, and Holland combined. California (north) has more soccer referees than most European countries. He can also provide a breakdown of the referees' age groups, and a hint at which U.S. referees will likely be officiating in the 2010 World Cup, for which the Federation is actively bidding. Games from amateur to professional, for both men and women, are assigned using an Internet Web page that every official is able to access. From a logistics point of view, this centrally arranged method of match scheduling is game-breaking, since it also allows additional hypertext links to "conference call notes," which are the result of after-match discussions that allow the referees to reflect on their performance. All match reviews are posted at the Web site.

This method of match allocation and assessment encourages openness and transparency. In addition to providing the highest level of officiating possible, all data collected is actively shared with Federation coaching staff and, more important, with the players themselves. The aim is to educate players from an early playing age about the style of referees in the U.S. and, more specifically, about how different surface and weather conditions affect match officiating. Accordingly, the director of coaching at the Federation, Bobby Howe, has integrated the results of the NRP into all coaching clinics. In preparation for the World Cup, Baharmast gave the WNT a specially prepared presentation that highlighted the type of officiating they could expect under tournament conditions. With the benefit of this kind of preparation, only two yellow caution cards were issued to the WNT during the whole of the World Cup. Esse Baharmast:

It is truly an honor for us to be able to make that extra one-percent difference between winning and losing. The laws of the game will absolutely be applied to all players, but we want to inform them of the consequences if they break the rules. If she does this, she knows she will be sent off. She can make an informed decision based on the intricacies of the game. And if that's what she wants to do, then she'll get sent off. On the other hand, we can help them adjust to the conditions.

The professionalism of the Federation's NRP has attracted widespread international interest leading to exchange programs with other countries. But for Bahramast, the most important part of the operation cannot be easily transmitted elsewhere.

The way we look at it is that this is a vehicle which has the four tires rotating. One is the players, and the others are the coaches, the administration, and the referees. You could have the best players, but if one tire is flat, the vehicle will never reach your destination. It's all about working together.

The Whole Team

When a core group of people stay together for a long period of time, there is always the possibility that they will develop unique attributes and skills that could not be honed and iteratively built upon without the sharing of knowledge and full engagement in mutual reflection. Mia Hamm is regarded as one of the world's premier strikers. She is also likely one of the smartest. Her thoughtful observations about corporate life, which clearly spring from her on-field experience, stand as an important illustration regarding personal and collective organizational responsibility.

Any type of management or company is similar to a team, in terms of everyone understanding what their role is. I think that's extremely important, and in particular, understanding that your role is not going to be the same every day. And how do you react to that? Do you sit there on your hands if you're not a starter and mope and be upset, or do you try to play the most positive support role you can? And when your time comes, do you make the most of it? In business, you might put together the proposal, but you might not get all the accolades. Do you sit there and say, "Screw this. I'm not going to help these guys anymore!" or do you say, "You know what, that's wonderful that our company has done so well." If you choose the latter, as you should, then you attack the next project with the same enthusiasm and the same focus as you did for the one before.

How does the Federation score on the dimensions outlined by Hamm? Unquestionably, all the various departments need to coordinate and integrate their activities on a daily basis. National team programs are inextricably linked with events, their marketing, and the officiating of the product on the field. As Hamm implies, each of these activities, at some point, may take center stage; yet it is their combined impact that makes the critical difference. Richard Matthys, who is the chief financial officer of the Federation, plays a critical role in allocating resources to each area of activity and is therefore well placed to observe the processes that nurture an appreciation of each others' roles. The budgetary process stewarded by Matthys offers a fascinating insider's view of the organizational footprint.

Matthys places considerable emphasis on "cash management and the implementation of financial policy." This is not set against a traditional strategic plan. A four-year planning cycle, or quadrennium, that captures the period between World Cups is put together from a sophisticated historical financial database that is based on the cycle of games played, which in turn might be affected by a championship year for one of the national teams. The result is a series of operational plans that take into account the constant changes occurring on a monthly basis. These plans are put together in conjunction with those of other functional department heads. Interestingly, this is a bottom-up process that relies significantly on trust and coordination. The preferred outcome is to ensure accurate and effective allocations.

The budgeting process is very creative here. Based on revenue strength, the more creative we are, we have a better chance to register more referees and coaches. In terms of dollars going into the operations, we are very heavily involved in the budget process as linked to the games. For instance, we have youth, fourteens, sixteens, and eighteens, and to identify what dollars we want to put in these budgets for a certain period of time, I rely on the operational staff, who are the ones that determine their requirements in conjunction with other departments. Through this office and working with the chief operating officer, the budget is further finetuned. All the players of the Federation form together as one team.

In stressing the importance of total involvement, Matthys provides copious amounts of information and data to ensure that fiscal policies are not experienced as a top-down squeeze play.

We try and make it as easy as possible. We are not just telling them what their budget should be. We give them a complete package with a lot of information so it frees them up to be creative about their own departments in terms of what their department goal is and what they need to do in order to accomplish their goal.

Most important of all, it was this form of budgetary management that enabled the Federation to invest in the development of the women's game. Richard Matthys:

In 1995, the Federation made a major investment in the WNT and the women's program. We didn't have anything banked; we simply didn't have any sponsorship revenue to cover the investment. It caused the organization to go into a deficit for a year. But our fiscal management, involving the whole organization, enabled us to get a little better so that we could afford those training camps and overseas games. It was one of the best investments the organization made.

The value of fiscal management, as part of the architecture of peak performance, is often overlooked, yet in the Federation's case it clearly presents important creative opportunities for expansion.

The hard numbers are difficult to ignore, yet the process of system integration, presented by the Federation's budgetary management processes, reflects deep commitment and passion toward the soccer family. Inclusion is the glue that helps bind the operations together.

As the organization continues its near-exponential growth, it is Nils Krumins, manager of human resources, who faces the daily task of piecing together the growing edifice of employee administration while trying to maintain the family atmosphere so cherished by all. There are some things that naturally pull in his direction. "Soccer has an allure. It attracts people. You share in everyone's passion for the sport and it helps to create a family ambiance." The home of the Federation, Soccer House in Chicago, comprises a pair of linked mansions dating back to 1873. Although substantially refurbished, Soccer House retains much of its nineteenth-century charm. Rooms with fireplaces and rich wood panels reside amid turrets, gables, balconies, and sweeping staircases. It is impressive enough to receive presidents and dignitaries alike. Even though it presents some physical communication difficulties, the overriding impact is that it is a familylike environment that encourages respect among employees. Indeed, it is seen by Krumins as a fortuitous gift that goes hand in hand with the need to transcend a job description mentality approach to work.

It would be impossible to write a complete job description for almost all our positions. So what we have done is to set out some broad parameters of responsibility and then attach related duties. Quite often it is in those areas of "other duties" that much of people's work tends to occur. We want to keep everything fluid, in a team context. You've got public relations, communications, marketing, sponsorship, events staff, and administrative support working on day-to-day trading issues, and of course you've got the team and the people who work with them. All of those people need to interact and be on the same page, and there can be no definition that says you are responsible to your team. It can't happen like that. So many different things are occurring and changing that all of those people work in different areas, playing off each other. Each one of them certainly knows the others' individual roles, but they all understand that each one of them must work across the lines. They can handle this. The team is alive.

Krumins was employed by the Federation to provide much-needed professional and technical expertise in the area of human resource management. However, his role also includes initiatives that relate directly to people's passion and need to belong. The emotional, psychic value of celebration is not lost on Krumins. Soon after the World Cup victory, he arranged for an in-house staff presentation of the trophy so that the functional staff could establish "their connection to the team that had just won the World Cup." This helped to close the loop from a visit that the WNT made to Soccer House at the start of the World Cup. An opportunity was provided for the staff to be photographed with the trophy, which Krumins felt would "build so much energy and maintain a positive atmosphere through a very literal personal attachment to the WNT's success."

The aura of association is, indeed, never far away. Krumins astutely notes that continual storytelling is an important source of information for the staff at Soccer House, helping to bind together the professional and the social.

Certainly it's a treat when the traveling staff come back to Soccer House and we get to hear some of the different stories and our connection to the team. It allows everyone based here in Chicago to feel on the inside. The exchange of different tidbits about their experiences can take place in a social setting. Different groups will head out for a beer on a Friday night, and they have that constant interaction and opportunity to discuss and learn more about what the others do, what their roles are, and all the different things they were involved with. It helps team building in terms of exposure to what other people's positions are.

For Krumins, the act of storytelling carries several useful properties that inspire high levels of cooperation and organizational harmony. Quite literally, this family is able to gather around the fireplace to hear the latest installment.

> Within the story are several different components. Functionally, you have the discussion taking place in the story, and the storyteller obviously relays in what context they were there and what their role was as well as their perspective and how they were part of the event they were describing. A more important aspect of storytelling is that it stirs the passion that everyone holds for the game. When you're discussing the things that happen with the players and the team, it brings up all the emotions and the passion helping employees to connect with the game. It's also positive from a friendship-building aspect, providing a stamp that emotionally involves everyone with the organization. The story brings it all together.

Throughout the 1990s and for some years prior to the first women's World Cup in 1991, the Federation faced a coherent, articulate, passionate, and very progressive women's soccer team who were clearly in the vanguard of women's sport in the United States. When he joined the Federation, Krumins solicited their perception of the Federation. Even though past President Alan Rothenberg and General Secretary Hank Steinbrecher had made significant commitments to women's soccer, the relationship between team and organization remained incomplete.

> Reaction certainly varied from one player to another. As players, they have never had a close-knit tie to the staff here. They have a connection with the coaches and the immediate staff from here who work closely with them. However, they were very interested to learn about the group that worked back here. They wanted to

know who the different people were and who worked in the different areas. I went out there to learn from them, to see what we could do for them, but they were interested in learning about the organization that they can't see for much of the time.

On one of his first visits to the team, Krumins was able to attend a WNT game where he witnessed an incident that for him captured the essence and passion that drive the organization.

During the regular run of play against an inferior team, one of their players came from behind and chopped the legs from under Shannon Macmillan. She was in full stride coming toward the bench where I was standing. So she comes sliding, literally on her stomach, face first toward the bench, and she just looks up and has the largest grin on her face that you could ever imagine. If it had been a man's game, you would have got the anger and temper tantrums. But the women just love what they're doing. It epitomizes the whole thing. I wrote it up in one of the reports I was submitting, to illustrate the concept that this is what we are working for. It's what they love doing. Without a passion for the sport, none of us would be here, and this incident epitomized it for me.

The manifestation of passion in the Federation office undoubtedly revolves around its inspirational secretary general, Hank Steinbrecher, who Richard Matthys calls "Mr. U.S. Soccer." Steinbrecher, who joined the Federation in 1990, stands at the heart of the soccer family. "Hank stories" are frequently told by all Federation employees. He is noted for being approachable and able to comprehend the big picture. His indelible mark includes a tripling in the number of people who work at Soccer House, many of them being able to cite a personal connection between the secretary general and their recruitment. In terms of all-important infrastructure, he has strongly supported women's programs, in particular the hiring of full-time coaches from only one in 1990 to well over twenty at the end of the decade. He is more noted, however, for the manner in which he relentlessly sells the game of soccer, particularly while traveling. Terry Johnsen provides a typical illustration of Steinbrecher at work.

> He is a very outgoing person. He was on a plane going from California to New York for the opening of the World Cup, and while on the plane saw a woman and her daughter who happened to be wearing a World Cup T-shirt. He invited them to the opening ceremony and the little girl got to go into the locker room. He's a one-man band promoting soccer. He invites everyone to Soccer House. This will include cabdrivers who are dropping off an official tour party.

Jim Froslid has no doubt about Steinbrecher's qualities and the impact he has on staff.

> Hank? He's very dynamic, he's very emotional. This organization needs a guy like Hank because he's truly inspirational and can mobilize people. Just by talking to a group for fifteen seconds he can inject a lot of energy into people simply by the way he speaks. Actually, his nickname is "the reverend" because he's such a tremendous speaker. That's good for our sport because we do need to be seen and heard if we're going to succeed in this country. He also has a very strong marketing background, which nowadays in sports is a fundamental requirement. If you don't have a grasp of marketing, you don't have anything, so there's a lot of respect for him.

From a policy and resources point of view, Steinbrecher's commitment to women's soccer is greatly respected by former national coach Tony DiCicco, whom he credits for his insight into how the future of soccer was going to unfold.

> Hank Steinbrecher was somebody who felt that it was the right thing to do—put a lot of money into the women's side of the game and to promote women's soccer and women's athletics. It wasn't

always popular. I can tell you, at times it was very unpopular. Alan Rothenberg, our previous Federation president, wanted to achieve certain standards for men or women, whereas Hank was more concerned about elevating the women's side of the game.

As an organizational inspirational player, Steinbrecher plays a critical role by providing staff with a strong sense of purpose and passion for U.S. Soccer. Externally, he has tirelessly represented the interests of U.S. Soccer to a sometimes skeptical media. Finally, he has been a positive influence and conduit between the Federation and the WNT.

The Women's National Team

Anyone who comes into contact with the WNT will tell you very similar things. Unmistakably, this is an extraordinary group of women who, over several years, have forged a tight-knit community. Yet they are not aloof, remote, or distant. They are inherently accessible, even at times when they deserve peace and seclusion. Federation employees who work closely with them in a professional capacity are constantly surprised at the team's ability to consider the circumstances of others. Thom Meredith, as director of events operations, has observed that their caring demeanor extends to autograph signings where they will go out of their way to dedicate their signature to an individual or to recognize some personal trait in a small note. He believes that this demonstrates "a profound difference in the way in which they approach the social part of being a team member."

This leads the team to extend themselves and to incorporate others into their routines and sense of play. Dana Schoenwetter became both accomplice and victim in the week leading up to the World Cup final when, after a training session, she was pestered by Mia Hamm and Julie Foudy to drive them to a bagel shop in Los Angeles to assuage their growing hunger. Since the two soccer stars were in their training outfits, neither had the funds to pay for the items. With Schoenwetter 30 cents short, and with the rest of the bagel shop still in the throes of celebrity recognition, the hapless national teams coordinator was mercilessly subjected to an endless stream of one-liners from Hamm and Foudy, who couldn't resist the opportunity to taunt their chaperone with her inability to look after them properly. This amusing story has happily "haunted" Schoenwetter ever since!

This innate sense of fun has an important role to play when more serious situations arise. During the inaugural game of the World Cup, the opening ceremony surpassed its allotted time, thus dangerously compromising the players' critical warm-up and mental preparation routines. Rather than allow the buildup of more nervous tension, out came the boom box, and their crucial pregame, on-field warm-up session was quickly translated into dancing to rock music in the locker room. This ability to improvise has been evident from the very early days. The inner strength and determination of the team was forged more than a decade ago when a core group of players began the long march toward gaining respect for their sport. When there were no dedicated youth programs, individual discipline was the only method by which standards and trust could be established. Brandi Chastain explains:

> When we started this whole thing, there were no such things as training camps and residencies. Apart from friendly matches, there were only a handful of games, so all the training had to be done on your own. It was really up to all the players to make a decision that they wanted to be best. In that, you had to trust that they were doing their job away from the actual training time that we had together as a team. It's easy to train in a residential camp, because you have to. But to get up in the morning at your home three thousand miles away from Christine Lilly or four hundred miles away from Joy Fawcett and Julie Foudy, and know that they're doing the same thing, that they're working as hard as you are, not only brings confidence, it builds trust, knowing that they're going to be there for you at the times when you need them most. It means that "I gotta just do it." I have to go out there by myself again for the four hundredth time in two years because I

know that they're going to rely on me at some point, and they trust that I'm going to do the job. Chemistry comes through trust, and when you get along with the people that you supposedly work with, then work is not work, it's more like fun, and I think that's what we have the most of. We have the most fun.

Chastain is not alone in these observations. All the players provided stories that confirmed the importance of trust that has been firmly established over the years. This has enabled the team to endure and develop phenomenal athletic ability. Principles of competitiveness, work ethic, and genuine belief in the team concept are the constant companions of the WNT. Along the way, they have also developed an internal sense of team management, which Chastain sees as the foundation for success.

Even in the hard times when we're out at practice and it's a hundred and ten degrees in Florida, and you're sweating profusely, and you're in a great deal of discomfort, Julie yells something totally asinine and then you start laughing and you forget that you're hurting so bad, and you remember that you're having fun. Eventually, chemistry is probably almost to the same level as trust. Relationships have never been a burden. We all get along, you know. I think in good relationships, even if you don't see eye to eye, you have communication about it, you have the type of relationship where you can express disagreement. And nobody holds grudges, nobody takes things out of context, so that chemistry has really allowed us to be creative, free thinkers, expressionists, and to be ourselves, within a group of twenty people.

Mia Hamm believes that the chemistry described by Chastain leads to a tough mentality where "nothing is taken for granted and everyone has to bring something to the table. I remember that from day one of my first ever practice." The core group from the 1991 World Cup, which includes Carla Overbeck, Julie Foudy, Christine Lilly, Joy Fawcett, Mia Hamm, Brandi Chastain, and Michelle Akers, is determined to ensure that the team retains its original characteristics. To this end, new team members are quickly brought into the fabric of WNT life. Julie Foudy:

> When a new person came, all the feedback we got was that it was terribly intimidating, so we make a point, very consciously, of the veterans rooming with a young player. I am rarely with Carla or Mia or another veteran. I'm always with one of the younger kids. This is a great thing because when you're living with them and rooming with them you get two days to bond with them and that makes a difference. One of the other things our leadership group has done is to make sure that during warm-ups and stretching, we do it with someone different each time.

Throughout our time with the players, it was evident that their obvious individuality both on and off the field was an expression of team identity. Even though many of the players retain iconlike status in the public eye, Julie Foudy insists that we "make sure that the group is the focus." From the outside, it looks even more impressive to Federation staff residing in Chicago. In his observations of the WNT, Jim Froslid believes that. "They live and die for each other." From the inside, we asked Mia Hamm for her own view and reflection.

> They are my best friends, you know. We've all been with each other so long that we've seen each other grow up. In sport, when you're out there training and you're playing, you pretty much see every side of people. You see them under pressure. You see them when they lose. You see them at their highest moment. So you know these players. They've seen every side of me, and I'm still accepted. I think that is wonderful.

As general manager of the NWT, Brian Fleming is the immediate net beneficiary of what the players have established for themselves. Fleming stands at the head of a Federation team whose role is to ensure that the eternal logistics associated with playing international events are tied down to the last detail. Reporting to him are trainers, coaches, equipment managers, and team administrators who book the hotels and flights and make sure that meal requirements are in line with dietary needs and personal preferences. As is usual under such conditions, many of the roles flow and intersect with each other. For Fleming, the best credentials in the world for these roles add up to nothing if the personalities are not right. In part, this requires an understanding of how to interact effectively with the team. As an ex–college athlete himself, and with a long history in sports management, including a stint as general manager of the men's national team, Fleming has an eye for hot spots or angst in the ranks that needs to be smoothed over. He is therefore well placed to empathize with the WNT, which already has a very strong sense of its own requirements.

> The women are deeper and stronger than the men, who can be almost superficial in the way they drink beer together. With the WNT, they are one for all and all for one. They are a lot more direct—if there is an issue, then they raise it and they deal with it as a group. Men are more likely to just ignore it as long as it doesn't bother them specifically. The WNT is definitely a team with twenty players who are all 100 percent together, so there is a lot more player involvement concerning day-to-day decisions—things that you do as a team both operationally and extracurricula-wise. No question you are going to get feedback. With the men, you put together a daily itinerary and hand it to them. Try that with the women's team and you are going to get an awful lot of arguments. You keep them involved in the decisions, you work with them so that they are part of the decision. This way you get a better feel for what the players want and what they are interested in doing, which can actually make my job even better, because once we have made that final decision there is nothing that will come up mid-stream because we have already discussed it. So it is unique working with these athletes. At first it was different for me to work this way, but now I actually look forward to it.

In keeping with the principle of vertical integration, each year the women's program brings the youth teams to the WNT camp, where the training and ways of working and being are handed down to the next generation of players. Here, the younger players can literally rub shoulders in the locker room with their idols. In this way, the special characteristics of the soccer family are reinforced, thus helping to create the future for the women's program.

A Hot Day in Pasadena

By late winter of 1999, the unique and compelling attributes of the WNT, known to Fleming and others who have been in almost daily contact with the players, are beginning to pass into public ownership. From a marketing point of view, the Nike Road to Pasadena had certainly done its job, leveraging effectively off athletic prowess, irresistible personality, and the promise of victory on the world stage. The week of the World Cup final itself, the organization that would otherwise be measuring its media impact via column inches in obscure publications now finds itself on the front cover of *Time, Newsweek, Sports Illustrated, People* magazine, and *USA Today*. Media coverage is so intense and time-pressured, that Jim Moorhouse, director of communications, actually contemplates, temporarily, refusing Tom Brokaw of *NBC Nightly News* the right to turn up at the Wednesday before the final training session and run the biggest good-news story of the year. Possible payback for NBC's atrocious coverage of soccer at the Atlanta Olympics? A hastily written personal note from Brokaw to Moorhouse, pleading for access, secures the slot. The scale of events unfolding is in stark contrast to Moorhouse's career experience. An admitted soccer junkie, Moorhouse notes that his current job is "the first time I've ever held a soccer position without the fear of the club folding on me." There were probably more spectators at the final training session than at many of the games Moorhouse had worked at in his early days with struggling clubs. The media frenzy had built to such a degree that police escorts to and from the training ground had to be organized. Film stars, Olympic gold medalists from the U.S. women's ice hockey team, and other notables made for a circuslike atmosphere. Melissa Mason, manager of event services, likened the occasion to a "mass stampede." The animated crowd became so raucous that at one point during a team discussion Mia Hamm turned to a noisy section of fans with a smile and, with finger to lips, signaled good-humoredly for them to shhh.

Clearly, the turnaround in media coverage was not lost on the WNT. At the last practice session before the final, the media are invited into the locker room as usual only to find the whole team huddled together in one corner. Julie Foudy, standing on a bench to gain attention, loudly instructs the scribes and assorted press to "Put your cameras down, put your pens down, and turn your tape recorders off." She then proceeds, on behalf of the team, to thank the press for their coverage and the important role they have played in helping them to share their dream with the American public. Unaccustomed to such thoughtfulness, hardened and cynical media hacks spontaneously break into prolonged applause.

Moorhouse credits *USA Today's* coverage with being an important breakthrough catalyst. In recognition of their role, the Thursday before the final, a special photo shoot of the team was arranged that resulted in a stunning front page 8-by-10 photograph. At the motel in Pasadena, the team is waking up to the most important day of their lives. Moorhouse, rising early, strolls down the hallway to see *USA Today* outside each room. It is an amazing sight, punctuated by the emergence of a half-awake Mia Hamm from her room, dressed in training cape.

> Mia opens her door still half-asleep, looks down at the *USA Today* on the floor and sees all her teammates smiling back up at her. She shakes her head in disbelief while managing a wry smile. I don't know. In any lifetime you can't expect this kind of exposure—waking up in the morning to see yourself like that. It was a very surreal moment for me!

At breakfast, the team is still able to exchange wisecracks while reading newspaper coverage of the events that are about to unfold; but in truth, there is now a strong desire to get onto the field and perform. Waffles, bacon, scrambled eggs, and fruit are, for the most part, quietly consumed. Fleming, who is known to carry the anxiety and nervous energy for the whole team, announces that "we are bound to win today because I threw up this morning!" Evidently, this is a longstanding good-luck omen. The team offers an ironic yet relieved cheer at this edifying news.

Meanwhile, Thom Meredith has arrived early at the Rose Bowl Stadium, as he always does, to begin preparation for the third-and fourth-place game that precedes the final itself. Even though Meredith is running the operations for the World Cup day, he, like many others, will fall victim to the impact of President Clinton's attendance at the game. Security is inevitably tight when the president comes to town, and this would be no exception. Thom Meredith:

> When he comes to an event, it really creates a lot of problems in terms of movement. I didn't pay attention to the competition office, because it wasn't in my area, but he needed a place to wait briefly while the teams were coming off the field. When I arrived in the morning, I left my duffel bag underneath the table in that room, so the Secret Service came in and moved it because he was going to be there for thirty seconds. That's fine, but they never returned the bag. It took over an hour and I had to go through five different people before I could get it back.

Rightly oblivious to these dramas yet to unfold, the team has taken an evocative bus ride through streets of adoring fans. In the locker room, game preparation, as usual, includes playing upbeat music from the ever-present boom box. As always, photographs are taken, not just of the team, but of the entire assembled staff who are working the game of their lifetimes. Melissa Mason decides to record the occasion by taking a photograph of each uniform hanging by the player's locker space. Equipment Manager Dainis Kalnins arranges for a red and a white rose to be placed across each player's uniform. Coach DiCicco then gives his pregame talk, which is heavily flavored with encouragement rather than detailed game analysis that had been covered earlier. In the week leading up to the final, Assistant Coach Lauren Gregg had prepared special personalized video clips of great moments from previous games, such as the Atlanta Olympics. The clips were then set to music chosen by each player. Positive reinforcement is the order of this and every day.

After an energy-sapping game, including a dramatic clearance from the U.S. goal line during the period of extra time, positive reinforcement is indeed the basic ingredient needed to carry the team through the heart-stopping penalty shoot-out. Briana Scurry's magnificent and game-winning save from Liu Ying sets up the final penalty shot from Chastain. At the other end of the field from where Chastain is about to make history, Brian Fleming, Dana Schoenwetter, Melissa Mason, and the rest of the field crew are at the end of their collective tethers. Minutes earlier, Fleming had expended copious amounts of mental energy in an attempt to assist Scurry's all-important save.

> I was a nervous wreck the whole game and totally dehydrated because of the hot sun that day. I didn't drink an ounce of water or anything the entire game and I am out there in a suit and tie and sweating my brains. When Liu Ying approached the ball, you could tell she wasn't totally confident. I thought Briana was going make this save. I was squatting down in the corner of the field with my hand up to my mouth and talking to myself and all I kept saying was, Be the hero—be the hero. I kept saying it over and over in my head.

For Chastain's penalty kick, Schoenwetter and the rest of the crew physically came together in order to cope with the pressure of the moment. "We were in a line of four or five and we just spontaneously locked arms together, waiting, waiting . . . when the kick went in everything became a blur."

Even during the mayhem and celebration, the sharing of the dream continues, as the team is brought together on the field to participate and be immortalized in the Disney "What's next!?" commercial. For this, Mark Noonan has to coordinate his entire operations so that the team can come together and feed the line to the camera, "We're going to Disney World!" The deal to make this commercial was set up on the Thursday prior to the final and went to air on the evening of the victory. According to Noonan, "This is the first time that soccer has been highlighted in this way. I got a call from the guys at Disney later that evening to say that it was the best spot they had ever done with this commercial."

The medal ceremony also offered another poignant moment. Michelle Akers, captain and one of the original team members from 1991, had to be brought out by the trainers on a stretcher to receive her winner's medal. As a sufferer of chronic fatigue syndrome, she was substituted late in the game and was put on a drip to help her recover. Julie Ilacqua, director of membership services, was sitting twenty rows back from the field with retired members of the 1991 World Cup team who had been specially invited by the Federation to the game.

> It was extremely moving. My section of the crowd began chanting "Akers, Akers." They brought Michelle out from the tunnel and helped her as she walked to the stage, where she was awarded her medal. All the 1991 team went down onto the stage and then the 1999 team came over to greet them. The crowd did not stop clapping until Michelle walked up to the front of our stand and held up her medal. That was really something, because she is the definition of an athlete and a champion.

In the locker room, Press Officer Aaron Heifetz faced the task of trying to organize the growing media frenzy and a presidential visit to the winning team. Some days later he told his immediate superior, Jim Moorhouse, "I was standing there and all the president's men were sitting in a semicircle and I'm saying to them, 'Okay, guys, this is how we are going to run this show.'" The sense of the near absurd is only removed when the president actually arrives at the locker room. As promised, Heifetz arranges a tiered section for the media to capture President Clinton's congratulatory words to the team. As the cameras swing toward the president, the players go about the task of shaving Fleming's head—a promise the general manager had made to the team should they go all the way and win the World Cup. Each player, starting with backup keeper Saskia (Sask) Webber, took her turn with the trimmer. The family continued to celebrate together.

The immense pressure and strain on the players at day's end is felt by Mia Hamm, who, like Michelle Akers, is in need of a drip to restore her energy level before she can leave the stadium. It is fully three hours before the bus finally leaves the scene of triumph and accomplishment. Improbably, there are still groups of fans waiting to catch a glimpse of their heroines. In a final astonishing act of sharing the dream, the bus driver is called to halt and the team opens their windows and tosses their cleats to the grateful fans. This treasured apparel is destined for the people's Hall of Fame.

Back on Tour

With World Cup fame assured, the ongoing media whirl involved talk shows, visits to shuttle launches, and White House presentations. The dream is still very much alive as the team reassembles several weeks after the tournament to participate in the Nike U.S. Women's Cup. The public spotlight knows no boundaries, and these days, wherever the team goes, they can expect a nonstop barrage of attention, welcome or otherwise. Although the team has been in the public eye for several years, the intensity has moved up several degrees.

The team has just completed practice, attended by several thousand season ticket holders at the Columbus Crew Stadium, where the international game against South Korea is going to be played on Sunday. The attendees are invited by the team to watch, cheer, and, at the end of the grueling session, obtain precious autographs. Gathered conspicuously together in the Adam's Mark hotel lobby in Columbus, Ohio, they are an impressive sight. Athletes together, they are in the prime of their physical and mental lives. The odd hotel guest blindly strolls through the middle of the entourage, oblivious to the space they have just violated. The players depart for their private social time, returning the hotel lobby, for now, to a semblance of normalcy.

The following morning the team takes another bus ride to a supposedly more intimate local training ground. Other than the locker room, there is probably no place that more solely belongs to the players than the team bus. Riding with them is a special privilege that confers temporary membership in the family. On board with the players are the ubiquitous children, assistant coaches, and administrators. As expected, the banter is lighthearted without being overly rowdy. Occasionally above the general bubble of conversation are more audible comments of irony and laughter that punctuate the relaxed environment.

Aaron Heifetz, the team's press officer, acts as the interface between the team and the insatiable demands of the media. More than this, he, is the choreographer who crafts each day for the team when it is on the road. From breakfast to lights-out, Heifetz orchestrates the day on a minute-by-minute basis. An avid soccer player himself, he also participates in soccer practice, taking potshots at the team's keepers or taking sides in a pickup game. He is not alone in this. Other members of the Federation, such as Greg Drozda and Melissa Mason, can be found working the field to the satisfaction of mercurial coach Tony DiCicco. If there are any doubts that this is the family at work, they are dispelled by the presence of several of the player's children, who, with baby-sitters in tow, fit easily into the training routine. Muscle-stretching exercises are accomplished with the smallest of the entourage being used as impromptu weights to be lifted and passed among the prostrate players. Squeals of delight emanate from child and parent, surrogate or otherwise, as the rituals and values of family inclusion are effortlessly woven into the fabric of game preparation.

Even at this far smaller venue, a swirl of peripheral activity consisting of prying TV cameras, anxious reporters, and young autograph seekers flaps around the edges of the training session. At the conclusion of the workout, players are quickly surrounded as they endeavor to oblige the never-ending requests for autographs and interviews for the evening news hour. Without interfering with the team's insistence upon sharing themselves, Heifetz is ready to gently move his charges back toward the bus and the short drive to the hotel. A quick shower and change before attending the next event—lunch at the All Star Café. Unlike training, this appearance by the players is a staged media event that is specifically designed to showcase the WNT to the nation. To avoid uncontrolled public disturbances, the team is ushered in via the back door and through the extensive kitchen complex. As the team snakes its way among pots and pans and workbenches, the several dozen chefs and kitchen hands spontaneously break into loud cheering and applause. This is heard by patrons in the large café, who likewise begin their applause long before the team actually emerges into the dining area. The group is dazzled by a bevy of flashes, TV cameras, and attendant anchors who waste no time in singling out for interview cocaptain Julie Foudy and the ever-popular Mia Hamm. It is, however, Kate Sobrero, one of the newer additions to the squad, who captures the limelight by winning a televised contest to concoct the most variegated ice-cream sundae, which is then passed to the youthful audience for consumption. Sobrero is a natural comedienne who personifies important aspects of the team's culture and the public's perception of it. It is a happy marriage.

Late afternoon and time for some interviews. Heifetz emerges with Julie Foudy, who wastes no time in providing an articulate history of the team. Although unrehearsed, it is not difficult to surmise that Foudy has heard these questions before. In an apparent maneuver to see if she is being fully understood, the interview takes an unexpected turn.

Researcher: Could you please give us a sense of the type of environment that encourages you to excel?

Foudy: Hmm. Well, doughnuts and beer really help, personally.

Researcher: Say what?

Foudy: Potato chips and Jerry Springer?

Minutes later and Foudy reverts to a more deliberative period of reflection and concludes the interview by offering her deepest observations, which are the opening quote to this chapter.

It is now game day against the South Koreans. Buffet-style breakfast is held in one of the hotel's larger weight-training rooms. Four round tables are provided, which allow the team to converse with each other. Brandi Chastain, who joined the team a day late, is making up for lost time with loquacious and animated conversation at the table, which also includes coaches Tony DiCicco and Lauren Gregg. Chastain has natural charisma, which easily blends into the team dynamics. Like the rest of her teammates, she cannot escape the chores that accompany their fame. Throughout breakfast and beyond, all of the players, staffers, and coaches go through the ritual of signing soccer balls, shirts, posters, and cards. At this session alone there are more than one hundred signatures each to complete.

Breakfast also doubles as the final game briefing. After announcing that the team is to play South Korea later that afternoon, DiCicco explains the game plan and, in doing so, Socratically involves the players by asking for their input and ideas. It is in this situation that the older players are best able to impart their knowledge. He uses this method to emphasize the importance of the team playing to its own standards rather than concentrating on the opposition. With the debriefing over, DiCicco moves around the room in a relaxed manner, sharing, at one point, stories from his youth that contrast sharply with the more recent experiences offered by some of the team. As the players slowly drift off to complete their own personal mental preparation for the game, cocaptain Julie Foudy and Brandi Chastain are the only ones left in the room to complete their signing duties.

The team bus to the Columbus Crew Stadium departs from the hotel. Just hours away from an international game against South Korea in the U.S. Cup, the atmosphere is more subdued than the previous day, although the chatter and laughter that is a constant companion to the group is still evident. As the team arrives at the stadium, many of the fans located at the top of the bleachers who are already watching the Brazil–Finland game preceding the main event are able to catch a glimpse of the bus as it slowly makes its way around the stadium's inner perimeter. By the time the bus arrives at the players' entrance, thousands of screaming supporters are squeezed into every conceivable vantage point. Security personnel anxiously watch as thousands of young girls and a healthy sprinkling of boys dangle perilously over elevated railings and staircases, all in pursuit of an elusive sighting or, perhaps more improbably, a cherished autograph.

At the game, United States supremacy is quickly established when Cindy Parlow powerfully heads home a pinpoint corner from Shannon MacMillan. Although the crowd is well pleased with the conversion, Aaron Heifetz is not. The stadium announcer fails to mention how many goals Parlow has now scored in her international career. In the pressroom where reporters are busy crafting the story of the day for tomorrow's papers, Heifetz, over his much-employed cell phone, barks out an order to a stadium official instructing him to rectify this important detail. The Federation is ever mindful of the public's fascination with sports statistics. If U.S. soccer is to achieve traction with a skeptical media as well as a growing posse of adoring fans, it is such last-detail professionalism of Federation employees like Heifetz that will win the day.

The team confirms their expected superiority with an emphatic 5–0 victory. At game's end, the players waste no time in sharing the dream with what Coach DiCicco calls "their extended team." Long after the final whistle, half the crowd have yet to depart. They can be found pressing themselves tightly against the perimeter railings as the whole team spends close to a full hour signing autographs on any item related to their beloved soccer team. Ingeniously, two fans situated over the player's tunnel ferry down, via a long piece of string, a U.S. Soccer shirt with the plea "Please sign me!" An American flag is also attached to the string. Even though the players have been signing hundreds of times, none can resist such tenacity, and as the team troops back to the locker room they reward this innovation with more autographs.

But it's not over yet. The media room awaits. Here the newshounds must also obtain their quotable quotes, and the TV cameras need another telling shot for their shortly-to-air sports digests. Fully two hours after the victory, the team heads for the bus. Mia Hamm, who is usually quiet in social surroundings, epitomizes the relief felt by all at the conclusion of the formal proceedings. On entering the team bus Hamm picks up the microphone and starts to mimic the mantra of airline cabin attendants. Seeing the opportunity for group involvement, as each member of the team enters the bus they dutifully carry out the instructions imparted by Hamm. Tiffany Roberts gesticulates wildly in the direction of the exit doors as her mentor reminds passengers that "for some people, your exit door may be behind you." Captain Julie Foudy makes an elaborate display of how the safety buckle should be employed, while Kate Sobrero is left to indicate the potential danger that lies behind the overhead bins. Hamm concludes her soliloquy by informing the "cabin" that contrary to everyone's hopes, "in the event of a water landing, it is regrettable that the cushions will not act as flotation devices."

Monday morning and it's off to Kansas for the next leg of the U.S. Cup. A swift change of planes in Chicago causes the team to sprint from one terminal to another, although several of the players still find time to purchase pizza on the fly. Arrival in Kansas signals it's back to business. A quick change in the hotel and the team is whisked away for a brisk training session. The family has now been back together again for several days and the sense of trust and mutual respect for one another—forged across a decade or more—comes to the fore in the form of self-ridicule. National icons they may be, but that is not sufficient to stop wicked, but never cruel, send-ups. No one is spared. Starting with Brandi Chastain and Mia Hamm, the team begins to read aloud extracts from their published bios, ruthlessly nuancing various phrases, satirizing themselves. This is an important mechanism that ensures that despite the fame that is now theirs, everyone is reminded to "keep their feet on the ground and their heads out of the clouds."

Humor turns to horror as the bus pulls up alongside the training fields revealing an "unscheduled" 2,000 fans, ably accompanied by network TV crews, "Heifetz, Heifetz!" is the exclamation. "What happened?" No one was supposed to know of this training session. The beleaguered press officer quickly recovers the situation, enabling the players to go about their business. While the team begins to stretch, Heifetz has already calmed the baying masses, promising autographs after the session and TV interviews at intervals as the players circle in and out of the drills. All is well. Despite a hard day of travel and some aches and pains from the weekend game, the training session still motivates the team. Their commitment and discipline is most evident in their personal exhortations to push for better and better results. Julie Foudy is the obvious dynamo in these situations. Her drive and enthusiasm are immediately picked up by teammates who scream purposively at each other in an effort to attain still higher levels of performance.

With training over once more, the whole team, coach and assistant coach included, sets about the task of quenching the fans' thirst for association. It's Heifetz's job to ensure that the balance between playing and appeasing fans and the media does not get out of hand. It is an almost impossible task under normal circumstances, but this day has stretched the limits of what the team can physically and mentally endure. Back at the hotel the coaches, trip organizers, and administrative staff start their own evening shift. Planning gets under way for three tours to Australia in the upcoming months, including, of course, all the necessary logistics for the Sydney 2000 Olympics. Sarah Whalen, one of the new players on the team, interrupts the meeting to ask if a group of them can start going through the videotapes of the Korean game. It is all of 10:00 P.M. and the hotel is still buzzing with activity.

The Ball Was Kicked Deep to Mia's Feet

Heifetz is well prepared for training the following morning. Indeed, he already has Hamm headed out for an early-morning photo shoot and, by the time the rest of the team arrives, has instructed the autograph seekers to wait patiently until the end of the workout. Moreover, in an inimitable avuncular style, he has walked up and down the high wire fence that separates the team and the fans, recruiting ball girls to retrieve stray potshots at goal being taken by Brandi Chastain as she practices free-kick set pieces. For a handful of girls, on this day, their dreams have come true. Heifetz also ensures that Chastain knows the names of the ball girls, and when she calls for the ball by name, the aura of association is complete.

Meanwhile, Hamm has completed the photo shoot and is now practicing hard with the rest of the team. It does not shape up to be a good session for the most feted female player of all time. Shots at goal are going anywhere but in the net. Hamm is visibly irritated. Even in practice such outcomes have an important impact on players who are dedicated to be their competitive best. Questions of whether a player is still able to deliver can be raised at any time and from any quarter—teammates, the press, spectators alike. Toward the end of the session, questions such as this are supremely answered. Shannon MacMillan drives a long cross-field ball right to Hamm's feet. A one-two with another forward places Hamm at an acute angle to the goalposts. With no hesitation, she powerfully threads the ball between the near post and astonished keeper, Briana Scurry. Spontaneous applause from all around is followed by Coach DiCicco publicly shouting his appreciation of Hamm's consummate skill and choice of action. Under game conditions, explosive moments such as these are recognized as inspirational. Clearly they motivate Hamm to be the very best goal scorer there is. Should anyone wonder why Hamm is the subject of such intense public scrutiny, they have just received their answer.

Being in a position to both assist in and proclaim the virtues of soccer players like Hamm cannot be easy to surrender. However, the Nike Women's Cup proves to be one of DiCicco's final tournaments as head coach of the women's team. With several years and many miles behind him, DiCicco, the coach with a brilliant win record that will likely never be beaten, decides to resign at the close of 1999 and take up the position, most aptly, as commissioner of the soon-to-be-established Women's Professional Soccer League, itself a vital part of the WNT's commitment to create their own future.

Preparation Down Under

The new coach, April Heinrichs, has little or no time to settle in; 2000 is an Olympic year. Many a sports squad has been turned upside down by the demands of performing in someone else's hemisphere. For this reason alone the WNT, after some wrangling over contractual terms with the Federation, are more than happy to participate in the pre-Olympic Pacific Cup tournament alongside China, Japan, Canada, New Zealand, and the host nation, Australia. The event also provides another crucial opportunity for the team to get used to the novelty of working with their new coaching staff prior to the main event in Sydney. Earlier, Heinrichs began her tenure by immediately bringing in a sprinkling of younger players. Inevitably, this was made possible at the expense of some of the original World Cup squad not selected for the 2000 Olympic squad. Despite these changes, the core veterans have embraced the challenge of working under a new regime. Julie Foudy:

> This in an interesting transition. April was one of us as a player, so she shares our mentality and core values. But she is also a firm believer in growth and change. There was a lot of anticipation that things would be rattled, but it's also a new voice, a new philosophy. That's wonderful.

Heinrichs was initially surprised at what she found when she rejoined some of her former teammates. With Olympic gold and a second world championship secured, Heinrichs could be forgiven for assuming that the players nearing their retirement might be lacking in passion and drive. She found the opposite.

> The natural assumption for most coaches when you take over a successful team is that they will be resting on their laurels. They

could possibly revert to living in the past and stop satisfying themselves. Even though I've known them for twelve or fifteen years, I was taken aback by how hungry they still are. They are just genuinely humble people. They believe in keeping your feet on the ground and being humble is the way you approach life.

Heinrichs began her training sessions by instilling some basic patterns into simple issues, ranging from the frequency of water-bottle usage to training uniforms being worn appropriately. More substantively, each player underwent a detailed objective assessment to enable Heinrichs to develop more "keys" and methods of play. Her aim is to provide structure to the process of learning, but then to take a step back and allow the players to make the necessary decisions once the game, or even practice, has begun. This, she believes, allows for greater creativity and flair, as well as de-emphasizing mistakes. On several occasions, Heinrichs has recorded examples where the set plays have been developed further, beyond her expectations. Fortuitously, this philosophy is a variation of the team's long-held desire for involvement. However, Heinrichs's method of coaching also clearly envisages passing full responsibility to the team once play has begun. Although this appears to be a players' dream, it brings with it potential problems when increased pressure pushes the players to want more certainty and less freedom.

To avoid this tendency, Heinrichs calls for even higher levels of trust between players, including the necessity to be openly critical of teammates who are not following training routines. Brandi Chastain believes that "she's giving us the responsibility to be tough with one another in order to get the job done, which is a nice addition to the way we work. Now we can bring things out into the open, in front of everybody, and talk about it." Accordingly, Chastain values open channels of communication, even if the conversation leads to unexpected observations.

What I like about April is that she's willing to understand someone else's perspective. I feel very comfortable going to talk with her, even though sometimes I might not hear exactly what I want to hear. But I'm still able to have that conversation with her. She can quite easily emotionally connect with the players.

When Heinrichs took over the position of head coach of the WNT, some press reports indicated that her style was distant and that she would not be able to connect with the players. This belief was tested during a three-week residency camp in San Diego. The players, who entered camp lacking fitness to the previous year's level, were put through their paces by Heinrichs.

I was driving them as hard as I could because we definitely came in on our backs this year. The fitness test I took them through lasted much longer than I anticipated because of the way they approached it. They approached it with such excellence. Rather than cutting corners, they were really doing their sit-ups properly— legitimate push-ups—and at the end of that I said, "You guys were so good. You absolutely did every push-up, chest down to the ground, elbows up, chest down to the ground, elbows up. You did every sit-up hands behind the head, elbows to your knees, you did it so well, such excellence. You can have the day off now." Players cheered, screamed, and yelled, and then they picked me up off the ground. They were really excited.

At least while in Australia, Heinrichs does not have to battle the voracious demands and attention of the U.S. media. Australia's interest in women's soccer has been sparked, to some degree, by their national team's seminude calendar portrait, which has earned them the rather dubious title of "the naked Matildas." For the U.S. team, there is modest attention toward Mia Hamm, whose exploits on the field have begun to transcend country, sports code, and culture. Apart from this, the team is relatively free from close public scrutiny. Constant demands for autographs and interviews give way to personal indulgences. At mealtimes, groups of players bring out empty and half-completed albums that purport to be running histories of the events of the past twelve months. Photographs, press cuttings, personal artwork, and small items of memorabilia are carefully and quietly assembled. Format and content are subjected to collective judgment. Some of the album's lines of development include award ceremonies, spin-off holidays, and social events shared among the players. All the time, stories are being told and retold, ensuring that new members of the team are able to comprehend the recent past. Sharing the dream this way ensures that future generations of players will have a reference point to build upon.

As the process of album compilation unfolds, clusters of players quickly coagulate only to disband and re-emerge with a different cast of characters. Although there are undoubtedly close friendships among the players, there are no permanent social groups that can be defined by exclusion. Minisocial systems among players, travel logistics people, and administrators rise and fall each day. Such intuitive associations reflect the on-field creative flair much encouraged by coach Heinrichs, who, as a past player alongside some of the existing team members, is eager to allow her charges the space to establish maturely their own responsibilities. Professional attributes are also associated with this mode of operation. For the international event in Sydney against New Zealand, Heinrichs takes the opportunity to "rest the best and test the rest." Sitting unemployed on the substitutes' bench are several star players who together can boast nearly a thousand appearances for their country. At the conclusion of the game, united by their unusual match-long inactivity, the core of the team who won the World Cup spontaneously take to the unpretentious back streets behind the stadium and run hard against no one but themselves. Bedecked in USA deep-blue track suits and running three abreast across the sidewalk, the motivated and focused phalanx of athletes establishes a blistering pace that attracts the attention of the local residents and those arriving for the evening game between Australia and Canada. It is an impressive sight that stops others in their more sedentary tracks. A clearly fascinated teenage male offers the observation to his upstaged skateboarding friends, "It must be them." Indeed it is.

Following the defeat of New Zealand in a round of the Pacific Cup, the team is eager to eat. Returning to their hotel, they find that an arranged 7:30 P.M. mealtime doesn't quite fit with their current state of hunger. An interesting impromptu mixture of fast-delivered pizza, breakfast cereals, and red wine quickly emerges, onto tables initially intended to host more traditional fare. The atmosphere could not be happier. Laughter, the constant companion of the team, once again underscores the proceedings. News of the early-bird smorgasbord reaches the remaining players resting in their rooms, and the group quickly swells to include the whole family.

Being invited into the inner sanctum of the U.S. women's soccer team is a privilege that carries with it responsibilities. Having spent several days with the team across two continents, our continued intrusion will do little to assist the accomplishment of their goals. It is time for us to leave. This is their soccer dream, and our association can only be temporary. Still, we have made many friends who have graciously matched all our requests for time in what is plainly the time of their lives.

Conclusion

In late June 2000, Dan Flynn is announced as the new secretary general to U.S. Soccer, replacing the much-admired Hank Steinbrecher. He inherits a Federation that has harnessed the passion for soccer that the United States has now awakened to. Unquestionably, this has occurred because of a very small group of talented women who have successfully kindled, ignited, and inspired those around them. April Heinrichs believes that "it is the players who have the dream, the players who have the idea of the future." Through their supreme efforts, the imagination of the next generation has been well and truly captured.

The Federation has in place the organizational infrastructure to be in contention for years to come. The challenge to "win World Cups forever" will require the continued integration of its collective experience and professional ability. However, for the women who began the journey more than a decade ago, the challenge of the future has inevitably changed. Christine Lilly:

> When I first started with this team, Anson Dorrance was coach and he would always tell us that we needed to sell the game of soccer. I was a young sixteen-year-old then and I didn't understand. But through time, with our hearts and with smiles, we began selling the game. It has taken ten hard years or more to make the sale. And that has happened. Now, as we fall away from the national team, the professional league for women gives me the chance to compete against my former teammates. I love to compete against my teammates! This will be something that is just incredible.

Julie Foudy loudly echoes these sentiments. "We are anything but complacent. I don't care what we've accomplished, even with the World Cup. We've set a great stage for soccer in this country and we've done remarkable things, but there's another level we can get to. There's always another level."

Shannon MacMillan, one of the most skillful forwards on the NWT, looks beyond her own playing career to embrace the aspirations of others.

> We don't want to walk away as if we're all done with this. We want to be able to come back and go to the games to see these young kids playing, the ones who are now asking for our autographs. We want them to have it that much easier because of the groundwork that we've laid. I challenge them to go out and choose their dreams and stay true to them as we have tried to do.

2

The San Francisco 49ers: Tilting the Field

> *"Why do the 49ers win? From the beginning, our owner has wanted to win. After we won the Super Bowl in 1981 it took off. It is amazing that through all the changes that have taken place, we have been able to sustain our winning record. As coaches and administrative people have moved on to other teams, they have taken with them the '49ers system' that is so successful. And yet that system is not written down anywhere. It's a learned process—an understanding of the operation, with buy-in at a very personal level. We don't have a formal doctrine; it's all up here, in our heads."*
>
> —MURLAN C. FOWELL,
> DIRECTOR OF STADIUM OPERATIONS

Bill Walsh is back. The coach who started it all, by winning Super Bowl XVI in 1981, returned to the 49ers in time to see the team post its worst record in twenty years. A four-wins, twelve-losses season doesn't make sense in San Francisco. The team that led the NFL in the nineties with a 75 percent win record left the decade uncharacteristically out of play-off contention. Walsh appreciates that with "more player mobility, with free agency, dynasties that once existed are more difficult to sustain, or to rebuild and sustain." For several years, the 49ers had tried to escape the seemingly inevitable. Bill Walsh:

On the financial side, we faced a salary-cap overrun. The club had been, in recent years, mortgaging the future very heavily, with no way of coming out of it smoothly. We were on a collision course with financial disaster, so that is being addressed. There were a number of very good players who could still perform adequately, but because they had aged, they had lost the championship edge we had previously held. We have to move them along in their life's work and meanwhile replace them with younger men. So at this point, we expect one of the youngest teams in the league, whereas, just two years ago, we were the oldest team.

Naturally, a losing record enabled the 49ers to start rebuilding the team with draft picks previously not available to them. But Walsh is not overly concerned that a team composed of mostly younger players will be overwhelmed with the task before them.

The worst-record drafting first put us back into a competitive mode, because we were able to take the early choices and manipulate the draft to where we drafted eleven players, rather than six. So we helped our team immeasurably. Nowadays, the dynamics for the games have changed so much, meaning that a younger team has a chance. A younger team can be very competitive, as long as you don't keep telling them they're younger and using it as an excuse. You can use it as a real strength because these young players are so full of vitality and intensity. They just want to play football. So it's our job to develop it, to regenerate the attitude that we once had.

Walsh's observations and influence are anything but restricted to the field of play. An author and authority on management and organizations in his own right, Walsh returned to the 49ers with a perspective on organizational peak performance that has enabled him to pinpoint and swiftly assess what needs to be done to re-establish a winning franchise. Nevertheless, Walsh's initial reflections on how well the business was performing are not harsh.

Anyone could come to one of our practice sessions or one of our meetings and they would say, "Gee, they just aren't this progressive elsewhere." We are still ahead of the curve in that sense, but in this form of sport, you just can't sit with a pat hand; you just can't expect to function in the same way each year. You must be continually evaluating your performance level and be quite willing to listen, to observe and glean from others, anything that can help you, and not feel that you need a purist way of doing something.

Not surprisingly, Walsh's comfort zone is rarely stable. His more deliberative impression of the front office was that "people were still doing things in a virtually identical way to what they had been doing when I was here the first time." This was not seen as a compliment.

Well, you know, I was a little disappointed it hadn't moved forward. I didn't see much creativity and vision that had been a feature of the organization. So I'm hopeful that we can move to a new vista and be much more contemporary in everything we do.

One critical principle of organizational life, that for Walsh is non-negotiable, is that the executive branch should not retreat into its own fiefdom, making all the decisions in isolation from day-to-day activities. His argument is that each employee, top to bottom, needs to have complete clarity of his role, position, lines of communication, and, significantly, interaction with others. These are seen as the preconditions for wider involvement.

One of the critical factors that put us in the forefront of our sport is the full participation by every employee. Open communication and full participation. Everyone is expected, in fact it's demanded of everyone, to participate in the decision-making process. Not that the decision won't be made by a single source, but everyone's expected to participate. So when we sit in a staff meeting, I'll go around the room and everyone knows they're going to be asked their opinion and their feeling. At the same time, we don't hold people to thoughts or positions they've taken earlier. We understand change, we understand people learning more and finding out through the process of ongoing interaction. We don't point fingers saying, " I thought you said . . . ." None of that goes on.

This fundamental tenet is also reinforced by the return of John McVay to the 49ers as director of football operations. Together, Walsh and McVay were responsible for implementing many of the practices that define the organization. Travel Manager Dave Rahn, who has been with the franchise for sixteen years and who previously worked in the public relations office, has seen duty in a number of positions, and could be considered the quintessential example of a 49ers man. He understands the significance of Walsh's and McVay's return. Rocking back on his swivel chair, with arms outstretched, Rahn tries to communicate the essence of the picture by exclaiming, "You know, they built this world." Rahn knows them to be inspirational players who are determined to see the 49ers return to their winning ways. However, he believes that Walsh, in particular, is appreciated for his integrity regarding their immediate prospects.

We had some talks where he was very up-front and honest in saying that this was going to be a rebuilding process. He was not trying to hide anything or pull the wool over anybody's eyes. "We'll make it as short as we can, but we have to do this."

Longtime 49ers security coordinator Fred Gualco noted that Walsh began his new job in typical fashion. "He just watched; he observed and gave input where he thought it was necessary. It's a pleasure to watch him at work again, getting the best from what people are capable of doing."

Walsh and McVay also brought in Terry Donahue as director of player personnel. As a recent inductee into the College Hall of Fame, Donahue is rated by Gulaco as being "an asset to the max." Donahue was instrumental in developing the 49ers strategy in the 2000 draft process and is seen as fundamental to the future direction of the organization. Moreover, Donahue is central to the issue of succession, since Walsh expects to hand over his portfolio to Donahue "within the next year or two."

Completing the reconstitution of the 49ers front office is the transfer of power from long-standing owner Eddie DeBartolo to his sister Denise and her husband Dr. John York. York, whose sporting interests also include horse racing, is the executive vice president of the DeBartolo Corporation. Such weighty corporate responsibilities have not precluded York from a high level of involvement in 49er affairs. Dave Rahn:

> When John and Denise took over, this was not a big change in ownership. In fact it's nice, because it was kept in the family—it wasn't like shifting gears. Both of them had been around for some time anyway and knew how things were done. The veteran players are very familiar with them. Dr. York has been hands-on, spending a lot of time here trying to get familiarized with what was going on, including all aspects of the organization, from marketing to PR to football operations. He was even sitting right in the draft room, really doing his research. He's never been involved in something like that before, so he's definitely shown a real interest in wanting to succeed, along the lines established by Bill Walsh, John McVay, and Terry Donahue.

The 49er Way
The first minicamp of the 2000 season is under way. It is taking place at the Marie DeBartolo Center, 4949 Centennial Boulevard, which was built in 1988. This is the home of the 49ers. Situated on a sparsely populated tract of land where the dramatic backdrop of the Sierra Nevada mountains creates an aura of rural tranquillity, the two-story center is the only building nestling at the tip of a large dead-end road. Behind it, shielded by high fencing, are ten acres of land—the carefully groomed training ground. Passing through the front door, players and office workers exchange relaxed greetings with the security staff. Players swerve left or right to enter a maze of media, conference, and briefing rooms, or the weight lifting and

locker rooms. The arriving rookies, who account for sixty of the one hundred or so hopefuls at the minicamp, desperate to make the cruel cut before the season starts, try not to stare too obviously.

Administrative staff go directly ahead to a sweeping flight of stairs, passing a display cabinet that boasts an improbable and decidedly magical five Super Bowl trophies, alongside many other artifacts of conference supremacy. The top of the stairs opens out to a reception area, behind which are several eye-level shelves supporting gleaming gridiron helmets from other teams. Unmistakably, this is NFL territory. Further yardage gained reveals 49er magic on every wall, along every corridor, in every available nook and cranny. Awards, milestones, personalized plaques, and literally hundreds of carefully framed and mounted photographs give us the unmistakable impression that we are mere mortals in the midst of icons. These trappings of greatness include mementos of those world-famous inspirational players who are indelibly associated with 49ers glory: Joe Montana, Steve Young, and Jerry Rice. The mere mention of these names to enthusiasts of the gridiron code is likely to elicit wistfulness and ignoble jealousies, instigated by respect for talent and ability beyond earthly comprehension.

For the 49ers, this particular minicamp has multiple benefits. First and foremost is the opportunity to start the year afresh and to assess the assembled talent. The grass is still lush, perhaps greener than some of the hopefuls, who are wearing for the first time the coveted 49ers outfit. It's a long way to the Super Bowl, but the enthusiasm, commitment, and adrenaline are patently obvious. This is also an opportunity for the family to come together. As is always the case on these occasions, the front office turns out en masse. Save security at the front door, everyone crowds as close to the sideline as the coaches allow. Bill Walsh, accompanied by a small group of friends and colleagues from glorious campaigns of yesteryear, is also evident. He misses not a second of the day's proceedings, although he plays no part in directing the on-field activities. This is left to Head Coach Steve Mariucci, who spends his time striding among players issuing words of encouragement as they go through their punishing routines and set plays. Watching the minicamp unfold is Fred Gualco, for whom this is a familiar scene.

> There's definitely a sense, now, that there's a focus on the family, on loyalty and a dedication to this organization. Whether you're a player, an administrator, or a coach, you know that this is a unique family and that they'll care for you, they'll develop you, and if it's that time for you to move on, they'll help push your career. That's the way it's always been, a career foundation for a lot of people.

Yet on this occasion something is new. For the first time, the dream of the 49ers is being shared with others. The minicamp has been opened up to corporations who either already sponsor the 49ers, or who might want to invest in a formal association with them. Unsurprisingly, in attendance are an array of the new breed of dot-coms who are eager to establish themselves with one of the most recognizable brands in the world. Stalwarts of the e-commerce world such as Dale Fuller, president and CEO of Inprise/Borland and ex-manager of Apple's PowerBook unit, can be seen on the sideline trying to figure out "which of the ubiquitous players is Jerry Rice." The executive vice president of Endwave, Doug Lockie, has already figured out that Rice wears number 80 and is tracking his every move. And he has also already decided that he wants to establish a strong sponsorship relationship, the only question is "the amount."

For Kirk Reynolds, director of public relations, and Rodney Knox, director of communications and marketing, these sponsors represent key opportunities to build important relationships that will help the 49ers maintain their infrastructure. Before the activity on the field gets under way, Coach Mariucci is brought over to those assembled and, by way of a handshake, vigorously introduces himself—an act that clearly confers both a sense of legitimacy and importance to the event. Promotional packets that include player information and identification sheets provide a strong sense of inclusion. This is amplified when members of the front office join the sponsors during a specially prepared barbecue lunch.

The day's proceedings conclude with the obligatory media crush as the invited press circle both Mariucci and Rice. Mariucci believes that, once securely in the locker room adjacent to the field, Rice will almost certainly be asked for autographs by a healthy posse of the possible new recruits. This can hardly be surprising. Jerry Rice is the greatest wide receiver in NFL history. His personal statistics will, in all likelihood, never be matched again. Over a full career, the constant pressure of eluding defensive cover might weigh like a nightmare on lesser beings. However, when we interviewed Rice in the twilight of his brilliant career, his passion for the game, his legendary fitness routines, and his glorious capacity for fun signaled by his infectious smile remained undiminished. It was impossible not to be completely charmed by him. More than most, he has the right to lay claim to being a major contributor to the 49ers' winning ways, yet when asked for his assessment of the origins of the team's success, he chose to highlight a strategic explanation:

> I think the San Francisco 49ers have been so successful because of the people upstairs—the organization. We had the best owner in the NFL. He was a very caring individual, and it really made you want to go out there and leave everything on the football field for this guy. He took care of his players. When I first came in, he was just like a father figure to me. I have so much respect for Mr. DeBartolo, and we still have such a good relationship. When we took to that football field, we always said that we're representing this guy.

Edward J. DeBartolo, Jr., president and CEO of the DeBartolo Corporation based in Ohio, purchased the 49ers in 1977. The turnaround, from two seasons with only two wins to the championship in Super Bowl XVI, has been well documented. Less well known is the deep personal impact this inspirational owner had on the 49ers organization. Any conversation with a member of the 49ers about how their twenty-plus year winning record has been sustained is guaranteed to start with "Mr. D." Until the transfer of ownership at the beginning of 2000, DeBartolo played an enormous part in establishing the organizational imperatives that remain powerful and acutely tangible to all. Recently retired quarterback Steve Young:

> We had an owner who valued winning more than just the bottom line. If only the bottom line is valued, then you don't have any incentive to win. He really had a desire to win football games, even though it might not have been in the best interests of his bottom line. Having said that, he set a tone of accountability. In a game like football, usually, the first thing that happens if you start to go downhill is that everyone starts pointing fingers at who is supposedly responsible. We had an owner who was willing to ask, "What did I do wrong? What do I need to do?" He set the tone for the rest of the organization, so that every person in the building says, "Well if the owner says 'What did I do wrong?' then what did I do wrong myself?" This is how we avoid the culture of finger-pointing, which will ruin an organization.
>
> In 1993 we lost the championship game to the Cowboys for the second year in a row. It was clear that if we didn't find a way to beat the Cowboys, we weren't going to win the Super Bowl. So Mr. DeBartolo said, "What do I need to do to beat the Cowboys?" He started that whole feeling. By the time it got down to the players, it was like, Okay, we've got everything we can to help us beat the Cowboys. We ended up beating them and won Super Bowl XXIV. That's a perfect example of accountability.

In addition to accountability, DeBartolo engendered an atmosphere of caring and support throughout the organization. Players and administrators alike now access a mutually supportive network. Fred Gualco saw, firsthand, DeBartolo's effect on the players:

> If there was something wrong with them he was always involved, deeply involved, and that's important. It is just phenomenal that our owner cared personally for the players and staff. When you see that, it has a tremendous impact. He stepped forward if there was a problem, no matter how small, and this gave everyone the

feeling that the owner cared for them. It is now a large family, and everybody cares for each other. No other teams in the NFL have this to the same extent. We've been to five Super Bowls, and we've watched other teams just show up, with their players wondering about how their mother and father and brother and sister are going to get there from different locations and about their flight reservations; but we do all that for our players. We make them as comfortable as possible.

Newer members of the organization, like Jim Mora, who joined the coaching staff (defensive backs) in 1997, are quick to pick up on the contrast with their previous experiences. As he rattled off a series of personal reflections, Mora's enthusiasm for this topic was evident from the sheer delight that accompanied his observations on the 49ers.

The number one difference that I have noticed since I have been here is the way that people are treated in a professional sense. Everybody in this organization is made to feel that they have a part in winning football games, and yet everybody understands that the most important people in any organization are the players and the coaches. Moreover—and I think that this is really important—in the other organizations I have been in, there hasn't been an effort by the front-office people to make the players feel as if they are special. The players have always felt, in my opinion, that they are a little more on the subservient side. Yet in this organization there is a concerted effort to make the players feel that they are special, that they are going to be taken care of so that they can concentrate on their job.

For instance, I had an experience in the first training camp last year. I had a flat tire. I asked a guy where I could get my tire fixed and he said, "You don't get your tire fixed around here. We do that. Give me your keys." This organization allows you, as a coach or a player, to focus solely on football and playing the game. They do a great job of making the players feel special.

Feeling special is not confined to the players. Sandy Fontana, who works closely with the chief financial officer and vice president of business operations, provides insight into the texture of the organization's community. In addition to her duties for the CFO, she works on benefits and health insurance and is moving toward human resources. She previously worked on travel, the portfolio now held by Dave Rahn. Fontana has been with the 49ers for fifteen years, but held her first 49er season tickets while still in high school. A self-confessed gridiron junkie, she still watches all the games from the bleachers with the rest of the fans, rather than from the more palatial surroundings that she could easily access. She describes a heady combination of magic making and strong community affiliation:

> It is very rare in almost any organization to establish, as our owner did, the foundation for a genuine family-type atmosphere, rather than a nine-to-five routine. Mr. DeBartolo always did something for the staff and the players—not just the players, but the staff as well. One year he hired a plane and we had our Super Bowl party in Hawaii; absolutely everyone went. In 1994 the whole organization went to Colorado Springs for three or four days. We had a barbecue one night, and at the Super Bowl party the rings were actually presented to the players. There was horseback riding, golfing, hot-air ballooning, and you could spend the entire day at the spa. It was absolutely wonderful and relaxing.
>
> At these Super Bowl retreats you really get to know everybody in the organization and their spouses or their own special guests—and it isn't like, "That's Jerry Rice and I can't talk to him." He is just another person. It brings more of a family and a human element into the organization. Even though we have a lot of superstars on our team, they are not, "Don't touch me, I am special." They are down-to-earth, normal people. Down-to-earth millionaires, that is! Mr. DeBartolo made this a family. He knew everybody's name and most of their spouses too.

Murlan Fowell, director of stadium operations at 3 Com Park, is another fourteen-year veteran of the organization who wastes no time in locating the origins of the 49ers' success.

> As the owner of this franchise, Mr. DeBartolo was generous to a fault in that he gave everything to the team, the players and the employees. He was a very generous man, and I think he built a loyalty and a camaraderie, so that you wanted to do the best you could for him because of what he did for you. I don't know that there's a lot of teams that can say that. You really take pride in your job and your responsibilities, and you want to make sure you get it right. You're part of the team.

Since the DeBartolo era, the structure of the 49ers organization has remained uncomplicated. In part, the community itself acts as a substitute for hierarchical complexity, and there is no evidence of artificial mechanisms designed to achieve integration. Formally, the general manager/vice president reports to the owner; under them are two more vice presidents, one of football operations and one of business. On the business side are several departments, including stadium operations, ticketing, marketing, travel, public relations, and accounts. The formal organization chart is not used in any operational way. Interestingly, it is hand-drawn (given the names associated with each portfolio, it is also several years out of date) with a series of dotted lines that indicate the possibility of multiple task activities where organizational participants, irrespective of their own functional expertise, are expected to relate to and cooperate in managing any number of ongoing scenarios. There are no teams or project leaders with official responsibility to make this happen. This $150 million operation, with up to 100 direct staff and players, and up to 2,000 part-time stadium workers, is run on simple, informal lines.

Unquestionably, the stability and continuity of the 49ers staff has enabled the 49ers to create the future. A solid cadre of coaches and administrators have been with the organization through many triumphs and, along the way, have inevitably learned how to deal with defeat—"turning the page," as it is described here. Coaches such as Dwaine Board and Tom Rathman played with the 49ers, and most long-serving administrators have worked in several capacities, adding to their overall fund of knowledge.

The reappointment of Bill Walsh as head coach is often seen as a pivotal moment in the long-term fortunes of the franchise. His initial tenure with the 49ers lasted from 1978 until 1989. Technically, Walsh is famous for the development and innovation of "the west coast offense." This method has been adopted by other teams whose coaches were once with the 49ers, thus enabling direct competitors to share in the 49ers' knowledge base. Mike Shanahan of the Denver Broncos and Mike Holgrem of the Seattle Seahawks, formerly coaches with the 49ers, have each tasted Super Bowl success based on their apprenticeships in San Francisco. Indeed, Steve Mariucci, who joined as head coach in 1997, spent part of his professional career under the tutelage of Mike Holgrem with the Packers. Mariucci notes the irony of his outsider status, coming as he did from the collegiate ranks as head coach at the University of California: "Mike Holgrem taught things the 49ers way. That's where I learned it. So they hired a guy from the outside, but I wasn't really an outsider. Hey, I was going to be a guy that was going to keep the continuity!"

Walsh's legacy is also managerial. The simple nature of the 49ers' organizational structure can be traced back to Walsh's philosophy of loyalty to and focus on a single command structure. His managerial style had the most lasting impact on the organization. The late Bob McKittrick, whom Walsh described as the finest offensive line coach the world has ever seen, explained to us how the 49er system began to take shape. McKittrick had more than twenty years with the 49ers and nearly thirty years in the NFL. He went to all the Super Bowls won by the franchise, as well as three college Rose Bowls, and along with the owner, was one of the few inspirational figures who experienced a losing season. With a generation of experience in pro football, McKittrick's reflections have immediate currency.

When Bill Walsh came into the organization, it had been decimated by defeat. The previous president/general manager had not been able to overcome the alienation of the people within the organization. The very first thing he did was to stress that we were going to be a first-class organization and present a good image for football. With Mr. DeBartolo unable to be here every day, Coach Walsh was essentially the man in charge.

Very early on he held an important meeting with everyone except the players and coaches. He told them that their job was to assist the players and coaches in anything they needed to help the team win football games. Stressing involvement and innovation, Walsh told us that anything that we thought might help the team play a little better, to win football games, would be welcomed. Coach Walsh asked everybody for ideas, so he would get the equipment man's opinion and the trainer's opinion and the video person's opinion as well as those of the assistant coaches and general manager and other people too. You could be standing at a urinal next to him and he would ask you, "What do you think about this?" He got information from everybody. Soon, the team buses ran on time. The players had a single room instead of doubling up, they traveled on a nicer aircraft, and ate better. All these little things were hard to notice, but if you had been somewhere else you would know the difference. All this laid down the foundation for an informal atmosphere.

A chance meeting between one of the authors and a cabin crew member on a Pacific flight reveals a similar story, confirming, even for those on the periphery of the organization, the kind of convivial, inclusive atmosphere established by Walsh. Margie Lince-Boris, who used to work the 49er charter flights at the start of the Walsh era, vividly remembers "advising" Walsh that it was about time that "young Joe Montana" be given the opportunity to start as the 49er quarterback. Lince-Boris is "entirely convinced" that since Joe actually started as quarterback in the next game, this was ample evidence of Walsh's ability to listen to sound advice.

In this early period of the Walsh era, all other official positions answered to Coach Walsh, so everybody was headed in the direction established by this informal consultative process. Crucially, the key aspect lay in the close working relationship between "football" and "administration." Understandably, no one on the administrative side calls any of the plays during a game, and each side of the business works through a season according to its own rhythm and heartbeat; yet all elements unite to maintain their focus. As the organization has expanded and taken on new operating characteristics, the simple command structure Walsh adopted, almost by default, has long since been replaced with decentralized decision making amid multiple sources of inspirational leadership. Nonetheless, the driving ambition of the administration to do anything imaginable to help the players focus on their game remains powerfully intact.

The ability of the 49ers organization to create success in the future also rests on its ability to hire the right people and to slide them into critical positions without extensive upheaval. Bruce Popko, director of marketing until his departure in late 1998 to join the Cleveland expansion team, was himself "watched" for two years as his career in football took him from the New York Jets to the NFL. He was actively head-hunted for the position, giving him an interesting perspective on how the 49ers acquire new staff:

> I don't know—it seems like the 49ers just have an uncanny knack of being able to pull out or just lose one or several pieces of the puzzle and are then always able to replace those pieces of the puzzle with a worker or coach or player just as effective as the one that departed. In a lot of other organizations, not just professional sports, there can be a total vacuum, a total void, created when certain individuals leave, but the 49ers are able to put people in there who are as effective as, or even more effective than, their predecessors.

Care is also taken to ensure that the personalities on the field mesh well. When the high-profile and controversial Deion Sanders became available to the 49ers, many of the key players were canvassed to see if they thought he could fit with the rest of the team. This process helped smooth Sanders's induction and acceptance by all the players. More important, for the one season he spent with the 49ers, Sanders proved to be a popular catalyst, and helped to inspire victory in Super Bowl XXIX.

One of the key appointments to the organization, made in 1996, was that of Bill Duffy to the position of CFO and vice president of business operations. Even though Duffy was only with the 49ers for a short period of time, he quickly reflected and readily accepted the 49ers philosophy that no one is above the team. Like the famous quarterback legends Joe Montana and Steve Young, whom the 49ers proudly parade as their own, Duffy was extremely adept at making swift judgments that helped carry the organization forward. His field of vision, like that of many hands-on managers, had to stretch from gritty day-to-day detail to the highly strategic and crucial deploying of finite financial resources. Fontana confirms that "When Bill came in, I don't think we missed a beat. We were able to keep going, because everybody knew what needed to be done and how to help him." Duffy's appointment was indeed a key piece of the jigsaw; so much so, that Mr. DeBartolo's personal intervention is worth noting here. Bill Duffy:

> One of the things that I found interesting about my interview process was that at the time I didn't know I was in the process! I had met with the president for a couple of hours and had a discussion about my philosophy and my business approach. A couple of months later he asked me to come on down for dinner on a Sunday night with Mr. D., where there would be five or six people from the organization. Additionally there were many other DeBartolo family members—cousins, this and that. I kind of picked up that it was a big night for me to do well with the universe of people there. We sat down for dinner—it was a very informal big Italian dinner, "Get this, pass that"—everybody is reaching and sharing—and by the time everybody has settled in, there is Mr. D. right across the table from me at maybe a twenty-person-long table. I didn't think

anything of it at the time, but realized later that this obviously wasn't an accident. I handled a lot of questions that night.

Ensuring continuity of purpose through careful recruitment is a way of life with the 49ers, which makes it possible to lose or replace key personnel without disturbing the existing community. Such stability can also be found in stadium operations, where the tradition of working 49er games is all about family and preservation of identity. Murlan Fowell:

> Many of our 2,000 employees go back to the previous ownership. We have grandfathers, fathers, and sons who between them have worked throughout the fifty years of the franchise's history. In fact, our game-day coordinator who organizes the ushers and gate men is seventy-one years old and has been here since 1946–47. We had an usher who we finally had to retire a couple of years ago because he was ninety-five years old. It was his life; he lived for the 49ers. We used to provide a chair for the guy, so he could sit down, but finally his family forced his retirement because he just wasn't capable of looking after himself. The family had to move him to his son's (his son was over seventy years old, for God's sake) in Los Angeles to get him away from here so he couldn't work anymore.

The SF logo on the side of the helmet is one of the most instantly recognizable brand images in all of pro sports. Sharing the dream is an important element of the magic that the 49ers have brought to pro football. It starts with the players and coaches. Those who go on to other teams take part of the dream with them and get to see the magnitude of the 49ers' overall influence on the NFL. Running backs coach Tom Rathman, who believes that "living and dying with the 49ers start when the players walk through the front door for the first time," had the opportunity to play for another NFL team before retiring from the field. This gave him an opportunity to compare firsthand the 49ers and his new club.

Rathman's observation is clinical: "The difference was night and day. It wasn't even close in the way the organization was run." While players are most viscerally at the center of the dream, the paying fans are only a step away from the snap, and with a highly competitive entertainment industry also scrambling for scarce dollars, the 49ers must provide a reason to fill 3 Com Park each season. The stadium has a capacity of 70,000, and it has been sold out since 1981. Lynn Carrozzi, ticket manager, estimates that there are approximately 20,000 people on the waiting list for the existing 65,000 season tickets, which can be passed down through family. Since the stadium is currently owned by the city of San Francisco, the 49ers are severely restricted in their ability to customize and market the 49ers brand according to their specific needs. Nevertheless, the existing, long-standing fan base has developed its own way of sharing the dream of the 49ers. For a 1:00 P.M. Sunday game, the huge parking lot that runs all the way from the stadium down to the water's edge starts filling up at around 7:00 A.M. Those with motor homes will arrive the night before and wait for the parking lot gates to be opened. The NFL tradition of tailgate barbecues and parties is in full swing by midmorning. At Christmas, the carnival-like atmosphere includes bringing tons of snow down from the mountains, and Christmas trees with lights are rigged up all over the lot. Most seasoned fans will enter the stadium only forty-five minutes before the start of the game. When they enter their section of the stadium they are sharing an experience that has been passed down through each generation. They will see the same families, gate men, and ushers who have enjoyed the same rituals for years. Stadium staff go the extra mile for their customers, sometimes visiting season ticket holders in their seats in order to address an issue or concern raised in correspondence with the ticket office. Fowell describes this technique as "turning negatives into positives." Sponsors, too, are very aware of this captive audience. Bruce Popko:

> The mystique of this organization and its success, year in and year out, continues to help us sell. The nice thing here is that we have been able to be more selective with the partners that we are doing

business with. We don't necessarily have to jump at whatever opportunity is there. We can be a little bit more selective and say to ourselves, Let's not only align ourselves with partners that are going to help us maximize our revenue and accomplish a lot of the business, Let's align ourselves with companies that we think are going down the same path that we are, philosophically. We want to partner with those at the top of their industry. That is remarkably different from a lot of the other teams in the league.

Winning the right way, with class, makes sharing the dream that much more potent. Popko argues that "This creates a much larger fan base that enables the 49ers to sustain their position, while other teams temporarily shine and then disappear from the radar screen."

Getting It Done

The pressure on the 49ers to perform is intense and stressful. Jerry Rice personifies the way the organization reacts to its environment:

You know, the expectations out here are so high. You start that winning tradition and the fans are very unforgiving. This team is supposed to win. It's a lot of pressure on you, but I love pressure. Life is nothing without pressure. If you could come out here every day and just run around with no pressure on you, or go on that football field on that given Sunday and there's no pressure, then I don't think you're going to have a good time. I love the game so much that I challenge myself during the off-season to get better. I never feel like I've really played that perfect game, and that's the extra incentive to go out there and get into the best shape of your life.

The determination to win has created a climate where the organization is able to channel individual effort successfully, according to an unremitting focus that is recognized by all. Everyone strives to be the best that they can be—to exceed their personal best. From a player's point of view this is very much de rigueur, even more so with the advent of the salary cap, which ensures that all the NFL teams spend roughly the same amount of money on salaries. Mariucci argues that this "puts everyone on an even keel, making things more challenging, with a premium on superior personal performance." Mora believes that the organization is well placed to deliver, noting that "You are stepping into an environment where I believe your level of performance increases because it's expected of you." Andy Sugarman, a relative newcomer to the 49ers with coach Mariucci, immediately grasped the importance of exceeding personal best:

> I've noticed in my time working here that every day you show up for work you've got to be ready to go a hundred miles an hour, and it's expected that you take it to another level, higher than you first thought you could. The hard part is probably getting to that level, but once you are there, it snowballs and it becomes what is expected.

Organizationally, the impact of almost two decades of winning seasons has led to a reinterpretation of what winning means. Winning better than the last win drives the organization. All portfolio holders are constantly looking to improve on their previous performance. Whether it is travel, marketing, or stadium operations, the sense of dissatisfaction is always present. Murlan Fowell:

> In stadium operations, we don't have a direct competitor, as the guys on the field do, so I am driven to be the best in what I do. In our job, we're playing against ourselves, so we've got to be able to see how far we want to go. It's not a competition; there's not an opponent. We have a function and we want to do that the best we possibly can.

High expectations throughout the organization, aided and abetted by a culture of constant improvement in all aspects of the business, naturally lead to game-breaking ideas. At the same time, change is profoundly difficult when operations appear to differ little from year to year. Murlan Fowell explains how Jim Mercurio from stadium operations was determined to help the 49ers redefine industry practice:

> Let me give you an example. It's easy in this business not to make change; it's easy just to do the same old thing year after year. But when Jim came to work here several years ago, one thing he grabbed onto was our credential and security system. He came to me with a system that we then developed over a couple of years and now it is the best, not only in the NFL, but probably in professional sports in the United States. Other people are coming to us and saying, "Explain your system to us!" It pretty much reversed the way we did things, simplifying it and making it self-regulating. It's much more effective. Now another team would not typically have championed this initiative. We're open to new ideas.

Every single day the 49ers broker, support, and develop better ways to make things happen. Efficiencies, savings, and resource investments are continually calibrated to serve the focus of the organization. According to Popko this means that "We are always able to stay one step ahead of the curve at every point, and we do it without showing our hand to everyone else."

Being the most successful franchise in the NFL means that all aspects of the operation are always subject to close critical scrutiny from other NFL teams as well as the media and the broader entertainment industry. This creates an added incentive to avoid negative commentary, although it is next to impossible to find evidence of organizational neglect. The defining quality of the 49er system is that of ensuring that the players can focus on the field of play, which has led to a near obsessive devotion to looking after the last detail. Every organization in this study exhibits the ability to cover detail competently, but the 49ers elevate this aspect of their work to a level of intensity that words do not adequately convey. The passion in Dave Rahn's voice was evident when he explained to us the "details details details" of travel operations. As well as organizing bigger planes, better hotels, and better food, his department looks after everything from the players, coaches, and their extended families to the logistics and layout of the hotel. In reconnaissance visits to away venues, bus and truck travel times from hotel to stadium are assiduously logged, as are the eating arrangements, right down to the condiment selection. Dave Rahn:

> I will look at the specs from a hotel that we have not stayed at before and they are always extremely vague. When I ask for more information and request certain things to be done, the hotels invariably come back and tell me that other NFL teams have never concerned themselves with such matters. Once we provide direction, they actually appreciate the detailed outlines.

On occasion, such care for the last detail is not without psychological costs. During the 1997–78 season, as the 49ers won the divisional title and prepared for their conference championship game against the Green Bay Packers, Rahn was part of a large senior management team working on arrangements for a possible Super Bowl appearance in San Diego.

> I still have a filing cabinet that is full of stuff. We were in San Diego three times, mapping it all out. We had to imagine moving about 1,000 to 1,200 people. Much of this fell on my shoulders. My timetable was that we would have to be there on the Monday after winning the conference game. We didn't want the players worrying about tickets so we would have had to get them out by Monday or Tuesday at the latest. I have a whole stack of manila envelopes with names written on them, ready for the tickets that never came.
>
> I had my timetable and logistics in the computer, and individualized letters for everybody, ready to be printed out for another set of envelopes also to be handed out on Monday, saying, "Here is all your Super Bowl information." I had the whole thing orchestrated. Everything was detailed. I had every office laid out, every office diagrammed at the hotel, every phone, every com-

puter, everything, down to the last detail. I had it all mapped out because I had to. You have to prepare for the unknown. But going right to the brink and getting knocked out . . . it was terrible.

Lynn Carrozzi, responsible for ticketing, is similarly inspired to cover all possible outcomes, for which there are no written procedures. Indeed, not for the first time, we heard the incantation, "It's pretty much in my head and their heads." Where a task has a direct impact on a particular customer, personal attention overrides automated systems.

If season ticket holders change their seat location, I do that manually—one of the girls will then input what I have done manually into the computer and a third one will check it to make sure that they match. We do a lot of what seems to be double work or overwork, but since detail is so important in this office, I would rather overkill than neglect something.

This level of care for the last detail can be found among all staff. Fontana believes that "it is something that carries through the entire organization." The same level of detailed planning that accompanies the players on away games is replicated when the 49ers take the organization on retreat. All arrangements, including ground transport, flights, and accommodation are taken care of, right down to personalized gifts being placed on the bed in the hotel rooms when everyone arrives.

The ultimate goal embraced by the 49ers is the removal of all impediments, all negative forces, to enable concentration on the game plan. Collectively, this state of flow can lead to powerful surges of self-belief. Recalling his first Super Bowl ring, Jerry Rice described how it felt to know that he was about to write a page in the sports history book:

We won Super Bowl XXIII on the final drive of the game. The game had been back and forth the entire time and now, with three minutes left, everything was on the line. When Joe ran into the huddle, even with the crowd screaming, you could hear a pin drop. The focus was so strong, with so much excitement, we knew we could get the job done, because we'd been in that situation before. In the huddle, we were all smiling because we knew we were going to win. Taking a ball over ninety yards, to win the Super Bowl—one mistake, and it's over. You lose. But we were so sharp and we made the right plays, and won. Man, that's the ultimate.

Those in administration express similar sensations of superior performance, invariably commenting on moments when time seems to distort and pleasure, tension, and exhaustion collide. In contrast, following a tightly disciplined training session, Steve Young described to us a distortion in "space," and in doing so provided one of the most evocative stories encountered on the project. His job is to move the ball forward; this is the essential measure of greatness in the NFL. And Young fulfills the criteria for greatness in every way. A peerless record of play-off contentions, divisional and NFL championships, as well as a Super Bowl ring, help to define the man and his craft. There are few more powerful images in sport than that of the gridiron quarterback who, in the face of organized opposition, inexorably drives his team down the field to secure a touchdown. Ever since the game was first played, this mesmerizing progress has been seen as symbolic. The running game represents the hard yards of life, with the promise of occasional rapid breakthrough. The passing game offers the seduction of quicker, more immediate progress, but can be an all-or-nothing gamble. On every play, these elements appear to be in balance:

I focus on tilting the field so that we are going downhill. The sheer momentum is carrying you that way. It's funny; I've had the experience of sitting on the sidelines when the quarter finishes, and we have to switch ends. Now, psychologically, we were just running downhill in one direction, and we don't want to go uphill. I really have to concentrate to make sure we are going downhill again, but in the opposite direction. Mentally, I have to retilt the field.

In metaphorical terms, the whole of the 49ers organization is dedicated to helping Young both tilt and retilt the field. This becomes most evident in the preparation and lead-up to the Sunday football game.

A 49ers Weekend

The trust between the players and administration is supreme. This is clearly evident when the players assemble on a Saturday at the San Francisco Marriott airport hotel for a Sunday-afternoon home game at 3 Com Park. The players are greeted by administrative staff who have made all the logistical arrangements for them. The atmosphere in the hotel lobby, where the 49ers have set up their own check-in system, powerfully exemplifies the community. One by one, the players muster at the 49ers' desk, staffed by the familiar face of Dave Rahn, who obviously maintains a close personal investment in the players' welfare. Their response is one of affection. Humor and good-natured banter echo around the lobby; the family is coming together. Security, though unobtrusive, is necessarily ever present. Senior administrators are also on hand. They also travel to away games, and on this occasion stay at the team hotel the night before the Sunday game. They waste no time in moving easily between players and administrators alike, softly sharing brief words of mutual recognition and support and, occasionally, more lively dialogue. There are no high fives here, or any of the overt physical demonstrations of manhood that are habitually associated with the NFL. Partners and children are a vital part of this community.

Early Saturday evening, the players enter a series of team briefings in readiness for the game on Sunday against the Indianapolis Colts. In between these meetings, which are run with clockwork precision, the players graze on inviting bowls of M&Ms, chilled sodas, or healthier fare. The ambience is both relaxed and focused. At one point, future Hall-of-Famer Jerry Rice attempts to coordinate a can of soda, a cocktail napkin, and a small morsel of food. This is evidently one task too many, and soft hands notwithstanding, Rice unceremoniously drops all items to the floor. A group of administrators who have witnessed this horrifying sight hope that it is not an unwelcome omen for the upcoming game.

The final briefing is attended by all the players, assembled administrators, and the odd invited guest. Coach Mariucci starts the session by showing a video montage of the previous game where the 49ers demolished the New Orleans Saints, which is set to evocative music and interspersed with humorous asides inserted from TV shows. The atmosphere is highly charged. The coach then hands out several shirts to selected players for their meritorious contribution in the victory over the Saints. Their dollar value is nominal, yet it is clear that they are prized possessions. Finally, Coach Mariucci winds up the session with a passionate, hard-driving invocation on how and why the 49ers are going to win their game on Sunday. Using finely measured oratory, he strides among his players, momentarily becoming part of the audience. A hand touches a shoulder as he slowly pivots around, incorporating the whole room into his field of vision.

> We're not going to win tomorrow because we're much better than them or because they're the rookies, or because we're at home and we're the good guys. Those aren't the reasons we're going to win this game. Don't ever kid yourself that that's how you win the football game. That stuff doesn't mean anything, doesn't mean anything. We play harder than them, we play more disciplined than them, we execute our game plan better than they execute their game plan. We take care of the ball better than they take care of the ball. That's why we're going to win the game. You've got to play to that plan.

The locker rooms at 3 Com Park are spartan and unpretentious. They have obviously seen better days. Unsurprisingly, they are in sharp contrast to the 49ers' pristine, though modest, training facilities at Santa Clara, an hour's drive south on Highway 101. Nevertheless, the functional locker rooms provide a sufficient, perhaps even appropriate setting for the team to go through the rituals of game preparation. On entering the facility there is a small anteroom off to the right where the head coach can work with players without distraction. The primary locker room area is split into two levels, making overall communication somewhat fragmented.

No matter, the 49ers have obviously long since made peace with their physical circumstances. They are at home here, preparing for their upcoming game against the Colts. Naturally, access to this hallowed place is restricted, but in keeping with the family orientation, a number of players' children are in evidence.

One of them is the son of Steve Mariucci, who is intent on getting a personal photograph alongside Jerry Rice. He is successful in this endeavor, but Rice takes the opportunity to bind the boy's hands and feet with masking tape. Once he is apparently securely trussed and immobilized, the rest of the locker room grinningly enjoy their adult superiority, but only briefly, as the boy upstages his hero by simply slipping off his sneakers and calmly walking away. This is evidently a team and an extended family that embellishes its strong professional work ethic with fun and empathy.

After a close-fought, thrilling 34–31 victory over the Colts, secured in the dying seconds of the game, the locker room is transformed. It is pure mayhem. The artifacts of victory in the form of binding tape, pads, helmets, and endless layers of clothing are strewn around the floor, but this growing mountain fails to impede the animated movement of coaches, administrators, security guards, and family. Outside in the parking lot adjacent to the stadium, thousands of fans have fired up their celebratory tailgate barbecues. Two hours after the end of the game, enthusiastic fans still congregate at the players' exit gates waiting to cheer their heroes as they and their families drive off in search of solitude. The greatest cheer is of course reserved for quarterback Steve Young. The roar of delight honors the organization's most inspirational player. The dream is shared and a community's belief in itself is upheld once more.

The morning after is soon lost to a nonstop series of the inevitable thorough game debriefings. By early lunchtime, without apparent design, administrators and players can be found eagerly lining up for salad, burgers, hot dogs, and related trimmings. Ritually, and for longer than anyone can remember, lunch is brought in each week by a different outside caterer, to be consumed communally in one of the briefing rooms, canteen-style. The whole organization is at ease and together.

First Down

In the face of considerable internal upheaval, together with constant turbulent external change, the 49ers have been able to establish consistency, continuity, and stability in their operations. Recruitment, selection, advancement, retention, and letting go are the most visible techniques used to create the future. Although the franchise has grown in extraordinary and significant ways, the organizational footprint remains clearly mapped. Getting the job done is a sharp phrase that carries discipline and expectations beyond its cliché-ridden origins. Personal and organizational sacrifice are the defining contours of the footprint. Players and office staff who pursue interests, personal or otherwise, outside this tight configuration of values eventually leave the 49ers. There is no place for those who do not share the dream. Bill Walsh, apart from winning three Super Bowls, established the guiding principle that administrative functions needed to be constantly and unceasingly focused on helping the players win football games. The respect and affection afforded Mr. DeBartolo provided the necessary glue that has been successfully transferred to the new ownership. The results have been remarkable. Dave Rahn:

> Since 1981 the bar has been set so high. We have been through and won five Super Bowls, and have worked with some of the greatest players in the game. One day we will sit back and say, "Man, that was incredible, that was just an incredible run that we were part of."
>
> You know we've had people who tell us, "You've been around for so long, and maybe it's good that you got to experience a losing season." No! It's not good! I never want to experience something like that! It makes you really appreciate what you had.

However, Bill Walsh is not yet prepared to preside over the demise of the NFL's long-standing elite team.

> We are alive and well. In the April 2000 draft, we rediscovered ourselves. We did this through our method of drafting, the people we drafted, and now we manipulated the draft through trades, prior to the draft and during the draft. We did this to get the men that we wanted. The mechanics of doing it were in place, and people from all over football could see that we were back. We demonstrated that from now on, they are going to have account for us when it comes to the championship.

3

The Atlanta Braves: The Eagle Has Landed

"There's a great sense of pride, here. You really have to pinch yourself every now and then to remind yourself that you're living through something that is very, very rare in any sport—to be at the level of success that we've been, for the last eight years, and with a reasonable expectation of continuing that success for the next four or five years, considering our team and the popularity of Turner Field. You really don't see our run coming to an end anytime soon."

—BOB WOLFE, SENIOR VICE PRESIDENT,
ADMINISTRATION

Many people in the Braves organization had little love for the old Atlanta–Fulton County Stadium. Hank Aaron might have slugged his 715th home run there, thereby eclipsing Babe Ruth's improbable long-standing record, and it might have hosted a World Series victory in 1995, but the day it was razed to the ground, few seemed to mind. Most, like the president, Stan Kasten, were glad to see the end of it. Perhaps the old stadium was forever tainted with pre-1991 memories of lost games, dwindling crowds, and an organization that had lost its way. Somehow, the Braves staff were able to divorce the greatest winning streak in baseball history from the very stadium where the feat began. They disliked the cramped offices, the lack of atmosphere, and the poor facilities. Quite simply, this peak-performing organization had outgrown its home.

Since the turnaround season of 1991, when the team went from worst to first in major league baseball, the Braves have won nine consecutive divisional titles, five national league titles, and the World Series title in 1995. Their total attendance at the beginning of the nineties was less than one million. At the conclusion of the decade that figure had climbed by a factor of three to well over three and a half million. No other team in the history of baseball has matched such a ten-year level of sustained peak performance. Archrivals from the American league, the mighty New York Yankees, trailed the Braves during this period by more than seventy games. Put simply, the Braves franchise currently wins more games in the major leagues than any other team. Inevitable comparisons with the undoubted "team of the century," the New York Yankees, who earned three World Series victories during the nineties, promises to set up one of the most enduring rivalries in modern professional sports.

For the Braves, their new home stadium, Turner Field, symbolizes their hard-earned change of fortunes. It trumpets both a successful ball club and an entertainment brand second to none within the sports industry, which competes intensely with other outlets for the disposable dollar.

Turner Field was the original venue for the Atlanta Olympic Games held in 1996, yet the Braves did not simply inherit an Olympic stadium. The reality is a little different. Stan Kasten and Billy Payne, who was the president and CEO of the Atlanta Olympic Committee, had the strategic vision to fulfill the needs of both organizations by contracting for the specs for the stadium to be drawn up in such a way that when the Braves took ownership, its conversion to a ball-park would essentially be a reconversion. As far back as 1989, when Atlanta city leaders were talking about putting in a bid for the Olympic Games, Stan Kasten suggested to them the idea of an Olympic stadium that could be converted to a baseball park later.

Around this time, the Atlanta Falcons of the National Football League had a new stadium built for them—the Georgia Dome. This left the Braves as the sole tenant in Atlanta–Fulton County Stadium, a thirty-year-old facility that wasn't ideal for either football or baseball, but was plausible for both. Given that the city had assisted the football team, the Atlanta Braves began busily investigating their own options. Bob Wolfe, senior vice president of administration:

> That's when Stan started laying the seeds for Turner Field. This was before the team on the field took off with any level of success. By the time the city won its Olympic bid, we had already hired architects to start plans for an Olympic stadium that could be converted to a baseball park. It was really a baseball park that could be used temporarily as an Olympic stadium. We had invested in those plans even before the city succeeded in the Olympic bid—we were well ahead of them on that. Once the city got the bid, a deal was put together that ultimately provided the Braves with Turner Field. Knowing that in 1997 we were going to open up the baseball season in Turner Field affected our planning year by year.

Sharing the dream of a new baseball stadium with the Olympic community ensured that the Braves and the city got a new park for a fraction of the real price. Virtually custom built for the Braves, Turner Field is now the new field of dreams—the "rarest of diamonds,"[2] where making magic on the ballpark's opening night took some shrewd planning, boosted by a large slice of luck. The intention was to keep the opening ceremony fairly elegant without being too glitzy. The evening began with a relay of the home plate from Atlanta–Fulton County Stadium to Turner Field. Bill Bartholomay, chairman of the board, who had once owned the Atlanta Braves and sold the club to Ted Turner back in the seventies, carried the plate out of Atlanta–Fulton County Stadium and handed it over to a group of young

[2] Caruso, G. *Rarest of Diamonds*, Marietta, Georgia: Longstreet Press, 1997.

children who lived in the neighborhood. The kids then brought the plate over to Turner Field and handed it to Hank Aaron, who was waiting behind the centerfield wall. As the fence opened up, he came walking out with the plate. Amy Richter, director of advertising, describes the scene:

> The whole stadium went crazy. He is just an icon, a baseball legend. He walked toward second base and was met by Tom Glavine. The past and the present came together—the two people who have helped make this organization what it is. They set the home plate down to complete the Turner Field diamond. We then had the Georgia Massed Choir sing the national anthem, as they had during the opening ceremony for the Olympics, thus recognizing the ties between the Olympic Games and the opening of Turner Field. As they sang, we let loose an eagle, an American bald eagle, from the top of the ballpark. While the choir sang, the eagle, with its huge wingspan of seven feet, circled around the field and landed at home plate on the last note of the national anthem.
>
> It was the perfect ending to a perfect night, the culmination of an incredible six months spent getting this facility ready. It was surreal, and one of the most magnificent things I have ever seen. The look on Ted Turner's face, President Jimmy Carter, and all the other dignitaries who were in Ted's box—they were like kids when they saw this eagle landing at home plate. They were like little kids getting a puppy for their birthday.

The move from Atlanta–Fulton County Stadium to Turner Field, a baseball theme park of a type that the industry had not seen before, was indeed a game-breaking idea, symbolic of a first-class organization spreading its wings.

The Anatomy of a PPO: Creating the Future

Ted Turner bought the Braves franchise in 1976. Fortuitously, a year later, he met a young Stan Kasten at a Braves–Cardinals game in St. Louis, where Kasten was celebrating his graduation from law school with a tour of major league baseball parks. Impressed with Kasten's savvy, Turner appointed him in-house legal counsel for the organization, a role that quickly became a baptism by fire. In 1977, during a seventeen-game losing streak, Turner, who was at this stage flirting with micromanagement of the team, went the whole way on a road trip to Pittsburgh when he decided to replace the team manager, Dave Bristol, and take over the dugout duties himself! Stan Kasten was just out of law school and employed in a legal capacity to "watch over Turner," who at this time was under suspension for making comments at a World Series party the previous year. Kasten takes up the story:

> In my first week on the job I got home to my little apartment, I turned on the TV and damn, what did I see? Ted's running the game from the dugout—in the middle of this suspension. I called our counsel from our outside law firm and I said, "Are you watching the Pittsburgh game?" He said, "No, I just got in. Why?" "Maybe you want to turn it on," I said. "Why? What's up?" he replied. I said, "Ted's taken Bristol out of the game and is calling all the plays. I'm not quite clear on this yet. I just turned it on myself." The next day I was a twenty-four-year-old trying to explain to the world what my client had just done and why this was a good thing. Ted was gone that day, as Commissioner Bowie Kuhn banished him upstairs. Ted's tenure in the dugout lasted only one game. He lost to Pittsburgh 2–1.

Of course, this colorful event is now firmly entrenched in Braves folklore, but it also helps to explain the origins of the current management style of the Braves organization. Turner's attempts, in the early days of his ownership, to manage the team game by game gave way to Kasten's vision of creating the future from a tradition of development.

Kasten is one of the top sports administrators in the United States. In 1979, at the age of twenty-seven, he was appointed president of the Atlanta Hawks basketball franchise, later adding the

Braves to his portfolio. His office in the CNN building in downtown Atlanta is a working office. Seated behind a large desk littered with work in progress, Kasten is articulate, passionate, and thoroughly engaged in the conversation about how the Braves turned everything around. He has told the story many times before, but is eager to provide the full explanation—this is not just another rehearsal. Scattered in the midst of his narrative are several friendly, yet revealing anecdotes (none of which can be reproduced for public consumption) that provide essential color and understanding. With his good humor and genuine love of conversation, Kasten is riveting to listen to. His insights are many and valuable, particularly in the area of Braves history.

From the seventies to the mid-eighties, although the Braves won a divisional title in 1982 and a couple of second-place finishes in the following years, the organization was suffering from the disease of "short-termism." Kasten was responsible for altering, root and branch, the direction the Braves had followed for many years. The team had the highest payroll in baseball and were placed last in the league, an embarrassment about which he dryly notes: "You almost can't do that if you are trying to." To compound the problem, the Braves did not have the excellent minor league system that is so critical in professional baseball. The philosophy up to this time had been based on a short time frame, driven largely by the fact that the organization was very much a TV entity. The result was that each year management pursued the best team for that year, necessitating a never-ending, frenetic search for viable free agents. Kasten saw the problem:

> When things work and you spend two million bucks on a great pitcher (which today would buy you nothing), you get one great year out of one great player. But if it doesn't work, that money is gone, you've lost the draft pick that you had to give up to sign the free agent, and the money that could have been spent building up your minor league is also gone. Doing this from year to year is not good. But if you take that same two million bucks, and you immediately plow it into development and add minor league teams,

minor league instructors and scouts, the same two million bucks down the road might produce ten great years out of ten great players. Remarkably, the formula is not secret; it can be replicated anywhere, and has been from time to time.

The problem for Kasten and any pro sports team is how long can you continue to lose before the media and fans eat you alive? Ted Turner, an owner who had already learned the hard way, gave Kasten the precious gift of time. Frequently, many teams begin with a long-term plan, but lose two games in a row and, in time-honored fashion, abandon projects and fire the general manager. Turner allowed Kasten to do it his way. Musing on the short-term outcome of this strategy, Kasten realized that:

> It means for the next two to three years, every day in the newspapers we are going to be idiots, we don't know what we're doing, we're clueless. And I understand that. If you're a fan or a shareholder, all you care about is how's that team or organization doing today. You don't care how good you're becoming in the minor league systems, and so I understand, I really do. But we have an owner who said, Just get it going your way, just do it.

Turner clearly deserves much credit for investing in time. This new direction also found favor with the general manager, Bobby Cox, who arrived the year before Stan Kasten. He responded immediately to Kasten's philosophy of replacing the yearly quick fix with building up the minor leagues, by expanding the multiples of what could be obtained for the money that had been sunk into free agents. Kasten and Cox, hand-in-glove, simply turned the dial all the way in the direction of minor league development. Minor league teams were bought and at the same time scouting and coaching were expanded. Chances were taken with young players who previously would have been sacrificed in favor of free agents.

Despite the obvious importance of investing in the future, Kasten still expresses surprise at the results:

We stopped giving away those drafts and started developing. It meant being a couple years more in the basement; it meant a couple years more of being the last-place team. But I didn't know that our success was going to be so incredible. I thought we would succeed and we'd become a good team, able to compete every year. I didn't think that we would win eight straight divisions. I didn't know that, I didn't know that we'd have the greatest pitching staff maybe in history. I couldn't know that. But we couldn't have done it unless Ted had given us the chance, or if I didn't know that Ted wasn't going to fire me the first time we lost two games, and of course I knew that very well.

I have been with Ted for twenty years now, and I tell everyone the blame for everything stops at my desk, because I have complete authority to do anything I want. He's never turned me down on anything that I said I needed, ever, in twenty years. On the other hand, if Ted feels strongly about something, that matters to me because he is one of the world's smartest people. That still doesn't mean we don't disagree, but if I feel strongly about doing something he's never, never contested me, and I can't tell you how rare and important that is. If you don't have that, you go off course very quickly. So that was the most important thing for us. The singular, most important distinction when I came on was that Ted allowed us to change our philosophy and gave us the time to do it—that was the one way the infrastructure could work.

Stan Kasten's vision of sustained peak performance on the field also carried over into the heart of the organization itself. However, unlike many corporations that seek to start afresh by removing existing staff and replacing them, Kasten had a different approach:

The main challenge for me in my first sixty to ninety days was really getting a hold of who should stay and who should go. There were a lot of rumors from the outside—some people often got a lot of blame from the newspapers, which affected my mind-set going in—one guy in particular, who I thought must be at fault. After ninety days I learned that on the contrary, he was very good; he knew what he was doing, and had a plan—maybe he needed to be deployed a little bit differently. He became a star in the industry. The first thing a lot of people told me to do when I walked in was to get rid of this guy; but although we did replace some people, we kept almost everybody there. We focused them, and gave them the challenge of building from the bottom up, and it was a lot more fun for everyone. It gave them some breathing room, because everyone would like to do it that way if they were ever given the chance—start from scratch, go from the bottom up.

Bob Wolfe, senior vice president of administration, who started with the Braves in 1980, has continued the theme of player development. Loyalty to staff and providing opportunities for everyone to grow through constant challenge have been the principles by which the Braves maintain what Wolfe calls "a first-class organization"—sentiments echoed by all the staff. In return, Wolfe implicitly receives the confidence of the Braves staff, and carries it with consummate ease. His relaxed style flows unobtrusively yet effectively throughout the front office. Records show that almost all administrative staff in director-level positions came into the organization at entry level and worked up. The management ethos includes a conscious effort to hire or promote from within—although not always possible, this is the Braves' initial intent. Low turnover and high retention rates mean that most of the staff have had the experience of running the organization when the team was not successful. This has helped to establish an organizational memory that maintains a balanced perspective on the Braves' current sustained run of success. Bob Wolfe notes that:

> The people who we have hired since 1991, good employees as they are, have no perspective on what it's like to be in last place for five years running. It is valuable to know that side to be able to enjoy the success that the team is having now. This franchise

moved here from Milwaukee, Wisconsin, in 1966, and as a contrast to our newer employees, there are some people still here from the day Atlanta–Fulton County Stadium opened. There is a great deal of loyalty among our workers. When we played the last game in the old stadium we honored the staff who had worked there from the beginning. Including our game staff, close to thirty people had been there in excess of thirty years. That's a lot of baseball games.

Although Kasten's commitment to long-term development both on and off the field was a major sea change for the organization, this policy could not come to fruition unless the staff were organized around an overarching inspirational dream and, more important, a method of achieving it. By 1989, as the benefits of investing in the minor-league system started to become apparent, Kasten undertook an extensive search for a new general manager, an inspirational player who could take the Braves to the highest level in baseball.

Kasten first turned to John Schuerholz, who was then general manager of the Kansas City Royals. Under Schuerholz's stewardship, the Royals had already won one World Series and, more important, in the process had garnered the reputation of being the "IBM of baseball." Schuerholz had been with the Royals for twenty-three years, so Kasten's approach was initially to ask Schuerholz if he knew of any good GM prospects. Inevitably, they found themselves discussing Kasten's dilemma at a baseball game in New York. Schuerholz now admits that at the very moment when Kasten broached the issue of the GM position with the Braves, unbeknownst to Kasten, he was hooked:

I have to be honest with you. At the moment when he said that, the lightbulb went on. I said to myself, "This is pretty startling," and I began to build some interest in the position myself. I vacillated between accepting and rejecting the Braves position. Finally, our owner in Kansas City, Mr. Ewing Kauffman, said, "If you are interested enough even to entertain going, you need to go and satisfy yourself and to take this opportunity." So once I got past that decision emotionally, I was ready to dive headlong into the challenge. Mr. Kauffman gave me that little push and I was on my way.

When Kasten finally realized that after several months of probing and discussing he might be able to snare Schuerholz, he moved quickly.

I brought him in twice under cover of darkness, so no one knew he was here. I didn't let him go over to the stadium because it was shabby and, obviously, not the Olympic stadium. That would have turned him off, so he didn't even see his office until he was already hired. We met here at CNN, which is very nice. He told me afterward, that was a very smart move. The fit between us was very good.

The organization needed a general manager who would complement Kasten's blue-sky thinking and consummate deal making. John Schuerholz brought with him what he describes as "an unrelenting, uncompromising, total commitment to being a first-class organization."

It is not easy to imagine John Schuerholz finding himself lost. Walking briskly toward his office through the mazelike corridors and walkways of the brand-new spring-training stadium at the Disney complex in Orlando, Florida, his stride is uncompromising and purposeful. A very clear-thinking, clean-cut figure, there can be no mistake that Schuerholz relishes a challenge. He maintains the trappings of a renaissance man, writing poetry and identifying with the endeavors of others. His favorite baseball player is George Brett, the Kansas City Royals offensive star with a lifetime batting average of .305, 3,154 career hits, thirteen all-star appearances, and batting titles across three decades. Yet the qualities that Schuerholz cherishes in George Brett are more to do with attitude than numbers. "No one loved the game more than George. His infectious enthusiasm was legendary. No matter what the circumstances, when George came to play, he was going to have fun, work hard, and give it his all." Likewise, Schuerholz exudes selfless commitment and honesty.

Unsurprisingly, the Braves organization that he inherited did not fit his image of what and how it should be. This was compounded by the wider perception that the Braves were not well respected within the baseball community. Schuerholz's observations were brutal and direct:

> It was an organization that, in the eyes of the industry, was simply floundering administratively—it didn't seem to have direction. There was no clear goal. The development plan for the team, driven by Stan and Bobby Cox, was working, but administratively it was as though there was no continuity, and no clear plan for how the organization was going to function. The organization was in dire straits in terms of operations, management, direction, and administration. The biggest stumbling block was apathy. There really wasn't a sufficient energy level, either individually or collectively, with the administrative staff. They were beaten down. Apathy had taken a stranglehold and people didn't think they needed to care, because no matter how much they did, it wouldn't change anything.

One man's inspiration began a transformation in the Braves organization. Schuerholz felt that many people who were department heads had not been given the opportunity to express their own individuality or function effectively, so initially he involved himself in many organizational functions beyond baseball. These included public relations, marketing, promotion, and even ticketing operations. The key point of this involvement was to enable him to communicate more effectively with people who were responsible for these areas. Schuerholz wanted them to understand what the administrative direction and goals of the organization were going to be. The aim was to establish a clarity of focus that technical experts could work toward:

We did that through communication with the various department heads and through group meetings. We talked about how we were going to redefine this organization, how we were going to establish new and higher goals. Next, we talked about what the goals were, and about how we would reach them. Then, more than anything else, we empowered the staff who were already here, who had previously been viewed as nonproductive and not very talented, to make this plan work. Through communication with them and considerable exchange of ideas, thoughts, and emotions, we began to create a very effective organization. Mundane things such as demanding people dress properly at work, because that is a reflection of your personal self-esteem and your job self-esteem assisted the process. I've always believed that how you present yourself is a reflection of how you care about yourself, how you care about your job, especially in an administrative and management setting.

Schuerholz intended to engage people individually, and to encourage them to talk about the importance of having pride in their work:

I'd walk down the hall and another person would be passing me and they would drop their eyes. They couldn't look you square in the eye and feel good about themselves. We began to talk continually about feeling good about ourselves, having the power of good thoughts and positive self-image, and making a commitment to doing the things that needed to be done—working harder, working more intelligently, working a bit more aggressively. Remarkably, the people who were there proved to be capable professionals. Our goal was direct. We wanted to become the premier professional baseball organization —to become a world-championship team.

Both on the field and administratively, Schuerholz's goal for the operation was to become the world champions of baseball in every facet.

After he had established that specific, clearly defined goal, the entire organization became aware of it. At the very early stages, staff were provided with a road map that enabled them to envisage how the goal could be achieved, including how to work, and in some cases how to go about implementation, and finally how it would all come together. Most important of all, however, was the complete transfer of ownership, so that the master plan belonged to all the staff. This was achieved by informal means, other than the occasional large staff meeting where Schuerholz communicated his beliefs directly:

> I hoped they heard the passion in my voice and saw the commitment I had to doing what needed to be done. Once we reached that point, there were a lot of willing partners in this new enterprise. We lived it. We lived it by our work ethic, by our commitment, by our passion, by our professionalism. They were meaningful and people saw that. Stan gave me great support; everything I wanted to do, he allowed me to do. We made substantial changes and now we are what we are—champions in the industry.

These changes had a dramatic impact on personnel inside the Braves organization. In the first place, they enabled Bobby Cox to return to his earlier role in the field as manager of the team. Second, the sharp focus on administrative excellence seemed to galvanize people throughout the whole enterprise. Jim Schultz, director of public relations, who joined the Braves in 1987, describes the immediate impact that Schuerholz had on people:

> John saw no reason at all why the Braves shouldn't be the best organization in baseball. When an attitude like that came down from top management, the impact was almost instantaneous; it was incredible. He made it a point to go from office to office on a regular basis, to stick his head through the door to introduce himself. "What are you working on, how or why are you doing things this way?" et cetera, and you know, that was the first time some-

one at that level had shown an interest in lower management or middle-level management. His commitment is to excellence. I attended a lot of speeches he made early on, and he still makes them regularly. His whole theme is, "We are committed to provide you, the fans, with a first-class product, and a competitive world-championship contending team."

Amy Richter, director of advertising, expressing similar sentiments on the impact of John Schuerholz's arrival from the Kansas City Royals, notes that he picked up where Bobby Cox had left off, and by adding some new ingredients, put a winning team on the field:

> I can't tell you what a difference that made then on the front office. Within a couple of months, once we had a real clear understanding of what his vision was, everybody was on board. John was completely dedicated to winning, and would not accept any excuses, not a single excuse from himself or anybody else, and it really had an incredible impact, I think, on everybody. It increased our confidence level significantly. You felt safe in being able to do things, and try new things and be successful at it.

Tom Glavine, who came through the Braves farm system to be a two-time Cy Young Award recipient, multiple All Star game participant, World Series MVP in 1995, and currently the most successful left-handed pitcher in baseball, also saw the difference when Schuerholz arrived:

> During the winter of 1990, when John Schuerholz came over as the general manager, we all sat down and talked, and the word commitment was used, and used a lot. We decided right then and there that there was going to be a commitment from top to bottom to making this organization a class organization and a winning organization. That started in 1990. It was simple things at first: the way you conduct yourself as a team, the way you go

about your business. The next thing you know you're winning
ball games, and getting all the respect that comes along with that.

It is perhaps even more remarkable that Schuerholz started the
turnaround without the benefit of any formal strategic planning.
Although the Braves have a variety of marketing plans, financial
plans, and objectives for every season, understanding how it all actually organizes and coheres is another matter. Stabbing an index
finger in the general direction of his temple, Schuerholz indicates
the location of the organization's strategic activity. "Here's the
strategic plan I'm sorry, this is where it is." Jim Schultz echoes
these sentiments:

> We have a unified theme to everything we do, but not catch-
> phrases. We have found that catchphrases, whether they are mar-
> keting phrases or sales pitches, can backfire on you. If you try to
> keep them generic, they are not effective. People will poke fun at
> them because they can apply to anything and have no real mean-
> ing. In other words, you can't make a promise in a phrase that can
> guarantee a World Series championship.

The organizational purpose that Kasten and Schuerholz established
from the 1986 season onward clearly had a cathartic impact on the
spirit of the organization. For Tom Glavine, the Braves community
that has subsequently emerged is about commitment, loyalty, and
family. "A lot of guys who don't play here look at us and say 'I want
to play for those guys.'" The front-office staff are now located together at Turner Field, with offices that dramatically look out over
the baseball diamond—very different from the sprawling and fragmented work environment at Atlanta–Fulton County Stadium. A
sense of community surges through the new facility, although it
deeply reflects Schuerholz's penchant for dignity, elegance, under-
statement, and humility. Amy Richter sees the new office space as one
that encourages "pride, decorum, and professionalism, a good thing
for all of us. The heartbeat of this community is nine players on the

baseball field, and around that you have a broad, diverse collection of people in administration who have found some common ground, a common thread that holds us together."

Naturally, the office walls are covered with items that celebrate the Braves. Photographs, montages, mosaics, and memorabilia are around every corner, providing vivid reminders to staff and visitors of hard-earned victories. In each office are personalized commemorative cut-glass plaques that gratefully recognize the contributions of all employees. Perhaps most poignant are the championship rings that are presented not just to the players, but to all staff throughout the organization. Amy Richter:

> It's not a huge event. They come around and distribute them somewhat discreetly. It is not really a very attractive ring for a woman to wear, but it symbolizes something very special and unique. When the time comes to hand out those rings, you can sense the uplift in morale. Every year that we have won the pennant and the World Series we've received rings, which, I think, demonstrates the organization's generosity.

Schuerholz also sets the tone for how this community celebrates its success. "Win with grace, lose with dignity" is his key phrase. This is not an organization that flaunts every pennant victory. Being thankful for reaching five World Series rather than complaining about lost chances helps maintain perspective. Nevertheless, the hunger for victory remains undiminished. Stan Kasten:

> The focus is to be World Champions, no question about it, and it hurts that we didn't get it in 1999. I am disappointed that we didn't win, but I don't feel that we failed particularly. I feel we didn't get what we were good enough to get—it just didn't happen for us. There is great disappointment and frustration, but it didn't diminish, for me, the pride I have in the work that everyone did to get us there. To say that our goal was to get to the world championship is not right. Sure, our goal is to win the world champi-

onship and I hope to do it again. But you can have a successful season and still not win the world championship; otherwise twenty-nine teams out of thirty are losers every year. I don't buy that, I do not buy that.

Kasten offers a simple explanation as to how the Braves maintain their drive to convert National League pennant titles into World Series rings, even though they have failed to do so on four occasions out of five.

We care about having a product that gives you a chance to win. Because everyone in the organization feels that way, it's not hard to muster morale—to have people excited and confident that every day you have a chance of victory. The organization has the fundamental strength that we are all very proud of, not just to contend but to actually reach the very top, to get to the World Series, something that other organizations cannot sustain.

In this way, the Braves community is constantly charged, and recharged, to drive toward contention. The nonstop whirl of day-to-day tasks works its way through all the functions of the organization. Wayne Long, vice president of marketing and broadcasting, says that the Braves community is continually invigorated with new challenges, each and every day, spliced with a healthy dose of fun:

When we were acquired a year or so ago by Time Warner, they sent some HR people in to talk with the department heads, and they had their questionnaires. I think the first question was, "Take us through one of your normal days; what is your day comprised of?" I said, "Which one? I have been here twenty-five years and I have never had two days exactly the same." That is the challenge for me personally. I wouldn't have been here for twenty-five years if it had been routine. It's a new challenge every day, and that's what makes it fun. Fun is an important word, because I keep repeating to my people that they have got to have fun while they are doing this.

Lisa Stricklin, director of human resources, also recognizes that the Braves community is much more informal than the parent company, Time Warner:

> We've learned, because of our business, to be more flexible when it comes to human resource practices. There's never a dull moment. We have employees with a strong sense of loyalty. There are people here who have worked for us for thirty years, primarily because they enjoy working in the game of baseball and, more specifically, because they enjoy working for the Braves organization.

Stan Kasten echoes these sentiments:

> How can you not have fun? I mean, even if you've lost, you're probably having fun. You get to work in a baseball park, for goodness' sake. I think you might have problems away from your work if you're not having fun. It's an inherently fun workplace.

That important sense of fun and organizational harmony was severely tested during the winter of 2000 when the Braves' sensational closing pitcher, John Rocker, made derogatory remarks to the media about ethnic minorities in New York. Disliked by fans in New York, Rocker faced a constant stream of abuse during the titanic play-off series against the New York Mets and again during the 1999 World Series against the New York Yankees. His comments quickly garnered media attention well beyond his dugout duties. Even the *Wall Street Journal* of April 18 saw fit to provide an in-depth analysis of the situation, focusing in particular upon the organizational pressures faced by the Braves. Stan Kasten fully appreciated the significance of the situation.

> In truth, John Rocker's comments were a body-blow to the morale of the organization. First of all, it cast us in a negative light when we hadn't had a sniff of negativity in a decade, you know. And all of a sudden we were tainted with the association of racism. It's the

last thing in the world you could expect out of us, so we had to explain it, particularly to our own staff, since many people in the organization are themselves minorities, or of different ethnic origins. They were offended. People who had worked with John never suspected any of this in him.

Kasten was aware of the potential negativity in the locker room that would almost certainly "put the collective unit at risk." Rather than trying to control the situation artificially, players such as Tom Glavine and Brian Jordan were able to make their concerns and criticisms of their colleague publicly known. This key component of the organization's reaction helped to communicate the seriousness of the issue and, more important, the depth of commitment to an inclusive community. "Everyone spoke out. It was unprecedented. Normally you don't get teammates speaking out against each other, but there was no other way to preserve what we have achieved together." However, alongside these sentiments, Kasten had other considerations to contend with. Although he was convinced that Rocker's comments were more about personal arrogance and immaturity rather than pure racism, the organization still had to accept that the community might be less inclined to share the team's longheld inspirational dream of baseball supremacy and the American way. This required an appropriate organizational response at the executive level.

We simply had to work through this thing to get the community to accept us again, even those people who were very critical of us. Being as open as we could be, this was something John Schuerholz and I tackled ourselves. We weren't going to delegate this to a functionary level. This was an issue so important that we, John and I, had to get out there, man to man, and deal with it. So we did. And that turned out to be the best decision we could have made. There are things that you delegate and then there are things that you can't delegate. When the purpose of the organization is at stake, this is one of them.

Another key consideration in the Rocker affair relates to the Braves' commitment to creating the future. John Rocker was picked by the Braves in the eighteenth round of the 1993 draft. He represents the uncompromising belief in creating the future through the minor leagues. Kasten argues, "If your plan is good, you should give yourself the time to let the plan work." Rocker, who saved thirty-eight games in 1999, is part of the plan, meaning that a trade, although possible at any time in baseball, was not the knee-jerk reaction of the ball club. By the start of the 2000 season, after a brief period of suspension, Rocker rejoined "the show" with a measure of both public and, more critically, organizational rehabilitation. The outcome, however, did not surprise the mercurial president of the Atlanta Braves. "We had a tumultuous winter, but given the people we have in our front office, we expected a good ending." The nightmare that had been played out on talk shows and in column inches ultimately assisted the organization's ability to look at itself and regenerate the dream.

Turner Field: Sharing the Dream

It is hard to conceive of Turner Field, or indeed the spring-training facility in Orlando, as being workplaces at all. The overall sense of belonging, pride, and identity, rather than just moving up a few notches with the opening of Turner Field, took a quantum leap into the realm of magic making. For the first time, the Braves were in their own home, and with that came a significant shift in responsibility. Possibilities for new signage, corporate sponsorships, and renewal of relationships with customers and clients expanded hugely with the opening of the new stadium. The opportunity to share the dream with many new clients, extend the product, and amplify the brand placed enormous pressure on the staff to deliver. The chief idea was to create a baseball theme park so that when people went to Braves games they would not just sit in the stands watching the team play on the field, but would get an opportunity to have a more intimate experience with the game and its history. In Turner Field, the Braves have established a new standard in baseball entertainment. Every stadium built subsequent to Turner Field will probably contain elements that will be directly attributable to the design and the construction of the Braves' new facility. Amy Richter explains that the opportunities presented by the converted Olympic stadium were hard to quantify, since the concept of a baseball theme park was quite new to the industry:

We have an area called "Scouts' Alley," which is an interactive games area, mainly designed for kids. It's a combination of interactive games and mural-sized scouting reports of former and current players. Museum-type exhibits allow people to compare the various weights of bats and different kinds of mitts that players use. Fans can also learn about what the sweet spot of a bat is and what it means for a player to hit the sweet spot. The anchor of Scouts' Alley is a museum that traces the history of this organization back to Boston.

So we've taken all these different elements from the game and brought them a little bit closer to the fans. We have bands. We have the "bleacher brigade," young college-age students who run around in the crowd and play with the kids and do all kinds of crazy things that just give it a little more of an upbeat festival atmosphere. There are people who argue that it's just not traditional enough for baseball, but the reality is that kids growing up today aren't tied into the traditions of the older generation of fans. Clearly we need to develop this new generation of fans.

Appealing to the fans, new and old, is precisely what Kasten wanted to achieve. He recalls only too well the problems at Atlanta–Fulton County Stadium.

I remember standing on the concourse in the eighties at the old stadium during the game, looking out, and the fans would come thirty minutes early, and they'd just be milling around. There was nothing to do, and as I've often said—it's not a joke, I mean it very seriously—"Milling is bad, buying is good." I hate milling; milling doesn't do them any good at all. Remember, milling is bad, buying is good. People will spend money if you give them something that they like, if you give them something to spend it on. If you give them a reason to come early, they will come early; if you give them a reason to stay late, they will stay late. And with those thoughts in mind, we went into our stadium and we developed our plaza.

The ballpark design that Kasten wanted necessitated the removal of almost half of the Olympic stadium to make way for a sweeping plaza that greets the fans before they enter the actual grounds. The pillars that supported the stands to the Olympic stadium remain as an oval perimeter, providing a dramatic link to the original purpose of the facility. Fans are greeted with evocative statues of Hank Aaron, Ty Cobb (a famous Georgian who did not play for the Braves), and knuckleballer Phil Niekro. Bob Wolfe:

One of the things that has made this park successful is the entryway into the plaza. As people come through the turnstiles, their first look at the stadium is from the plaza area. There's a video board, a retail store, concessions, and a huge billboard picturing an oversized baseball. We put characters, jugglers, and microphones there—full entertainment that people who come to the park can experience. That's the unique part of our ballpark. I've never seen it anywhere else, and it's one of the big reasons for our success.

Once inside the stadium, fans are greeted with wide concourses where they can continue to watch the game while purchasing from concession stands. For those looking for an upmarket experience, there is the 755 Club, an exclusive restaurant that honors Hank Aaron's record home-run tally. Entertainment is everywhere. Kasten clearly recognizes that the Braves are an entertainment vehicle that has to compete with every other entertainment vehicle under the sun and that their safest bet is not to think of fans as fans, but as customers:

You don't owe them a thing, but you're an idiot if you don't give them some reason to patronize you. I think you are safer in just thinking of it as any other business. To succeed you need to satisfy your customers. Your customer is always right—if they don't like what it is you are selling, you need to sell something else, period! They don't owe me anything, they don't have to buy their season tickets. We need to wake up every day and give them a reason to want to patronize us. It may be the game, but it may be the other things too. It may be the whole evening's experience, which is what I think, and that's why we worked as hard as we could to make this the ultimate fan/consumer's baseball park ever.

Hard-core baseball fans naturally attend games no matter what the conditions. Kasten, above and beyond this, had to make the ballpark appeal to both young and old, and more crucial still, females of all ages.

The All Star Game, held at Turner Field in 2000, provided further impetus for developing the theme of baseball in all its possible representations. For the occasion, Kasten commissioned new statues, murals, paintings, and artwork using various materials, all in the cause of "jazzing the place up to maintain and expand the baseball theme." As well as catering to critical tastes of the more traditional fan, the demands of a new generation of potential customers have also been answered. A new digital dugout has been added to the plaza area, housing eighteen Sega Dreamcast machines that enable would-be coaches to play their own game of baseball using the Dream Squad software. Reaching out to the potential fan base remains a core feature of the Braves' activity, especially when cooperating with the broader interest of major league baseball. Nowadays, Kasten sees the brand image of his organization as firmly located within the industry:

> The frequent-user program, available to all major league teams, uses a swipe card that enables you to accumulate points all through the season. The award program gives us local information in terms of database tracking, which is part of the Internet and e-commerce initiatives developed with America Online and major league baseball.

The Braves participate through an MLB monster portal that establishes a Web site for each team with each aspect of the site being constantly updated to reflect "best practice." Kasten approves of the way in which teams have "agreed to throw all our assets into the one pot to work together," creating an overarching superbrand that will enable the game of baseball to compete effectively within the entertainment and sports industry. Naturally, this multiplies the opportunities for the Braves to leverage effectively off their own individual brand. Stan Kasten:

> Our brand is very near and dear to us. Now, there is so much more out there in terms of merchandising, in terms of apparel and other memorabilia, not to mention being able to do a much better job selling tickets and doing a better job with customer service in terms of tailoring to our customers' needs. Then there's the whole business of selling membership, statistics, and many other e-commerce initiatives that work through the MLB central monster portal. These are the critical business initiatives that have been really coming alive in recent years leading to significant brand expansion.

All these developments help to attract the interests of corporate sponsorship. Turner Field remains the key focus. Long-standing sponsor Coca-Cola was clearly eager to push the envelope with its concept of a Sky Field. Kasten explains:

> When Coca-Cola came to us, we were thinking they would have the name of the plaza, and they would write us a check and it would be the Coca-Cola Plaza. We gave them the plans and they said "Do you mind if we take them and study them for a few weeks?" "Be my guest," I said, and they came back with a use for absolute dead space, on the roof, for Christ sakes! On the roof! I said two things about the space itself: You come back and show me what you want—but two things. It can say Coke, that's fair, you're spending money; but you also have to say baseball. It had to be baseball—that's what this place is—everything had to be

baseball. When they first unveiled the plans to me, I thought damn, they took me literally; it says Coke and it says baseball!

Coca-Cola had come up with a unique Sky Field that sat 23,000 square feet on top of the left-field, upper-deck stand. The chief feature is a forty-two-foot-high Coca-Cola bottle made from thousands of pieces of baseball equipment, such as gloves, bats, balls, helmets, Braves shirts. It spews out fireworks on command when the Braves hit a home run. The field also includes a real pitchers' mound with a regulation ninety-foot base path that kids run along throughout the game. A dugout replete with bench and bat racks, nine twenty-eight-foot-tall baseball cards featuring pictograms of players, and, most magical of all, the promise of $1,000,000 for anyone who catches a home run hit into the Coca-Cola Sky Field.

Turner Field has enabled the Braves to share their dream with a much wider spectrum of fans, customers, sponsors, and clients than before. It is the heart of this peak performing organization. The impact has been staggering. There are now nearly 30,000 season ticket holders and they, along with 20,000 other patrons for each game, do come to the park early, as Kasten intended: "We used to swing the gate two hours before the game; no one would be there. Well, now we swing it three hours before a game, and you know what, they are outside the gates an hour before we swing the gates."

The success of Turner Field was followed by the opening of the new spring-training stadium in the Disney complex in Orlando, Florida. Strategically and symbolically placed in the heart of the entertainment world, the new facility demonstrates that from start to finish, the Atlanta Braves are a first-class outfit.

The Performance Zone

The full apparatus of the Braves organization, including the minor league system, players, front office, and stadium personnel, numbers more than 1,500 employees, with revenues from various sources measuring in the hundreds of millions of dollars. Formally, the organization is arranged into multiple specialties along functional lines.

Each department has its own game plan, following the focus articulated by Stan Kasten and John Schuerholz. Nowadays, the notion of a first-class organization that provides topflight entertainment and contends world championship status each year has long been adopted, owned, sanded, varnished, and polished by all organizational participants. The mode of putting this collective vision into operation is intriguing. Even though the quality of the product needs to be reaffirmed in every game played throughout the season, the coming together of all the functional or system elements does not rely on, or even use, formally organized teams.

At the individual level, employees hold themselves supremely responsible for the impact that their particular job has on the final product. Exceeding personal best is a way of life that means as much in the office as it does on the baseball diamond. In the earlier days, Schuerholz would look outside to other preeminent baseball franchises to get a fix on what individuals should do to try to be the best. In more recent years, however, he has shifted decisively toward internal assessment:

> Now, we use ourselves as the benchmark. The spotlight is brighter here. The heat is turned up a notch higher. Our expectations have grown higher. We have high internal expectations; the external expectations are high too, but more important to us are our internal expectations. That's where most of the pressure comes from, not from the outside expectations, because you can rationalize those any way you like..It's intimidating in one sense, but invigorating in another. It primes the engine. It makes you, as an individual, as a professional, want to be at the top of your game. Wearing this uniform, or business dress, is representative of the finest organization in baseball. You can play up to those expectations.

Larry Bowman, director of stadium operations and security, faces more than most unrelenting pressure to deliver time and time again at the highest professional level of peak operating condition. A mosaic of tasks, which includes ticket-taking, ushering, guest relations, security, police, first-aid coordination, telecommunications, maintenance, and engineering, needs specific attention to the tiniest detail to get the ballpark game ready. Bowman has an impact on several hundred employees. He faces the ultimate paradox where the unexpected is the norm. Bomb threats, special requests for prayer facilities for different religious orders, and on-field runs by spectators are all standard fare. Bowman explains: "You can have a general plan of action, but each game is unique. If we try to set something in stone, certain portions of it will become obsolete the very next day." Managing in this environment does not lend itself to formal rules, job descriptions, and routine lines of command. Bowman has a different approach to deal with constant change:

> No one here is ever really satisfied. There's room to do more. Always. Each individual has, in large part, a desire to reach perfection. But I think my staff perform better when they are focused on reaching it rather than actually achieving it. And no organization ever gets there. I have the type of personnel here who are never satisfied. That is typical of this organization. Moreover, you realize that you have to be innovative in coming out with solutions.

The expectation of innovation and creativity and game-breaking ideas is another significant factor in enabling Bowman's staff to address the constant whirl of change:

> All my staff have to be innovative, simply because we are constantly confronted with situations where we might not have the resources to get something done. And we live or die by getting the job done. Whatever the circumstances, my staff needs to be creative, resourceful, and even visionary. These are key questions when we interview for this department: How flexible are you? Can you adapt to change? How well do you operate under stress?
>
> Here's an example of what I mean. Last year, after an on-field spectator incident, the officer that was responsible for that part of

the field instituted some changes among his personnel in their deployment and positioning. He talked about what to look for, what to listen for, and how to make sure they wouldn't be caught napping again. This was good, because I got to see what this guy brings to the table. He felt personally offended by the fact that somebody got on the field while his unit was out there. And then he took steps to make sure that it wouldn't happen again. During the remainder of the regular season I noticed that the other teams saw what he did, and when they rotated onto the field, they not only wanted to do what he did, they wanted to add their own wrinkle to it.

Capturing the ideas and creative juices of the staff so that everyone in the organization is in a state of flow with each other begins with functional strength. When Bowman is searching for new staff his primary concern is to hire people who are strong in their areas of expertise. From the position of functional strength, cooperation and working in formation become the default practice. The activity is informal, unspoken, and unexceptional. Larry Bowman:

> You don't want a general practitioner; you want a specialist in each area. You look for the best person for player development, and the best general manager you can find, and you build your organization around those goals. It's mandatory to have the skills to do the job, but those skills are rendered useless if you can't interact and interrelate with the people around you. No department here is truly separate. They all interact—they have to for the ball game to happen. That is the organizational footprint.
>
> People here really buy into the organization and support it, and they want to see the organization fare well. Their concern for the organization supersedes personal agendas. To have a successful team you need to have folks that view it as a team, see their stake in it, see their interest in it, and act on their interests for the overall good. That strengthens the organization because you don't have people tearing at it from within. Everyone looks at that over-

all goal, and if they see something in your area where they can be of help to you, then that's what they do.

Bob Wolfe, senior vice president of administration, puts the practice of flow into an organizational context. While he acknowledges that formal job descriptions can be found for most employees, he is quick to point out that very few of them are more than eight to ten written lines, and they're not specific in some cases. "We have a philosophy of, 'This is your job description,' but at any time, if something comes up, you can find yourself doing something else. We have a very good level of cooperation." According to Wolfe, this type of work activity is also reflected in the way departments themselves avoid a purely functional mind-set:

> I would rather leave it to departments to develop their own ideas. One thing that can't be emphasized often enough is the importance of communication among departments. There are very few departments within this organization that can act with complete independence from other departments. The marketing people can't get their job done without the cooperation and knowledge of the people who are running the ballpark. They go hand in hand.

Information sharing, even when there appears to be little utility in doing so, is another important dimension that encourages different groups to work together:

> In our periodic staff meetings we encourage each department to talk about what they have going on, even if it doesn't seem to relate to other departments. Different departments may be able to offer some help or assistance, and are at least aware of what's happening in the organization. One hopes it makes them feel part of the ball club as a whole.

Although the Braves do have a formal organizational structure chart, it has languished in someone's office drawer for quite some time. It contains numerous boxes with job titles, plenty of lines, and perhaps two discernible hierarchical levels. Beyond that, its utility is unclear. Bob Wolfe, after studying it quizzically for a brief moment, apparently for the first time in ages, gestured and said, "You should certainly have this, but it's not going to tell you a whole lot about the flow of business around here. Communication across departmental lines is as important as communication within a department."

The impact of the organization, and the manner in which business gets conducted, is not lost on the players. Tom Glavine, who has seen the Braves during the good times and the bad, truly represents the Braves' decisive move to create the future by investing in long-term development. More than anyone else, he is in a position to observe and comment on how the organization has contributed to the most remarkable, sustained winning performance ever witnessed in the game of baseball. This is how Tom Glavine explains the Braves' success:

Number one is a commitment from Ted Turner, who put good baseball people in charge of running this organization. They have the commitment to make it a first-class organization in everything they do. This commitment has existed ever since I got here in the late eighties. The trend was toward being a team with a first-class organization from top to bottom, both at the big league level and the minor league level. What you're seeing at big league level is a direct result of hard work that was put in at the minor league level. A lot of us came through the system.

The Braves have also reaped the benefits brought in by the business side, by the owner, the team president, the general managers. They're the ones who are getting the players, signing the players, and developing the players, so they get most of the credit, but it goes beyond that. You're not just a successful organization by how you play the game on the field, or at least I don't think that's our philosophy. You also have got to have a group of guys and an organization that's committed to the community, to doing things for other people—that goes a long way toward getting people behind your team and involved in the program. If you've got a team full of good guys who are doing a lot of community things, that helps with that relationship an awful lot. I think the front-office people below the general manager and the owner, the public relations department and the community relations department, do a great job of making sure that it all takes place. When you see that commitment from your front office, it motivates you as a player to have that same commitment.

The next thing you know, you've got tremendous confidence in what you're doing. I think it's true of anything in life. The more confidence you have in what you're doing, the better the chance you have of getting the results you want. That's what happened to us.

Conclusion

Ted Turner, Stan Kasten, and John Schuerholz were the inspirational players who moved the Atlanta Braves off the bottom rung of major league baseball. Turner provided Kasten with the time he needed to create the future by investing in baseball players through the minor league system. In parallel, management of the club was allowed to re-group and find a common thread that helped to define the organizational footprint. John Schuerholz was given a free hand to provide focus and direction, which managers quickly adopted and re-created to their own specifications. Bob Wolfe's supremely balanced handling of the organization benchmarks the industry.

One inspirational player alone cannot turn an organization around, no matter how charismatic he is or how deep his pockets. The Braves are the ultimate example of how long it takes, and how hard the organization has to work, to become a peak performer. The greatest starting pitching rotation in the history of baseball, of Glavine, Smoltz, and Maddux, with six Cy Young Awards among them, is a rare gift delivered by a peak performing organization. Stan Kasten has no doubt about what lies ahead for the Atlanta Braves.

I do believe that we are not in the middle of a run that has a finite life. Even if we have to stop for pitfalls, which you can't predict, we will rise above it quickly and regain our former position. We employ a process; we have an organizational focus and a way of doing things that leads to success. Some years we may not win a pennant, some years we may not win a world championship, but barring catastrophes we should always be competitive, and when things go well, we should be able to contend for the very highest achievement you can have in our sport.

4

The New York Yankees: Business in Pinstripes

"This is not a job, it's a life;"

—JASON ZILLO,
**ASSISTANT DIRECTOR OF MEDIA RELATIONS
AND PUBLICITY**

The cacophony overwhelms you. The subway to the161st Street station has carried generations of baseball fans to the shrine that is Yankee Stadium. The pounding noise from the nearby bands of drummers penetrates the station's stairways and pedestrian tunnels. Emerging into the half-light, the hypnotic rhythm joins the raucous voices of Yankee fans already high on the adrenaline surge induced by sighting their history-rich amphitheater. River Avenue runs down one side of Yankee Stadium. Dominated by an elevated rail track, which measurably amplifies the ambient noise level, the narrow street captures the growing medley of sound, rendering normal discourse impossible. Street vendors vie for quick business against a backdrop of more permanent sports memorabilia shops. Avuncular retail service, provided by "Baseball Land" and "Stan the Man," whose facades are replete with flashing neon lights, pace this strip of Yankee heaven. The iron canopy provided by the elevated rail track and the darkening of night provide a sense of enclosure reminiscent of a stage set at Universal Studios. The milling fans, ever familiar with the rituals of postseason play, know their parts so well. They are the film extras. This is the World Series.

Earlier, the opening game of the World Series against the Atlanta Braves at Turner Field produced a different earsplitting crescendo of its own. A dramatic flyover by a squadron of F-17 fighter jets underscored the final notes of the national anthem and the conclusion of the pregame entertainment that included the obligatory celebrations of all things American and baseball. The meeting of the "team of the nineties" and the undoubted "team of the century" offers a steady stream of comparisons. The fan-friendly vistas and walkways of Turner Field are a different world from the narrow corridors and spartan concrete of Yankee Stadium.

Could it be that the organizations are different too? Perhaps the Braves and the Yankees have found different paths to glory. The popular version of the Yankees is that George Steinbrenner, as principal owner, leads a franchise that is aloof, impenetrable, and willing to bludgeon its way to success with money and attitude. We were eager to find out if this was so. Would our observations of the Yankees organization strengthen and broaden our theory? The results surprised us, but not in the way we had anticipated.

Down in the Dugout

On a cool day in April when the bright sun has yet to dull the biting edges of a stiff spring breeze, Joe Torre, the Yankees manager, seeks temporary shelter in the Yankees dugout. The upcoming game against the Minnesota Twins is still a few hours away. He has time for some reflection. Torre is a man who can afford to be relaxed. His record since joining the Yankees organization in 1996 is peerless in modern times. During his short tenure with the Yankees, apart from 1997, he has won the World Series every year. Joining baseball's most famous franchise cannot be considered an ordinary rite of passage. Even though Yankee Stadium has been refurbished, partially rebuilt, painted, and overhauled yet again, it still remains, in everyone's mind, "the house that Ruth built." The echoes from the past are as loud as ever. Their names are indelibly written across the generations—inspirational players who continue to map the contours of the Yankee landscape. Babe Ruth and Joe DiMaggio, names that enjoy instant recognition on the world stage, lead an unparalleled phalanx of players whose uniforms have been retired by the Yankees.[3] With an enviable record already secure, Torre, like the Yankee icons who preceded him, flirts with greatness and a special place in the pantheon of baseball legends. He is well positioned to understand the pressures his players must face when they enter Yankee Stadium. This applies equally to those who have yet to make their mark and those who have had performances that have already captured the imagination of their generation. Roger Clemens joined the Yankees in 1999, thereby picking up his first coveted World Series ring. With his previous employers, the Toronto Blue Jays, Clemens a.k.a. "The Rocket," won his fifth Cy Young Award—the only pitcher in history to do so. Yet his record in a Yankee uniform has been enigmatic. Sitting alone in the dugout, Torre freely ruminates about the difficulties associated with players such as Clemens, integrating with the Yankee organization. His cadence suggests empathy and respect for one of the finest hurlers the game has ever seen.

We always hold people to their highest accomplishments. I went through it as a player. I hit .363 and .290 the next year and everybody's wondering what the hell's wrong with me. But it was closer to my lifetime average. So it's understandable that everybody would hold "The Rocket" to the five Cy Young Awards. I hate to use the word struggle, but he's clearly not been as comfortable as he has been elsewhere.

I think that gives you an indication that this place is different. Given the fact that we won a few World Series, I think he came over here last year trying to fit in, as opposed to being Roger Clemens. It wasn't until about midway through the year that I had my first talk with him about that. I told him—go ahead, be selfish.

---

[3] The immortals are, Mickey Mantle, Roger Maris, Thurman Munson, Billy Martin, Don Mattingly, Lou Gehrig, Yogi Berra, Reggie Jackson, Bill Dickey, Phil Rizzuto, Whitey Ford, Elston Howard, and Casey Stengel.

Pitchers are supposed to be that way, anyway. They pitch once every five days, and you have to be yourself, be animated. He was trying to control himself but he's fine now, he's out there, yelling. He's just motivating himself.

Even though Clemens's pitching was uneven upon his joining the Yankees' roster, Torre refused to launch into a tirade about failed expectations. Instead, using his vantage point, he offers an astute reflection on the pursuit of perfection and exceeding one's previous personal accomplishments. It is a rare glimpse of what it is like to manage extraordinary talent. Joe Torre:

I'm not sure if he was caught by surprise when he came here, considering he felt he had to be something other than he was. A lot of it was analyzing and trying to have a game plan for himself. I think he overprepared, but that's him. Unless you're in the dugout with him, you can't tell a whole lot from the other side of the field. But you know, he's his own worst critic and he wants to be as perfect as you can possibly be. I'm not sure if he could be that perfect, but that's him. Am I going to tell him he shouldn't be that way, after what he's accomplished? Not a chance. We try not to complicate things for people. Mel Stottlemyre, our pitching coach, and I try keep it in the simplest form because that's what we can understand. You try to increase the positive, whereas pitchers in general always try to accentuate what they didn't do.

Allowing people to do their jobs without unnecessary interference is undoubtedly a trademark of the Yankees organization. In this regard, trust and respect are not undermined simply because performance appears to be less than anticipated. Torre clearly sees no value in berating or exhorting his players to improve. Personal responsibility is the unspoken expectation of everyone. This is also evident and amply illustrated in the lead-up to the game against the Minnesota Twins.

The Rituals of Game Preparation

Hours before the first pitch is thrown, the clubhouse or locker room begins to receive its first cache of talent. To get to this hallowed place, it is necessary to descend into depths of Yankee Stadium and "follow the blue line" that twists and turns several times along narrow corridors where, in some places, both walls can be reached by outstretched hands. In several places security personnel are placed to ensure that only those with the right credentials continue. Even though the complex has undergone dramatic external alterations in its eighty-year history, it is impossible not to speculate that these are the very same steps that Ruth, DiMaggio, and Gehrig took more than two generations before.

The doorway into the clubhouse is unpretentious and can be thought of as special only in that it immediately faces the short tunnel that leads directly to the field of play. Inside, the floor is clad with an incandescent light blue carpet. To the far left of the clubhouse is the physio room and on the opposite side is the recreational area where players not expecting to see action on any particular day are apt to congregate. Each player, with his name prominently displayed, retains his own permanent cubicle. In front of their personal space is a light-framed chair, each placed at exactly the same forty-five-degree angle to the cubicle. This is an ordered place. Upon arrival, most players swing directly to their area and begin the ritual of changing into the famous pin-striped uniform. Roger Clemens purposefully strides into the room, heading straight for his cubicle. He is a study in focus. A brief recognition of someone else's presence is acknowledged with a short comment, "Yeah, I'm pitching today." It is easy to surmise that this man needs space and no interference in his personal preparation.

Each of the players decorates his cubicle with personal mementos, which include photographs of family and loved ones, favored CDs, keepsakes, lucky charms, and the odd invocation. Derek Jeter's space is dominated by a cutout piece of print that simply says "Showtime." Across from Roger Clemens is another newcomer to the Yankee clubhouse, although he has a wider experience of the Yankee organization by way of the minor leagues. Ed Yarnall is a promising left-handed pitcher who has seen action with the Florida Marlins and the New York Mets before being acquired by the Yankees in 1999, the year in which he was the International League's Most Valuable Pitcher. His prognosis is that he will be with the team for a few days while a more seasoned arm is recovering. Torre is upbeat but realistic about his possible contribution.

> There is a chance he could stay because he gives us that second left-hander in the bull pen, but I think Mel and I have to talk it over and see which way we prefer to have it. As of right now, he's here for three days. He had a short planned outing on Friday, just in the event we needed him for this week. He's a lot better, you know—they wouldn't have sent him here unless they felt he was ready. I'm not sure I want to bring him in for a key situation, to get that one guy out, because he's not really a reliever at this point, even though he would be pitching out of the bull pen. We'll use him in a less-than-pressurized situation, not when the bases are loaded.

Yarnall himself understands the situation well. He does not feel that his treatment reflects his minor league status. The Yankee organization invests heavily in preparing players like Yarnall to be ready for major league action. This includes removing all impediments, which, in turn, allows players to concentrate on their game. Ed Yarnall:

> These guys really don't spare any expenses in terms of what the players need. Even in the minor leagues, they just try to make it a little bit easier for you. I think that the biggest thing is the way that they make you feel. The quality of the coaches, trainers, and medical staff is outstanding. We have weight rooms in the minor leagues as well as up here. We have a massage guy that comes in to make sure you keep your muscles stretched. They really try to do everything that they possibly can to make sure that you're ready to play baseball and that's the number one priority. If there

are any problems, they get everything taken care of. They really do everything they can to take your mind off everything else, so when you go out on the mound or onto the playing field, you can just concentrate on baseball. I'm focused and ready to go because we have quality people running the organization.

Looking after the players to the last detail places the Yankees alongside the San Francisco 49ers, who also focus relentlessly on providing a tranquil, supportive environment for their players. For the Yankees, this carries over to the administration side of the business, where new recruits can also rely on support and respect.

Rikki Dileo, a media relations assistant, has only been with the organization since December 1999, yet one of her tasks is to introduce a media relations intern to the warp and weft of the organization. It is his first day with the New York Yankees. Induction is a simple process of the new person tagging along watching what unfolds as Dileo fulfills her media obligations. Today she files the box scores and statistics for external consumption in real time. Because Dileo joined the organization after the last World Series victory, she had not completed the twelve-month period that is necessary to qualify for receiving a championship ring. All employees retain high expectations about their prospects of adding to their inventory of adornments.

Throughout the day, senior media personnel Rick Cerrone and Jason Zillo brush past Dileo and her nascent charge, slowing down sufficiently to inquire after their progress. Zillo joins them both for lunch in the media canteen. Exposure to the organization is disciplined yet gentle. There are no formal mantras about the importance and value of history. Whether you are Roger Clemens, Ed Yarnall, or the new media assistant, your entry into the Yankees organization rests on the contribution you have been hired to make. Rikki Dileo:

> When you first get here, you know about the history and all the great players from each era, but they don't push it down your throat. It gradually emerges in a subtle way around you. It gives you a chance to establish yourself.

The Workplace

Yankee Stadium is the prime medium through which stories are communicated. The paying public gets some of it, but not all. The perimeter of the stadium displays the most obvious trappings of a glorious past. There are separate clubs named after Ruth, Mantle, Munson, and Ford. Above the front office reception is the Yankee crest that proclaims "Courage, Tradition, Heart." Even at 9:30 A.M. there are several scores of Yankee fans hoping for a glimpse of their current heroes as they enter the stadium. High on the outside stadium wall that runs down the first-base line is the famous inscription bearing the words spoken by Joe DiMaggio, "I want to thank the good Lord for making me a Yankee." A more recent addition is the famous Yankee logo that now carries the proclamation "Twenty-Five-Time World Champions, the Team of the Century." A large version has even been placed on the side of a concrete walkway linking the stadium to an adjacent car park. Close to the entrance are three flagstaffs, each resting on an octagonal plinth. The eight sides announce the year in which the championship was won. Having run out of all available sides, the 1999 and twenty-fifth victory is recognized by a smaller plaque sitting on the shoulder of one of the octagons—space for another twenty-four.

Although celebration of a feted past, amply laced with current success, is never far away from the casually curious eye, it cannot be said that the stadium is awash with garish decoration. Nor is there any need. This is Yankee Stadium. Deliberately or otherwise, the organization has cut a supremely fine balance between recognition of its finest with breathing space for those who have to follow in the deepest of footsteps. This alone is an important statement for organizations wanting to create maximum leverage from their own, perhaps more modest, list of icons.

The real surprises, however, are reserved for those who are allowed to share a journey into the heart of baseball. Security guards, who elsewhere are notorious for their officious handling of potential interlopers, here are relaxed and friendly. Amid the crackle of radio talk sets that intermittently burst into life, there is still time to help unrecognized guests. If it were ever possible to be "welcomed" by a security cordon, this is the place. Such warmth cannot simply be an aberration. José Castillo, who is on duty by the players' clubhouse, while employed by an outside contractor, still sees himself as part of the Yankee organization. "Although I would rather work the field, I'm fine here by the clubhouse. I love working with the Yankees. It's a great experience." Visitors are provided with information that enables them to conduct themselves in a place that belongs to the players. Like all of his colleagues, Castillo transparently discharges his duties without fuss or pretension. Yankee officials arriving for the game greet each other with familiar smiles, handshakes, and words of encouragement. Contact time is brief; work has to be done.

The front office is accessed via a large-capacity, slow-moving elevator. Two floors from ground level the doors open. Move to the right and a glass partition and door are the only remaining obstacles to the reception area, wherein lies the proudly displayed 1999 World Series championship trophy. The area is quite small, certainly intimate. Two receptionists are busy fielding the never-ending line of callers. One of these callers is evidently quite persistent and aggressive, leading the receptionist to smile and whisper to us, "She calls every day and we try to be nice. I'll be with you in a moment."

Barely a yard away from the receptionist's bench is the trophy that excites the passions and hopes of millions. Behind it are familiar portraits of Yankee heroes. Ruth, DeMaggio, Mantle, Maris, and Jackson are all depicted in various action poses. On this wall are those who are revered by the Yankees organization. Most telling of all, however, is that between them is a portrait of Doris Walden, who for thirteen years was the Yankees' receptionist. The portrait is titled, "We miss you, Sugar." In all of our travels we have not seen members of the organization's administrative staff celebrated alongside the playing heroes. Evidence of this type of recognition is not isolated or restricted to the office area. In propitious places, plaques can be found that immortalize members of the organization for whom no batting or pitching statistics can be found.

The dugout naturally belongs to the players, so it might be assumed that inspiration for current players could be found from images of former Yankees. Surprisingly, however, both ends of the dugout carry half-busts of nonplayers: Pete Sheehy, Yankee equipment manager from 1927 to 1985, "Keeper of the Pinstripes," to the left as one faces the dugout, and to the right, Jimmy Esposito, Yankee Stadium superintendent, 1960 to 1986. The celebration of nonplayers is taken a step further with the celebration of those who assist in sharing the dream of the Yankees. Next to Esposito is a half-bust of Bill Greene, the *World Telegram* sports photographer with the tag line, "Just One More." Elsewhere inside the stadium are similar portraits of executives and administrators who have served the organization.

The juxtaposition of visibly celebrating players and administration alike is a powerful statement of a unified community. It is not just the players who get the attention. The theme of family and respect for those who have contributed to the Yankee cause can also be found in the way in which the organization publicizes itself. The 2000 media guide, which might be expected to trumpet the previous year's World Series sweep of the Braves, dedicates its inside page to Bob Lemon, 1920–2000, "A Gentle Man, a Consummate Competitor." The annual glossy brochure entitled "The Century's Team" contains a section headed "New York Yankees Family Album." Rather than featuring photographs of the players, the reader gets to see the families of the players and the coaches.

In keeping with the family and community theme, the original philanthropic foundation set up by principal owner George Steinbrenner in 1973 was extended in 1994 with the creation of the New York Yankees Community Council. It has broadened its commitment and raises funds for community outreach programs in the area of youth and education development. The charitable and nonprofit work carried out by the organization via dozens of annual initiatives is another vigorous example of how the extended family is fostered and the dream is shared. It is hard to square these images and organizational contours with the well-worn moniker of "Damn Yankees," a

phrase that allows less successful franchises the convenience of a subliminal accusation of arrogance. More appropriately, this is an organization that has established a self-confidence that results in harmony
and rhythm across all its activities.

Organizing for Peak Performance

Although the principal owner, George Steinbrenner, undoubtedly
plays a significant role in how the franchise operates, the operational
responsibilities fall to Lonn Trost, who, as the Yankees chief operating officer, has been associated with the organization since 1975.
Trost, an inspirational player off the field, brings a legal background
as general counsel for several sport franchises as well as a set of experiences that enable him to maintain perspective in the face of a star-
studded history.

> If I find anyone in the organization who can't get past the state
> of awe, I ask them how they put their pants on in the morning.
> Well, we all know that the answer is one leg at a time, so I just re-
> mind them that the great legends of the past and the heroes of
> today tend to do the same.

The COO's space is a working office, which overlooks the ballpark.
Confirming widely held suspicions that the architecture of the game
of baseball is one that involves intellectual pursuit, Trost has an expansive literary bookshelf behind his large, sturdy work desk. Time is
infinitely elastic here. Various vice presidents, managers, and assorted
administrators circulate in and out of the office informally, unhur-
riedly, and constantly. It is a scene that is not restricted to game-day
preparations. Early in the morning through late at night, Trost's office sees more traffic than home plate when the pitchers have lost
sight of the strike zone. A shirt-and-suspenders man, Trost is untroubled by the volume of activity around him. He is soft-spoken and
looks incapable of being severely ruffled by any impending event that
might befall the organization.

In trying to explain how the Yankees operate, Trost is able to quickly recover an organizational chart that resides in a close-to-hand drawer. The chart actually runs to three pages that sit on top of one another to reveal a skeletal outline. It depicts a classic functional structure that is organized around baseball operations, stadium operations, accounting, media relations, and business development. The administration group consists of vice presidents in marketing, finance (as chief financial officer), administration, and ticket operations. Those making up this administrative body call on a special advisory group that includes ex-Yankee players. Currently, the group comprises Yogi Berra, Reggie Jackson, Clyde King, Don Mattingly, Al Rosen, and Dick Williams.

Counting minor league operations but excluding all players, the full-time staff approaches two hundred in number, although the front office at Yankee Stadium operates with nearly sixty people. With part-time stadium staff and contractors, the operation can involve several hundred more. Each department head reports directly to Trost, who in turn reports to the principal owner. Effectiveness is born out of the deep development of functional expertise that sees most people spending most of their time working in their own area. However, when it is time to coordinate and determine the impact of one area's activities upon another, the organization is at its intuitive best.

This was evident at the start of the 2000 season when, most improbably, the world champions faced the prospect of having their opening day rained out and ignominiously canceled. The logistics associated with this scenario are difficult to comprehend. Technical, financial, marketing, media, and public relations issues are only the most obvious considerations. Predicting the weather, always a difficult task, caused an intractable situation for the Yankees. Lonn Trost:

Total functional understanding was paramount in this situation. Anything less and we would have not been able to integrate our responses. At around ten o'clock, prior to opening day, I called a general meeting of all relevant staff who had to understand the implications behind canceling our opening day. I told them it was important that they took responsibility for their own areas and even more important that they understood how that would impact on other areas.

From this point, Trost needed to translate broad participation into an executive decision that would be fully understood and acted upon by all parties.

I called another meeting at about two o'clock the same afternoon but asked that only those who felt the need to be heard should attend. Furthermore, they were asked to report on what they considered to be the key issues of concern. Finally, by five o'clock I narrowed down the number of people who had to make a decision and that was done jointly.

Although the final decision to cancel was not a popular one for the fans, beyond the loss of the game itself and all the anticipation that goes along with opening day, it was not associated with anxiety or a debilitating process of second-guessing. Everyone was kept fully informed and was able to participate within the context of an executive decision being made. The handling of this delicate decision ably illustrates how the Yankee organization is able to deal with situations and circumstances that might derail less well-managed franchises. A debacle right at the beginning of the season may well affect the team's preparation for the season as a whole.

The managerial style adopted for the opening-day cancellation decision has been effectively cultivated by Trost. Rather than creating a traditional command-and-control environment, Trost has sought to develop a more inclusive approach to managing.

When I joined the Yankees, I called staff meetings. Note, I did not say departmental meetings. To encourage personal responsibility, rather than stand up at the front of the meeting I frequently sit with the group. This is a better way to get our people to completely integrate their thinking, so that if we are giving things away on fan day, our approach and execution is consistent.

Coming together is revealed as an organic activity that occurs without the pretensions of formally identified cross-functional teams. Not surprisingly, the organizational chart doesn't contain references to any such artificial arrangements. During a game, the rhythm of the organization lies dormant for prolonged periods, only to suddenly kick into life. There is no obvious leadership role being exercised. A state of peak flow emerges and subsides without fuss or fanfare.

As the organization knows itself, so the participants know each other too. A heightened state of performance is linked to the way in which the Yankee community has arisen. As with the baseball players, organizational employees come and go, yet within the natural exchange of human resources the creation of the future is aided and abetted by consistency. Jason Zillo, who joined the media department as an intern in 1996, need only turn to vice president and general manager of baseball operations Brian Cashman for inspiration. "Brian began his time here as an intern, too, only a few years ago." Indeed, Cashman joined the Yankees in 1986 in the minor-league scouting department. By the age of thirty-one he became general manager, making his priority the acquiring of as much pitching talent as he could find. He also hired Kim Ng as assistant general manager, thus proving that in the Yankee organization, at least, one of the last bastions of the male preserve is collapsing.

Unquestionably, the continuity created by long-serving and young employees greatly assists the organization's ability intuitively to grasp the full picture. It knows how to run the base paths and when people should be rested, supported, and given additional resources. The organization has become its own proud metaphor.

Conclusion
Much has been written on the New York Yankees, primarily relating to performance on the field of play. This is as it should be. However, we differ from the mainstream in one important respect. The organi-

zation cannot be neglected as a source of important inspiration that contributes to success. No doubt the image and anecdotal evidence of the Yankees being driven by a powerful owner with both money and an attitude is unlikely to disappear. We note, however, that a more considered interpretation is that this organization displays all the traits of the other peak performing organizations in our study. And this includes the Atlanta Braves. We began this chapter by suggesting that their very different baseball parks could be seen as statements that the organizations could be operating very differently too. This is not what we found. Each organization has established itself as an elite team in the major leagues. It is perhaps fortuitous that they are located in different leagues, ensuring continued rivalry without the possibility of tedium setting in.

Although their routes to success are "path dependent," the principles by which they have achieved great things are essentially the same. Each reinforces the coherence of our theory. Essential difference is limited to the fact that the Yankees have experienced success for a longer period of time. In this respect, their greatest challenges differ slightly. The Braves are new to baseball supremacy; indeed, they have arguably yet to achieve it in the eyes of those who measure the finer points of winning and losing. Only a string of World Series rings will begin to satiate the thirst to succeed. The Yankees have already demonstrated their lock on the previous century. Twenty-five world championships tells it all. Their new challenge is to repeat or even surpass their previous century's work. It is the Atlanta Braves who plan to stop them.

The Yankees are a consummate PPO. Rather than arrogance, we found quiet yet firm self-belief that helps create a supremely relaxed environment exuding a warm, friendly atmosphere. These are the preconditions for peak performance. Herculean exploits on the diamond will continue, and the New York Yankees will celebrate and recognize its players accordingly. All of them.

5

The Chicago Bulls: A Bulls' Market

"I have been blessed to have been a part of, and to have witnessed at close range, the Michael Jordan era, the wonderful players who surrounded him, and all the championships that we have accomplished together as a team. I've been more blessed than any professional deserves, and the scary thing is that when you're as blessed as this, you face the challenge of the future. There never has been, and may never be, a sports team that has faced this kind of challenge—that will have to fill such a void like the Chicago Bulls will have to when Jordan retires. We will never see the likes of him again."

—STEPHEN SCHANWALD, VICE PRESIDENT,
MARKETING AND BROADCASTING

It is a regular season game day and the Minnesota Timberwolves are in town. In the early afternoon, the cavernous $200-million-dollar United Center, the custom-built facility operated by the Chicago Bulls and the National Hockey League team the Chicago Blackhawks since the 1994–95 season, is empty and silent. In preparation for the evening's event, the seemingly unnatural tranquillity is occasionally punctuated by the clatter of workers erecting courtside tables, TV equipment, and the like. Outside, game day or not, hundreds of fans throng excitedly around the Michael Jordan sculpture that guards the entrance to the building, photographing their hero in majestic flight to the basket. It is an evocative image, frozen in time, preserving the legend.

An hour before tip-off and the United Center, aided and abetted by 22,000 partisan Bulls fans, has undergone a dramatic transformation. Cacophonous sound from the relentless pregame entertainment show echoes around the concourse areas, pulling remaining spectators to their seats. These precious moments are only for those who have been fortunate enough to share in the remarkable Jordan era soon to draw to a close.

Deep below, the press room, thronged with 200 newspaper, radio, and TV personnel, buzzes with talk of the impending game, deadlines, and the scoop that will grab tomorrow's sporting headlines worldwide. Farther down the corridor is the Bulls' locker room. It is modest in size, but adjacent to it lie the generously expansive lounge and weight room where the team spends much of its pregame preparation time. In contrast to the frenzied courtside celebrations above, the Bulls' locker room remains insulated and unruffled. Luc Longley, the giant Australian import, stands awkwardly next to his locker and frets about an injury that prevents him from playing and relegates him to a three-piece suit.

> My diagnosis is that I have a bruise on the head of my femur and other various bone bruise injuries, which have come and gone, and come again. Bone bruises can take a while to heal. I was told to treat them like a fracture and there is nothing you can do about it. I was probably a bit ambitious coming back. I felt pretty good, but then the next day it was a bit sore, so we are going to take as much time as we need to get it right. I hope that won't be very long. We will have to see how it goes, but I suspect I will be playing in the play-offs.

He's unhappy with the situation in which he finds himself. Tony Kukoc and Bill Wennington, after a brief pregame workout on court, sit quietly in one corner of the locker room discussing the upcoming game. Dennis Rodman, the last to arrive, is greeted with smiles.

Nothing is said. Prior to the last-minute team talk, and as game time approaches, Coach Phil Jackson, looking deep in thought, strides purposefully in and out of the locker room.

Perhaps thinking about his upcoming retirement, the most famous athlete on the planet reflects on what it took to create the Bulls dynasty. Michael Jordan:

> I think we have been very fortunate. We've been together a little bit longer than some of the other teams. We know how to go out and deal with the situation. The team knows how to compensate; you miss key players and other players step forward. This has enabled us to survive without key players, and I hope we can continue to do that for as long as we need to. I think that's part of being a championship team. I am very happy with the way we have achieved things.

And so it was to be on this night. Jordan scored 41 points in a 107–93 victory over the Timberwolves, leading the team to yet another play-off berth and, inexorably, toward a sixth championship ring. Despite the turmoil created by his impending retirement, in the locker room after the game a dapper Michael Jordan was at ease with himself. We were eager to ask him about his personal philosophy of the game of basketball. Our assumption was that his considerable influence, and his attitude, might transfer across to the organization itself. Earlier in our research, the great New Zealand rugby All Black Jonah Lomu told us that he hated coming second best to himself. This concept of exceeding personal best appealed to us. Indeed, we found it in all the organizations we studied. So one of the key questions we posed to Jordan was whether he hated coming second best to himself. His initial reaction was one of surprise; this was one question he had not been asked before in the endless rounds of interviews. After raising his eyebrows, inducing a rare furrowed brow, he recovered quickly and shot back: "I don't mind coming second best to myself—at least I have got the first two spots wrapped up!" We got the message! Truly great inspirational players have no peers. For Jordan, a performance second best to himself is of sufficiently high caliber to be ahead of all the rest. That has been the story of the Bulls throughout the nineties.

Running of the Bulls

The Chicago Bulls have reason to feel smug about their organization, yet little or nothing is taken for granted. Like the game itself, the physical structure of the organization is supremely orchestrated. The Bulls' offices are a short elevator ride away from the ground-floor entrance to the United Center complex, and the security desk that screens workers and visitors alike.

The reception area bristles with basketball lore. A row of refurbished, wooden-slated bleachers from the old stadium, in addition to being a place to sit and wait, offers an evocative link to the past. On the walls action-laden photographs; enlarged, mounted press clippings announcing victories; hoops, nets, signed basketballs, and jerseys all celebrate the Bulls' history. In this space, it is simply not possible to keep one's eyes steady. In an adjacent corridor hangs the now-famous shot of Dennis Rodman hurling himself in horizontal flight as he attempts to retrieve a basketball that appears hopelessly destined for the courtside seats. Most intriguing of all is the floor. Wooden boards replete with court markings encourage fanciful thoughts that cannot be sustained elsewhere. While sitting on the bright red seats, it seems entirely possible that Jordan or Pippen might emerge expertly dribbling the ball past the reception desk. The boardroom lies adjacent to the reception area and, consistent with the integration of the game and the front office, the large boardroom table is furbished to scale as a basketball court. Black leather swivel chairs serve as bleachers and witness the metaphorically rich discussions of the Bulls' corporate offense.

Past the reception area, the front office pulses with the relentless intensity of a full-court press in a closely contested play-off game. Despite the obvious pressure of game day, smiles come easily here, reflecting a close-knit community that is fun-loving, respectful, and professional. Building a team as successful as the Chicago Bulls requires more than pure basketball skills. Irwin Mandel, vice president of financial and legal, and salary-cap coordinator, credits owner Jerry Reinsdorf, General Manager Jerry Krause, and Coach Phil Jackson for their respective abilities to utilize the draft and salary cap to the best advantage. Mandel argues that long-standing relationships among these three organizational players have ensured that drafting and trading have taken place with a long-term view in mind, and that they have not tried to invade the technical parameters of each other's expertise. "Loyalty, sincerity, and trust," according to Mandel, ensure that the owner does not second-guess the player choices and trading decisions of the general manager, who in turn will respect the tactically imperative requirements of the coach. Mandel is the final dealmaker:

> I try to understand the salary-cap rules as best I can. I work very closely with the general manager. We are always trying to think ahead: how much salary-cap room do we have now; how much are we going to have in the future—what is the right thing to do salary-cap-wise? The general manager will always talk to me if he wants to make a player move. I have been with the Bulls for twenty-five years and never once has the Bulls' general manager said to me, "Is this a good move basketball-wise, is this player better than that player?" I have never been asked that in twenty-five years, nor should I be. The owner shouldn't decide that and neither should the vice president financial and legal. That is not my job; but he will always say to me, "Irwin, how can we do this salary-cap-wise, does this make sense?"

What made great sense was perhaps the most important draft pick in the history of professional sports. In the 1984 draft, Jordan was passed over by Portland, who, with the second pick, wanted a center rather than a guard. Chicago, from their third-pick position, selected Michael Jordan. While the Bulls were certainly fortuitous in the draft, a critical philosophy of long-term development commenced with an ownership change the year following the drafting of Michael Jordan.

Mandel stresses that Jerry Krause employed a strategic approach to picking complementary players from the draft and obtained key players such as Scottie Pippen and Charles Oakley.

> The public and the press like to know what the Bulls are doing. But Jerry Krause doesn't inform the public or the press about his plans. He cares about getting the best team, and he won't tell you anything, on the record or off the record—even if you swear to him that you'll tell nobody, he still won't tell you what his plans are. His reason is that if he had let it out that he wanted Scottie Pippen, and that he was trying to move up to number five in the draft, then another team that wanted Scottie Pippen might move up to number four, so Jerry Krause played that very secretively. Nobody knew he wanted Pippen, and right before the draft he moved from eight to five to get Scottie Pippen. He was very aggressive and he made it happen. It boils down to this. Who do we love? We will do everything in our power to get the guy that we love. You make it happen. You do everything in your power, and that's what the Bulls did to get Scottie Pippen.

Mandel also credits Bulls owner and Chairman Jerry Reinsdorf with establishing a streamlined organizational structure that allowed for quick and responsive decision making. Directly under Reinsdorf are three vice presidents, Jerry Krause for basketball operations, Steve Schanwald for marketing and broadcasting, and Irwin Mandel for financial and legal issues. There are seven department heads who are responsible for thirty-two front-office staff and an additional twenty or so assistant coaches, trainers, medical staff, and media announcers. Together with the on-court players, the organization gets by with fewer than seventy people. Irwin Mandel:

> The Bulls, in my opinion, are set up very, very well. I really like the way we are organized. Jerry Reinsdorf gives his three vice presidents a great deal of leeway, a great deal of independence, respon-

sibility, and jurisdiction. I cringe when I see an organization that has too many layers. One of the brilliant things about Jerry Reinsdorf is that if I need any answer I can go to him directly. There are no layers in between; we can make our case directly to Jerry. We don't have to go to a president, a vice chairman, and then a chairman, which causes things to get lost in translation. Since Jerry is a decisive person, we get to make our case directly and quickly. There have been some teams in the NBA that have had many owners and those owners have appointed executive committees that decide things. To me this is not good. In my opinion it is much better if you have got one guy who gives the final okay, and he gives it to people who he has a lot of confidence in. A structure like this gives you a much better chance of success.

Keith Brown, senior director of sales, underscores the speed of decision making in the organization, noting that formal channels are less important than the cogency and leverage of a good idea:

A service rep, a sales rep, or an intern might come up with an idea for a way in which we can improve our game entertainment, or a way to be more efficient in a particular area, and we will do it. Unlike a lot of organizations that I have observed, from idea to implementation can take literally minutes. We don't have to go through an arduous or cumbersome chain of command. If there is something that I think will make my department or any area of the Bulls more efficient, I can go to my vice president, and we can debate the pros and cons, and if we like the idea the decision is made right there; it's done. Even if it's a decision that involves a substantial investment. If we like an idea, we can pick up the phone and call our owner, Jerry Reinsdorf, who is extremely accessible, and Jerry will give you a "Yes, go ahead it's a great idea," or "No, it's not," and things get done very quickly and very easily. There isn't a lot of red tape or paperwork. Our management structure is well defined and pretty streamlined.

Another critical aspect of the organization is the continuity of its staff, in particular the senior executives, most of whom joined the Bulls either before, or at the start of, the winning era. Keith Brown shoulders the burden of receiving and sifting through the thousands of job applications that arrive at the Bulls' front office every year. The business is currently built around a cadre of well-established people who collectively set the entry criteria for those lucky enough to be considered as employment prospects. Keith Brown:

> We came in at entry level and have grown with the organization. That experience and consistency certainly contributes a tremendous amount to the business success that we enjoy. Now, when we hire, we look for good people of good character, people who are happy and are fun to be with. They will be intelligent, enthusiastic, and willing to learn the business from the bottom up. They have to be good solid citizens with a strong sense of humor and a great work ethic. Those intangibles are every bit as, if not more, important than job skills. Chemistry, too, has an awful lot to do with the success of this community.

Mandel notes that the stability of the staff is vital to the Bulls' success. Sitting in his office, where some of the largest and most talked-about player contracts in the history of professional sports have been put together, he animatedly drives home the point:

> This is an important thing that I'm going to say. Most of our people have been here for twenty or twenty-five years. Our ticket manager has been here about twenty years. Our PR director has been here about eighteen years. I've been here twenty-five. Our controller has been here thirteen years. Our marketing vice president has been here thirteen years and our sales director has been here about thirteen years. These are experienced people. Every person here is a damn hard worker, has a great attitude, is capable, and works to the very best of their ability. If you ask other

people in the NBA, I think they would say that this is one of the best-run front offices in the league.

Steve Schanwald is unequivocal about the value of the Bulls' staff and, in particular, how the future of the organization rests squarely on personal development:

> Our philosophy has always been to promote from within. People know that they have a chance to grow within the organization. Growth is very hard; it's one of my biggest challenges as a manager because we have a small staff and the turnover is very low, with a lot of competition for jobs. I always tell people that my goal is to help you grow internally but if I can't help you grow internally my commitment to you, in exchange for your commitment to me, is to help you grow externally. I have no aversion to, and in fact take great pride in, seeing somebody go on to bigger and better things outside the organization.

The flow of activity in the front office benefits from the continuity of employees. Traditional forms of managing collapse when the staff can routinely access the inventory of accumulated organizational knowledge. For Schanwald, it is not a matter of leading or delegating. Using a familiar sporting metaphor, he argues for personal responsibility:

> With good people, you let them do their jobs. Give them an overall philosophy. Then you give them the ball and you let them run with it. That's the only way it can work. I don't have the time to be looking over people's shoulders. We've hired our people; we've agreed where we want the organization to go and how we're going to get there. And now, everybody just runs with the ball.

Coordination of administration and game-day preparations in the United Center are the most tangible examples of this philosophy. Tim

Hallam, senior director of media services and a twenty-year-plus veteran of the Bulls, has seen the bad and the good times and is uniquely positioned to witness how the place truly operates. Hallam, more than anyone else, has been the conduit through which the world has gained access to Michael Jordan. He is not one to stand on ceremony, and has a gifted comedic reaction to anyone who tries to grandstand or bluff his way through to the Bulls locker room. The public, pressure-cooker atmosphere has forced Hallam to ensure a maximum focus on getting the job done. In this, the organization is a source of strength:

> There's a lot of trust in allowing you to do your job, so from that standpoint, from an ownership or management style, it's very conducive to building the right frame of mind. You can see how it operates—the people here who are laughing and walking around smiling all the time are also doing a hell of a lot of work. It has to do with the atmosphere here. People are friendly. Probably ninety percent of the people in this building are here because they enjoy sports of some form or another and wanted to get into sports marketing and public relations.

This workplace environment enables the Bulls to pull together, as a team, without formal governance or explicitly identified roles. Organizational processes are transparent and transferable among people. This state of peak flow is critical to understanding how the Bulls sustain peak performance. For Hallam, the thrill of working with the Bulls is the way in which the community comes together, separates, and coalesces again:

> You can illustrate this by looking at the night of a game. For example, you have media services and you're worrying about the players, the locker room, the interviews, the brochures, and the game itself. You also have marketing; you're worried about the handouts, the music, and the promotions. You have another group of people helping out with the giveaways; you have the

ticket manager and his people worrying about all the departments that may come up with lost tickets or what have you. Everybody is out of formation, in his own formation. But we're really in formation. They may not be visible formations, but we're still following the same goal. We've all got our little different formations doing spins and loops, getting the job done. It's like a school of fish at times. We are in formation but at times it seems as if there is no formation—which is the beauty of it. And when needed, at the snap of a finger, we can all go back in the formation, which is fantastic. I think that's probably the key to this whole place.

This type of transparent activity produces an atmosphere conducive to creativity, which the organization also sought to encourage by establishing the position of manager of creative services, a role currently filled by Jim Hopkins. Unlike many other sports organizations that farm out all promotional materials to external agencies, the Bulls do all their brand imaging in-house. Hopkins is responsible for game programs, season guides, flyers, brochures, invitations, posters, and giveaway promotions as well as submitting designs for championship rings. In short, Hopkins, working very closely with Steve Schanwald, manages the image and messages associated with the Bulls. He argues forcefully that internal control leads to greater spontaneity and, of course, creativity, to the point where ideas can be changed on a daily basis. Game-breaking ideas are the result:

> This is a young, dynamic, and forward-thinking organization. Everyone is open to new ideas and, more importantly, is supportive and ready and willing to share ideas with one another. As a grassroots organization, we don't lose control of our message, which might well be diluted or changed by going to an outside agency.

As a relative newcomer to the Bulls, Hopkins wryly shared with us the following telling observation that every reader can surely identify with:

It's a lot easier to get out of bed in the morning, you know, when you're going to work for the Chicago Bulls, than it would be if I had to go work at the post office. I mean, I could sort the mail here, and it would be a lot more fun because I'm doing it for the Bulls. That helps a lot, I think, in making everyone a little bit more excited and maybe work a little bit harder.

The veterans translate this in a slightly different way. They argue that trust and the ability to rely on each other without the pretense of formal regulation or performance management review at every twist and turn is at the heart of the "running of the Bulls." Perhaps surprisingly, Tim Hallam believes that it "probably has nothing to do with winning," and that it is more likely that this community has been forged at a much deeper level of commitment. In reflecting on life with the Chicago Bulls, Hallam offers both an explanation for peak performance and a powerful charter for personal conduct:

I walk into work every day. It's friendly, informal, and yet respectful. You respect people's questions and jobs that they have. You're genuinely curious about their lives, their family and their children, as well as what's going on with the Bulls.

I've been here long enough to see Irwin's kids go from three years old to college. We've seen people struggle through deaths, personal problems, divorce, and at the same time we've all laughed ourselves silly. We've enjoyed ourselves and we've frequently worked ourselves to exhaustion. We've all had crises in our own areas. We've enjoyed the top of the mountain and some of us have started at the very bottom. We've seen growth in every aspect of the organization and in ourselves.

Sara Salzman, director of community services, who is in her twelfth year with the Bulls, shares similar sentiments. She observes that strong loyalty, pride, and tradition enable everyone to feel part of the organization. "We feel like we belong." Such feelings of community are amply fueled by the championship rings that are presented to all those employed in the organization. This is made all the more meaningful by the fact that the entire cast of the Bulls, along with spouses, is flown by chartered plane to away games for the championship finals. The organization pays for five-star accommodation, meals, tickets, and transportation. Marketing retreats are also held where work is interspersed with play. Salzman believes that these and other special functions help to build a genuine camaraderie that bonds people together. More important, she argues that these community-based getting-to-know-each-other activities encourage peak-performing qualities: "We have very high goals and strive for excellence. I don't think there are any real weak links in this organization. In this community there is a lot of grit and a lot of drive and determination."

Despite the self-imposed pressure, the tight deadlines, and the expectations of constant first-class results, the ambiance of the organization remains decidedly informal, creating what one director told us was "a chance to grow and a chance to learn." On game day there is a complete absence of formal meetings. In a very relaxed way, people talk all the time, sharing key information, and enjoying each other's friendship while getting the job done. Until Jerry Reinsdorf took ownership of the Chicago Bulls, the franchise had never made a profit. Since that time, a profit has been realized each year, and staff now receives a ten percent bonus on gross salary, plus $1,000 in cash. Keith Brown:

> One of the best things about our offices is that everyone is good fun. You can say anything to anyone. There is an awful lot of joking and teasing. Everyone is comfortable and on a first-name basis. It is not an environment where you are looking over your shoulder. It is a very casual atmosphere. People who are happy work harder and better. Our owners pay very well, including bonuses and good benefits. We are paid fairly and treated well. Other teams like to keep salaries down, but they end up losing good people.

Branding the Bulls

The Jordan era has seen a corporate marketing strategy put in place that assiduously builds the brand of the Bulls. There is no question that drafting the most gifted athlete ever to grace a basketball court provided a strong product to sell. Nevertheless, Irwin Mandel argues that the job still had to be done, and that Jordan's presence did not by itself guarantee a meal ticket for the rest of the business. He credits Jerry Reinsdorf, in the first instance, for being very marketing conscious. At Reinsdorf's insistence, and in order to maximize potential revenue, the marketing department quintupled in size. Irwin Mandel:

> I give Steve Schanwald a lot of credit—Steve is a brilliant marketer. So, at the same time that the team was improving, so was our marketing. In spite of how great our team is, I really respect Steve Schanwald, who gets the maximum dollars that there are to be gotten. If we had a less capable marketing department, we would still make money and we would still do well but we would not do as well. What his department does is maximize revenues. They do that beautifully. My guess is that there are very few teams in sports that have as capable a marketing department as do the Bulls.

Steve Schanwald joined the Bulls in 1987 when season tickets numbered fewer than 5,000, yet that year they began their sellout streak, still alive at the conclusion of the 1999–2000 season and slated to continue for several more. Whatever the popular image people around the world have of the Bulls, Schanwald is probably responsible for it. The branding of the Bulls in the Schanwald years is probably one of the most successful marketing operations in modern times. Building a successful sports team is one thing, but sustaining it requires encouraging long-term customer habits that roll into revenue streams that can then be deployed in the interest of team development. Steve Schanwald has made this possible. The office he works from positively drips with an astonishing array of Bulls memorabilia taken from the championship years. Appointed with personalized mementos from sporting icons across the world—Pelé, Muhammad Ali, Wayne Gretzky, and Michael Jordan—it is a jaw-dropping gallery of dreams. Schanwald is an inspirational player who exudes confidence and pride in his organization and its people. Unlike His Airiness, Schanwald has to keep both feet firmly planted on terra firma. The pressure associated with the Bulls' territory could easily unhinge the best of professionals, but through all the hoopla of six NBA Championship victories, Schanwald has retained a measured sense of purpose—to share the dream that is the Chicago Bulls. Each year the department sets out its strategic marketing plan for the up-coming year. Following a review of the previous year, discussion turns to the philosophy to be deployed in each area of the marketing prod-uct. Schanwald leads his team through the new goals and, step by step, how those goals are going to be achieved. Customer service be-gins with the administrative equivalent of the Bulls' famed triangle offense—intense marketing strategy to sell more than one million seats per season is amplified with the development of long-term cor-porate partnerships, and finally investment in the local community through the community service function.

Marketing is responsible for ensuring that season tickets are sold to capacity and that current holders continue to patronize the prod-uct. Schanwald's vision is clear:

> We tell all of our staff that everybody has to contribute in an ac-tive or passive way to a successful sale of season tickets. I want that to be the focus. I want people to understand that being able to market season tickets successfully is the lifeblood of any sports organization.

"Steve is ambitious and hardworking; it sets a tone," Keith Brown observes. "He always wants to push the envelope, to do more in bet-ter ways. This kind of thinking permeates the organization." As with "the basketball department," a term used by Steve Schanwald, ex-ceeding personal best in the marketing department is a natural goal. For Brown, "it boils down to not resting on your laurels." Game-breaking ideas are constantly thrown into the cauldron to ensure that, whatever the result of the game, the entertainment package wrapped around the total product is the best it can possibly be. Staff visits to Disney and NBA marketing meetings fuel the imagination, and the Bulls' marketing machine is in constant overdrive, supplementing, developing, and raising hybrid ideas. Given that the fans are in the building for more than three hours and that the game is only forty-eight minutes long, entertainment becomes critical. The Bulls squeeze every last ounce of magic out of every available second to enthrall their customers. A relentless, mesmerizing, sustained stream of audience-relevant promotions, audiovisuals, and cameo acts accompanies every game. Although the formula is familiar to many North American sports arenas, the Bulls simply do it better. Much better. Keith Brown:

> Our mission is to maximize the sales potential of the product by attracting people who aren't die-hard basketball fans. Our marketing philosophy is to make winning and losing as moot an issue as it can possibly be in terms of its impact on attendance and fan enjoyment. What you see here can be truly unbelievable. People who are attending a game for the first time can touch the magic. You will see grown men, women, and children crying or literally trembling because they are so excited just to be here.

As a direct result of Schanwald's marketing strategy, for well over a decade the Bulls have been able to cap their season ticket holders at 15,000, with the remaining 4,000 being withheld as street seats and for special corporate and group bookings. Finally, there are 3,000 corporate seats in advantageously located suites. The level of sustained interest in season tickets is remarkable, and has been the prime reason for the selling out of the United Center year after year. Even more remarkable is the 25,000-strong waiting list to apply for a season ticket! This enviable state of affairs is not lost on the Bulls' marketing chief:

We promote that list extensively. We promote our sellout streak, if nothing else to let season ticket holders and others know subliminally that they possess a valuable commodity, and that once the cycle turns down with us, as it inevitably does for all teams, they will want to hang on to that ticket because, as soon as they give it up, there's somebody standing in line waiting for the chance to get it. Once they give it up, it's gone forever. Our hope is that people will recognize this and that people will give us time to rebuild and that they will therefore hold on to their tickets.

As far as the floating seats go, Schanwald is determined to ensure that he gives people a chance to sample the product. Although all games are extensively televised, he wants to grow new fans who can attend games at the United Center, "especially the younger fans, and to create and instill habits in people that will be difficult to break. Sports marketing is about creating habits in people." Certainly, the television broadcasts are a critical component in opening up the Bulls product to a huge audience. They have helped to produce one of the most staggering statistics we have encountered in this study. In the city of Chicago and the state of Illinois alone, the Chicago Bulls have an active database of more than 500,000 fans who have expressed the desire to purchase a ticket to a Bulls game. In preparation for Jordan's retirement, Schanwald is ready to move: "When seats become available again, as they inevitably will, these are the people that we will market to directly."

In all of these considerations, Schanwald has resisted the view that the price of a ticket to a Bulls game is infinitely inelastic and that black-market prices of $1,000 and more, for a place at courtside, suggest that massive revenues can be generated by hiking the price of seats at the United Center:

One of my great worries is ticket pricing. As you continue to raise your price, the double-edged sword is that you've got more revenue, but at some point you will trigger a reduced fan base. The team owner's philosophy is to strike a balance. My greatest worry, in fact, is the escalation of ticket prices. This should not become an elitist sport.

Rather than drive up ticket prices to create a short-term advantage, the Bulls' marketing plan takes a more long-term approach. Creating equity in the product is achieved by building loyalty among season ticket holders in a very personal way as well as continually and aggressively seeking out new fans, thus adding to the incomparable database. Brown also cultivates and nurtures those who are already in the fold:

> This is unique to sports organizations. We have four full-time service representatives whose sole job is to meet face-to-face each year with every single Bulls season ticket holder. They actually go to their place of business or home, knock on the door, walk in, and say hello. They let them know that we appreciate their support of the Bulls. They ask if they have any questions or problems that they might be able to help them solve, and let them know that they are available to them should they ever need something from the Bulls. We always hand-deliver a gift to them at this time. We also correspond with them regularly, affording them the opportunity to buy tickets to other events. And throughout the year we send them other gifts and promotional items, including a monthly magazine.

Brown is well aware that without the gifts, the magazines, and the personalized visits of the service representatives, the Bulls would still easily sell out the United Center game after game. Yet he sees the salaries of the representatives and the costs of the promotions and gifts as investments for the future.

> By cultivating some goodwill, by letting them know they are appreciated, by giving them something back, by being proactive by serving them, we are creating what we hope is a good long-term

relationship. If we become a team that wins only fifty percent of its games and the guy is debating whether or not he wants to renew his tickets, and is on the fence, we hope those little things will push him our way.

Creating long-term loyalty is also central to corporate partnerships. Despite the obvious advantages of being able to market one of the most recognized and revered athletes in the history of sport, when dealing with sponsors, the organization has resisted the temptation to focus purely on its most obvious talent. Greg Carney, director of corporate partnerships, knows what his clients initially think about when they are toying with the idea of an association with the Bulls, but he quickly steers them in a different direction. For Carney, sharing the dream with corporate sponsors goes beyond current players:

We focus so hard on customer service and treating the people who we work with right. When I used to sit down and talk with clients, the first thing they wanted to talk about was Michael Jordan, Scottie Pippen, and Dennis Rodman. It was hard to get people out of that thinking. What I intend to work hardest on is our brand, our logo—the Chicago Bulls. If you want to do a promotion, do it with the Bulls' logo, don't do it with Michael, Scottie, or Dennis. The first thing is the logo. We've worked so hard to build equity into it, to make it recognizable. Now, you can take the logo and put it on anything and people know what it is. I can say, "This is going to be beneficial for us, because the logo is beneficial for you." That's really the strength and value of what we do. It's that branding. The Bulls' logo is always going to be there and that's what we want people to recognize. At the moment, the Bulls logo uniquely conjures up images of Michael Jordan, and championships. And that's just fine.

As with ticket sales, Carney looks to engage a family of sponsors who will be committed to the Bulls for much longer than the current run of success. The guiding vision is to reap the benefits of the association with Jordan without being completely reliant on a one-dimensional strategy to attract the interest of potential sponsors. Just as the Bulls try to make winning or losing a secondary issue in the purchase of a game ticket, they address corporate partnerships in precisely the same manner.

> We're all realists. We know that one day it's going to come to an end. It's our hope that we've created first-class relationships that are strong, that we've delivered value over the years, and that the benefits to their company will continue until the next great player comes along and plays in Chicago.

At any one time the Bulls maintain somewhere between 200 and 250 corporate partnerships. Each one is important to the Bulls, regardless of the money attached to the relationship, be it a handful of dollars or a $100,000 promotion. Sponsorship deals are always integrated with basketball, and Carney is adamant that the building will never host a straight advertisement. Each sponsorship promotion is directly linked to the entertainment package experienced by the fans, which in turn increases recognition and association with the Bulls brand. This coordination between "punters and partners" calls for consistency and fit between what the sponsors might like to do and what is deemed to be appropriate within a pure basketball context. Getting the right theme to a promotion, rather than merely signing big-money corporate deals, is a principle that Carney will not break. Nor will the organization attempt to deliver something that is out of its range. Rather, it will overdeliver on what it knows is possible.

> Sometimes we've walked away from dollars because potential sponsors have wanted to do something that we've tried before and that we know doesn't work. If it doesn't work for us, then it's not going to be mutually beneficial. We hope we have the expertise to come up with something different. That's the fun, creative part of my job.

As with the season ticket holders, the Bulls go to extraordinary lengths to cultivate their corporate partners. It starts with receiving, as a matter of course, monthly mailings, in-house magazines, and promotional items, and quickly moves to the more substantive area of block bookings for home games. Special clinics are organized where sponsors and their families have the opportunity to meet the players and obtain autographs and memories to last a lifetime. Each year a different mix of sponsors is flown out to Los Angeles to an exclusive resort for "golf, relaxation, and good food," while sponsors' birthdays and other anniversary dates will always be remembered with cards and phone calls. If during the season the pregame entertainment is going to profile a specific family theme, sponsors with families will be invited. Every last detail is painstakingly taken care of. Throughout all this, Carney knows as intimately as possible the industries that have created a partnership with the Bulls:

> This morning I went from cars, to hot dogs, to credit cards, and telecommunications. We have to be creative all the time. I sit in meetings with eight or nine people throwing out ideas and just think "Wow!" We are always looking for game-breaking ideas.

Before the marketing department became active, the only promotion the Bulls had to offer was a wastepaper basket, so in the early days it was not difficult to dream up exciting new ideas. In more recent times, the Bulls have been able to innovate using themes based on players' personalities. One of Carney's favorite promotions was a plastic drinking cup with a picture of the controversial Dennis Rodman on the side with yellow hair. A cold drink turned his hair red. This gimmick was so effective that McDonald's, despite being one of the most image-conscious companies in the world, hired Rodman to do a series of similar promotions.

> Now, Dennis Rodman and McDonald's, I ask you. You'd never think those two would come together. They did commercials with

him with different types of hairdos with four different sets of cups. Each week the cups changed to a new color. It was really fun. This is the magic of being able to bring something different to the table, being able to produce new ideas effectively.

The Rodman cups demonstrate how strong ideas create multiple benefits. In this case, the Bulls were able to forge an association with one of the strongest companies in the marketplace. Carney argues that these game-breaking ideas provide the leverage for revenue generation that "helps the organization put a quality player on the court."

The sale of season tickets and development of corporate partnerships are undoubtedly driven by business necessity, although these activities are far from exploitative. Corporate citizenship, however, is seen in a much deeper philosophical light. Steve Schanwald:

All our creative promotions and publications are designed to speak to the tradition of the organization and to reflect well on us as a company that does things in a first-class way. We also wish to be good neighbors and to perform good service in the community. Accordingly, we have a director of community services. It's very important to be active and involved in the community, to give back to the community, to be an organization that cares about more than just its profit, its bottom line, and so we work very hard at giving back to the community.

Sara Salzman, as director of community services, can count on complete support from both Jerry Reinsdorf and Steve Schanwald. While she is aware that the perception might be that all she does all day long is "give things away," Salzman notes that her eleven-year-old department, one of the oldest in the NBA, is still in the business of sharing the dream, and as such connects directly with the concept of passive revenue generation:

I hope, passively or otherwise, that everything we do will subliminally stick in people's minds and maybe one day down the road, people will say, "The Bulls did something good, and I am going to support them." We are grooming young fans, doing nice things in a feel-good type of way.

As with direct ticket sales and corporate partnerships, Salzman is rigorous in applying the highest of standards when it comes to dealing with her constituents. Everyone who comes into contact with the Bulls asking for assistance will receive an answer. And the number of requests is staggering: two to three hundred written requests and one-hundred and fifty phone calls each day, tens of thousands by the year, and more at play-off and championship time. Many requests, particularly the thousands that were addressed to Michael Jordan, could not be met easily, although Salzman's department always tries to compensate with something appropriate. Each year, more than $800,000 is raised for other charities that receive autographed Chicago Bulls memorabilia. With demands such as these, the organization had to respond with a formal institutional initiative. The CharitaBulls was established as a separate organization in 1987 to serve as a vehicle to improve the quality of life in the greater Chicago metropolitan area. In 1994 the CharitaBulls donated $4.5 million to establish the multifacility James Jordan Boys' & Girls' Club and Family Life Center. More than one million dollars has been donated to the Chicago Park District Programs to restore 140 damaged city basketball courts. Tens of thousands of dollars are regularly donated to Special Olympics basketball tournaments, computers for local libraries, school programs, and scholarships. Dozens of organizations in the Chicago area benefit from the community services initiatives undertaken by the CharitaBulls. In 1998, the Bulls donated $3.5 million to Chicago public schools.

Special dinners, raffles, auctions, local three-on-three basketball contests, player appearances, and straight corporate sponsorship programs are some of the many vehicles used to raise both awareness and the money necessary to make a difference. A network of former players, mascots, and Bulls' announcers ease the demand on current players by making appearances on their behalf. The strong youth and education orientation of the CharitaBulls' work sits well with the overarching theme that can be found at the heart of the Bulls' sustained sharing of the dream. Sara Salzman believes that, outside of NBA Championships, "focusing on the community, and doing long-lasting work that will have an impact in perpetuity," is the mission and principle by which the Bulls live. Although charity work is undertaken by most sports franchises these days, we have seen nothing to match the work of the CharitaBulls. This level of commitment to the city of Chicago is not a temporary aberration nor is it contingent upon continued NBA dominance. The rebuilding of the Bulls, post Michael Jordan, has everything to do with an organization dedicated to returning to the city of Chicago an elite basketball franchise able to win championships.

50 Minutes

At the end of the 2000 season, which saw just seventeen victories, Steve Schanwald is anything but a worried man. "The phone is certainly ringing less, the mail is bringing in less, and yes, the television ratings have declined—it's not all a bed of roses having to fill the void left by Michael's departure. But on the day he was drafted, we were already planning how to move the organization beyond his retirement." That planning began implementation with a dramatic meeting in the United Center, which directly followed the press conference announcing Jordan's retirement. Steve Schanwald:

The first thing I did was to bring in David Stern, the NBA commissioner, who had been attending Michael's retirement press conference, and I asked David if he wouldn't mind speaking to our staff. So Jerry Krause and Jerry Reinsdorf and I went upstairs and we had a meeting with everyone. We talked about the future and we talked about the future of the Bulls without Michael and we talked about the future of the NBA without Michael and we provided them with reasons for hope and optimism. This was the very first thing we did, literally, within fifty minutes of the ending of that momentous press conference. It was important from that moment to focus on the future and that is what we did. We focused our staff on the future.

For Tim Hallam, who joined the Bulls as a losing franchise, this was familiar territory, although this time around circumstances are significantly different. Indeed, Hallam positively relishes the prospect of taking the journey to success all over again. He sees the climb back to the top as entertaining, interesting, and challenging, especially the enjoyment "of watching people develop and change as we put the pieces and bricks back together, one by one." Tim Hallam:

> My sense of it, especially within my own area, is that it would be different if you were rebuilding and beginning that trip back up the hill if you had not had any success prior to your journey. But because there are six trophies sitting in the city of Chicago, it certainly makes that trip much easier when you have done it before. Your organization knows how to get there because they have a track record, a proven track record, of knowing what to do, so the journey makes for a heck of a lot more positive scenario because it is a trip that has been done before. It is very positive that the group that I am around enjoys what they are trying to do. Like the new players, they are young kids who are pretty wide-eyed and gung ho. They are very helpful and are not jaded. That is a nice change too. They are eager and they want to get back to where we have already been, so it is a lot of fun.

At the center of the rebuilding lies Jerry Krause's decision to create a bridge to the future by developing young players through the draft system while choosing to wait for the signing of free agents until the right players are ready and willing to move to Chicago. With plenty of salary-cap room available, the Bulls might have chosen to sign good free agents after the departure of all of their star players at the end of the shortened 1999 season. That undoubtedly would have created a better team, possibly able to contend for a play-off spot; but in reality, that would have resulted in nothing more than a mediocre team. For Krause and Schanwald alike, this would be the worse scenario of all. Steve Schanwald:

> Some people didn't like the fact that we had the second worst record in league. The alternative is that we could have had a better record with a mediocre team and won as many games as we lost, but the toughest thing to extricate yourselves from in this league is mediocrity. When you finish in the middle of the pack, you end up drafting middle-of-the-pack players. Worse than that, you end up spending more money than you should on players who don't deserve it.

Although NBA stalwarts such as Pat Riley have applauded Krause's moves to create a new elite team, there can be no question that the organizational stakes are of the highest order. The building of the team relies upon the organization's ability to remain committed and executing at its peak, while at the same time using marketing acumen to convince a potentially skeptical public that the dream is still alive. In this way, the team's and organization's fortunes are inextricably linked. Internally, Schanwald looks to what he calls the "4-H method" to maintain organizational performance at a robust level. These are hope, history, hoopla, and finally hoops. The hope side of the equation is to convince the staff who have recently joined the organization that they too will wear rings such as those owned by the staff who were fortunate enough to have been on board through the 1990s. The history and tradition of the Bulls is self-evident, but even in a season of uncommon defeats, magic or hoopla is built into every home game at the United Center. Finally, the promise of great hoops, "the best basketball in the world," as Schanwald calls it, will again be part of the Bulls experience.

The focus upon which the organization is crafted remains the selling of season tickets. In this regard, Schanwald is able to create a direct line of sight between the flow of internal activity and the need to connect with the Bulls' customers.

Everybody understands the challenge at hand, understands their roles and responsibilities, understands how they fit into the puzzle. Right now we are in the midst of calling people that we haven't heard from regarding their season ticket renewal. Anybody who hasn't renewed gets a phone call from us. We write out all the reasons why they should hang on to their seats. Everybody understands what their job is and that ultimately they still have to contribute in some way to our ability to market season tickets successfully. I have twenty-one people making these phone calls now and I have got them from all departments, not just ticket sales. I've got people in corporate partnerships making calls. I have got people in community services making calls. I want everybody to understand what we are about here so that it helps all the staff stay connected to that important focus of the organization. We work very hard to educate our staff internally that there is a reason for optimism and hope.

In typical Bulls style, the office sports a brass bell that is vigorously rung every time a season ticket renewal is confirmed. It is an audible event that links the organization to ongoing success. Evidence of the potency of the Bulls marketing offensive is that in the year when they were next to last in season victories, the Chicago Bulls also held the NBA attendance record. Every game was sold out, as it has been the past thirteen years, four of which were achieved without Jordan playing. By late spring of 2000, more than ninety percent of season ticket holders had renewed their association with the Bulls, demonstrating the continued habits and passions being captured by relentless brand management. Perhaps even more astonishing is that the waiting list for the few available season tickets has actually lengthened after Jordan's retirement. The ability to share a dream, that for some might seem more like a nightmare, is a story in itself. Steve Schanwald explains:

"What we have tried to do is make sure that our fans understand exactly what we are trying to accomplish, what our strategy is, and quite simply it is to create a great team." In October 1999, and again in March 2000, a letter from the owner, Jerry Reinsdorf, was circulated to each season ticket holder stating, "Our goal is to build something special with special players—something that will last."

Interestingly, the letter also refers to Phil Jackson's replacement, Tim Floyd, who Reinsdorf describes as "the best young coach in the business." Tim Hallam argues that Floyd is not only a great coach, but also a superb media-savvy communicator, much appreciated by the press who admire and respect his honesty. Likewise, Schanwald is effusive in his observations of their new coach.

> Jerry Krause needed to find a good person to steer the ship, and that was Tim Floyd. He found us a great coach who understands basketball and the business side of basketball. I can't say enough good things about Tim Floyd and the way he perceives and understands the big picture. He is a totally dedicated, focused coach, teacher of the game, and student of the game. Importantly, he relates well to all kinds of people, he has got great people skills, and what is important to me is that he understands that a basketball organization is about more than just playing basketball. And he gets it, he truly gets the business side.

Dealing effectively with the public and press alike is a critical part of the Bulls' rebuilding strategy. Coach Floyd's ability to keep negativity in the media to a minimum helps to establish with the fans a mind-set that a Bulls season ticket remains a valued commodity. Unashamedly, Schanwald reminds people of fans who gave away their season tickets in 1984, the year before Jordan was drafted. Volume 10, number 4, of the magazine *Basketbull*, entitled "Looking Forward," contains commentary and articles that explicitly outline the Bulls' intentions. In signaling that "we are committed to winning championships," the Bulls' general manager, Jerry Krause, forcefully states, "This is going to be a process. We've done it before, we're going to do it that way again." For Schanwald, the message to his customers is clear. As he hammers out the point once more, you have the privilege of being treated as if you were a temporary season ticket holder.

If you are thinking about giving up your season tickets, now is not the time to give them up. However, if we don't execute our plan and if things don't go well this year, then maybe I couldn't blame you if you didn't renew your tickets, but this is not the year to give up your tickets. You recall very well how valuable those tickets were and they could be that valuable again. Once you give them up, they are gone forever. So we have had a very high rate of renewal and for the most part, our fans understand our plan. We didn't get any boos all year in spite of our record. No, the fans were very understanding and patient and that was really our challenge—a public relations challenge with our season ticket holders who really are the group of people who set the stage for the sellouts.

A large part of the marketing strategy is to help the city of Chicago bond with their first post–Jordan era draft picks, Elton Brand and Ron Artest. According to Tim Hallam, these new young players are fun to work with and inherently appealing to new fans who want their own heroes. Brand in particular carries the mantle of responsibility until new draft picks are secured and free agents are signed. Meanwhile, brand awareness is very much a part of the way in which the new dream is being shared.

As much as most are prepared to embrace a new order, some still cast their eyes to the perimeter of the United Center basketball court in hope of seeing Michael Jordan cheering on the team in the place that was his home. Tim Hallam, who admits to missing Jordan tremendously, is however pleased that the organization is moving ahead. At the same time, Hallam believes that Jordan is also well aware of the problems that might ensue should he be a constant feature at Bulls games.

Michael is the type of person who knows the chaos that he creates when he shows up. I think he just needs to have time to get away from what was so dear to him, what was so important and what made his whole life. It is a little more difficult than people simply saying he should just show up and watch a Bulls game.

Hallam notes however, that Jordan has turned up at Bulls practices and, as recorded by the press, privately visited the Bulls' dressing room during an away game against the Atlanta Hawks. Even so, Hallam had to do a little coaxing to make the meeting happen.

> He was up in the suite in Atlanta and of course I got to say hello and was able to get him to come down to meet the team. I wanted to make sure that Elton Brand met him, as they had never met before. He also likes Tim Floyd very much and was eager to say hello to him and to tell him to keep his head up. When he came into the Atlanta locker room, all of our young players just gawked at him. They were just like little kids. Usually guys shower and get up and go for the bus, but every member of our team sat there and just stared. Corey Benjamin had a video recorder going. Michael wished them luck and using your basic locker-room chat encouraged them to keep working hard. As they were walking to the bus they were saying, "God, I met Michael Jordan." It made me feel like an old man!

Hallam watched the Jordan era from start to finish and firmly believes that although Jordan could have played for a couple of more years, "he had the perfect exit and despite everything you may want to read, Michael left because he was ready to retire."

A New Page

The organization continues to execute what Steve Schanwald calls "the revenue-generating fundamentals of sports marketing." The prospects of the team rely heavily on Schanwald's ability to provide outstanding customer service through an unparalleled entertaining game experience and by identifying and growing new fans. At courtside, Jerry Krause has put in place the principles by which the team will be rebuilt. Even this is a precarious enterprise. Steve Schanwald:

> Lottery balls have to bounce the right way. You hope for a good strong draft with good quality players coming out in a year

that you have two of the top six picks in that draft. Moreover, you hope that it is going to be a deep draft, so that is luck. In terms of free agency, you have to have players that are willing to take less money to play for you because any free agent can sign for more money with their existing club. We have to do a good enough job of convincing top free agents that they will be better off here in Chicago and that it is not just a monetary issue.

Nor can the challenge of winning new NBA championships, according to Schanwald, be separated from the inspirational dream of the owner of the Bulls, Jerry Reinsdorf. Celebrating the city of Chicago by way of basketball championships is a tradition that Reinsdorf is reluctant to lose. Schanwald confirms that the dream starts with one man, the owner.

None of this is possible without Jerry Reinsdorf. The man at the top really deserves most of the credit for any success that we achieve because he is the person who approved the budgets. He is the person who formulates the plan. He is the person who says yay or nay to various ideas that cross his desk, and he sets the overall tone. So really, if there is credit for what we have been able to do, not only in the nineties but now in terms of trying to get as good as we can as fast as we can, it must go to Jerry. He brought everybody into the organization, including the coach, the general manager, me, and media services—all of the important people here. And we continue to have periodic meetings with him over how we are getting payoff from the plan. The credit really goes to him.

Conclusion

This is an organization that will continue to win championships. At the end of the Jordan era and in the aftermath, we did not find panic or a frenetic group of people perched dangerously on the edge of a precipice. Rather, we observed calm, confidence, clarity, and a community with an almost complete disassociation from the wild speculation swirling outside the confines of the United Center.

As all of the inspirational players have lived, learned, and grown together, so the organization has been able to maximize fully the business opportunities created by the Jordan era. Accordingly, they have developed their brand image, creating direct, long-lasting relationships with the ticket-buying public, with strategic corporate partners, and, finally, with the Chicago community. Yet as the opening quote from Steve Schanwald explains, no other sports organization has faced the retirement of a player such as Michael Jordan. Beyond the notion of a franchise or marquee player, Jordan has helped define the game of basketball as a global entertainment. The Chicago Bulls also recognized that Michael Jordan was not just a player to occur once in a lifetime, but that he is peerless in the life of the game. They have their glorious past and it is also the key to their future.

6

FC Bayern Munich: More Than 1–0

"You cannot separate the Deutscher Fussball–Bund and Bayern Munich."

—FRANZ BECKENBAUER,
"THE KAISER"

Dedicated fans travel to FC Bayern Munich (FCB) games from Austria, Italy, Switzerland, and all over Germany. On a cold, damp Bavarian winter's day, Borussia Dortmund, FCB's traditional great rivals in the German Bundesliga (premier professional league) are in town, and once more the Munich Olympic Stadium will reverberate to the sound of 63,000 partisan voices. Although the facility was built for the 1972 Olympics, it now "belongs" to Franz Beckenbauer—"The Kaiser." There, as a player, he led the German national side to a famous 1974 soccer World Cup victory. Beckenbauer rates this triumph as "the highlight of my life—the greatest of successes." Yet the German people count his winning the World Cup, as team manager in Italy in 1990, as an equally crowning moment of his career. In Germany, Beckenbauer is revered as a national hero. He continues to carry the torch as president of FC Bayern Munich, but his connection to the national side is ever present. He explains the origins of the link:

In the last thirty years, we all started as youngsters together. When we belonged to the German national side, we were also winning European Championships—there were always five or six players from Bayern Munich. You cannot separate the Deutscher Fussball–Bund and Bayern Munich.

For Beckenbauer, a home game inevitably leads to media attention on a huge scale. Prior to the match, an endless stream of dignitaries and hopeful press, not to mention thousands of fans, laid siege to the part of the stadium that houses the FCB offices and, in particular, the area that Beckenbauer inhabits before the game. To get within range is next to impossible. The cordon of officials and astutely deployed security is impenetrable except to those with special passes. By contrast, the right documentation dramatically clears the way. Doors open and minor celebrity status is conferred upon those who have been granted access to the FCB president.

Prior warning of this experience came during the taxi ride to the stadium. Upon hearing of our destination—the VIP gate—and, more important, the reason for the visit, the fare was promptly waived. Earlier, the hotel where we were staying got word of our agenda, courtesy of a carelessly left itinerary, and our rooms were automatically upgraded to presidential level. Requests for Beckenbauer's autograph followed thick and fast.

At the center of it all, Beckenbauer is relaxed and looking forward to the upcoming game. As usual, at halftime and after the final whistle, he will provide nationwide television commentary and analysis of the game from a studio within the stadium. He reluctantly accepts the fame that has robbed him of privacy and solitude, although to obtain a measure of seclusion he now lives in Austria, just a short drive across the border from Munich. His office in the stadium is unpretentious and functional. Dressed casually, with graying hair evident beneath an improbable baseball cap, Beckenbauer shows few signs of the youthful elegance and style that graced famous football stadiums around the world. But as he explains why FC Bayern Munich has been one of the global soccer giants for the last thirty-five years, it becomes clear that he has lost none of his passion and enthusiasm for the game: "Bayern Munich was founded in 1900, so we are coming up to our one hundredth birthday! You really have to go back to tradition. I think it is tradition that explains our consistency, together with location."

Beckenbauer has been the figurehead of German football for twenty-five years, ever since the famous 1974 World Cup victory. Even before then, Beckenbauer was a key figure in the German national side, playing in the losing team in the World Cup final against England in 1966 and scoring a critical goal, once again against England, in the quarterfinals of the tournament four years later in Mexico, which set Germany on the way to a famous 3–2 win.

He collected 103 international caps and sat on the coach's bench for sixty-six international matches. As president, Beckenbauer stands as the titular head of the FCB community, an extended family that definitely includes the thousands of fans in the Olympic stadium. The Kaiser is eager to tell us how the national side and Bayern Munich both succeed by planning and tracking every last detail, but it is now 3:30 P.M.—time for the kickoff. A hurried knock on the door, and we are quickly ushered up the steps toward the VIP seating area. As our party, with Beckenbauer at the head, emerges into the sunlit majestic amphitheater of the Olympic stadium, the crowd immediately recognizes the entrance of its finest inspirational player and roars its delight. During the next ninety minutes we chat about the game, tactics, and what it takes to build a great organization. At the final whistle, Beckenbauer is immediately besieged by the media. Cameras, microphones, and cassette tapes are dramatically thrust in his direction by journalists begging for commentary on the afternoon's victory. Time for us to leave.

Germany was the European champion at the time of our visit, as it has been twice before in 1972 and 1980. France, thanks to victory in the 2000 championship, is the only other team to have won the tournament more than once. The German team has been crowned

World Champion three times and placed second or third five times out of the sixteen contests since the inception of the tournament in 1930. Unlike all other European nations since 1950 (the team was not allowed to play immediately after World War II), Germany has never failed to qualify for a World Cup. Deutscher Fussball–Bund Youth Teams secretary Bernd Barutta told us:

> We are always criticized. If the German team is only one up we will be criticized. We will be murdered if we fail to qualify. All other countries in Europe—England, the Netherlands, France, Spain, Italy—all of those countries have experienced a failure in World Cup qualifying matches. But we have never failed. If we don't qualify nowadays we are in big financial trouble with our sponsors and partners.

While other national teams wax and wane, Germany is always in contention, always expecting, and expected, to win.

Continuous Contention

At the heart of Germany's soccer success story is FC Bayern Munich. FCB has ruled the thirty-six-team German Bundesliga[4] throughout its history, with fifteen Fussball–Meister titles and an additional seven second-place and three third-place rankings. In 1999, FCB was once again crowned Fussball–Meister, winning by a fifteen-point margin, the largest in the history of the league. The 2000 season proved to be one of the most dramatic in the history of the Bundesliga. In their centenary year, FCB clinched the title on the very last day of the campaign with a 3–1 win over Werder Bremen, which left them equal on points with Bayer Leverkusen, who, at the beginning of that final day, required only a draw to win the title. Incredibly, they lost 2–0 against the much lower-placed Unterhaching, leaving FCB to be crowned champions once again with a superior goal average throughout the season. The league title completed yet another double winning season

---

[4] FC Bayern Munich has always been there. Some have sunk into oblivion, and some have been relegated to the lower leagues.

for FCB, who two weeks earlier had also lifted the German Cup for the tenth time. No other German team comes close to this record of continuous contention in Europe's most consistently competitive soccer nation.

Within the elite of European soccer, FCB's record is also hugely impressive. During the 1970s they won the European Cup (an annual tournament played among the champions of the national leagues across Europe) on three consecutive occasions. In recent years they have clearly demonstrated their incredible resilience, bouncing back from what could have been a devastating defeat by Manchester United in the 1999 final of the Champions League (the modern equivalent of the European Cup), in which they lost two goals in the final minute after having led 1–0 for most of the game, to once again reach the semifinals in 2000.

A million fans routinely attend home games during a season. There are 1,500 registered FCB fan clubs worldwide and 10.5 million fans. "Kronen Wild Duck Haikon China" is not a new Chinese Restaurant—it is the new FCB official fan club in the People's Republic of China. FCB is a worldwide sports franchise of stunning proportions.

The Kaiser gave us his perspective on how this has all come about, but to explore the reasons for the relentless success of FCB more fully, we also needed to understand the national success of German soccer. A high-speed train ride took us to the headquarters of the Deutscher Fussball–Bund nestled within woodlands on the edge of Frankfurt-am-Main.

As our interviews progressed, the primary reason for the consistent success, both of the German national side and of the nation's crowning club, FC Bayern Munich, became clear—they are creating the future through investment in infrastructure, continuity, and community. The DFB has six million members, 27,000 clubs, twenty-one "Land," or district, associations, and five regional associations. Each of the Land associations has a sportschule fully equipped to provide world-class training facilities. The DFB is committed to offering the best possible organization for everyone, from the very young to seniors and players in fun-friendly leagues. Sophisticated scouting and development systems ensure that talent is identified and nurtured from a very young age. Club, district, regional, and national leagues for all age groups hone talent through intense domestic competition. The role models provided by the elite club and national representative players create an ever-present incentive to achieve glory and financial fortune.

DFB General Secretary Horst R. Schmidt explained:

> We believe that the consistency of our success is due to the strong structure of our clubs and our regional associations. That means that over the years we have been in a position to support talent. We can now look for talent at a very early age—under six. The kids in kindergarten are asked if they are interested in playing football. A lot of sports are competing for the children's attention, so it's understandable that clubs try to have them very young. By the age of nine or ten, coaches from the Land associations are already looking for talented players. They are invited to training lessons and that continues over the years. Talented club players are noticed first by the talent scouts from the Land association, then by the regional association, and the best players make it into the national squads for the various age groups. Clubs in the higher leagues look for talent in the smaller clubs. They used to have to pay smaller clubs a transfer fee before they would release them, but the European court outlawed this system as a restraint on work. This created an unbelievable loss of money for small clubs all over Europe. We now have a completely free market, and players can change clubs with no charge at the end of their contracts. This makes the wealthy clubs very strong.

Creating the future through development is therefore a responsibility shared by the clubs and the DFB in a mutually dependent and symbiotic relationship. Both know that the success of the national team and the Bundesliga is dependent upon the continuous nurturing of new talent. The small clubs play a key role as the foundation of the pyramid, but are coming under increasing financial pressure as economic forces drive money toward the elite teams. Many of the Bundesliga clubs, such as FC Bayern Munich, have alliances with smaller clubs to extend the dream and build for the future. The very best young players move to the Bundesliga clubs at an early age, which suits the DFB, as Schmidt revealed:

> The talent scouts of the regional associations and the clubs work together because they have a mutual interest in ensuring the talent gets better and better for the club and national squads. The Bundesliga clubs try to attract talented players from the age of fourteen or fifteen from all over the country. That makes it easier for the DFB coaches to look for talent and to see how the players develop. Eighty percent of talented players are members of the Bundesliga clubs and play in their teams by the age of sixteen or seventeen. The normal way is that these youngsters come to a Bundesliga club and then show up in the nationals.

The DFB coaching system is sharply focused on the development of talented players for the national squads for each age group from under-fourteen upward. It is a systematic and relentless process, where the constant goal is to hone the skills of the very best inspirational players who will secure a place on the elite, senior national side. For the DFB, all roads lead here. This focus on the national side is certainly not mirrored in other European countries, and it is hard to separate the unparalleled success of the German senior squad from this focus. Schmidt described the process:

> The coaches think that the most important age for talent is between twelve and fourteen. We have an under-fourteen national side, then every age group through to the elite national squad. We have eight coaches. The coaches stay with their teams throughout the age groups and then start back with the under-fourteens. The best players become professional at eighteen, but often much younger players will have training contracts with Bundesliga clubs, and parents are very interested in this kind of contract. Our

members number six million people, and we have to work to maintain the number of people in football. Three or four million are really playing. A third of our members are parents, officials, referees, or supporters. We have to ensure that these six million people become more, and we want to develop talent very early so that there is a good future for our national team.

Although elite sport is but one of three DFB goals, along with popular sport and social responsibility, it is clear that elite sport drives the dream. Without a successful national team, soccer would subside in popularity, meaning fewer funds and minimized magic with which to develop the broader goal of social responsibility.

After clearly setting out for us the relentless DFB development process, Schmidt introduced us to Bernd Barutta, DFB Youth Team leader, who provided us with further detail:

Through the fifties, sixties, and seventies, youth football developed all over Europe, and finally all over the world, with different age groups, from under fourteen up to under eighteen, when players become seniors. The main work is done in our clubs and our regional associations. We pioneered a tournament for the twenty-one regional associations for the under-fourteen age group. Our coaches can take a close look at the players in the tournament, and we then take about fifty players and invite them to training sessions. We now do this for every age group. This way we can build up young players for the national representative squads. Nine out of eleven players in our World Championship winning team in 1990 had been youth national players first. Altogether, we have about sixty full-time paid coaches. We even have a football teacher's degree, run by the University of Cologne. The DFB educates their players and they gain experience. Without a successful national team the Bundesliga would decline, and the clubs realize this.

The DFB organization is unique in Europe in that it organizes everything having to do with German soccer, including professional leagues, the amateur leagues, the referees, and relations with the press. In most countries, the amateur and professional leagues are divided. Schmidt:

> We have been lucky enough to have both professional and amateur soccer managed by DFB. This is not the case in England, France, Italy, or Spain. We are convinced that ours is the right way. The fact that we have a strong, concentrated organization has helped us to be very competitive over the years in our national squads, and this makes it attractive for youngsters and players from overseas to play soccer in the German leagues.

Over the years, powerful DFB presidents have ensured that the amateur and professional leagues have remained under one roof, despite the short-term financial considerations of some Bundesliga clubs that have led them to create pressure for greater ownership of the Bundesliga. Continuity in organization is a notable feature of the DFB. Since 1900 there have been just seven presidents, and while other nations sack their coaches at the slightest sign of a losing streak, in Germany just seven coaches have developed the national representative squad in more than seventy years. Schmidt sees this continuity as an important ingredient in creating the future:

> Almost everybody in this association has played soccer, and this is what we prefer. We always have the same people from the DFB supporting each of the national teams, which means they know each other well, how they all think, and what their needs are. The key players on the staff of the DFB have all been here for more than twenty years.

Just as continuity builds success over generations, so the tradition of winning is self-perpetuating. Schmidt:

> The art of administration is directly related to what happens on the field. It is very important for the motivation of the people

working in this association that we have successful teams. We are a powerful association, which has always been very successful, and people are proud to be members of staff or members of committees. People want to belong to the DFB because of our traditions and our success. It does not matter if we are not always champions, but we have to be there, and to be a successful team playing football at the level that is expected. Winning is important, but the way you play for the public is very important. If you play with all your prowess, but you lose, people will accept this. If you win, but you don't play very exciting football, people will not accept this. We played one championship in Spain and got to the final, losing against Italy. Everybody in Germany was unhappy, not because we lost in the final but because of the way we played.

Wolfgang Niersbach, DFB press, publications, and public relations director, described the intensity of the media spotlight that is continually focused on German football:

We are sitting in a house of glass! In Germany we have a market with thirty TV channels and a hundred and seventy radio stations, and now we have the Internet. Thirty million people buy newspapers in Germany every day. Let me give you an example. The national anthem is sung before international matches. Our [then] coach Berti Vogts does not sing the national anthem because he needs that time for focus and concentration. So after every match I get about ten letters from fans asking why our national coach is not singing the national anthem!

Both the DFB and FCB embrace a symbiotic relationship with the press, and systematically share the soccer dream through managed media relations, thereby extending the horizon of business possibilities. Niersbach:

We created a system whereby not all the players are available for the press every day, but we offer something each day. We give them certain information and make available three or four players for special interviews, and the next day we offer other players. We work very closely with the clubs in this way.

According to Niersbach, the DFB wants to share the dream globally.

We want to host the World Cup in 2006 based on our ideas of the relationship between professional sport, amateur sport, and social action. This is not just about the German FA. It's about the whole country. We are a peaceful country, a new country, after reunification in 1990. This is not a development of soccer only; it's about our country.

No sport in our study has found its way into the soul of a nation to quite the same extent as soccer has in Germany. The passion of the DFB was palpable. Enthusiasm and energy infused our meetings, and were evident in the care with which the DFB ensured that we understood every detail of German football organization, and that all our questions had been answered to our satisfaction. Sharing the magic of the DFB community, even if only for a short while, was seductive. Niersbach summed up:

Everybody feels proud to work for the DFB. Nearly everybody will say, "I have too much work, but I'm happy, I'm happy to work here, because it's not normal work, like for a bank." It's a great feeling to be part of a success story. Personally, I am convinced that the secret of success is to work in a quiet atmosphere, with discipline, in a strong organization. Look at the [1996] European Championship in England. We didn't really have the best team, and we had so many injuries, but we won because of team spirit and the mentality and character of the team.

On the Deutsche Bahn high-speed train back to FC Bayern Munich, we reflected that the formula of passion plus precision should put German soccer continuously in contention for a long time to come.

By this time, we had completed most of our global peak performing organization studies, so we believed that we could predict some of the reasons for sustained peak performance. But would they apply in Germany, where the language, culture, and management traditions are very different from those of North American, English, and antipodean sporting organizations?

This was the question we had in mind as we prepared for our interviews with the staff of FC Bayern Munich. Our earlier research had revealed that the organization is studded with German soccer stars of the seventies and eighties. Our first meeting was to be with the legendary stars Karl-Heinz Rummenigge and Uli Hoeness. In his playing days, Rummenigge's name itself was enough to horrify opposing fans. He was the scourge of many a defense, breaking on a regular basis the hearts and hopes of spectators not sporting the colors of either FC Bayern Munich or Germany. As an inspirational player, Rummenigge had it all: seemingly unlimited stamina and strength; a vicious turn of speed; lightning reflexes; and a poacher's instinct for goals that was reminiscent of Gerd Muller, another FC Bayern Munich and German player still working with the organization after his retirement from the field. We wondered whether Rummenigge had made the transition to organizational life with the same ease with which he had sliced through opposing defenses in his prime.

Robbed of a full playing career by injury, Hoeness was a dangerous inside forward who always maintained a flamboyant style of play, whether pulling on the shirt for FC Bayern Munich or Germany. A ubiquitous chaser of the ball, Hoeness was a celebrated member of the victorious 1974 German World Cup side, and is now FCB's manager.

We arrive early for our interviews at the FC Bayern Munich headquarters and training grounds in the sleepy Munich residential suburb of Harlaching. Celebrated in soccer circles, Säbener Strasse 51 is the FCB Scbaltzentrale (nerve center). Decorated in the distinctive Bayern Munich colors, the buildings symbolize the scale of activity carried out at FC Bayern Munich. With 64,000 members, FCB offers professional and amateur, women's, youth, and school football as well as basketball, handball, squash, table tennis, and more. It is both a social club and a superbly successful global business in one.

Despite the early hour, fans, players, and the press are moving in a disciplined manner toward the FCB offices. We follow, keeping in the central area. This is clearly a place dedicated to fans. They are buying tickets, making inquiries, and soaking up the FCB magic. There is a family atmosphere, and people seem at home here. TV crews and the press are all around, although quite who or what they are interested in never becomes apparent, since this appears to be an ordinary working day. Throughout the building, symbols of Bundesliga supremacy appear to be accepted as natural by the polite yet persistent fans who are purposefully going about their business. We are more easily distracted by the impressive array of trophies, pictures, and soccer memorabilia, which dates back to the club's foundation in 1900. No corner could be found without magical representations of the tradition of winning.

We are expected. The FCB logo is etched into the smoothly polished dark wood table in the interview room, and more memorabilia adorn the walls. Hoeness appears moments later, relaxed, informal, and immediately understanding and sympathetic toward our project. He exudes organizational energy and passion. It is clear that this inspirational player continues to lead his organization with all the flourish, drive, discipline, and tenacity that he exhibited on the field. We suspect Hoeness has much to do with FCB's fame and fortune, and Rummenigge confirms this: "For the last thirty years we have always had big players, thanks especially to Hoeness, who has been here for twenty years. He is always buying more."

Hoeness is forever famous for bringing down Johan Cruyff, thus conceding a penalty in the first minute of the 1974 World Cup to a rampant Dutch side that had already dispatched favorites Brazil 2–0 earlier in the tournament. When we asked him how he felt about securing his place in history in this way, his demeanor still betrayed depths of guilt and disbelief. From this shaky start, the West German 1974 World Cup squad went on to a great victory in which Hoeness's

flamboyant football played a major part. We asked what it was like
to win the World Cup. Honess's evident pride in this achievement,
even twenty-five years on, really needed no words: "It was incredible.
We hadn't won the World Cup since 1954, twenty years before, and
to win in Munich in our own country, you know . . ."

"He won it," said Rummenigge. "I lost it twice in the final. Let
me tell you what that's like!"

> We lost to Argentina in 1986. I was very angry about that, be-
> cause we had played very hard. The German Chancellor Helmut
> Kohl came into the locker room, and we were damaged and hurt.
> I was the captain, and he came to me and said, "Oh, Mr. Rum-
> menigge, the team was fantastic today, and you are a really good
> ambassador for our country." And I said "* * * * off, Chancel-
> lor!" He said, "No, really. You were very good." We were so dev-
> astated that I walked away. He just did not understand our passion
> to win. We didn't need to be told we were very good just then!

With world-class players like Beckenbauer, Rummenigge, and Hoeness engendering the passion to win, it's not hard to understand the
growth of the FCB franchise. Hoeness gave us his explanation:

> The most important time for German football was in the seven-
> ties. FCB won three European Cups in succession from 1974 to
> 1976, a record never since equaled. Then, in 1974, Germany won
> the World Cup with five FCB players in the squad. These successes
> formed the foundation for our subsequent preeminence. When I
> was injured in 1979 I was twenty-seven. I hadn't played for six
> months, and FCB president Neudecker asked me to become man-
> ager. I discussed with my doctor how long my knee would be sta-
> ble and he convinced me to finish immediately. When I came here
> in May 1979, we had revenues of 12 million marks, eighty percent
> of which came from entrance fees. This year we had revenues of
> 165 million marks and only sixteen percent came from the gate.
> Next year we will have 200 million. Opel and adidas are

big sponsors, and we make a lot of money from royalties on various merchandise. Back in 1979 we had twenty people in our organization—now we have hundreds. The team brand is a fantastic name known throughout the world—even in Japan and China everyone knows our name. It was necessary to build our story around this town, and I think we were successful in that from early on. Many of the great names from the past help us today. The way we select inspirational players for the future, and combine them with the personalities of the past, tells you everything you need to know.

Many players who have been inspirational on the field in the past are positioned throughout the organization to pass on the dream of greatness. These living legends are the conduits from the past and the drivers of the dynasty, providing constant reminders of FCB's legacy of greatness. They have known success and continue to expect it. They encourage others to exceed their personal best.

Even though the players of Germany's famous seventies soccer squads were the catalysts for FCB supremacy, there are clearly other ingredients that lead to sustained peak performance. Echoing the infrastructure and commitment to long-term development that is also the hallmark of the Deutscher Fussball–Bund, Franz Beckenbauer emphasized continuity through the ranks of the organization, from the team to the administration:

> The financial situation in the seventies was very, very limited. We couldn't afford to buy Pelé, but at this time the youth program was very, very good at Bayern Munich. So all of us—Sepp Maier, Paul Breitner, and Uli Hoeness—we all came from the youth levels. And many of the Bayern team of the seventies are now working in the organization itself.

Hoeness agreed, explaining that this strategy continues to the current day:

> When I was young, everyone played football; I could play on every street corner. Today, the interests of the young kids are so

different: some play with computers, and they play ice hockey or basketball, so we have to look after them to keep young players coming to the club. We have fourteen flats for young players, and we have young players from all over the world. We have people who look after them, and teachers who help them with their classes in the afternoon. We always try to bring fresh blood into our main team of twenty-five players. We have a third-division team, and about five players from the main team play in the third-division side, with the rest made up from normal amateurs. We also have junior amateur teams. About half our team comes from our youth program, and the other half we buy in to fill certain positions as they are needed. We choose people for their character. We don't buy people who are just fantastic players. In this age when people get so much money, it is important that you buy character and vitality. We don't have too many people from outside Germany, because they don't usually intend to stay here for the rest of their lives, and we don't get the same commitment. It's into the money machine for them and then they go back, so they cannot create a special identification with this club. Players from South America find it hard to learn the language and don't like the snow!

Andreas Jung, manager of sponsoring and event marketing, told us how FCB uses alliances to help create the future:

We have an agreement for technical cooperation with a second-division club in the suburbs of Munich. Our younger players will go there so they get good experience, and if the club has any very good players we have first option. We have eleven league teams, eleven youth teams, two women's teams, and two women's youth teams. We have one chief coach, and all teams—from the eldest youth team to the youngest—play the same system as the FCB professional teams.

The continuity of inspirational players and staff, combined with the systematic way in which FCB creates the future through a carefully constructed game plan of development and judicious buying, harmonizes the community. Gwen Lloyd, administrator in the manager's office, who is English by origin but a fluent German speaker, explained the inside story of working for FCB:

> It's really really great. It's like a big family; you have complete trust and you feel that you could go to anybody at any time if you had a problem. It's such a different job. Most office jobs tend to be dull and boring, and here the work is not that much different·from that in another office that I left to join FCB. But everything that happens around the work is interesting. We patent people I suppose . . . people who you know other people admire and go to the stadium every week to see. We all get involved with the football. Every worker gets two season tickets. Everyone works very well together, and it doesn't really matter what department they come from. Downstairs, whatever . . . they'll call us, we'll help them. If we need something then they help us. Everyone's prepared to help everybody else and I think that's the main thing that makes everything work and flow smoothly.

Jung offered some more examples of how the organization makes magic and builds community:

> If at the end of the season the team is successful, the staff gets a month's extra salary as a bonus, and they get a paper personally written and signed by the president, Mr. Beckenbauer, congratulating them on their hard work and how it contributed to the success of the team. One year we were invited to go on a ski trip for three days. Next week we will have our end-of-year party where everyone is invited, including the players. All these things mean that now, at Christmastime, or when there is a big match, you don't say, "I'm starting my work at 8:30 A.M. and I am going to finish at 5:00 P.M.," if there is a crowd of people here waiting for tickets. People are not looking at the clock, and they do what needs to be done. The players and administrators are

all part of the FCB family. The majority of staff will have personal contact with the players because they come here to practice. They are known by name and none of them are arrogant.
They go through the building, say hello, and talk small talk to
the staff. There is no hierarchy. Most of the staff have played
football themselves, so we all talk the same language. We get
thousands of applications, so we choose people who we think
can do the job, have a passion about the game, and fit into the
FCB community.

Germany is known to scholars of management as the home of Max
Weber, father of the theory of bureaucracy. We were interested to
know the extent to which Weber's bureaucratic tradition would play
itself out on the field of German soccer organizations. Since we had
found very little of rules, regulations, policies, and procedures in our
peak performing organizations thus far in the study, we approached
FCB with, we confess, an expectation that here we would find an out-
lier.[5] We asked Hoeness whether job descriptions and formal performance appraisals are used, and whether strategic plans, mission
statements, goals, or objectives are in existence. He replied, "Nothing
really, no. We have no plans. I only know that we will make a profit
every year!" This is not the death of bureaucracy, since it has never
lived in FCB.

In response to our rather persistent questioning about job descriptions, Gwen Lloyd smiled: "People don't have detailed job descriptions because the jobs change so quickly and everyone has too
much work!" We were a few kilometers from Max–Weber–Platz and
no vestiges of bureaucracy were in sight. We persisted with our prej-
udices, causing Gwen increasing amusement. "Perhaps your managers will sit down and discuss performance over the year with you?"
She exclaimed, "At FCB they don't even start—because we are working closely together, and we get told all the time that we are doing a
good job."

[5] Data that does not fit with the general theory.

Focus substitutes for bureaucracy. Crystal-clear understanding of, and deep belief in, the organization's purpose minimizes the need for policies and regulations. Franz Beckenbauer confirmed the importance of focus on the field:

> German football is not as creative as Brazilian football. It is simple, but with ambition, spirit, and willpower. Some countries, for example the southern countries in Latin America, are more sensitive than the Germans. If they get to a certain point in a tournament they become afraid when they realize that they can win, and they get the shakes! But the Germans say, "Come on, let's go."

Jung emphasized the same focus in the off-field team:

> I think the most important difference is that our players do not have to do anything else; the team focuses on the match, on playing football. Our task is to do everything around the match: the allocation of ticketing, the event itself, the trip of the team, and all the technical questions for the team. We do these things perfectly down to the last detail. Everyone is focused on winning goals and the goal of winning.

The passion to win and the focus on winning is universal. Hoeness told this story:

> The most important thing is that the team is successful. We once had a coach from Argentina. The Argentinians play creative football; he worked hard and the players liked him. Then I read an interview with him and he said he cannot understand these people who are always willing to win, and he likes to play creatively to entertain people. Two or three weeks later he was off—chop. I told him, "You play a very attractive ball game; very entertaining. Please do it wherever you want, but not in Bayern Munich!"

Hoeness sums up the FCB focus in a simple phrase: "We have to abolish losing!" Everyone knows this.

FCB has continuity and tradition that come with its rich history and strong community, but at the same time flexibility, learning, and the relentless pursuit of game-breaking ideas are ever present. Hoeness described to us his relaxed style of management, which we had already sensed. "I never know when I come in here what my plan is for the day, after lunch and so forth. The most important thing is that you are flexible. For me it is a laugh every minute. I cannot imagine working for another club. It is something special to work here."

Rummenigge was proud of FCB's tradition of winning through game-breaking ideas on and off the field:

> Our 1974 team were intelligent guys, clever guys, winners. This was the first generation to make big money out of soccer, but nothing like what we see today. Generation by generation, soccer is changing. It's different and harder than before, because you always have to come up with new ideas. But the organization knows how to have success and the economic side is very successful. So our job is to convince new people that these are the right things to do. We ask whether a new player is really confident. Is he willing to believe that the team must be perfect?

If we couldn't find stereotypical German bureaucracy, surely we would see much-vaunted German precision. Indeed, it was everywhere. Franz Beckenbauer confirmed the perfectionist attention to the last detail:

> Yes! The organization is great—well, you know the Germans—the planning and the tracking of every last detail. I was team manager for six years and my assistant, who died two years ago, Horst Schmidt, planned everything, like a cake for us to eat. I tried to overturn some of it, but he told me not to bother him—told me to shut up—to go and do something else, and at the end of the tournament I found out he was right!

The Munich Olympic Stadium holds 63,000 people, and all of these seats could be sold as season tickets. However, unlike in North American sports franchises, where season ticket sales are kept high as a protection against poor performance, FCB is sure of its success. Hoeness:

> We have 65,000 members of FCB, but that doesn't mean they are all season ticket holders. We sold about 20,000 season tickets. We didn't want to sell more, because if you always have the same people in the stadium you don't make money on merchandising. We have six to eight million fans in Germany, and if you have so many fans and nobody is able to get a ticket, the dream fades.

FCB sells symbols of association through four FCB shops, four mobile vans, and by mail order. The distinctive red, white, and dark blue colors and logo extend the FCB brand into a range of clothing, memorabilia, and merchandise as diverse as mountain bikes, watches, school equipment, kitchen equipment, and toys. The FCB Meister Katalog offers a rich array of branded goods for squads of enthusiastic fans worldwide. The range and extent of these dream catchers is the most impressive and comprehensive among all our project organizations. With a print run of one million copies, the Meister Katalog is big business, and the financial payoff feeds the dream. There are about 120 people in distribution of tickets and merchandising. Service and image drive the dream, with "everyone treated very friendly," according to Jung. "You do not know what they want to have; maybe they want a ticket, maybe a tie, magnet, shirt, you don't know but you treat everyone the same. And if you treat them friendly, the chance that they will buy is better." Sponsors are partners in extending the dream:

> Opel and adidas are our two premium sponsors. Then we have other sponsors to whom we offer standard packages of benefits plus further special options. Cross-promotion is very important between our sponsors. We often suggest that a sponsor goes together with another to get greater benefits. Also, we want success-

ful sponsors, because then we have a transfer from sponsors to the club and from the club to the sponsors. We had 350 hours of TV coverage last season and 3,467 million people contacts. About twenty-five percent of our income comes from sponsorships.

The revenue derived from sponsorships, merchandise, and ticket sales enables FCB to fund the development of youth players and to play a role in the DFB's commitment to social responsibility. For example, inspirational players take decisive positions against drugs and smoking in nationwide and local campaigns aimed at the young. The FCB is at the forefront of an ongoing "Say No to Drugs" campaign. Rummenigge was one of its initiators. "Drug abuse caused a tragedy in the family of a close friend of mine. So I immediately agreed to do whatever is necessary to warn our youngsters."

The FCB dream is more than just winning. More than filling the stadium, year in and year out. More than selling symbols of association. More than just a 1–0 win. Winning attractively is important, but beyond winning, FCB is committed to being a partner in society, and takes its social responsibilities for popular sports and, especially, youth seriously. This commitment extends throughout the DFB. Niersbach:

A key moment happened at the World Cup in Mexico, when we saw homeless children a couple of meters away from the World Cup stadium. We were there as guests of the country, but we wanted to help. The Mexico Foundation in Queretaro has now existed for more than ten years. It was not just a momentary reaction to say, We have brought you money for the homeless children. We established an orphanage, and now we have raised more than two million marks for Mexico, and we feel that our whole association understands the idea. So you have a referee meeting or a Christmas meeting and afterwards they bring money to the foundation: 20 marks, 200 marks, 1,000 marks. The German embassy in Mexico is involved and each mark goes directly to the children.

One million volunteer coaches throughout Germany teach young players skills and values that go beyond the football field. "A young girl or boy in an amateur club should learn good social attitudes for life, for example, how to win and lose, and to accept a weaker partner," says Niersbach. "It's the task of sports, whether it's Munich or a very, very small club, to offer training and match competition, but also to offer a certain social attitude. Most clubs think this way."

The inspirational dream of winning attractively with passion and with social responsibility brings meaning to the German soccer logo "More than 1–0." The dream is the theme. Soccer can contribute to the greater good of society. We continue to share the dream and follow their fortunes. The official song of the Deutscher Fussball–Bund, sung by Anna Maria Kaufmann and Joey Tempest, summarizes our story.

> Running with a dream,
> Burning deep inside,
> Don't let them bring you down,
> Don't let the chance go by.

> Running with a dream
> Only we can show
> How far this road will lead
> And what it means
> To be running with a dream.

> Sometimes it seems like you've got it all
> And everybody wants a share;
> Sometimes your back is against the wall,
> And nobody seems to care.
> We've tried so hard and we've come so far,
> We are the ones who don't give in;
> The world will take us for what we are,
> Whether we lose or win,
> But we're running with a dream.

7

WilliamsF1:
We Are All Racers Here

"What really makes Williams tick is that it is one huge great family and every single member of that family has got one goal. That is to be a winner, whether that is by their technical contribution or in some other way. Every single one of us is completely focused on one thing. Winning."

—JANE GORARD, MEDIA MANAGER

The numbers are simply staggering. On the sixteen race weekends that comprise a full Formula One season, more than two and a half million spectators will visit the race circuits. Each Grand Prix is watched by an estimated worldwide TV audience of more than 351 million, making an aggregate total of 56 billion loyal viewers. The "need for speed" makes Formula One the world's most popular spectator, and breathtakingly spectacular, sport. For the past twenty years, WilliamsF1 has established the best record, outpacing by a substantial margin the Ferrari constructors' team, which is more obviously associated with the romance of motor racing.

Having won the coveted FIA Formula One World Constructors' Championship nine times, and the better-known FIA Formula One World Drivers' Championship seven times, the trappings of victory are all around the Williams factory at Wantage in Oxfordshire. As managing director, Frank Williams's opinion is that "Grand Prix racing attracts and creates more true passion than any other sport." This can clearly be seen in the people who work for WilliamsF1. Yet in the mid-sixties, Williams was sleeping on a sofa in a shared flat in Pinner Road, Harrow, on the outskirts of London, trying to establish a spare-parts business. Twenty years later, that business had become Williams Formula One.

The present Williams factory has been in operation since the beginning of 1996. Employing more than 360 highly skilled employees, it has an output that is at best modest, making just seven cars each year. However, it takes 250,000 person-hours to build a single car, produced from more than a thousand complex technical drawings, and finally constructed with more than 3,000 machined components worth more than $1.5 million U.S. Additionally, each car is completely stripped down between races, subjected to more than 200 diagnostic checks, and then rebuilt. Overall, the factory machines more than 200,000 components each year. The organization also boasts one of the most advanced, fastest, and most accurate half-scale model wind tunnels in the world, allowing year-round aerodynamic testing. The Williams car, like other Formula One vehicles, can reach 200 k.p.h. from a standing start, and then stop within seven seconds. Straight-line speed is well over 340 k.p.h. Just as important as the Grand Prix cars are the test cars that complete more than 30,000 kilometers each year, a vital element in ensuring that the work carried out by everyone in the organization is directed toward making the car go faster.

The atmosphere in the factory is a heady mixture of engineering and the romance of victory. The entranceway into the facility opens out to a large atrium. In the middle of this space lies a vivid reminder of the raison d'être of the organization—Jacques Villeneuve's peerless 1997 World Championship–winning car. One corner of the atrium is reserved for an assortment of trophies, shields, plaques, and other mementos that celebrate the winning years. Elsewhere, the walls offer a rich array of framed photographs, memorabilia, and nuggets of information that provide tantalizing glimpses of Williams's history.

The shrinelike qualities of the atrium are amplified by the Formula One museum. Close to the reception booth a pair of sturdy double doors opens to a priceless collection of Formula One cars that represent twenty years of Williams's engineering. The cars, all in pristine running condition, carry the names of the great drivers who helped take Williams to the peak of motor racing. The cars of World Champions Alan Jones, Keke Roseberg, Nelson Piquet, Alain Prost, Nigel Mansell, and Damon Hill, along with those of many other Grand Prix winners, are all on display. If there is an inner sanctum to the world of Formula One, it is here. Adjacent to the museum is the plush, state-of-the-art Ayrton Senna Lecture Theater, which hosts conferences, media presentations, and launches of new products from Williams's sponsors.

The production areas that adjoin the atrium and museum bear little resemblance to a traditional engineering factory. It is an unparalleled, world-class facility where the highest skill level is employed. Every section or workstation maintains a surgical cleanliness. Only the racks of titanium rods and alloys reveal the true nature and intent of the operation. Placed near each other to ensure maximum coordination are computer-aided design systems, which play an integral part in the research, design, development engineering, production, and testing. Three autoclaves that deal with new carbon-fiber composites are housed in a clean room that would not be out of place in a NASA launch-vehicle assembly area. The bays where the cars are finally constructed and tested have the ambiance of a large hospital operating theater.

High technology, precision engineering, and a strong sense of professional discipline are immediately apparent. The in-house factory capabilities include composites, fabrication, machining, electronics, pattern and model making for the half-scale model wind tunnel, hydraulics, and various ancillary support functions. Approximately half the total workforce is directly involved in vehicle construction. Echoing the traditional working methods of skilled artisans, some forty design and research engineers collaborate closely with craftsmen to ensure that all tasks related to the making and assembly of each car are effectively conceived and executed. The race and test teams are each staffed with a mix of twenty engineers and mechanics. Another forty people working in administrative capacities round out the morphology of the organization. Within this latter group are sixteen marketing and media personnel who are responsible for sponsorship deals, public relations, and generating more than $100 million U.S. in annual revenue.

During the year the facility holds several open days when friends and family of the workforce can see plant operations for themselves. In preparation for such occasions, some of the work spaces display small pieces of wreckage from spectacular accidents that are undeniably part of the thrill of motor racing at its fastest. Poignant reminders of the hazards, dangers, and expense of Formula One motor racing, they offer a surprisingly immediate connection for those peering in from the outside. "This is a mangled piece of suspension wishbone from Jacques's [Villeneuve] shunt in the Belgian Grand Prix," factory worker Bernie Jones explains. "Course, we don't expect an apology," he adds with a wry smile. As long as there is no proprietary engineering involved, and the driver suffered no more than a dent to his dignity, these trophies, once seen by 350 million television viewers, are carried off to many an Oxfordshire mantelpiece.

Even though the Grand Prix season winds up in late October, a week later and the factory is already in high gear, designing and preparing new components for the following year's WilliamsF1 car. Many of these activities began during the racing season itself. New FIA technical regulations governing the specifications for the coming season are made available to the constructors well before the last Grand Prix race has been run, giving them time to design components afresh to conform to the new rules. The off season is also an important opportunity to begin experimenting with reconfigured components that offer the tantalizing hope of a faster car. One workstation is honing a newly designed wheel nut that might reduce the time it takes to change a tire during the all-important pit stop. "This innovation might cut two-tenths of a second off our pit-stop times," explains craftsman Steve Pieri. Although the component looks immaculate, Pieri is not impressed. Meetings will take place among the design engineers, the technical director, Patrick Head, and the factory specialists over this and an unspeakable number of other critical components. However, at the end of the day, it is craftsmen like Steve Pieri who have to machine the impeccable part, a responsibility he is proud to hold. During the race season this process may need to be concentrated into a much shorter period of time. David Williams, general manager:

> It is not unusual for the company to design a part today, manufacture and test it overnight, and fit it to the car tomorrow. Naturally, this means that the emphasis is on each employee to take full responsibility for his or her work, with maximum freedom to act.

Work activity is seemingly relaxed and unhurried, yet Alan Challis, race and test team coordinator, a twenty-year veteran at Williams, observes in understated fashion that "At Williams, every day is a defining moment."

Celebration is never far away. In the canteen facility hangs a large, evocative photograph of the Williams pit-lane crew at Suzuka, Japan, in 1996 cheering the final checkered-flag victory that secured Damon Hill the Drivers' World Championship that year. The enlarged picture is personally signed and dedicated by Hill to the Williams team. Similar artifacts, including scaled models of Formula One cars, can also be found in and around the offices. These objects embody a magic-making environment and a relentless ambition to be first, to win. This clear organizational focus comes directly from its two iconoclastic inspirational players, Frank Williams and Patrick Head, Frank's partner and technical director of the team. Head explains:

> Frank and I have relatively straight aims that are clearly visible to our organization. We're just motor racing nuts really. Everybody in the company is aware that we have very, very focused aims. I'm sure we have degrees of complexity, but, put simply, we worked out quite a long time ago that if you can be successful on the track, other things, particularly the commercial aspect of the com-

pany, tend to look after themselves. They tend to be a hell of a lot easier to run when the technical and the performance side is right. A company is more difficult to run if you turn that focus around.

We've always been very focused on the purpose of the company. I don't think that this is totally the case with all the other team principals. There are some teams in Formula One who give the impression that profitability comes first, and then they try to do the best job they can within the level of profitability. Whereas nobody here has any confusion about the Williams company. They know that the driving motivation is always to be successful and to win, not just to be profitable. And if becomes necessary to sell assets in order to be successful, that is what we would do.

The Driving Forces

Kay Young, head receptionist, observes of Frank Williams, "We still think of him being a mighty figure." It is a sentiment easily understood by the observer, although Williams himself is more matter-of-fact in his personal assessments. "Since the age of four or five, I have always been interested in cars. In the late 1940s maybe only one family in twenty had a car. To ride in one was a major event. To race them with friends—it just happened." Frank Williams is the consummate inspirational player. While fulfilling his own passion for speed he took a corner too fast and "cocked it up." The crash, which happened in France in 1986, left Williams tetraplegic and permanently wheelchair-bound. Despite this setback that almost cost him his life, he has continued to lead Williams successfully.

Apart from having amassed a lifetime of Formula One motor racing knowledge, Williams is known for his great business acumen and, in particular, his skill at making critical deals with suppliers, sponsors, and contractors. In the early days of Williams, his ability to find sponsorship funds was about survival, whereas his current dealings are more likely to be about fine-tuning the organization to enable it to maintain its success. In conversation, Williams misses nothing. Urbane commentary combined with razor-sharp observations ensures the maximum attention of those within earshot. Whether in the office or in the pit garage, his presence lifts those around him. His friendliness and kindly demeanor sit uneasily with the popular belief that Williams is the hard man of Formula One.

More important, his sheer grit and determination have provided the platform for others to establish their engineering and racing credentials and make real their dreams of speed as well. Patrick Head, who as a promising racing-car engineer joined Frank Williams in 1977, is a Formula One icon in his own right, famed for his unrivaled expertise. Dave Jones, chief inspector, notes:

> He is totally committed to racing. Patrick can walk into your department and if you have ten bits on the table, he can look at them, and if one has something slightly wrong with it, he'll pick it up. He knows every little bit of that car.

Head's legendary knowledge and passion for his work are truly inspirational. Although he has the appearance of a grizzled factory superintendent, he combines unparalleled engineering skill with an avuncular and infectious joviality. He is always willing to demonstrate his love for motor racing. While relaxing in the pit garage, only hours before the start of the Canadian Grand Prix, Head toys with a small, irregularly shaped defective engine component. Fixing his gaze purposefully on the offending object resting on the tips of his fingers, he animatedly launches into a detailed technical explanation of why the engine part had recently failed. Quick to recognize that his audience is somewhat out of depth, he generously wraps up the one-sided discussion with the simple observation, "It's a design fault really. We'll fix it next week." Still, he leaves the strong impression that he is personally insulted by the presence of the compromised object.

He talks effortlessly and very positively about the great drivers associated with Williams, although he has a more reflective and deliberate cadence when referring to the great Ayrton Senna, who tragically died in a Williams car three months after joining the team.

"You knew you were in the presence of someone special when working with Senna. After testing or qualifying he would never discuss the session until he had seen the telemetry on the tires, which he considered to be the key variable in motor racing." Contrary to uninformed opinion, Head also considered the Williams FIA Drivers' World Champion of 1996, Damon Hill, to be "a very fast driver indeed." Coming from Head, this is little short of the ultimate accolade in the racing world.

Head is also effusive about the Williams drivers for 2000, Ralf Schumacher and the young Briton, Jenson Button. Schumacher joined Williams from Jordan, bringing a reputation for being impetuous and accident-prone, while Button joined the prestigious Formula One team untested in the top flight of motor racing. However, Head sees both drivers as carrying the necessary skills to put the new BMW engine through its paces during the important developmental period of racing.

Peter Yonge, chief buyer, describes Frank Williams and Patrick Head as "the prime movers, the shareholder owners who from day one have been the common denominator." For Lindsay Morle, media executive, their presence creates a special aura of association:

> It is very hard to describe actually, but there is something magical about Williams. It took me two years to get this job. There is such a history to it, especially with what Frank has gone through, and with himself and Patrick coming from the bottom to be a winning team. I think it inspires people to work as hard as they have done to get where they are. Everyone wants to be part of the Williams team.

Having created such a passionate desire to belong, the WilliamsF1 organization does not need to search for a mysterious formula that will unleash seemingly unlimited employee motivation. Jim Wright, head of marketing, offered an eloquent testimony as to how the organization sees its key inspirational players:

The magic of Williams can be summarized in four words: Frank Williams and Patrick Head. They are the inspirational leaders. We all draw our motivation for our quest for supremacy from those two guys. This is where the commitment to sustain peak performance starts. Clearly, in a marketing role, I don't have too much contact with Patrick, so my inspiration comes mainly from Frank Williams. He motivates me in what I try to do, and that obviously penetrates down to my staff, who I try to motivate in the same way. But Frank is an extraordinary man. This is probably the only organization that I have ever come across where everyone reveres the boss. That is a very, very rare thing. Everyone loves Frank, because he has got time for everyone. He's tough, but he's fair, and he will always, always support his staff. I have never seen an occasion where he hasn't supported his staff. Even though they may have been in the wrong, he has given them support, and sorted it out later.

The daily impact of inspirational players cannot simply be captured by reference to the art of delegation or overwhelming charisma. These attributes clearly apply to both Williams and Head, but another defining feature, observable in the organization at all levels, is that there are no followers. Each and every person plays a key role in the life of the community. Not surprisingly then, Williams attracts those who strive constantly to better themselves.

Jane Gorard, media manager until 1999, personified peak performance under pressure. She and another colleague were the conduit through which a stunned world learned of the tragedy of Senna's untimely death. In addition to dealing with the external demands of the media, who maintain a voracious appetite for any tidbits of information, Gorard also handled the internal dispersion of information throughout the organization. Adroit and astute in her professional dealings during the Grand Prix season, Gorard brought a balance and perspective to her work that helped to define the contours of the Williams community. Equally at home on the factory floor or in the finely appointed visitors' room, she talked of pushing for improvement in everything, everywhere. In this she was not alone. The Williams community thrives on personal accountability. Gorard believes that the maverick instincts of the two giants of Formula One act like a magnet for those who may be lured to experience other pastures:

> There is so much respect for Frank and Patrick, because of what they have done and, in particular, how they haven't always toed the party line—they have bucked the trends. They have done it because of their desire and their passion for motor racing, and that filters through to all of the people who work here. Although people have left Williams and gone to other teams, the grass is greener on the other side of the fence only for a while. Many have returned, because they lose that feeling of being part of a big family. I don't believe you get that in other teams. Internally, we benefit from their attitude, which is wonderful. This is something very special, that you probably wouldn't ever get anywhere else. Frank and Patrick have enormous respect for all of the 360 people who work here.

On the back of sustained success spanning two decades and a growing public fascination with the Williams organization, and in particular the respected persona of a wheelchair-bound Frank Williams, an extensive global exercise was carried out to determine the core brand values of the enterprise. This led to an all-important name change from Williams Grand Prix Engineering to WilliamsF1. Jim Wright, head of marketing, well recognized the importance of this initiative, in particular the opportunities that might accrue in terms of acquiring much-needed sponsorship dollars—measured in the hundreds of millions, of course. At the same time, Wright was and remains determined to ensure that sponsorship alliances are consistent with the brand values associated with Williams. The BMW engine partnership, which began at the start of 2000, provided the perfect springboard to establish the principles upon which the Williams dream is shared. Unequivocally, according to Wright, "every sponsorship contract contains a clause that says, 'the sponsor recognizes that the prime purpose of the racing team is to win races.'" Jim Wright:

> Through exhaustive international research we determined a very clear set of brand values. We stand for technology, team excellence, strong leadership, and above all for sustained success. We take those brand values forward into sponsorship programs and align our brand values with potential sponsors. Sponsors play an enormous rol in the future of the Williams team. Sponsorship is about more than just cash. If we can find a sponsor who contributes technically to our programs to make us go faster or improve the way we work, then by giving us a performance edge, that makes it the richer for us.

For Wright, emerging alliances are seen as a two-way channel rather than cash simply flowing into the Williams coffers. The most important illustration of this hardwired principle can be found in the relationship between BMW and Williams, which marked a decisive move away from traditional Formula One tobacco sponsorship. Wright explained to us how this new alliance has created a crucial focus on the synergies between like-minded organizations.

> The BMW relationship is game-breaking in many ways. It's not just about engine supply, as some of the other automobile manufacturers have become involved in Formula One; it's also about a technical and marketing partnership. And this is where it's unusual. Our deal with BMW enables BMW to put their stamp upon the whole look of the team, including styling rights. That is something which sits very well with other sponsors coming on board, because they know that they are going to be presented in a very good way and they also have an association with BMW—a marketing legend. From 2000 onwards we will be the BMW Williams F1 team, and clearly that's a two-way communication channel.

Wright sees the relationship with BMW as part of the wider inspirational dream that provides unswerving meaning and purpose to Williams's staff.

> The dream for everyone at Williams Formula One is to carry on the enormous success which we've had over the last twenty years. In itself that puts some pressure on us because we are all aware of our history and we know that we have to perform at a peak level in order to sustain that success. What we have in BMW is a partner who also has a great history and heritage of success in motor sport. We feel very comfortable that in BMW we have a like-minded partner.

Sustaining Peak Performance:
A Magnificent Obsession

Frank Williams knows that constant peak performance is not the same as sustaining long-term contention at the top of motor racing. For this reason, he sees that humility and winning go hand in hand:

> There is not constant supremacy. I never believe that we are supreme in any way. We are always fearful of being given a good thrashing the next time we turn up at a race. It is not an exaggeration to say that we know that we are not that sharp. We think that there are better-organized teams out there in Grand Prix racing. It is very competitive, but no more competitive than any other world-class sport like American football or soccer. There are some very clever people working here, but the biggest advantage we have is magic.
>
> Most people here are nuts about what they do. People here love cars, and the epitome of competition, currently, is Formula One Grand Prix Racing. Once you are involved, it is a whirlwind that sets up a nonstop challenge. Just participating, just being around the cars and entering a race is exciting. The drivers are very special human beings. All twenty drivers on the grid would

give you the ride of your life in a touring car. Their control is prodigious, especially in the wet. They have seven-hundred-fifty horsepower to control, and the car weighs, with them on board, around six hundred kilograms. In the wet they can't see anything and yet off they go. I once said to Nigel Mansell, "How do you know when to brake in all that spray?" Nigel replied, "I wait for the front wheels to lift off, pause, and then I brake." It wasn't exactly what I expected.

The magic and excitement of racing reaches everyone. No one gets left out at Williams, and a strong sense of ownership prevails. Kay Young sums up the community atmosphere: "Everyone wants to be fast and successful. When we win, everyone's part of it. Not just the engineers and the aerodynamics people, it's not just them. Everyone plays a part in it." Bryan Lambert, test team manager, offers additional confirmation that inclusion is a natural feature of the organization: "It is the group of people as a whole. It is not just Frank Williams and Patrick Head. All of the employed people here work as a team."

Each race during the season provides an opportunity for the organization to come together. Watching the race from afar, however, provides only a partial explanation for the extraordinary bonds between people who do very different jobs. Bringing back the trophies and displaying them is another powerful mechanism of inclusion, but there are also far more important activities that are critical to the maintenance of a tight-knit family environment. In this organization, everyone is kept informed. On average, thirty-five people out of the total 360 actually go to the Grand Prix. After each race there is a technical debriefing among Head, Williams, and the engineers who were actually at the race, where they will discuss whether the race strategy was correct, or whether new parts worked, and what emendments might be considered before the next race.

Equally important, if not more so, are the debriefings that Head conducts after several of the Grand Prix races. They are attended by all members of staff. Jane Gorard:

Patrick, who is never lost for words, will talk about the buildup to the race weekend, he will talk about "free practice," he will talk about qualifying, and, if appropriate, something specific that happened to one of the other teams. He communicates the whole tone of the weekend. He will congratulate and if necessary chastise, if that is the right word. If there is a department that has to pull its socks up, because that is where we were let down at the weekend, then he will say so. Patrick discusses exactly why the team believes that, for example, the suspension broke. It could be a fault in manufacture, it could be a fault in materials, or it could be a fault in the building of the car. Depending on which it is, then obviously that particular area has to be focused on.

He will also talk about gossip, pointing out that one of the other teams obviously had a good weekend because they had topless models all around their car, but that unfortunately it did not make their car go any faster. It always adds a bit of humor, but really the purpose of it is to bring the race back to the team, so that we all feel that we were there. Even if we have all sat and watched it on TV, it doesn't matter. There isn't a single person in this place, or member of the family, who is not going to be glued to the TV when a Grand Prix is on. For the Australian Grand Prix they will all be sitting there at 4:30 or 5:40 in the morning, having had parties the night before that just run through until the race starts.

The debriefing is not taken lightly by anyone. Kay Young is absolute when describing who actually attends:

Everybody does. When we are down there, nobody takes any calls. We just tell everyone to call back. Patrick's got a booming voice, he's got presence, and when he talks everyone takes notice. Everyone listens.

Held frequently throughout the racing season, these informal gatherings in the race bay are special occasions that create strong ties and loyalty to the Williams community. The race bay also features during times of celebration. Jim Wright:

> Success is obviously very important to the team and it's important that we take time to enjoy and celebrate. After our world championship titles in 1997 we gathered in the race bay of the factory. Every single member of the WilliamsF1 team was brought into the race bay, all 360 people who had played a part in winning those championships, and they were addressed by Frank and Patrick.

Notwithstanding such scenes that indicate the contrary, the external wisdom is that the organization is a cold and clinical engineering outfit. The most dramatic image that fuels this perception is the television view from each Grand Prix, which always shows Frank Williams in the pit-lane garage staring, expressionless, at a bank of monitors, absorbing an endless stream of data transmissions. Jim Wright dryly reflects on a fundamental misunderstanding:

> That is the difference between the workforce and the viewing public. The first comment I get when I tell people what my job is, "Oh, Frank Williams. He's such a miserable git. You never ever see him smiling." That is the TV image, but I carefully explain that you have to remember that he's looking at several monitors, and he's listening to two radio channels, and he's concentrating. He's working! The reality is that he is one of the most fun-loving people you would ever meet. Any one of the 360 employees can walk up to Frank's office and request to see him. There is never a problem with that. He knows all of them, and if any of them has got a problem, they go to Frank. So I think that's pretty important.

Frank Williams himself ensures that the organization does not slip into the habit of adopting a deferential attitude to authority figures. Standing on ceremony for either himself or Patrick Head is positively discouraged. His arguments are simple yet persuasive:

There is no room for formality in a building full of pressure. We are a Christian-name company, which is something I am very proud of. I don't know all the surnames, but that is partly by design. When you are starting off on a Christian-name footing, as we do with new people, they tend to get on better and they are more productive.

The informal and friendly attitude that Frank Williams cherishes so much is embodied in people like Dave Jones, chief inspector, who has worked at Williams for twenty years. He draws a direct link between atmosphere and doing great work:

Informal? Yeah. People outside think we are pretty serious. I have got a new guy in my department who has just come from Benetton and he was told, "You don't want to go and work there, they are really serious and they do not know how to have fun." But we are always larking about in our department. People enjoy themselves. Many people have been here a long time—the actual staff turnover of senior members is negligible. Most of the guys in the shop have been here for twenty years. It's continuity. Everybody knows what's going on. If you want something done quickly you know who to talk to and you can get it done. They came in last Friday to get a new flap to go out to Australia. The jig was drawn by the office, machine and finished by Saturday afternoon, and was in the composite department by Sunday morning and then winged out by Sunday night. You can get things done that quickly.

Knowing what to do, who to talk to, and how to get things done is a competency that Williams has built up in the organization over many years. Guidance, however, does not come from formal job descriptions, and individual performance is not driven by detailed appraisal systems. The organizational chart simply drawn shows the two directors, Williams and Head, followed by a layer of senior managers that includes the general manager, chief designer, chief aerodynamicists, marketing manager, and financial director. This, according to David Williams, is, "the group that manages the company." Annual informal assessments are carried out in the factory between foremen and workers, but the structure of the organization is relaxed. Frank Williams:

> From time to time communication takes place by formal meeting. But really, informal corridor meetings are taking place morning, noon, and night, seven days a week. You might say that that is a bit strange—a bit sloppy—but it works most of the time.

By contrast, in the mid-nineties, Williams began a fruitful relationship with Andersen Consulting, who developed an Enterprise Resource Planning (ERP) system that was designed to tighten up the working cycle for building a Formula One car. ERP linked design and production with purchasing, inventory, and financial controls throughout the continuous cycle of design–build–test–implement. Alongside the ERP system, informal teams spring up and disband as needed. There are no formal cross-functional or self-managed teams that have official status or can be identified as part of the formal governance process within the organization. Structure, such as can be recognized, ebbs and flows around functional expertise. For this to work, the stability of the workforce is a vital element in creating the future. The security of employment enjoyed by the workers is underscored by Frank Williams's observation:

> I don't think we have ever made anyone redundant. I remind myself that most great companies make people redundant in their time. It has to be coming to us one day. I worry about it all the time. However, when we expand we try first to promote from within.

With the benefit of the trust and commitment that this attitude engenders, ongoing corridor meetings and focused, yet impermanent, teams are able to create a firm basis for working in a state of flow. For Dave Jones, this way of working has hidden dividends:

Someone might come up with an idea to improve the speed of the car, but because we have worked together for many years, we can say, "No, it didn't work. We tried that four years ago." At some of the other teams, because they tend to change staff quite quickly, they will say, "Oh yeah, we should try that," and that way they make costly mistakes.

The constant nature of iterative change in Formula One has its greatest impact in the area of aerodynamics. Geoff Willis, who is the chief aerodynamicist at Williams, describes an engineering process whereby one technical change automatically causes a new generation of design issues. The ability to understand how these changes are interrelated is best suited to a relatively stable workforce that has been able to digest past knowledge to be dispensed under new situations. Geoff Willis:

One of the difficulties with Formula One design is the way that all the parts are all so interconnected that you tend to have to go round the car evolving one part and then finding if it makes a change to how another parts should be designed. You are aiming for a spiral of improvement. But everything has to be looked at every few months because things constantly change. You can never say, "I fixed this bit and this is now perfect." It'll never be like that. In a month's time, you'll come back and you'll think, "Oh, there must be another way I can do this." Every year we manage to make the car go faster and at the end of every design you think, "That's the best I've done. The best I can think of." But in the back of your mind you know that next year you'll make it better. So it must be possible at all times to make a faster car.

Members of Willis's team are likewise encouraged to identify with the end product of their labors and, more important, to take personal responsibility for the tasks before them. Willis believes that this sets up the environment necessary for worker commitment and creativity.

One way to get the best out of people in an environment like Williams is to make sure that they see the consequences of what they're doing. We run a lot of our work on a project basis, where the person who is initiating the work will see it all the way through to completion. So they see all stages of it, particularly from the design point of view right to the shop floor. They know what they need to do and when they need to do it by. Individual responsibility is what you need to drive good quality. You get the best people, give them the resources they need, and then expect the best from them.

Formal job specifications for each employee do not sit well within such a complex engineering environment. What works in the factory goes for the office, too. Lindsay Morle:

We are not really that formal. There is a lot of banter. It's a lot like a community. If someone is snowed under we will all pitch in. It is not like, "That is not in my job description. I'm not doing that." You do it because you know it needs to be done. We are always working together, pulling as a team. We don't use performance appraisals to get things done. No. That kind of structure just doesn't exist.

The demands of Formula One ensure that the synergies of informal teamwork are used to their maximum potential. All aspects of organizational life are influenced by the quest for improvement and, in this respect, a Formula One car is never finished being built. The car that Williams rolls out of the box and tests for the first time at Silverstone at the start of the racing season has made leaps and bounds forward, from a technical point of view, by the time it performs at the opening Grand Prix in Melbourne, Australia. This process of development and design continues relentlessly throughout the season.

The informal and flexible yet disciplined processes that define the Williams organization are well suited to demands for constant iterative change and game-breaking ideas. Although much of the design and precision engineering is carried out by a cadre of highly skilled, qualified craftsmen, no stone is left unturned in the quest to find extra speed. Bryan Lambert:

> Ideas come from lots of people. Obviously, the main people are in the drawing office, in the design office, but they will listen to anybody who has an idea, whether it be from the design office, or the guy sweeping the floor to keep the place tidy—anybody—if they think that the idea is worth trying, then we will try it.

The ever-increasing technical sophistication needed to compete in Formula One inevitably pushes involvement in the direction of those who are scientifically qualified, yet Frank Williams has no intention of cutting off a powerful supply of innovative ideas—the shop floor.

> As engineers in a highly competitive environment, we have to respond to the continuous staircase of change. People working with the suspension, carbon-composite material, etc., must all contribute ideas, especially if it is a critical change that involves safety. Certain directors or the chief designer approves the drawings, so there are procedures.

Patrick Head argues that innovation can flourish only when the fear of failure has been taken out of the organization:

> We try to create an atmosphere where innovation gains credit, where it is recognized. However, innovation often goes through considerable periods of failure before it is seen as a visible success. If you have an environment where failure is not tolerated and is openly criticized, or where people are looking for failure in others, you can get an environment in which nobody will innovate for fear of failure. You have to run the organization in a manner that is not inward-looking, where each department tries to pick out

faults in the other. We have values here so that the first response to failure is not to pick out the individual and crucify him. The focus is on how you're trying to put it right, not to blame someone for why it's not right.

The constant move forward with new ideas creates an ongoing sense of urgency. Expectations are extremely high, both in the factory and in the office. People who join the organization from outside are well positioned to reflect on the pressures to contribute from the moment they enter the organization. Jim Wright:

When I arrived, no one took me by the hand and led me in gradually. Here you were, joining an elite workforce, and you were coming into a position where people were already expecting you to deliver. In fact, I've seen that since I have been here. I had been here for a couple of years when we hired an in-house lawyer. We had never had one before. People just expected him to know all the FIA rules. You have to really get onto it.

Peter Yonge, another twenty-year veteran of the organization, has observed similar experiences when new people join the workforce:

There are people here who have come from other industries, the Air Force in lots of cases, who can't initially understand speed and the immediacy of things. They are used to a machining environment where they make something that might sit on a shelf somewhere in Malta or Kuwait and never see an airplane. Our guys can make a component on Thursday afternoon and watch it going round a track in Brazil on Sunday afternoon. This makes for very good morale. It is very immediate.

Christian Vine, manager of new business development in sponsorship and marketing services, has observed the impact of the speed of decision making upon those who have come into contact with WilliamsF1. He notes that more than any other facet, the speed at which management operates is the single most valuable lesson that corporations can take from the Williams workplace.

> Organizations can't believe the speed at which we need to make decisions. We need to make progress, take positive action, and not delay decisions. We have a race season that will start in March and if we're not ready for the season, the sport is not going to wait for us and our competitors will beat us; it is as simple as that. Time and again, people from outside who have worked on F1 projects in engineering have subsequently gone back to their own organizations and shot up through the ranks because they have a new attitude toward getting things done and getting things done quickly and positively. So, for us, one of the biggest challenges is trying to make other companies work at our speed.

Although the drama of working in the world of Formula One has its share of pressure and tension, the high expectations create an invigorating atmosphere that is conducive to innovation and change. Jim Wright:

> This is an enjoyable experience. It is an ever-changing experience. It is not something for which there is an established routine. It is a constantly evolving process. I have been here three years and four months, and it is ever-changing. You are always focusing on something new, a new program or something else to go out and sell. So it is very motivational from that point of view—you don't feel as though you are doing a routine job week in and week out.

These sentiments are typical across all occupations at WilliamsF1. There exists a strong suspicion that all employees represent the very best in their personal field of expertise. Personal responsibility counts for a great deal here, and individual pride ensures that state-of-the-art knowledge is employed at every turn. This is most evident in the test teams who pursue to the last detail improvements that can be measured in fractions of a second. As the test team manager, Bryan Lambert has one of the most demanding jobs in the organization. He is responsible for overseeing the thousands of test miles that are the backbone of Formula One success. His role is to drive engineering capabilities to the very edge, a task that calls for precision and discipline:

> The people who work for me are people who are interested in development—they are not interested in just working on a car. We are there purely for development, and obviously if the development is successful the car will go quicker. We are not there to beat other teams' times; we are there to beat our own. For me personally, it's important to make sure that the test goes like clockwork from start to finish, because it is all down to me at the end of the day: the logistics of the trucks; the people; the organization during the day; every element; and, yes, every detail. This type of organization is very important.

In a similar vein, Chief Inspector Dave Jones bristles with confidence when describing how commitment to technological innovation and exceeding one's personal best is a natural component of the work ethic. "I think everyone has such commitment to new technology. Part of your job specification is that you keep up-to-date with the latest technology and you maintain all your equipment. It is the individual's responsibility." Head himself admits to a perfectionism that motivates him to improve constantly: "Frank and I, we're always looking at ourselves to see what we can do to improve. Organizationally, anything that is running well tends to get pushed out of my head, because there are always plenty of bits that I'm not happy with." Satisfaction is fleeting and quickly subordinated to the next task at hand. Jim Wright experienced this at the 1997 British Grand Prix during a brief discussion with his mentor.

> After the British Grand Prix in 1997, where we won our hundreth Grand Prix, I went over to Frank and said, "Frank, fantastic. One hundred Grand Prix wins. You must be delighted." And he said,

"Yes, I am, but in ten days' time we are in Hockenhiem, where Ferrari will be very strong, so we need to get our heads down and come up with the right package to win." That says a lot about how this organization performs. Our way is to focus on the next race and try and win that one.

The relentless focus on winning and the passion to exceed personal best are best revealed when the organization turns up to race. Senses are sharpened as the effort of many is concentrated into the frenetic activity of the few, which in turn is vested in the two drivers who carry the final burden of performance.

In the Pit Garage

It is midafternoon and the qualifying session for grid position in the 1998 Canadian Grand Prix is over, as are the seemingly never-ending, impromptu prerace press conferences that the Formula One drivers have to endure. Apart from the sound of the occasional pneumatic drill, the pit garage has for once fallen silent. Standing alone in front of one of the monitors is Jacques Villeneuve, the 1997 FIA Formula One World Drivers' Champion. Like his father, Villeneuve is already a racing legend, respected and feted by the Grand Prix community and especially by the Williams crew in the pit lane. He is watching one of the junior Formula Atlantic races that helps to fill the race weekend. As he focuses on studying the form of the drivers who aspire to claim his coveted title one day, the odd mechanic drifts by unnoticed. A casual reminder from one of the engineers about the upcoming drivers' race briefing is greeted with a knowing smile and a nod of the head.

Closer to race time, Villeneuve is apt to pad around the garage with his racing full-body jumpsuit undone and the top half sprawling around his hips. The idea is to ventilate body heat to stave off possible dehydration toward the end of the race. In the pit garage at least, glamour takes a backseat. Humor, on the other hand, is very much in evidence. At one point during the race weekend, Villeneuve accidentally spills his hot drink all over one of the computers that processes the race car telemetry and in the process wrecks the critical keyboard and mouse. The entire garage nearly collapses in stitches as one of the crew dryly observes that this is the cheapest accident Jacques has had all year. Prior to discovery of this minor calamity, the world champion, aided and abetted by a willing accomplice, actually contemplated an elaborate cover-up of the deed, but in the pit garage nothing goes unnoticed for long.

Such a relaxed, informal atmosphere seems barely possible. By definition, the pit garage is the focus of all the raw power, high technology, and surges of adrenaline that are associated with Grand Prix motor racing. Notably, the unexpected burst of noise as a Formula One engine kicks into life is startling, but in other respects the pit garage offers seemingly transparent activity conducted with a minimum of tension. The highly visible pit stop, conducted at breakneck speed against an unforgiving stopwatch, is usually cited by management gurus as a fine example of teamwork, yet this activity represents a mere fraction of race activity. More important, the pit stop consists of a preordained set of maneuvers that is barely related to the rest of the weekend's efforts. The pit garage calls for far more complex activities—many discretionary, invisible, coordinated decisions are made in a split second. And no one is obviously in charge.

Throughout the Grand Prix weekend the pit crew is in a constant state of activity. Making the car go faster rests on supreme technical knowledge applied against an ever-changing backdrop of conditions. Air temperature, track temperature, track conditions, circuit layout, and a whole host of new iterations brought in from testing between races have to be factored into the settings on the car. A mixture of free practice and qualifying sessions allows the team to adjust, recalibrate, and try again. Small group debriefings on tires, engines, gearboxes, suspension, and, finally, race tactics take place in trailers at the back of the compound. This seemingly endless flow of interaction sees both race cars being built and rebuilt many times during the weekend. However, technical advantage, while precious, amounts to little without a feel for it all. Intuition and personal judgment rest not simply with the driver, but with every single person in the garage.

Unquestionably, the pit garage is a special place to be. Cramped and seemingly chaotic, it offers a surreal experience. Sitting unobtrusively in a corner of the garage is one of the disassembled engine blocks that generates more than 750 horsepower, the grunt at the heart of the raw attraction of Formula One racing. There is a stack of wings here, a row of nose cones there.

In among the computers, the boxes of spare parts, and the tables at the back of the complex are tires—lots and lots of tires. And then there is the crew, engaged in an endless flow of activity. The stacks of tires are constantly rotated, as each set of boots nears its turn to take to the track, while the ones already used are taken to the back of the garage. Parts of the car are being assembled, drilled, honed, attached, disassembled, and reassembled. Few words are spoken among the pit crew. A brief nod, a longer than usual meeting of the eyes followed by a raised eyebrow or a facial expression contain information as vital as telemetry from the state-of-the-art pit-garage computers. The ability to communicate this way was probably born out of necessity, since the deafening roar of a single Formula One engine renders traditional conversation ineffective. The advent of the radio headset provided for more normal discourse, but this is usually restricted to formal confirmation of a known situation. Being in the pit garage feels as if you are walking through a basketball court while the Chicago Bulls are in a play-off game, and the ball is going around and over you while your presence remains largely unnoticed. The level of sustained concentration needed by the pit team is phenomenal. James Robinson, senior operations engineer, believes that it takes at least two years, possibly three, before a member of his team is fully able to understand his role:

> I think it's fair to say the Williams way is that everybody is focused on their particular area, their particular expertise, and getting down to it and trying to do the best job they can. It needs very little paperwork, very little in the way of formal systems. You don't have to go over a problem twice; you don't have to ask if something has been done. You identify the problem and you can

walk away, knowing that in a week's time the problem will be solved. You are looking at a period of two to three years before you think that person is in a position to be truly trusted.

If we have a problem this weekend, we know somebody has got to look at the design side of it, somebody has got to look at the manufacturing side, and someone will be generating the right parts, either internally or from outside of our own process. But those parts will be available in the factory before the next race. There is no follow-up system to say has it happened, has it been drawn, has it been stressed, has it been made, are the materials right, has it been painted, has it been tested in the labs, has it gone to the track to be tested, if so was it quicker, was it slower, did it break, did it not break, and, finally, did it need looking at again? A lot of that is basically done with two lines on a piece of paper. Every two weeks we are racing and we are problem-solving in that time period. As long as that is managed in such a way that it produces a safe and quicker car, then I think that is a very good way to operate.

For the pit-lane crew, especially, this calls for high levels of individual technical ability and accountability.

However, individual technical skills alone are insufficient. More important still is the network of relationships among crew members. Intense awareness is also a vital part of the working landscape, both in the factory and, more decisively, in the pit garage, where the rubber literally meets the road. Task and process unite in a state of flow—a combination of head and heart. For James Robinson, this is not accidental:

Williams has always been run on an engineering basis, creating a very strong group of focused, purposeful engineers. A lot of it is knowing your job. Our people have come through the ranks, whether they be mechanics or even Formula One drivers. You have to learn quickly what is required and what is needed. No one says, "You should be doing this now," or "This should be happening." It needs very little guidance or management. Rather, it needs pointing, not leading.

Heinz Harald Frentzen, who joined the team upon the departure of Damon Hill, has a unique perspective on Williams. Coming from the much smaller Sauber team, Frentzen was surprised that Williams was "so well organized." Reflecting on his two years with the team, Frentzen points out the difference between Williams and other constructors:

> People here are workaholics. They live day and night with the problems. Patrick Head, the technical director, has so much experience. From his experience he already knows so much, and yet he still wants the chance to learn more and more things. As far as I know, as a technical director, there is really no comparison that can be made with him. He is the motor.
>
> I also think that apart from Patrick, the flexibility in the team is based on many good people who have lots of very good experience. They know the research and the direction they must go—the team knows itself perfectly. Here in the pit garage they have a very special procedure; it's a kind of special rhythm.

It is a rhythm that can incorporate disruption, distraction, and the demands made upon it by the external world. Ffiona Welford, motorsport press officer for Williams during the 1998 season, dealt directly with the journalists who constantly want access to the world-famous drivers and any pit-lane action that will land them the big story of the Grand Prix. Sponsors, too, and a bevy of celebrity superstars have to be kept happy during a Grand Prix weekend. She had to maintain a delicate balance between the pressure-cooker atmosphere of racing and the need to satiate the media. It is a crucial interface that has to be managed to perfection. Ffiona Welford:

> I am the main point of contact with the media on circuit, so technically speaking I need to know what is happening throughout the

race weekend. Frank, Patrick, and the crew will give me anything I need to know, things that I should probably be telling the media, and then I can go out and keep them up to speed with what's going on. The trust has to be there between us. When I need to ask them a question for the media, the fantastic thing about them is that they can be absolutely rushed off their feet busy, but if I say, "I need to ask you this," they've always got the time to tell me, always got the time to give me an answer. From my first year here, nobody has ever brushed me off and said come back later. They answer straightaway because they know I need to keep the media informed. Nothing is too much trouble for anyone.

Cooperation among the different roles in the pit garage takes place in a seemingly effortless, tranquil zone, which contradicts the popular image of Grand Prix racing as drama-filled, frenetic, and frequently dangerous. Although drama and tension are always just below the surface, the pit-garage experience rests at the confluence of a well-oiled organization that knows how to win.

Conclusion

Frank Williams feels that his organization is "not important to the central thread of life," yet those who either work for, or who are associated with, WilliamsF1 will tell you a different story. Although Frank Williams and Patrick Head are most strongly associated with the history and current direction of the organization, the dream belongs to all. From Head's Grand Prix storytelling to Williams's insistence on informality, the traditional mental model of hierarchy and separated occupational classifications collapses in favor of personal discipline and identification with a collective purpose—the goal of crossing the winning line before anyone else. The whole organization is geared up to ensure everyone's total contribution toward this end, and, without fuss or fanfare, the people at WilliamsF1 continually contribute by exceeding their own personal best performance at work. There is a relentless pursuit of development that includes coming forward with new, game-breaking ideas to make the car go faster, and ruthlessly dealing with each and every last detail. A positive attitude toward failure is encouraged as part of the critical development process. This keeps WilliamsF1, if not in, then at least knocking on the door of, the winner's circle. Finally, there is a seamless integration of all aspects of organizational activity without the traditional methods of managerial control.

The legacies Frank Williams and Patrick Head are manufacturing at WilliamsF1 will remain long after they have retired. The powerful stories and mystique associated with these inspirational players have influenced the very fabric of organizational life and sustained the dream of winning.[6]

---

[6] In recognition of his services to the motor sport industry, Frank Williams was knighted in the 1999 New Year's Honors list. On 23 February 1999, Sir Frank Williams proudly received his knighthood from Her Majesty the queen on behalf of everyone who has worked for the Williams team, both past and present.

8

Team New Zealand: The Making of Black Magic

"If it was going to be easy, it wouldn't have been worth trying. We have taken on the rest of the world at the hardest game available—the America's Cup—and won. This project was a two-year, heads-down, blinkers-on campaign. It was a long-term project where only total commitment could succeed and where a win was never guaranteed. But as long as everyone could put their hands on their hearts at the end and know that they had given everything there was to give, that was all I could ask for."
— SIR PETER BLAKE ON THE TEAM NEW ZEALAND
1995 AMERICA'S CUP CAMPAIGN

The America's Cup for international yachting is the oldest continuously contested international sporting competition in the world. Queen Victoria awarded the Cup in 1851 to John Stevens, owner of the schooner *America*, for his crushing victory against a fleet of sixteen of the best of England's racing fleet. The Cup's deed of gift specified that it should be the subject of ongoing friendly yachting competition among countries, and it has been a symbol of national pride ever since.

Six years after his initial victory, Stevens handed the trophy—in fact, a pitcher rather than a cup—to the New York Yacht Club for safekeeping. Since then, the names of subsequent winning yachts have all been inscribed, but the trophy itself remains nameless. It is an irony of history that countless millions of dollars have been expended in the pursuit of an unnamed cup that is actually a pitcher.

The New York Yacht Club kept winning for 132 years, the longest winning record in international sporting history, thereby cementing the myth that the cup actually belonged to the United States. During much of this period it was bolted in place, with no thought of it ever being lost. The history of the cup is marked by the successes and failures of some of the world's richest people—Vanderbilt, Rockefeller, Lipton, Turner, Bond, Koch, Gardini, Fay, McCaw, and Bertarelli—vying to demonstrate their technical and sporting prowess in defense of national pride. Business manager Alan Sefton, who until 2000 had been on board all New Zealand's America's Cup campaigns, explains:

> It's been an American institution. It still is, by the way. It's quite extraordinary. If you go to the East Coast of the States there are generations of American families who have grown up with the America's Cup. It's dominated their whole lives and those of some English families, too. For example, when Tommy Sopwith was inducted into the America's Cup hall of fame a couple of years ago, three of his family came over from Britain. They were so emotional. And Britain has never won it in 150 years!

In 1983, wealthy Australian businessman Alan Bond went to New York with a much-publicized "golden spanner," to unbolt the Cup and take it home. Skipper John Bertrand came back from 3 to 1 to even the contest at 3 all, and then sailed through from behind in the last race to squeeze over the line first, and into the history books. Dennis Conner achieved lifelong notoriety as the first American skipper to lose the cup, and he vowed to get it back. The winning yacht club takes possession of the trophy, and is responsible for organizing the next defense in its home waters. So in 1987 Dennis Conner set course for Australia, where he successfully atoned for his defeat and recovered his nation's honor.

After sailing straight into contention with two narrow losses in the Challenger series finals in 1987 and 1992, Team New Zealand convincingly removed "The Auld Mug" to Auckland after a perfect 1995 campaign. They sailed away with only one loss on the water in the Challenger series (preliminary to the finals), and a 5–0 wipeout against Dennis Conner's *Young America* in the America's Cup finals. In Auckland, and nationwide, it was carnival time for weeks, with welcome parades and parties the length and breadth of the country.

In the Auld Mug's illustrious and often controversial 150-year history, it has changed hands just three times, going to Australia in 1983, back to the United States in 1987, and to New Zealand in 1995. In 2000, New Zealand successfully defended its 1995 triumph with a 5–0 victory over Italy's Prada team in the glittering waters of the Hauraki Gulf off Auckland, New Zealand. This victory was the first successful defense of the Cup by any team other than the United States.

The America's Cup is the fourth most-watched sporting spectacle after the Olympics, the soccer World Cup, and Formula One. Tony Thomas, manager of the America's Cup 2000 Regatta events (AC2000), gave us the facts:

> The year 2000 regatta was over five months, and up to three months of that was covered live on TV. This is up to twenty-eight days of live coverage and three hours plus per day. Last time there was a cumulative total of 600 hours of television coverage and a total reach of 382 million homes. This equates to viewers of more than 600 million.

This is a sport where campaigns can cost more than $60 million U.S. The course to the America's Cup is long and arduous. Years of preparation (normally three to five years between competitions) are required, leading to months of trials during the Challenger elimination series for the Louis Vuitton Cup, then weeks of competition in which the current holder of the America's Cup competes against the winner of the Challenger series. So how did New Zealand, a small Pacific island nation with a population of 3.5 million (about the size of San Diego), take on the technological and financial might of wealthy syndicates from the world's richest and most technologically advanced nations, and win so perfectly? This is the story of the making of Black Magic.

New Zealand has the highest proportion of boat owners of any nation in the world. No New Zealander lives far from the sea or a lake, and the mild climate enables year-round, cyclone-free sailing. From as young as five, Kiwi kids start sailing blunt-bowed Optimist dinghies competitively. They graduate to eight-foot, yachtlike P Class dinghies, a class that has been raced competitively in New Zealand for more than fifty years.[7] And then, as they grow older, they go on to Starlings and Lasers. Most of New Zealand's greatest yachtsmen, such as Russell Coutts, Sir Peter Blake, and Chris Dickson, grew up racing P Class. The New Zealand Yachting Federation creates the future of New Zealand yachting through an infrastructure of school, regional, national, and international races for all age groups. As a result, New Zealand professional sailors have dominated world sail racing for more than a decade, from windsurfing to the Whitbread Round the World Race. Kiwis are to be found in the yachting crews of most nations. Tom Schnackenberg, Team New Zealand technical and design specialist, explains:

> One of the key factors is that the sailors become, by a process of natural selection, very self-reliant. They have to demonstrate ability at a very early age or they won't make it through the junior ranks. You can imagine the first time Dad takes them down to the beach, and Mum gets them organized in their Optimist and rigs the boat and unrigs, while the kids just play on the beach! But the ones who are keen find that Mum and Dad's enthusiasm runs out, and pretty soon they are organizing their own boat. They are bullying Dad or their neighbors into fixing things, or they are work-

[7] The P Class was founded in 1943 and is named after the Ponsonby Cruising Club in Auckland, which sponsored the original design. It is said that the P Class is so difficult to sail that if you can learn to sail in it, you can sail anything.

ing together, and then starting to do the work themselves. Then they end up as late teenagers competing internationally. They really have to be able to manage themselves around the world. So we have got this big team of yachties who are independent, innovative, and self-reliant. When the Team New Zealand guys show up in some town, they will come in from different parts of the world, either hitching a ride in a boat, being flown by someone in a private jet, or just coming in conventionally on an airliner.

From this foundation in competitive sailing, New Zealand has developed a world-class marine industry that attracts wealthy sailors from Asia, Europe, and the United States for cruising, construction, and comprehensive refits. Cutting-edge designers, skilled tradesmen, Kiwi innovation, and exquisite quality can all be obtained at competitive prices. So the winds were fair for a quest for the cup. In an age of tumultuous change and instant images, the America's Cup provides a sense of history, challenge, romance, and adventure.

The Kiwi quest for the cup started spectacularly in 1987, with wealthy merchant banker Michael Fay bankrolling the project and Match Race champion Chris Dickson at the helm. The Kiwi America's Cup debut was controversial. *KZ7* was made of fiberglass. This provoked protests from other syndicates, because traditionally the 12-Meter Class had been built of aluminum or, in the early days, of wood. The affair, which became known as "Glassgate," was resolved in New Zealand's favor and "Plastic Fantastic" went on to win thirty-seven races out of thirty-eight in the Challenger selection series (i.e., the series of races in which the teams compete to qualify for the Challenger final). In the final, it was *KZ7* against Dennis Conner's *Stars and Stripes*. Alan Sefton analyzes the failure.

We didn't know how to win. We didn't have the campaign experience to take the last step, and there were certain cracks appearing in organization and in the chemistry of the team right at the last, when it mattered most. There were some changes made to the boat. The boat can be configured in various ways. *KZ7*, which is the fastest light-winds twelve-meter the world has ever seen, was configured to produce even more light-air speed for the series against Conner. Now, Fremantle is a strong wind area, and we struck a period of quite strong winds. In Western Australia the weather pattern is dictated by a low-pressure system in the interior that sets up the "Fremantle Doctor" phenomenon. It sucks in the sea breeze. Now, that pattern is dominant until the first cyclone comes ashore in North Australia. The first one was sitting just off the coast. If it had come ashore it would have destroyed the Doctor, which was at its peak. We struck a period where it blew nineteen knots plus for six weeks and lo and behold the night we got knocked out the cyclone came ashore. And from the next day on the America's Cup was sailed in light winds. Conner beat Australia in a set of conditions in which *KZ7* would have murdered him, which we proved later in the year in the world twelve-meter championships. Knowing we would have light-air speed to burn away, we should have protected ourselves by configuring more at the other end of the scale. But hindsight is a wonderful thing, and it was a fabulous campaign by anybody's standards. We just had not got every last detail right and we didn't know how to win.

Having come so close, Fay did not intend to give up the dream easily. In 1988, he changed the rules of the game with an early challenge, which was legal under the Cup's deed of gift. The Kiwi challenge came not in the twelve-meter class, but in the form of a massive monohull yacht, colloquially known as "the big boat," which was dramatically different in its design from the traditional yachts that had featured in the America's Cup for much of its history. Fay wanted to take the contest back to the glorious J Class days of the early twentieth century, but the San Diego Yacht Club defended in a catamaran[8] and won easily. The next two years were spent in the courts debating

---

[8] Catamarans easily outpace monohulls of similar or larger size because of reduced wetted surface and the ability to skim over the water rather than plow through it.

the legality of both vessels. The Kiwis won in the lower court, but lost on appeal. This sorry saga, however, had a silver lining, because the outcome was a radical update in design that created a new International America's Cup Class yacht, spectacular in its speed. The way was clear for the America's Cup to become a massive media and marketing extravaganza. It now offers multinational sponsors excellent value for money, and opportunities for professional sailors to pursue both fortune and national glory.

The first of the competitions with the new design took place in 1992. The new class opened up the opportunity to develop the most sophisticated technology in all dimensions of design and construction. The America's Cup campaigns attract the world's best designers and engineers, boat builders, sail makers, and sailors. We even found people who had worked on America's Cup campaigns at WilliamsF1.

Michael Fay and David Richwhite, his merchant bank partner, did everything they could to make sure the 1992 campaign was successful, and it nearly was again, Alan Sefton affirms. The campaign lacked for nothing in funding, and had New Zealander Bruce Farr as designer. Farr was recognized as the world's best. Alan Sefton: "The campaign was designer driven. It was knitted around the Farr office, and they wanted to make decisions ranging from the design of the boats to signing off PR releases."

In this second challenge, New Zealand again reached the final of the Louis Vuitton Cup, winning with ease all the way. At 4–1 up against *Il Moro di Venezia* of Italy in the final, *NZL 20* looked unstoppable. But a legal judgment cut her challenge short. The bowsprit that was used to help gibe spinnakers was ruled illegal by the international jury. A previous jury had approved the bowsprit earlier in the competition. One more match and it would have been all over, but the jury ruled that one match be taken away as penalty. Alan Sefton describes the consequences:

> Our focus went completely. We concentrated on contesting the allegations at a time when we should have been concentrating on boat speed. The bowsprit had certain boat handling advantages,

but it probably didn't contribute anything to boat speed. This eroded the confidence of the crew. They had spent the whole time sailing with the bowsprit which had been approved for the first round-robin races, so they had become very used to the system. When the Italians got the jury to reverse the original ruling, the whole handling system had to be completely changed, and that's very difficult. It was hard in the original configuration, but they had perfected it. Peter Blake's call early in the controversy was to cut it off and accept defeat on the legal front. He intuitively knew the effect it was having on our psyche.

As the Kiwi confidence was eroded, so was their edge in boat speed. NZL 20 was then fitted with a tandem keel. According to Sefton:

> This was a fabulous piece of engineering. It was slim keel blades at the front end and the back end, with this twenty-ton torpedo attached to both of them. The key to it was that both blades turned. That offers some very exciting prospects on the start line, but the reality was that the potential was finite. So, while we were performing close to the top of our game in the finals, *Il Moro* was still able to improve. Once the keel went on, there was no going back because of the structural changes that had to be made. I think possibly the keel was put on because it was sexy and full of excitement, and maybe people got carried away with the potential, as opposed to the reality of it. This was part of the problem with having a designer-driven campaign.

After the jury ruling, NZL 20 did not win another race or lead round another mile against the experienced Paul Cayard of *Il Moro*. The campaign was at an end. *Il Moro* went on to lose in the America's Cup against Bill Koch's *America3*, and the Auld Mug stayed in the United States once more.

Michael Fay and David Richwhite decided they would not try again. Peter Blake had become involved in the last part of the 1992 campaign, with the confidence of earlier success in winning the grueling Whitbread Round the World Race after seventeen years of trying. But he became disenchanted with the politics of the America's Cup and was uncomfortable with the competitive management style that had characterized Fay's 1992 campaign. He preferred the cleanly competitive, open-ocean environment of the Whitbread, where sailors pitted themselves against the elements.

Alan Sefton was convinced that New Zealand had come too far and learned too much to give up without another attempt, but he had to find new financial backing:

> Michael rang up to arrange a game of golf, but really he wanted to talk. I think we played four holes in two and a half hours. You are left with this big hole in the bottom of your stomach, and you don't know what to do with yourself. It was a major hurdle to overcome. I spent the next three weeks in San Diego, watched the finals, and helped wind up the campaign. Then I told Peter Blake I was coming over to England to talk, but he clearly wasn't ready, so I disappeared up to my mother's in Wales and got my head out of it for a couple of weeks. Then I went down to Elmsworth and spent a weekend with Peter, and we talked it through. He agreed that he should at least come back to New Zealand and find out what was possible. If you are looking at supporting the campaign entirely out of commercial sponsorship, then that's a different kettle of fish entirely.

Sefton knew there was a lot of support in New Zealand, and he knew the value of "the psychological support and the boost that you get from knowing the whole country is watching." But he and Peter Blake did not know whether this would translate to sponsorship. So, with Michael Fay's advice, they did the rounds of potential New Zealand sponsors. Alan Sefton:

> Yes, it could be done. But there was a very definite ceiling in everyone's mind, and we couldn't get past that ceiling. You realize that there are only so many players in New Zealand that can look at it.

We couldn't afford many misses, because we would run out of candidates very quickly, but we were enthused by the reaction. Peter mortgaged his house to pay the entry fee and I paid the running expenses of the campaign. They weren't large, because we were lucky enough to have an office in the Royal New Zealand Yacht Squadron clubhouse, but by my standards they became quite large until we actually got the first sponsorship in.

World Match Race champion Russell Coutts soon joined these inspirational players as skipper. Alan Sefton:

Obviously, the skipper appointment was very important. I think we canvassed about fourteen different opinions from the yachting community, and the call for Russell was absolutely unanimous. It was quite unbelievable. He brings much more to the campaign than just his ability to steer a boat, and he is the best in the world at that. He is an engineer by profession, so he's got a different mind-set to other sailors. The America's Cup is a design contest as much as a sailing contest, and he can bridge from one aspect to the other. By being able to talk on the level of the designers, but from a sailor's perspective, he was instrumental in how that side of the campaign was structured.

With sponsors on board—Telecom, Steinlager, TVNZ, Toyota, and Lotto—the campaign got under way rapidly. Limited funds gave the campaign focus. The challenge was to win the America's Cup, but the focus was "making the boat go faster." Peter Blake says, "The limited budget was a plus, because it forced us to concentrate on what would give us a quicker boat around the course."

At this point, Team New Zealand realized that a peak performing organization would be needed to succeed against intensifying international competition. Alan Sefton:

Everything very quickly became team focused and a team decision. And that really is a Blake trait. He is a natural leader, but he doesn't just act arbitrarily. If a decision needs to be made, Peter will make it; but his normal way of going about things is to get people around him whom he has complete faith in. He canvasses opinion constantly, listens, and then finds the right consensus. That was also Russell's inclination from the sailing perspective, so the team just grew along these lines. Some America's Cup campaigns have been skipper driven, as with Dennis Conner or Paul Cayard, or our 1987 campaign with Chris Dickson. Then we went to the other extreme in 1992 with a designer-driven campaign. Neither of these approaches worked, so there had to be a smarter way. It was agreed that this would be a campaign managed by the whole team.

This decision inevitably led to a break with designer Bruce Farr, as Tom Schnackenberg describes:

He is a really good designer, and he had been the designer for all the campaigns in the past, so he was the logical choice. But there was a desire to manage the design, to let the sailor customers be in charge of the design team, and to have it in-house so that it was a very open process. Bruce wasn't too keen on a lot of that process, because he is a very powerful designer, very good, but used to making his own decisions. He sells his designs and he works with his customers, and he lays out options for them, but he controls the work and the intellectual content. So the sailors hired the design team, and Russell charged off round the world to interview potential designers. Most of them took time to talk to us, and we just asked them how they would go about winning the America's Cup. They were quite forthcoming, because they realized that we were implicitly asking them if they were interested in working with us. We built the design team from that start.

There is a design language and a yachties language, so we had to work on communication, and the designers had to unbend to try to understand the questions they were getting. And, of course, the sailors had to come some way to understanding the design process. The design team would meet each morning all through the summer as the boat was being put together. There was constant interplay between sailors and designers.

Peter Blake says, "It was important to learn by our mistakes and not to have too many repeats—so our collective knowledge was built into the boat." For example, a wooden mock-up of the deck was built to enable the sailors to pinpoint perfect positioning for winches, leads, and workstations.

The Team New Zealand management style was born. It was decided early on that since the sailors would have to take what was delivered around the course, they would be the customers. They made it clear that they did not want a boat from one side of the design spectrum, like *NZL 20*. They wanted a boat close to what everybody else had, but they also wanted boat-speed edge! There is no substitute for boat speed.

Alan Sefton says, "Team New Zealand actually runs as a team." To achieve this, there is a raft of meetings at different levels so that everybody is always fully informed. Alan Sefton:

> For example, in 1992, if you tried to find out anything about the boat you would not have succeeded unless you had a triple A CIA classification. Even lots of people within the campaign were not allowed to go under the skirts and see the keel. We went absolutely the other way in 1995. We decided it was everybody's campaign. We always told everybody on the team exactly what we were doing—if we were in the test tanks in England, they knew why we were there, what we were testing on this visit and so on.

Security around America's Cup events has to be very high, and this helps foster family—it reinforces the belief in being part of something that is very special. Sefton:

> In 1995, the policy of keeping everybody informed didn't let us down. It worked very well because everybody bought into

the campaign and, in particular, they understood that the dollars were finite.

Tom Schnackenberg confirms that the sailors were central to the development process. In 1995 the two Black Magic boats, known by their registration numbers as *NZL 32* and *38*, were almost identical, so that it was possible to make small changes in one to test for an improvement in boat speed. Team New Zealand delayed the building of the first boat until the design process had been completed, so that the two boats could be built together. The Australians, French, Japanese, and Americans all built their boats sequentially, so their boats leapfrogged each other, whereas the Team New Zealand pair had a similar performance spectrum, and both were kept up to scratch right the way through. This matched-pair, two-boat campaign was a game-breaking idea that has now been adopted by most syndicates and is central to Team New Zealand's relentless search for speed.

> America3 did the same thing, but the design team operated as scientists. They would change the boat but not tell the sailors what they had done, because they did not want them to have preconceived notions that might prejudice the results of the test. Whereas we did the opposite. The sailors were involved in making the decisions as to what to change. Their involvement meant that the quality of the testing was much higher due to increased focus and concentration. I was part of the design and sailing teams, and I could see we wound up making much better decisions. The sailors were the customers, and everyone else was supplying them.

Through inclusion, Team New Zealand built community. Because people have been together for a long time, and some of the relationships go back to the formative years, there is a strong sense of family. Tom Schnackenberg:

> We squabble just like families do, and there is a sort of openness that you get in normal families, yet, just like a family, you stay

tight and you work through problems, and when it comes to meeting the outside world, you depend on your family members. You defend each other against attack, and even if you agree with the criticisms, you say, "Just a minute, you can't say that about one of us." And we deal with the issue in the family. Admission to the family takes time; personnel decisions are made very slowly and very carefully. We are lucky in New Zealand, because there are enough good sailors around to run several teams, so we have the luxury of choice. Enthusiasm is often the important criterion. When we are deciding on a person, one of the key factors is whether they are compatible, so that everyone is a team player. You don't want team players in the sense of "me too" people. The interplay of strong personalities in an open family setting builds strength. Because it's a family, we try to get a genuine consensus when hiring somebody so that the person is accepted.

Tom went on to explain the extended nature of family:

We are really a family. That includes everyone, the sponsors as well. It's not just the team, the shore crew, the sail makers; everyone feels part of one big family. The family of sponsors for the team in particular have been with us for a long, long time and they feel a sense of ownership, so they have been very much a part of everything we have done, including the transition from the old structure to the new one for the 2003 campaign. The public and the sponsors realize there is a huge team there and the front people are only just one part of it.

Russell Coutts says that this approach extends to all significant decisions in the sailing and design teams:

Team is a big word. Team New Zealand is not as it may be perceived, with strong leaders directing all the operations. It is actually very much consensus led, and ideas are aired to the group.

Key decisions are made quite slowly and discussed thoroughly. There is a high degree of individual responsibility.

Peter Blake confirms the importance of the Team New Zealand family. According to him, success comes down to "forward planning, a united team approach, and a clearly focused goal," but to do the planning and make the correct decisions, the right people are needed:

This includes not only the sailing crew, but also the shore manager and secretary, designer, boat builders, sail makers, computer wizards, engineers, i.e., the overall team. Everyone has to buy in. There are no small jobs. Everyone is important. The weather boat up the course is as vital as the man on the bows. Every person's input is valued, and all ideas are welcome. The finer details are outlined to everyone, because if you haven't got trust, you haven't got anything. Success comes from a combination of all the factors, so the less meaningful jobs must not be overlooked. We keep the team small by the standard of other syndicates, and we pay them as well as we can. We don't pamper people too much, and we don't force them to live in each other's pockets or impose curfews, as happened in the 1992 campaign. They are all given their own space and trusted not to let the team down. The chemistry has to be right, the attitudes have to be right, and people have got to be able to have fun, or they won't give everything of which they are capable.

Both expertise and a good attitude are essential. Peter Blake continues:

We have to have people with specific types of expertise: sail makers, riggers, spar makers, boat builders, electricians, engineers, people with medical knowledge, helmsmen, sail trimmers, bowmen, mastmen, navigators, winch grinders, etc. Each person has an area of expertise for which he is totally responsible, but most people have two or three jobs, and can turn their hands to almost anything. Everyone knows from the start that if they don't perform they will let the rest of the team down. We expect them to perform right from the beginning, so we take great care about who we take on. Most of all the crew, the team, have to want to win more than anything, and be prepared to give up everything to achieve that aim. It's important to make people feel that their contributions are worthwhile. People who realize they are appreciated and that their views will be listened to will give far more of themselves.

Team New Zealand emphasizes the importance of continuity for the strength of community, but knows that new blood is always needed to sustain the dream. "Russell and his guys know the new talented sailors and they pull them into Team New Zealand," explains Sefton. Coutts describes how they go about recruiting:

Obviously, sailing ability and an ability to work with the current group as a team player are important. New sailors must also take ownership of an area that will improve the speed of the yacht as a secondary function, e.g., sail development, weather program, spar program, boat building, and deck layout. They should therefore have skill or training in one of those areas. We also have an eye for creating the future, so we tend to employ and try out younger people. It is often easier for them to buy into the culture. We generally put new sailors on a six-month (or more) trial. The selection process usually comes down to a vote among those affected, or who will be working closely with the new candidate. We try to give new people feedback if they have some negative points but are showing overall potential.

Tom Schnackenberg had his own reasons for choosing Team New Zealand for the 1995 campaign, having previously worked for John Bertrand's Australian syndicate:

I felt that I could make a bigger contribution in this team, and saw that there was a need for me. John Bertrand had gathered a big team around him. I could see people there who did exactly what I did, whom I respected, so it was time to move on. It was nothing to do with money, because I hadn't even asked either team what they had in mind for salary. I hadn't any notion whether I would get more or less or the same. The question for me was whether I could make a difference.

Team New Zealand expects that everyone will make a difference throughout the campaign. It is clear to everybody that they go to meetings to contribute, not just to listen. Alan Sefton reveals how this approach has led to game-breaking ideas:

> We made several very significant speed gains this way. One was in the sail area, where two or three sailors had developed a particular idea on their own. Under normal circumstances, sail design would be left to the designers and sail makers, but they raised the idea, were encouraged, and were given a bit of a budget and time. They developed a sail shape that was very significant.
>
> We got to the stage in San Diego where we could go straight from design to manufacture through computers. We could take a design for a set of wings for the keel straight to the milling machine. Now, there are endless combinations of position and pitch shape, and you could spend the rest of your life twitching around getting them right. The first set we made in stainless steel cost us nearly $30,000 U.S., so we weren't going to be making too many! The boat builders thought about this and came up with a system using plywood and carbon fiber, and we were making wings for $300, so that changed the ballgame completely, because we could test all sorts of combinations.
>
> Tom Schnackenberg wanted to develop a twisted wind tunnel. A normal wind tunnel is a bit artificial because it has smooth surfaces, whereas the ocean is not smooth. The wind actually does a lot of different twists and turns over the wave pattern, and the wind at the top of the mast is quite different from the wind at the bottom. So Tom, being the techie he is, came up with this idea.

Everyone looked at him a bit sideways, but we knew that Tom comes up with game-breaking ideas, so we said, "There is no budget, but if you can fund it, off you go." So he went round to people like Ross Blackman in administration and me, begging and borrowing to come up with a result. Because it was for boat speed, we all found some money out of our budgets, and it proved to be a great idea.

The sense of family encourages people to contribute, and to develop game-breaking ideas. It also facilitates information sharing, which assists everyone to exceed their personal best by drawing on ideas and encouragement from others.

Internal competition and politics are minimized through community, based on a key insight from the 1992 campaign. In 1992 there were three would-be skippers and two crews competing with each other. Each crew position had two crew members who were set against each other in selection trials to get picked for the final crew, thereby destroying any sense of team unity. The result was infighting and lack of focus. According to Peter Blake, "The 1992 crew didn't know why they were out there." Alan Sefton explains:

That was very destructive within the team. One bowman wouldn't talk to the other about procedures and better ways of doing things. Michael Fay, using market principles, thought that competition would bring out the best team, but it doesn't work that way. In 1995 we named the sailing crew eighteen months out.

The intense community culture of Team New Zealand was at first strange to Tony Thomas, who was hired from a marketing background in 1997 to lead the management of the America's Cup 2000 event.

There are no HR procedures, no strategic planning, and no job descriptions. Just instant trust, to which you respond. At first I was annoyed, because everyone wanted to know what I was doing and to get involved. I interpreted this as a lack of trust, but it soon became apparent that this was the culture; everyone is interested in everything and wants to help.

Team New Zealand is organized along traditional functional lines—design, sailing, boat builders, rig, sails, sponsorship, PR, and accounting—as are all our peak performing organizations, and, in common with the others, there is easy movement across functional boundaries. The lines of hierarchy are flexible. As Alan Sefton says: "Peter Blake is the boss, but Peter also pulls bloody strings on the boat! Because he was willing to do any job that needed to be done, people realized early on that it was a different style of campaign."

The departmental heads meet two or three times a week, or more if required. Monday meetings are held with the whole team. Each department describes in a few minutes, with an overhead, what they achieved the previous week, and what they have planned for the one coming. Then, once a month, there is a full-scale team meeting where everybody is there unless they have good reason not to be. In these meetings there are more formal presentations. All the key decisions are made on a consensus basis. Tom Schnackenberg:

"If we couldn't agree on a decision, it generally meant that we didn't know enough to make the decision, so the normal course of action then was to go back and look at the question again."

Peter Blake would give team talks to inspire the team, and to impress on everyone the importance of careful cost saving and not leaving anything to chance. However, he rarely acted in the traditional manner of a syndicate boss when sailing. Tom Schnackenberg can remember only two occasions in the 1995 campaign:

Peter was invited onto the boat as part of the sailing crew, but he asserted his position only twice. Once was the day when the Australians sank. He was very quick to get on the radio as we were leaving the dock and start badgering the race committee not to run the races. Normally, you would not see him anywhere near the radio. Another time was when we completely ran out of wind. He was down below with a few others to concentrate the weight on top of the keel. Eventually we ground to a halt because there was no wind. All Peter's Whitbread experience came to the fore, and he leapt on deck and started whistling, tapping the boom, and doing all the little superstitious things that you do in the Whitbread race to be in the lead. It was very funny.

Blake created the focus that led to preeminence, but Team New Zealand is more than just Peter Blake. A crew full of inspirational players has developed the dream: Tom Schnackenberg in charge of design, Brad Butterworth the tactician, Russell Coutts, Bob Rice on meteorology, and Tim Gurr as boat builder. Altogether, there are about seventy people in the Team New Zealand organization, including sixteen in the sailing crew. Most team members are sailors and are involved with Team New Zealand because they love sailing. According to Peter Blake, "They are so keen they will walk over broken glass for Team New Zealand."

Responsibility for leadership lies throughout the organization. In fact, the idea of leadership, with the implicit corollary of "followership," sits uncomfortably, as Tom Schnackenberg describes:

> We've got a few followers, but not very many. Almost everyone is a part-time inspirational player. I don't see myself as a leader, but I can be a stirrer at times! Everyone is wild to get on, so they will poke at one of the other people who are maybe seen as leaders, and say you should be doing this or that. And because there is respect right across the group, they have impact. It's almost like the players are running it. So the team is managing itself.

This observation was brought home to us when we realized that Peter Blake has his home in England, and that he spent several months sailing around the world on *ENZA*, winning the Jules Verne nonstop around-the-world speed record during the buildup to the 1995 campaign. Tom explains:

> Peter was the leader, but on the boat and among the sailors it's really more Russell. Peter described himself as "just the catalyst," but he was much more than that. He showed a huge amount of leadership in keeping us going financially, and nobody would have gotten anywhere without him. The thing he did which was really good was to keep us thinking about what could go wrong. He made a big impact at the beginning, but we actually went through part of the campaign on our own while he was on *ENZA*, winning the Trophée Jules Verne of the Association "Tour du Monde en 80 Jours," awarded for the fastest circumnavigation of the world in under eighty days. Peter Blake and his crew completed their circumnavigation on 1 April 1994 in 74 days, 22 hours, and 22 seconds. He kept in touch by e-mail from the yacht, which were pretty garbled when it was going up and down in big waves. Listen, learn, help, and lead—that is Peter's style. He's in and out, but his inspiration is always there.

Peter Blake carried Fay's dream forward, made it his own, and shared it widely. His Whitbread Round the World Race and Jules Verne Trophy wins made him an icon in New Zealand and attracted world attention (later leading to an invitation to become president of the prestigious Cousteau Society). His knife-edge exploits were widely televised, and his understated manner gave him instant media appeal. As a romantic adventurer, Peter has it all.

Michael Fay's dream of wresting the America's Cup from the United States was shared by New Zealand's avid sailors, but neither the 1987 or 1992 campaigns, successful as they were, found their way into the national psyche. The publicity surrounding the campaigns was brash and corporate. From the outset, Peter Blake resolved that the 1995 campaign would be based around deeds, not words. This approach appealed to sponsors such as Telecom, Stein-lager, Toyota, Lotto, and TVNZ, and massive public support developed as the regatta progressed. Typical of this was the "red socks" campaign. As Black Magic's voyage to victory progressed, Peter appeared in the after-guard wearing what quickly became known as lucky red socks. From a joke within the sailing team, the red socks became a national symbol of support for the sailors. Red socks were on sale everywhere, with proceeds going to assist the campaign. And so the dream was shared.

As Alan Sefton explains, "All you have got to sell is your dream. You are asking others to invest in your dream to win the America's Cup. Some might think it's an absurd dream or a pathetic dream, but that's really all you have got to sell."

Sustaining a dream that has been achieved requires imagination. Alan Sefton describes the America's Cup as "a sporting Everest; the pinnacle of the sport." But, like all personal or organizational Everests, once climbed, the incentives to do it again are reduced. It is in the nature of the human spirit to seek constantly extended challenges, to sustain the dream. For the 2000 campaign, the Team New Zealand challenge was reimagined as being the first team outside the United States to defend the trophy successfully. But for individual team members the challenge has to be more personal. Tom Schnack-enberg revealed to us how he retained the magic second time around:

It's difficult, because it's a longer campaign; people come and go. Last time we were together for a short time, and we had this adrenaline surge that we can win the cup. We all had something to prove. I said this to a few of the guys, and one said, "Well, I have got something to prove." He was one of our dozen or so new guys. They revitalize the team.

When you start to see a dozen challenges lining up, you see what a huge task lies ahead, and that focuses people's attention. The public actually helps to keep us focused by saying, "You have got to do it." They sense the magic behind these boats. But what really sustains the magic for me is a feeling that we can actually improve a lot from last time. I think that is the main thing that motivates people, born as individuals and as a team. I think the idea of continuous improvement, even though nobody actually talks about it, provides a focus, as does the sense of being able to hang onto the cup for a long time.

Personal challenge lies at the heart of Team New Zealand, as it does for all human endeavor. The focus on "making the boat go faster" provides direction for the dream. The testing process has been likened by some to watching the grass grow. However, according to Tom Schnackenberg:

Having the sailors buying in, knowing what is going on all the time, and even leading some of the ideas, means they become intensely interested in the process. The intensive testing system gets them focused, and then it's just having fun, skylarking around. If there's a sense that people are getting bored or not concentrating, we just go home. There is no big hand like Peter Blake saying we have got to stay out until five o'clock. The people out there just want to stay to get the job done.

Russell Coutts explained to us that the sailing team does not use policy manuals or job descriptions.

We have developed a crew manual, but more for recording items such as breakdowns and safety procedures and our current thinking, rather than for laying down the correct procedure. Sometimes we try to record a method just to be sure that we can define it correctly for ourselves, and that we all agree.

This flow of information through easy relationships is readily evident throughout the Team New Zealand headquarters at the Viaduct Basin in Auckland. During our several visits we were treated as guests of the family, receiving courtesy and care from everyone we met. Despite the relentless media pressure, and visits from sponsors and friends of the family, we observed the same friendliness extended to all. Here is an organization that truly shares its dream.

Security there is tight but not oppressive. The premises are spartan and open plan. The design team, weather forecasters, sailmakers, engineers, electricians, boat builders, and sailing team all have their separate areas, but they flow easily into one another. The site is pristine and has a feeling of understated perfection and commitment to precision. Peter Blake's office is central to the action. The Team New Zealand headquarters exudes energy, but there is a calm, relaxed rhythm of activity. No orders are given; no voices are raised; they all know their roles.

Team New Zealand livery is proudly displayed at all vantage points, while sponsors' logos adorn the buildings and the boats. At the center of it all stand the twin Black Magic boats *NZL 32* and *NZL 38*, sleek and evocative, reminding all concerned of the central focus of the action—making the boat go faster. The silver fern, New Zealand's national symbol, is displayed along the aft topsides as a statement of national pride, alongside sponsors' logos, the symbols of those who have chosen both to share and to finance the dream.

We are offered the opportunity to observe the twin Black Magic boats in testing at close quarters and arrive at the Team New Zealand dock at the appointed time to find the boats being prepared for sea. The crew is focused, just doing the job with quiet efficiency. Each boat has a captain, but there is no outward sign of who is in charge. Occasional social remarks are passed about the weather, or last night's activities; conversation is routine about the day ahead. It is all very businesslike. The activity is structured, as everyone has his own job or responsibility, but as soon as one area is tidied away, then those who have finished look to help the others. People know if help is needed—they don't have to be asked. Everyone lends a hand to carry the mainsail because it takes at least six people to pick it up, and it gets easier if you have seven or eight. Highly specialized teams, such as those dedicated to winches or electronics, calmly go about their work.

The Team New Zealand work boat and the Avon chase boat are already attaching tow ropes to *NZL 32* and *NZL 38*. The sailing team members have checked their crew assignment from the daily lists and hop on board their respective boats. Murray Jones, our captain for the day, invites us onto *NZL 38*. He explains that the Black Magic boats are out sailing every day, weather and repairs permitting. Some days the emphasis is on testing innovations, but today it's to be race practice. We have already signed indemnity forms accepting the risks involved in sailing on these high-performance racing yachts. We are reminded that the previous week a Spanish America's Cup sailor was killed when a block exploded under load. We have also signed to the effect that we will abide by the Team New Zealand secrecy rules, a reminder of the extreme lengths that competitors will go to in order to discover Team New Zealand's winning formula.

As we are towed out to the racecourse, crew members relax, munch carbohydrates, and share good-humored banter. It was the feel of a family day out sailing, and we are treated as guests of the family. We are warned in a friendly way of potential dangers, and team members share a quiet word or a joke with us as the day races by. Once out in open water, the chase boat drops our tow and planes out 3.3 miles to windward[9] to drop the orange marker for our day's course. The start line is marked by the work boat at one end and by another orange marker 200 meters away.

The crew take their positions in a well-rehearsed rhythm. There is intense focus and concentration; hardly a word is spoken; there is just the occasional comment or gesture. In no time, the mainsail is attached and hauled up the mast. A crewman is whisked 32.5 meters to the masthead to look for wind and check that all is well with sails and rigging, and is back down again almost as fast as we can watch. The

[9] The Cup races start by going upwind 3.275 miles, then down and up for four legs of three miles each, then a final run of 3.275, for a total of six legs and 18.55 miles.

headsail is set with similar speed, and we accelerate rapidly to 10 knots to windward. *NZL 32* has replicated the exercise just astern of us, and we are ready to race. The ten-minute gun sees us inside the start line, vying for the favored windward position.[10] Close-quarters tacking at a closing speed of 20 knots provides heart-pounding excitement for us, and calm fun for the crew. The only words spoken now are the countdowns to five minutes and to the start, and the occasional comment from the headsail trimmer. *NZL 38* wins the windward position and we match tacks[11] until *NZL 32* sheers off onto a split tack.[12] *NZL 38* powers up to 11.5 knots, the mainsail is tensioned down until it is a perfect airfoil,[13] and the running backstay[14] is tensioned to 6 tons. We are warned not to hold it!

Attention then turns to the battered, yellow-covered computer sitting on the afterdeck just next to us, which provides comprehensive real-time telemetry for both boats. The navigator, Clay Oliver,[15] explains the readings to us, and points out that, contrary to expectations, *NZL 32* is getting more wind pressure and lift[16] on the leeward side of the course. We eye the skyline and suspect that the wind may shift to the southwest and that a squall may be building. The first cross of the boats shows that *NZL 32* is five lengths ahead, having benefited from the more favorable wind, and so it remains to the windward mark. *NZL 32* ahead of us sets the spinnaker perfectly and sails off downwind. We follow. Again this complex routine is handled with scarcely a word and we are off "downhill" with a black squall

[10] Being upwind of the opponent provides advantage because you can block the wind getting to the opposing boat.

[11] Sail in parallel as close into the wind as possible.

[12] Goes off on a diagonal course.

[13] Shaped like the wing of an airplane.

[14] The backstay is actually a set of four wires, which converge on the runner block at the back of the boat: the topmast backstay, the runner (which takes most of the load), the upper checkstay, and the lower checkstay. These have varying amounts of tension, but the total amount is about 6 tons when sailing upwind.

[15] Oliver is a key member of the Team NZ design team, having been recruited especially for the 2000 defense. He is the author of the velocity prediction program that underpins the Team NZ design process.

[16] Lift refers to a better angle of wind giving a better angle to the mark.

building to leeward. The headsail is prepared, ready for the anticipated windshift. Rain and wind come more quickly than expected,
and the spinnaker has to be let go quickly to keep excessive pressure
off the mast and the backstays. The crew meets what is high drama
for us with rhythmic, wordless, high-speed, confident action; the sail
is gone. We are tacking to windward again after a 180-degree wind
shift. And so the afternoon goes by with good humor, good comrade-
ship, and intense, high-performance sailing on the world's fastest
matched pair of America's Cup yachts. *NZL 32* maintains her five
lengths' lead at the first mark to the winning line, as happens in
ninety percent of America's Cup races. The headsail is dropped and
stowed, and the mainsail disappears from the boom into its cover in
the time it takes for us to turn around and watch the squall disap-
pearing out to sea. We are again under tow back to the dock, as the
crew holds a debriefing session in the cockpit on the key lessons of
the day. The telemetry will be downloaded and analyzed later.

The state of flow that we witnessed in the organization and on
the water takes a while for newcomers to understand. As Tom
Schnackenberg explains, time takes on a different dimension for
Team New Zealand players:

> When you go out and race it's a natural adrenaline spur, win or
> lose. If you have won, you are feeling good. If you have lost, you
> are feeling good in an interesting way, and you are spurred on, ei-
> ther way, to rush around and fix things up, and there is an urgency
> which keeps you going. You can run into a twelve-hour game pro-
> gram very easily, as time just flashes by without you even noticing
> it. Then, when you have a little break between the races where
> you go out testing, that's like a holiday, even though you have just
> as long a day. It's just different, like the difference between the
> weekend and a weekday.

"Making the boat go faster" becomes a focus in itself. As a
consequence, individuals and the organization are constantly seeking

to be better than they have been, to exceed personal best. Tom Schnackenberg:

> We don't think about the competition very much. We say we have got to go faster than last week, so we are out to beat ourselves. We had some weaknesses last time. We didn't lose any races, but we sure had some close calls, and we were getting overtaken downwind by a couple of boats. But we just focused on improving our own boats. We have to be self-reliant and create our own competition to beat ourselves, to achieve some sort of perfection. It's up to us to make sure that our in-house racing is better than anything you will see on the Challenger course.

Alan Sefton confirms this enthusiasm for exceeding personal best: "In 1987 we stopped developing during the finals. That cost us the regatta. In 1995 we made sure we kept developing all the way through."

Tom Schnackenberg explains the process of exceeding organizational best:

> For Team New Zealand, development was a process of continual adaptation, but once in a while we had a little jump, a lucky jump that hadn't been thought of before. If you keep intellectual pressure on a particular area, you skip along, and you take a bit of a walk, and if you have all of these people knowing what is going on, somebody will come up with an idea, even by asking a question, and the next minute, puff, you have made a little jump forwards. And you work on the find, and for a while things are easy because it opens up a few possibilities. We don't really expect jumps, but as long as we keep the pressure on they just happen.

Russell Coutts says that this "constant focus on improvement and continuous search for new ideas" is the primary ingredient of Team New Zealand success, along with good communication, especially between the sailing and design teams.

The last details are considered to be important, and organizational flow ensures that none are overlooked. The America's Cup is a game of seconds, according to Peter Blake:

> One second a mile is a twenty-second gain on the course. Races have been won or lost by less than three seconds. So a one-second-per-mile gain is worth spending a week on to get the little bits right. Speed gains came through making minute changes to one boat during two-boat testing to measure the difference. In the Whitbread Round the World Race, sponging out a few liters of bilge water—first having to clear away a pile of heavy and wet sails, lift the floorboards, sponge out, then put it all back when you are leaping from wave top to wave top and the yacht is leaning on its ear—just to get rid of a few unwarranted kilos of weight, was seen as just as important as steering the yacht or trimming the sails.
>
> Before each America's Cup race we would have twenty-five people polishing the hull, having fun as they ensured that the most minute speck of weed or dirt was removed so there was nothing to impede progress.

Russell Coutts made a similar point about the testing program:

> The differences we are looking for in the research and testing program are often small. When we test, every component must be set correctly, or it will introduce more error into the results. There is a high emphasis on checking components to eliminate as many variables as possible.

To most people, Team New Zealand's attention to the last detail would seem fanatical. To Team New Zealand players it's just the way they do business. And this continued throughout the five years' preparation for the first defense. Relentless intellectual pressure was applied to all aspects of designing, building, and race testing. As the world leader, Team New Zealand realized that they had continuously to exceed all aspects of their previous best performance. Tom Schnackenberg describes the way in which they dealt with the intense media attention building up to the America's Cup 2000.

> *Prada* was in our design space. She was among all the things that we had tested and checked out. So we felt we understood her. The media portrayed *Prada* as the boat to beat. And we were seen as the underdogs at the start of racing. We thought we knew how we would go against *Prada* and it turned out that we were right. But there was no sense in trying to win a war of words at that stage.

Team New Zealand's best competition was itself. World match racing champion and current Team New Zealand skipper Dean Barker explains:

> Our philosophy right from the start of the 2000 campaign was that we were never going to have a race crew; it was always going to be a squad of sailors. So any one person could fit into their opposing role on each boat. We set about building a team that had an equal in every position. My role was to skipper the other boat in the racing that we did. It was really a great opportunity for me to build my experience in racing and sailing the America's Cup yachts against Russell Coutts, who is perceived to be the best in the business. I never expected to race during the Cup.

But Dean did get to race the final race. In a sacrificial play, Coutts relinquished the opportunity to become the first America's Cup skipper to win ten consecutive races and handed the helm to Barker. Barker describes the fifth race in 2000.

> The day that we went out for the last race to skipper the boat was quite an unusual feeling actually. I guess in a way it was Russell proving his point that it was a team philosophy and that anyone was replaceable on the boat. For me it was a huge opportunity to go out there and not let him down and not let the team down. Ob-

viously, I didn't want to let myself down either, but to have an opportunity like that you can't let it go because you don't get that many of them in your life.

The worst part of the day was actually leaving the base because we were towed out through thousands of people around the Viaduct Basin cheering and they were all expecting to have a big party that night. But once we got outside the viaduct, it just felt like another day, even though a lot of pressures were associated with it. We got down to the race area, the sails were up, and once we got into a daily routine, it became, through doing it so often, just like another day. Because of the strength of the team, the depth, we have so much confidence stepping on board the boat, knowing that everything was going to work faultlessly.

I was obviously very confident in my own ability and also the teams.' That put my mind at ease when we actually were out there and we started racing. Obviously, by that stage we knew our boat was fast and everything that we were doing was very positive, so it was easy to fit into a role like that. When we finished that race, it was just incredible with so many other boats swarming around *NZL 60*, just incredible.

And so Team New Zealand complemented their perfect 5–0 1995 challenge for the America's Cup with an equally perfect 5–0 2000 defense. A dynasty was born—or was it?

Renewal

Skipper Coutts, tactician Butterworth, and designer/navigator Schnackenberg, the most powerful triumvirate in America's Cup yachting, took over as syndicate leaders from Blake and Sefton after the America's Cup 2000 victory. The talk was of retaining the cup for the next generation or the next thirty years. And so the process of contracting the team for the 2003 defense commenced.

But the success of the spectacular America's Cup 2000 event attracted the interest of global billionaires intent on capturing the cup at any cost. Headhunting of Team New Zealand sailors and shore crew began in earnest. Speculation was rife for months as to who would stay and who would go. Sums beyond the imagination of New Zealand professional sailors were on offer from rival syndicates. To the great surprise and devastation of the nation, it was Coutts and Butterworth themselves who were the first to jump ship, lured by a lucrative deal from a new Swiss syndicate funded by Swiss pharmaceutical billionaire Ernesto Bertarelli. Butterworth explained to us that "the excitement of challenging for the America's Cup is much greater than defending it." As sailors, they saw their destiny as being on the water rather than navigating the business of the defense syndicate.

Other long-standing members of Team New Zealand departed for a Seattle-based syndicate headed by billionaire Craig McCaw. Tom Schnackenberg remained as Team New Zealand syndicate leader, and Dean Barker, fresh from his victory in the last race, became senior skipper. The seascape had changed dramatically. To outsiders, the Team New Zealand dream looked in disarray, and the prospect of development of a dynasty had disappeared. Tom Schnackenberg describes the new challenge:

"Beat the billionaires." That is the challenge! How can a little country like New Zealand compete against the likes of Ernesto Bertarelli, whose own shareholdings are greater than the total market capitalization of our entire stock market!

Dean Barker enthusiastically embraces this new greatest imaginable challenge:

It has actually provided an exciting new goal, something to really focus on. It has brought out a lot of good values and enthusiasm in the guys that have stayed with the team, and the young guys who are coming into the team as well. It is the best thing that has happened for the team in that we are going to have people just bubbling down here every day, just really excited about going sailing and the whole process of building an America's Cup team again. So although the initial reaction was pretty much of shock at what has happened, I actually think in the long run it is going to be incredibly satisfying. The biggest risk for us was having complacency in another campaign, if we had just carried on as we were. At first we thought, How can we possibly carry on without some of these guys? But people say to you from the business world and other sporting areas, No one is irreplaceable. It is actually so true that you might think that a person is a big loss but it just really opens the door for someone else to put their hand up. So it's got the potential to run so much better than it has ever run before.

Barker explains how the future for Team New Zealand will be re-created:

I guess the team feeling dissolved a little bit and then a lot of the team started having some big money thrown around and that is where it all started splitting the team up. But what that has done has shown who is wanting to stay for the right reasons. I would say that the feeling of family will definitely grow as a result of what has happened. There are obviously a lot of very strong bonds with the guys that have been here for all the America's Cup campaigns going back to '87, because they have shared a lot of experiences together. I see it as really like creating a future again for the next generation that will carry things on.

9

New Zealand Rugby Union: Any Color as Long as It's All Black

"Passion. Passion for the game. I think there's no one in this organization who doesn't have a genuine love and passion for what we do. Passion makes this place tick, along with good leadership and good governance. And the All Blacks are the pinnacle of that passion. They are the glue."

—EVAN CRAWFORD, MANAGER, RUGBY DEVELOPMENT

The All Blacks. Few brand names in the sporting world carry so much power. For more than 100 years, revered and respected by common acclaim, the New Zealand All Blacks have been the dominant force in world rugby union. Only a small number of sports teams can trace their lineage back to the nineteenth century, and none can claim a seventy-two percent win record over this astonishing length of time. The game of rugby union is played throughout the world, with local club sides forming the backbone of the test-playing nations. England, Ireland, Scotland, Wales, France, Italy, Canada, Argentina, South Africa, Australia and New Zealand, Fiji, Western Samoa, and Japan annually wage titanic struggles for championships in their respective hemispheres, yet the New Zealand All Blacks set the standard for the game. During the 1990s the All Blacks won 73.9 percent of all international matches (compared with next-place Australia at 73.7 percent), and since the advent of professionalism from 1996–69 won 75.6 percent (Australia 72.9 percent).

For more than a century New Zealand's national pride rose and fell with the fortunes of the team that wore the black jersey with the silver fern, but in 1995 this linkage nearly broke down. The fine line between sport and entertainment had been breached in the early nineties when both codes, rugby league (professional) and rugby union (amateur at that time), were eyed as potential moneymakers by media moguls who had little time or understanding for the subtleties of national culture and rugby traditions.

Rugby union in New Zealand was largely a provincial affair, with a representative national council of twenty-seven members (reduced to nineteen in more recent times) who met infrequently and tried to administer the game with a hardworking national office of two or three full-time workers. While the structure of the organization was less important when the game was being administered on a purely amateur basis, the advent of the professional era has required a far greater degree of strategic intent and large-scale operational ability. The impetus for change within the union code to move from strictly amateur status to accepting that union players could be paid—and therefore become professionals—came from two directions. Most important was the greater development of professional rugby league, played passionately up and down the eastern seaboard of Australia and in the north of England. A less fluent game than rugby union, rugby league retains an avid following that, in the early nineties, was beginning to translate into television rights, sponsorship deals, and a professional game in the form of a new Super League.

Lured by the prospect of lucrative, late-career deals, many of the star union players at test and provincial level began switching codes to the professional rugby league (which, according to the rules in force at that time, precluded them from continuing to play rugby union), thus potentially depriving the union game of role models for the young school children who for generations had formed the backbone of the All Blacks' international success. This was also a period when the joystick generation was emerging and where physical contact sport was played out on computer screens rather than in the nation's ballparks. The amateur game, which in terms of stature and status had had an unchallenged place in the hearts and minds of New Zealanders, was in danger of being lost. The NZRU also faced the further threat of a "professionalization initiative" from within its own code.

In 1995 the World Rugby Corporation (WRC), apparently backed by Australia's charismatic media baron Kerry Packer, threatened to sign a significant number of rugby stars, All Blacks included, to its own professionally based international competition. Although the WRC initiative was doomed to fail, like World Series Cricket two decades earlier, the impact of this intervention was both dramatic and traumatic. Unable to react to the new situation with sufficient coherence or strategic clarity, the NZRU council, which had successfully built the All Blacks into a fearsome winning team and a durable brand, had sufficient guile to vote in favor of its own extinction, to be replaced by a smaller board of nine members and a growing professional national office of fifty people.

Initial backing from Rupert Murdoch through News Corporation enabled the NZRU to maintain its position as the national regulator and steward of the game, although, from 1995, the elite players were paid. With the recognition that business acumen would be essential in the new era, the character of the board inevitably changed. Kevin Roberts, who in 1995 was the chief operating officer of the Lion Nathan Brewery, a major sponsor of All Blacks rugby, played a key role in establishing professional rugby by acting as a broker between the competing interests of the Packer and Murdoch camps. Appointed to the new board as an external member, Roberts immediately brought a range of skills that helped facilitate organizational transformation. Board Chairman Rob Fisher is in no doubt as to Roberts's importance to New Zealand rugby:

Kevin has a fearsome intellect and an ability to think much more laterally than anyone else around the board table, myself included. And he has a remarkable clarity of thought. I don't know too many other people who can say, "Guys, here are the six things that we need to do," and out of his head, from a complex set of discussions, lay them out. I might have thought of six, but by the time I get to articulate them, I'm struggling to recall what the first two were! He does it without writing anything down, so he just has that rare clarity of thought. And he's visionary. Of course, he absolutely loves the game and the All Blacks, so you put all that together, and you're well served.

Fisher has evidence he can point to directly. In 1997 Roberts, together with the then-CEO David Moffett, was instrumental in negotiating a major sponsorship deal with the adidas organization. This included the supply of state-of-the-art sports kits for the All Blacks designed especially for the 1999 Rugby World Cup. The overall dollar value of the sponsorship, rumored to be more than eighty million New Zealand dollars, including bonus payments for championship victories, spread over five years, effectively secured the future of New Zealand rugby union. Peter Ciulionis, director of finance and administration, is in no doubt as to its importance:

Are we happy? I think it's an absolutely brilliant deal. It's going to make a huge difference to rugby. It's a big exercise, managing an influx of money like that. Where do I want the money to go? I think it can go into the amateur grassroots side of things and, professionally speaking, we also need to preserve some funds for the best players, not for those who are already past their best.

Ciulionis neatly describes the two levels that New Zealand rugby has to consider simultaneously—amateur development and resourcing the elite players. Either way, the newly constituted board was aware that if the All Blacks were to remain all-conquering, the game would have to be rebuilt from the bottom to the top.

In order to excite the nation, the new "greatest imaginable challenge" facing the board required a far more sophisticated plan than just parading the boys in black once more. Accordingly, the board embarked on a wholesale restructuring of the relationship among itself, the provincial rugby associations, and local clubs. In simple terms, the focus is the creation of significantly wider opportunities to play, and identify with, the game. To achieve this, the board and its operational staff, while continuing to provide the necessary technical regulatory stewardship of rugby, set in motion formidable developmental programs at all levels of the game. Without a systematic approach to rebuilding, the broad base upon which the All Blacks had established their long-held supremacy risked rapid erosion. Moreover, according to its stated strategic intent, the union endeavors "to ensure rugby is the most exciting entertainment product for all New Zealand and [for it] to be recognized as a leading sports brand worldwide." The union's inspirational dream is nothing less than to maintain rugby's position at the heart of the nation.

The new organizational structure, or "family tree" as it is usually referred to, naturally places the board at the policy level, with the national office clustering around three functional directors. These are Jack Ralston for commercial and marketing; Peter Ciulionis for finance and administration; and Bill Wallace, who heads up the largest group—rugby services—which includes managers for rugby development, referee development, and managers for the amateur and professional game. The directors, including Communication Manager Jackie Maitland, all report to CEO David Moffett.[17] Together they are the "tight five."

A House of Brands

As part of the fallout from the move toward professionalism, the NZRU, rather than the club or provincial sides, contracted to pay the salaries of those players deemed good enough to earn a living playing

---

[17] Coach John Hart and CEO David Moffett concluded their contracts with the NZRU at the end of 1999 subsequent to the completion of this case.

the game in provincial or international competitions. Funds are derived from sponsorships, gate receipts at international matches, and television fees. While accepting responsibility for professional payments, the union clearly needed to establish viable competitions (such as the new Super 12 competition that is deemed critical for the continued success of rugby union in New Zealand and which will be considered in some detail in this chapter) in which contracted players could ply their trade. Despite the obvious significance of these game-breaking ideas, David Moffett constantly points out that:

> The professional part of the game represents only 0.1 percent of the people involved in rugby. The game in total has not gone professional. It is still the largest amateur sport in this country. What we have got is the splitting of rugby union into two. One arm looks after the professional part of the game and another arm looks after the amateur activities. The professional game generates the funds that are then, in part, redistributed to the amateur game, which in turn secures the future of rugby.

Without question, the All Blacks are the premier brand upon which the fortunes of the game rest. The sacrosanct black jersey is the uniting link between the amateur and the professional game. A run of defeats, as in the 1998 season, is treated as a national crisis with the potential to undermine the very roots of rugby and to inflict considerable damage on the confidence level of the country. Prior to the professional era, the All Blacks were a microcosm of New Zealand society. Bill Wallace, director of rugby services, notes, "We had this incredible ability to have the doctor, the farmer, the shearer, and the unemployed all playing together as equals." As a consequence of this, Wallace argues:

> The All Blacks brand is owned by New Zealanders. They are the stakeholders. That's the thing that has been profoundly illustrated to me so many times. We get heaps of letters and phone calls, and until you've actually read them or listened to them, you truthfully

don't realize how passionate New Zealanders are in their belief that they own the All Blacks. So you carry this very heavy responsibility. You know that it is extremely important that this brand remains a valuable icon in the national culture.

Recently, the NZRU set out to codify the brand values associated with its most famous charges. Inevitably, the values that capture the essence of the All Blacks brand are those of respect and humility combined with power, tradition, commitment, and masculinity—values that form the basis upon which any and all professional relationships, internal or external, are formed. Former coach and player Laurie Mains describes what these values actually feel like.

> Nobody in this world knows what it means to be an All Black if they haven't been there themselves. Even someone who has been on the periphery, such as a selector, can never fully understand this. If they have not pulled the jersey on, they can't actually feel what it is. I wasn't a great All Black, I only played fifteen games or so, and yet that jersey just did something to me. The day I pulled it on was something I'll never forget.

Over the years, the jersey has gone through many changes. Each time a new design is about to be presented to the New Zealand public there are claims that traditions are being sacrificed. However, Kevin Roberts,[18] backroom architect of the latest version of the Kiwi icon, rejects such ideas: "Down through the years, captains in every era have pulled on a different style jersey, but the common denominator is that every one of them remains an All Black." Chairman Rob Fisher, who, as the photographs in his office attest, has spent many years in and around the game of rugby, was reminded of the power of the jersey during a sports seminar that was being addressed by a New

---

[18] Kevin Roberts, as a member of the board of the NZRU, did not participate as an author in the research or writing of this chapter. Kevin resigned from the board in April 2000.

Zealander who had played in the National Football League in the United States and had justifiably earned his position as speaker at the seminar based on his winning of a Super Bowl ring. Rob Fisher explains what happened:

> I was chairing the session and it was most agonizing because he couldn't speak. He just absolutely choked up. One of the players put his hand up and asked a question, which enabled him to get started. But he froze because he was in a room full of All Blacks. Despite everything he'd achieved in the world of sport, he couldn't handle it.

Jonah Lomu, currently the most famous rugby player in the world, says of the impact of the black jersey, "It's like putting an S on the front." Echoing sentiments familiar to many players, Lomu describes a close-knit community:

> There is a saying that once you are an All Black, you are always an All Black. When the guys who are former All Blacks turn up, they are still treated as All Blacks. It doesn't matter what year you played, you still get the respect. It carries on.

As the game has become more commercialized, the issue of projecting the All Blacks brand in an appropriate manner has seen the NZRU reconstitute the way in which the dream is shared. Sponsorship dollars provide critical lifeblood for the game, but nonetheless the NZRU has recently developed a strict set of guidelines that are designed to protect the All Blacks brand from any long-term damage. No partnership is contemplated if it contradicts the core values of the brand. In this sense, although the All Blacks create significant leverage for the NZRU, they are never for sale. Jack Ralston, director of commercial and marketing who was lured away from the Nike organization in 1997, explains how the national office deals with these all-important brand issues:

We look for people who have the same values as the All Blacks. It's one of the things we are adamant about. We used to have sponsors who didn't quite fit with the values of the All Blacks. We've shifted and repositioned some sponsors, too. For example, McDonald's has moved from the All Blacks, which we didn't feel was the right fit, to a more appropriate brand. McDonald's agreed with us.

Prior to the professional era, building the All Blacks brand was largely a subliminal process, but with multimillions of dollars of sponsorship revenue generated annually, the development of the brand was quickly subjected to new pressures forcing the NZRU to examine what the All Blacks actually stood for. Jack Ralston gives a fascinating insider's view as to how the organization learned how to defend its brand values systematically.

In the early days of professionalism, there were no strict brand disciplines. For instance, if a company had an advertisement they wanted us to approve, it was virtually done by consensus. It was held up in the office and everybody commented on whether they liked it or not! On my second day in the job, this is what happened. An advertisement was held up and I said, "Well, does it fit our brand values?" Everybody looked bewildered, so we had a think tank to put together some basic values and the advertisement didn't measure up. Even though we liked the color and the copy, when you ran it past some values it didn't measure up.

So we spent a lot of time early on developing these very strong brand values against which we now measure any possible sponsor. And we'll only associate with people who fit. Recently, we had very heated discussions with a company who wanted to associate the All Blacks with the James Bond theme using Jonah Lomu as the front person. It absolutely didn't fit with our values, so we had to stand and put our hands on our hearts and say, because it doesn't fit our brand values, we're not going to do it.

Not surprisingly, the imagery, affinity, and performance of the brand resonate across all functions and activities of the organization. The team has its own management structure, but interaction with the board and operational staff, according to team manager Mike Banks, is now "running a lot closer together than in the past." This is a delicate balancing act, since for many years the All Blacks flourished as an independent unit, operating as a subsidiary company with a high degree of autonomy, in terms of accountability, from the board. The point of contact with the parent body is now provided by the manager of professional rugby, Cameron Harland, who faces the challenge of maintaining the traditions of the All Blacks brand while handling a complex set of competing professional pressures, including management of all the professional teams under the union house.

Harland is himself a product of the NZRU's dash to embrace the future. Before taking on the NZRU's professional liaison duties, as a twenty-something executive, Harland had already served on special projects reporting directly to CEO David Moffett, successfully managed the bid to have the 2003 Rugby World Cup hosted in New Zealand, and developed the NZRU's all-important perspective on brands, all the while acting as chief strategic planner for the organization. Harland states bluntly, "The success of this organization is about the All Blacks winning. Everything that we do drives towards that." He is able to articulate precisely what he has to do to ensure on-field success. As budget manager he has to ensure that the All Blacks have the resources to operate both efficiently and effectively:

> My job is to make sure that the coach can do his job, and the manager can do his job, which is to manage. It's also to make sure that the players do their job, which is to play. I'm directly in the firing line in terms of making sure that the coach, manager, and the players are looked after. So we need to make sure that any of the other issues that they have on their minds are removed. For example, I ensure that their contracts are sound and that they know what their future is with the NZRU. We also deal with their

worries about what they're going to do after rugby—who will take them on board?

These activities are far more problematic than might be imagined. It is not simply a question of looking after the last detail, although contractual issues naturally require this. Harland has a far greater level of responsibility. The emergence of professionalism for the elite rugby players means that seemingly trivial decisions relating to players and teams carry significant impact with respect to overall policy coherence. Important issues such as player retention can be influenced by equity considerations among players, different treatment of elite players at different levels of skill, and continuity of policy with respect to team selection when considering players who have been lured to play for overseas clubs. What appears to be a simple liaison role is in fact project-based management with strategic significance. Alliances have to be contemplated between the NZRU and rugby union organizations in other countries. The loss of elite players, or "player drain," is one of the major concerns of the NZRU. Losing players to overseas clubs subverts the sharing of the dream, as inspirational players are no longer available to represent the game on an everyday basis in New Zealand even though they are still eligible to play for the All Blacks on the international stage. Fostering a strong sense of community within the rugby family is therefore a fundamental objective.

The stability of the community, including both the amateur and professional game, is complicated further by the potentially competing needs of several brands that have only recently become part of the NZRU's operations, and by the inspirational dream of keeping rugby at the heart of the nation. Providing players with the opportunity to compete in tournaments outside international test matches is a vital part of the NZRU's strategy of robustly supporting the elite squad. At the same time, the NZRU also needs to appeal to thousands of rugby players who will never make the professional grade. Cameron Harland:

Yes, the top of the heap is the All Blacks, but we've only got fifteen guys who run out for them! There are at least 135,000 people in this country who play rugby, most of whom are never going to play for the All Blacks. We would hope they won't stop playing rugby just because they know that they're not going to wear the black jersey.

This translates into broadening the base of the game. The most important development in the world of rugby that addresses this need has been the advent of the Super 12 competition played between franchise clubs owned by the unions in South Africa, Australia, and New Zealand and run as a partnership among the three countries. Regularly lambasted in the press and by every pundit imaginable, this critical initiative was put in place both to support the professional game and to attract a broader spectrum of spectators. As the Brand Book, which describes each of the portfolios under the NZRU's care, says, Super 12 is about "entertainment, flamboyance, color, and razzmatazz." Deliberately lacking the symbolism of All Blacks rugby, these games are designed to appeal to nontraditional fans, including women, families, and teenagers. With bonus points for high scoring, the Super 12 competition produces fast, risk-taking rugby that is full of extrovert play and flair. Semifinal places in the competition have been dominated by the Kiwi teams, and, more important, every Super 12 final has been won by a New Zealand franchise. These events have a very special flavor, which illustrate the NZRU's success in adding to its brand portfolio.

The 1999 final was played at the Carisbrook Stadium in Dunedin, New Zealand—one of the world's most celebrated rugby grounds—between the 1998 champions, the Canterbury Crusaders, and the Otago Highlanders. Super 12 rugby is little short of a revolution. Prior to the game, passengers disembarking from flights into Dunedin are piped into the airport, reflecting the region's Scottish ancestry that is deeply imbedded within the brand values of the Otago Highlanders rugby franchise. The taxi ride from the airport reveals the passion for the game ingrained in Kiwi culture. Throughout the length of the journey balloons, ribbons, flags, and banners display the Highlanders' blue, gold, and red colors. Cars, lorries, letterboxes, houses, and shops are all adorned. Even the city center clock has a Highlanders scarf tied around it!

The Super 12 competition uniquely combines provincial and international pride, since players compete both for the nation and for local supporters. The passion is intense—all 41,000 tickets for the stadium were sold out within thirteen hours of going on sale. This game, featuring—according to *NZRU* chairman Rob Fisher—"the world's best two provincial teams," will be watched by 100 million people around the world.

This is a big occasion for the NZRU. The president, inspirational former All Black Andy Dalton; David Moffett, director of the NZRU; and Rob Fisher, both chairman of the Union and current chairman of SANZAR, the alliance among the New Zealand, Australian, and South African Rugby Unions, are all gathered together at a hotel, as are representatives of the alliance partners and key sponsors, UBIX and Ford. Symbolic of the significance of this event to the nation, then–prime minister Jenny Shipley attends the game and the pre- and postmatch functions.

The NZRU contingent, dignitaries included, leave by coach for the prematch function in the Otago Rugby Union boardroom. Here, national and local officials, past and present, together with their families, enjoy waiting for the upcoming game from a vantage point in the main stadium while the crowd and the atmosphere build outside. David Moffett, in his carefully balanced scarf of gold, blue, red, and black, reflects quietly on the joy of experiencing the drama of the buildup to the match just four years after he was instrumental in the implementation of the Super 12 competition. Already the low-cost, outdoor "scarfies" seats are awash with the gold and blue of the home-side supporters, intermingled with the black and red of the invading Crusaders. Painted faces and hair portray unmistakably the partisanship of the fans. To leave absolutely no room for doubt, parents and kids alike carry banners or flags proclaiming their support, or brandish their mock Crusaders swords or Highlanders axes to great effect. This is an occasion to dress up, and an opportunity for the good-natured crowd to indulge in an afternoon's enjoyment.

Prematch entertainment, consistent with the Highlanders brand, is in evidence everywhere. By finishing top on points, the Highlanders have earned this hometown advantage. Thousands of balloons are released into the stadium and float skyward. And there is the usual mock intimidation of the visitors, as the Highlanders' evocative song is sung and resung by 30,000 partisan voices. The words appear on the scoreboard, although few need to read them. The atmosphere is electric. The Crusaders team runs onto the field to a crescendo of applause, and a sea of red and black banners and flags appears. As kick-off approaches, the Highlanders are piped onto the field by a full Scottish pipe band to an eruption of approval from the supporters. The rituals are complete; the game can begin.

Bone-crunching tackles, followed by awesome breakaway speed, strength-sapping scrums, brilliant set plays, precision shots on goal, and roar-inducing tries, all combine to invoke the intense concentration and involvement of the 41,000 fans. Here is a brand in the making. The game lives up to the eager anticipation, and the outcome is in contention until the very end. The Crusaders claim victory for the second year in a row. Red and black flags and banners prevail, home fans move away quietly, and Dunedin is deserted that night. Gold and blue banners and balloons hang forlornly and the party is over for another year.

With cups awarded, congratulatory speeches made, and media interviews given, it is time for the after-match functions. Along with the prime minister, players from both teams, national and local rugby officials, sponsors, spouses and partners, children and babies mix in the easy harmony of an extended family of hundreds. Satisfaction in achievement or wry resignation betray the players from both sides more readily than their smart team blazers. Victors and defeated players alike converse about competitions to come now that this challenge is over, and through their concerted efforts the position of the inspirational dream of rugby in the psyche of the New Zealand nation has been strengthened once more.

Away from the roar of the crowd and the entertainment of the Super 12 final, Bill Wallace understands that if the union is to create the future successfully, it must continue to generate new revenues that can be driven down to the all-important club level. From a technical point of view, the Super 12 franchise format has seen the development of new structures that encourage and stimulate innovative administration. Bill Wallace:

> Infrastructure. We will live and die by our infrastructure. The Super 12 is a fascinating study in itself. We decided to go the franchise way, even though no one had actually done it for rugby before. Here's how it works. We said, "Here is the franchise of that brand, it's on a risk or return basis, and we'll charge nothing. You take all the gate, it's all yours and we'll provide you with the players and the coaches, all paid." The franchise clubs are accountable to us under their contracts, so there is a bottom-line responsibility there. The Super 12 clubs appoint the rest of the management and do the marketing, so their responsibility is to build the brand. Typically, in any arrangement such as this, we communicate frequently as a franchise group. We put coaches on incentive programs, and all the players are highly motivated because they only get paid if they get selected. In the first year the Wellington franchise made $900,000 profit from zero and kept the lot. They then distributed it to their unions. A little union like Poverty Bay got $20,000. That's trickle-down. This is what we wanted to achieve.

Servicing the Super 12 brand also necessitates constant review and reflection. At the end of the season, Wallace and a small group from the NZRU hold debriefing sessions with all the players. Questionnaires and open-ended notes are made available and collected to ensure the widest possible feedback on all matters relating to the conduct of the season. Separate workshops are arranged where major problems can be tackled head-on. Some of these sessions deal with postcareer advice and skill building for life after the paddock. Even though the Super 12 competition is still in its infancy, the supportive community focus provided by the NZRU has given the five New Zealand franchises a solid basis for success. In recognition of this important addition to the NZRU's portfolio, visitors to the offices in Wellington are immediately greeted by the five franchise jerseys displayed together behind the reception area. It is a reflection of the era that these flashy, brightly colored icons of a new generation are flanked by All Black jerseys, which remain the most powerful image for sponsors.

Even though sponsorship interest is inevitably largely focused on the All Blacks, Jack Ralston has had little difficulty in marketing the Super 12 brand. It is a high-profile competition with an international flavor, which expands opportunities to share the dream with sponsors and the public at large. Moreover, its unique brand values led Ralston to look for a different type of sponsor for the Super 12. This caused McDonald's to move their sponsorship from the All Blacks to the Super 12, where they could appeal to the broader section of the population newly attracted to rugby entertainment. Ralston's aim is to build on New Zealanders' natural passion for the game:

> There's a whole raft of extended identities that have fallen out from this exercise. As a result, we can now legitimately appeal to both sexes. In a nutshell, we had to define clearly the values for our core products, the All Blacks and Super 12. We talk of products in a marketing sense in this office, but we don't use that publicly. We talk about teams and competitions.

The search for clarity and focus is far from being an academic exercise. The extensive deliberations around brand identity have seen sponsorship revenues and television rights totaling close to fifty million New Zealand dollars a year. This is a far cry from the early nineties, when annual income barely scraped into seven digits. Now the future of the professional game depends on this financial structure.

In addition to the All Blacks and Super 12, the NZRU maintains the National Provincial Championship (NPC), which is embraced by the premier clubs in the nation. Although the union does not control the club sides who compete for the NPC and the Ranfurly Shield, NPC rugby is still seen as fundamental to the brand portfolio. Coming from the heartland, the NPC fosters local pride and unrivaled fervor. The Brand Book distinguishes the NPC in the following manner: "NPC rugby is played in every major town in New Zealand. It is the rugby of old—raw, gritty, and real. It is the fundamental backbone of our game." Ralston attracts sponsors who reflect these values, where "It's the people, the passion, and the pride that's associated with being back on your own turf. For the NPC we clearly delineate those things." The Super 12 and NPC competitions attracted more than 1.2 million spectators in 1998 divided roughly equally between them, while almost half the nation could claim to have watched at least one Super 12 game on television. Traditional Ranfurly Shield games evoke passionate tribal instincts, similar to those of Super 12 finals.

Apart from the three major rugby brands, the NZRU also stewards several other teams. Most notable is the national women's rugby team, the Black Ferns, who in 1998 thrillingly captured the world championship title for the first time. The New Zealand Maori Team held an undefeated tour of England, Scotland, and Tonga, while the New Zealand Sevens Team won Commonwealth Gold in the 1998 games in Kuala Lumpur, as well as winning several other high-profile Sevens tournaments. In 1999, the New Zealand youth team took the Youth World Cup in Wales.

The NZRU has firmly embraced the challenge of the professional game by developing a number of highly successful brands, which have broadened the appeal of the game. The audience is larger, the revenues greater, and the rugby experience is more varied and robust.

From Small Blacks to All Blacks

The success of the youth team in particular is indicative of the NZRU's massive commitment to grassroots rugby. According to former All Blacks coach John Hart, "For rugby to continue to flourish, we can never lose sight of the grassroots requirement to cultivate the game and to encourage people to participate." Historically, the strength of the game has been at the local level, and the great players are forged here. John Hart's predecessor, Laurie Mains, explains the system.

> We have got huge drawing power from within the provinces, which nurtures talent for international rugby. At club level, competition in the first, second, and third divisions keeps tossing up players. Carlos Spencer, Christian Cullen, and Jonah Lomu all came from the lower divisions. While playing for a small club, someone in second division snatches them out of third division, and gives them a promotion. Then someone in first division drags them out of the second division. Nowhere else in the world has got this foundation, this structure that discovers, nurtures, and develops players.

Additionally, one of the most recent initiatives aimed at improving elite development is the Institute of Rugby, based at Massey University and cosponsored by the New Zealand Sports Foundation. Cameron Harland has no doubt that the institute is "the single most important commitment that this organization can offer professional rugby. Each year we focus on twenty young up-and-coming guys, so we're talking about development of the young elite." The cohort group go through nutrition education, media training, alcohol abuse recognition, budgeting, and, finally, career advice. The purpose is to prepare potential All Blacks to a level of professionalism worthy of the black jersey, including exposure to off-field duties the players are likely to encounter. Harland notes the meticulous planning that goes into the program.

> We really work hard to provide the right environment for these guys. This includes preparing them appropriately for the professional game. As future role models, they have to be able to handle themselves in the public glare, so we established a basic code of conduct for off the field as well as on it.

Little of this preparatory work with elite players has any meaning unless it sits inside a broader framework of player development, beginning with club and school rugby. Until the professional era, responsibilities for administration of the game were clearly understood and well segmented. In simple terms, the NZRU looked after provincial matters and the All Blacks, while the provincial associations dealt with the local club sides. At board and national office level it has, however, been recognized since 1995 that the benefits of the professional game must go well beyond a handful of stars at the top. Channeling funds into the amateur game has seen the unprecedented development of programs and initiatives designed to create the future of rugby in New Zealand.

The NZRU has created a fully integrated program known as the "rugby stairway," which can take the youngest players of the game, aged five, from Small Black rugby to All Blacks. There are seven intermediate steps along the way, each one with its own distinctive characteristics. The size of the field and length of playing time gradually increase as the children progress from junior and Super Small Black categories to teenage levels at school, alongside club and colt rugby. Simultaneously, the skill levels are also amplified at each step. The penultimate sixth step, before the All Blacks themselves, is the NPC and Super 12. Manager of Rugby Development Evan Crawford coordinates this extensive program. He can count on more than fifty regional development officers (RDOs) to work in conjunction with the provincial associations, who pay a portion of their salaries, and formally retain responsibility for club and player development. Some top-up money is also received from the Hillary Commission, a government-sponsored body that provides funding and policy direction for all sports played in New Zealand. Recently, the union has employed additional national RDOs who help to deploy the nonstop activities of the RDOs more effectively.

The RDOs' brief is to work primarily with the provinces, to deliver the development programs. Evan Crawford:

The RDOs' primary role is retention and recruitment of players, coaches, and administrators. The provinces sign a contract that advises the RDOs of the strategic direction and the job specification that we have outlined for them. They help write the program and deliver it. When the Small Black kids have their weigh-in with the RDOs, the parents who are going to be coaches take a simple course that talks about coaching ethics. The RDOs also give them free resources and as much assistance as they can.

To this end, Crawford has in his possession a plethora of manuals, diaries, pathways, handbooks, and guidebooks. Brightly colored coaching guides, invariably carrying the distinctive golden McDonald's arches, containing introductions to training methods, injury prevention techniques, and plain skill building, can be found all around his office. Apart from being intrinsically valuable in their own right, these documents exist for a more urgent purpose. A drop-off in the number of people playing rugby necessitated the development of a strategy to reenergize the nation's interest in rugby union. Although attracting new players and keeping them would seem to be the most appropriate response, it is also vital to maintain the commitment of young players as they progress up the rugby stairway. Creating the future for rugby union rests heavily on the ability of coaches to provide support and ongoing technical advice for emerging players. Crawford's problem, however, begins with sustaining continuity of coaches:

> It would be fair to say that the direction we've taken in the last two years in development is geared less toward recruitment and retention of players and more toward recruitment and retention of coaches. The belief is that if we get coaches and we educate them, we will attract players. At the same time, the players that we already have will be better catered to. In the past, it was just, "Go out there and get as many kids playing the game" as possible. We did that, but we didn't have the people on the ground to coach and help them; therefore the playing numbers dwindled.

Crawford confirms that although the Union has more than 8,000 coaches, it loses half of them each year. This means another 4,000 have to be recruited just to maintain existing coverage. This unsustainable drop-off led Crawford to concentrate on developing resources aimed at making the coaching role as attractive as possible.

> So what we're trying to do is educate them. We're trying to provide them with user-friendly resources so that anyone—mum, dad, sister, anyone—can take and adequately coach a little junior team. If they get a taste of it and like the experience, we can encourage them to progress through and become more advanced coaches.

In order to be proactive with grassroots rugby, the NZRU also set up a Provincial Advisory Group under the auspices of ex–All Black great Brian Lochore. This reviewed player progression from club rugby to higher provincial levels and reported in 1998. Historically, this might have been seen as provincial turf, but the NZRU's resourcing of the game through professional revenue has created a greater responsibility, and increased opportunity, to develop secure pathways for player enhancement and progression to the elite level. A club and junior rugby manager now oversees this aspect of the NZRU's grassroots work.

The developmental aspect of rugby, in terms of coherent policy toward coaching, player attraction, and progression up the stairway, has no realistic counterpart in the preprofessional era. In less than four years, the NZRU has systematically identified what it needs to do to create the future of New Zealand rugby.

Less well recognized, but still vital to the NZRU's inspirational dream, is a commitment to playing the game a certain way, with flair, and in an expressive, free-flowing manner. As rugby became ever more professional, the union had the foresight to establish a referee development program with a view to maintaining both a particular style of play and the quality of officiating. In rugby union, perhaps more than any other sport, the match referee has a keen influence on the manner in which individual games are played. Depending on the attitude a particular referee adopts, a game can be transformed either into an open running and passing spectacular of exciting rugby or a stop-start fragmented game punctuated frequently by the shrill sound of the official's whistle. According to Keith Lawrence, manager of referee development, "The board and David Moffett recognized that refereeing could no longer remain an adjunct to the game. It had to be part of the mainstream." Beginning in the early nineties, funds allocated to this aspect of rugby increased from a few tens of thousands of dollars to millions in 2000. Lawrence can call upon five full-time regional referee development officers who also work closely with coaches in the field, thus providing a coherent infrastructure. At the elite level, Lawrence points out, "If you are going to have a really good NPC or Super 12 Championship, you need more than one good referee at that level." As well as cultivating good referees on home turf, the NZRU has been at the forefront in bringing officials in from overseas, in recognition of the fact that certain refereeing styles are more influential in different rugby-playing regions, which in turn has a significant impact on the way the game is played in those areas. The manner and style in which rugby union is played is not the same the world over, and refereeing has a major part to play in this fragmentation.

> One of the interesting things we have done is to encourage visiting referees from the UK, South Africa, or wherever. Over time we have been able to get across the southern-hemisphere psyche of the game. We've looked after them very, very well, showing them all the sights of New Zealand, made available our best training facilities, and we've involved them in our referees' meetings, just so that they can have a presence. Generally speaking, they come around to our way of thinking. We don't do this necessarily just to suit the All Blacks; we do it because we have a really strong belief that rugby, if it is to be sustained, needs to be played in a free-flowing, positive fashion. Within New Zealand, we try to encourage our referees, throughout the grades, to take on this philosophy.

From the most unexpected of quarters, referee development, the NZRU has found an intriguing way to express the flavor of one of its inspirational dreams: to have the game played the way it should be played as an "entertaining product, recognized as a leading sports brand worldwide." Through its international links, it is also able to share the dream with those who manage the game on the field for its foreign competitors.

The Union Makes Us Strong

The developmental picture of the organization begins with a recent personnel initiative. Given the riches available, the NZRU has properly understood the importance of retaining the services of those inspirational players who in years past brought a nation to its feet. Without exception, every single person who works for the NZRU, either in Wellington or out in the field as an RDO or unpaid coach, understands the magic of the All Blacks. But without the continuity provided by those best placed to communicate hard-earned lessons, there is a danger of losing the sense of community that the All Blacks themselves have built across the generations. "Once an All Black, always an All Black" is a phrase well known to every New Zealander. With this simple statement in mind, the Union has astutely made key appointments to ensure that the organization benefits directly from the All Blacks' memory and experience.

Andy Dalton, currently the president of the NZRU, was an outstanding, inspirational All Black captain from 1981 to 1987 and now plays an important role as a figurehead for the NZRU. Dalton states:

> I attend functions from club level to board meetings to the international arena. This way I am able to promote rugby to players, supporters, and the public at large. On behalf of the NZRU, I also host visiting officials, sponsors, and visiting teams and personally address special functions and events.

This largely ceremonial position, which purposely does not carry any job description, puts Dalton in the position of visible representative of the NZRU's values. Sean Fitzpatrick, who was captain from 1992 until his retirement in 1997, is widely recognized as probably the greatest All Black captain of all time and one of the greatest players in the history of the game. He gained a reputation for being a consummate professional who, better than any other, maintained the spirit of All Blacks rugby. In his new role as consultant, he is uniquely placed to transfer his experience back into the NZRU's activities in a variety of organizational settings. He brings a perspective that is both inspirational and aspirational:

> What's the magic of the All Blacks? I loved the All Blacks because we were so successful. We created a wonderful environment to be involved in. We were the best at our job, the best rugby team in the world, ninety-nine percent of the time. As we ran out onto the field, we knew we'd worked harder than anyone else. We had a real resolve to make sure that we were going win.

Fitzpatrick now approaches the organizational challenge before him from a player's perspective:

> My primary objective is simply to create a good environment by accessing the necessary resources so that the players can be successful. Second, I'm responsible for creating a line of communication from the players to the board. I use my career experiences to connect with the new breed of professional player, which includes assisting to set up a players' association.

Fitzpatrick considerably enhances organizational continuity from field to office. Maintaining the presence of inspirational players as the NZRU's activities rapidly expand transfers legacies from one era to the next while fostering a strong sense of community in the organization at large.

Sustaining a robust community requires more than habitual exhortations from managers or coaches. "How, then, do the All Blacks constantly set up personal challenges for themselves?" was the question we asked of rugby superstar Johan Lomu. His response was crystal clear. "All the players—we hate coming second-best to ourselves."

This formulation neatly reengineers the sports mantra of exceeding personal best. It also lies at the heart of the NZRU. Personal responsibility and an overwhelming passion to improve and do better sum up the attitude and actions of the staff at the national office. The search for self-improvement on the rugby field is matched by those who manage the affairs of the union. David Moffett:

> We want people in here who are going to be self-starters, motivated to actually go off and do it. People here understand that we are not going to be just reactive. I encourage that. I don't want to run this business; I want my people to run it. We foster a culture of hard work, commitment, and passion—passion for everything we do, but specifically passion for the All Blacks. There are no half measures. If you're not passionate about the All Blacks, don't come and work here.

Jack Ralston sees Moffett as the catalyst responsible for many of the successes associated with the organization:

> I think you need to know the important part that Dave Moffett has played. He has the ability to get down to what needs to be done, rather than get lost in the woods. He has terrific vision of where this game needs to go and is a true agent of change. You can't underestimate what he's done in pulling the whole group together and in identifying the right organizational players. That's the story here—David's ability to attract the right people.

Given the relative infancy of the "new" NZRU organization, in conjunction with the board, Moffett was able to clarify the focus. Building new brands, solidifying older ones, and setting up new development programs has all been carried out at breakneck speed. There is within the NZRU an active attempt to make first plays in the industry. Executing projects as planned and then taking them as far as possible introduces discipline to each aspect of the NZRU's affairs. Six key measures of success are each addressed by a twenty-five-goal game plan against which progress is matched. This, and a sense of strong engagement, enables a level of intense and sustained peak performance to be achieved. Jack Ralston:

> Everybody has input, everybody is listened to, everybody is a valuable unit in here. It's the little things that count, like the Monday morning work-in-progress meetings where we all find out what's happening and where we are at, so that we are absolutely accountable for what we do. This makes our teams very fluid. We know each other's jobs pretty well, so that we take responsibility for the total result, not just our component of it. We love breaking down walls.

Conclusion

In less than half a decade, the NZRU has helped to usher in the professional era. The NZRU has established brand identities and equity, and developed all aspects of the grassroots amateur game at breathtaking speed. In terms of its overarching purpose, the organization quickly realized that following the advent of professionalism, the maintenance of the inspirational dream—to keep rugby union close to the heart of the nation—required the sharing of new dreams, additional to the traditions and long-standing values of the All Blacks. The NZRU is now a house of brands. Although the greatest imaginable challenge remains All Black supremacy in all international matches, the NZRU is also able to point to its other domestic and regional brands as evidence of its success. The focus now involves relentless brand building alongside extensive player and organizational development. Through these activities, the NZRU is creating the future—today.

10

Netball Australia: Finding Flow

"We both said exactly the same answer at the same time. Like somehow there's this mental link; it's quite amazing. I think we all just learn; it's not taught to us. It's intuition."

– CARLEY BAKER,
NATIONAL MARKETING MANAGER, NETBALL AUSTRALIA

In netball you must pass the ball or shoot within three seconds or incur a penalty. There are no time-outs, and few set plays. As a consequence netball is a fast, free-flowing sport, that requires supreme athleticism, agility and anticipation, consisting of four quarters of fifteen minutes each, with brief intervals between quarters. As a spectator spectacle, it has an attractive media profile because of its intense action. Netball has a higher number of active participants than any other sport in the Commonwealth.

Karen Miller, Australia 21 elite player explains the magic:

I saw the World Championships on TV and from then on I became very involved in netball. They were winners. When you are a kid growing up you always want to play for Australia, and once you start at the club and district level you can see the progression from there. We play because we love the sport. I have been playing since I was six years old. Netball was within our family I suppose, and that's really why I chose it. When you are ten you put a whistle in your mouth and you start umpiring; when you are thirteen or fourteen you start coaching. I think Australia is ahead of anywhere in the world in players, coaching, administration; everything all comes together and that's what makes us World Champions.

World Champions

Netball Australia has globally dominated this 100-years-old-sport for more than three decades. The Australian Netball Team has won eight of the ten World Championships since their commencement in 1963,[1] and won the inaugural Commonwealth Games gold medal in 1998. They are the champions of one of the world's most popular women's sports, with more than seven million participants in forty-five countries around the globe. The team's last minute one point victory over New Zealand in the 1999 World Championships brought both nations to a standstill. 'Why don't you have a brand name for your elite team, like the New Zealand Silver Ferns netball team, or the British Lions rugby union team?' we asked National Executive Director Pam Smith. She replied, 'We do, its World Champions!' They have achieved this record, the best of the international teams in our research, because they have long understood how to organize for peak performance.

Australian netball provides participants with the opportunity to excel and achieve recognition in an exciting and entertaining sport that attracts huge public interest through a range of escalating competitive challenges in club, regional, state, national and international championships. It also encourages lifelong participation in a range of different activities within the local, regional, state, national and global netball communities, including administration, coaching and umpiring.

Netball Australia's focus is to develop the netball brand as Australia's number one participation sport, both nationally and internationally. Competition for the elite athlete, both in relation to other

[1] In the remaining two World Championships they were placed second.

women's sports such as hockey and in relation to non-sporting activities, is intense – it is vital to ensure that new generations of players are both attracted to and remain involved with the game. The recruitment and development of potential elite players provides the foundation for achieving the enduring challenge of remaining World Champions.

Recruitment and development require infrastructure. With over 375,000 registered competition netball players in Australia, the demands placed on central co-ordination are acute, but because Australian netball is organized federally there is only a small central group of professional staff at the All Australian Netball Association Ltd (Netball Australia) national office. Each netball association in the states and territories of Australia is itself incorporated – they are completely separate legal entities with considerable autonomy from Netball Australia. States, territories, regions and local clubs maintain their own vigorous identities, as evidenced by separate web sites, brands and sponsors. All the states have their own professional staff who make their own sponsorship, events and marketing arrangements, independent of the national body.

Independence breeds fierce inter-club and inter-state competition, innovation and diversity of coaching and playing traditions. This intense domestic rivalry is the driving force behind Netball Australia's global dominance. Inter-dependence comes into play when external challenges need to be faced. The states and territories meet twice annually in the form of the National Council for administrative and governance purposes. The Council operates with sixteen members, two from each association, and has a significant measure of stability in the membership. A separate board of eight people, elected by the Council on the criteria of skills and passion for the sport, together with an appointed National Executive Director, has overall governance responsibility for Netball Australia. 'We have a proactive board,' explains National President Sue Taylor; 'It's a mostly female board. All debate is open, frank and to the point. We are all busy people with other lives and can't afford to 'pussyfoot' around.' Pam Smith, National Executive Director, attributes their enduring success to strong leadership:

I honestly believe that the major reason for Australian netball success has been the fact that it has been run and led by women. Business is controlled by the old boys' network. Our female athletes are the most successful in the world, but they don't have the same social standing as their male counterparts. Because we have had to struggle in this difficult environment we have got to put in that much more effort and try that little bit harder to get our piece of the profile, but we know we can do it. We've got the perseverance.

Pam Smith is the only appointed director of the board. As well as being a full voting member she is also the driving force behind the national office that operates the business. The board's brief is to develop netball as a global sports entertainment brand, while remaining true to the dream of grass-roots netball as the foundation of elite player potential.

Pam Smith explains that the basis for working together rests on infrastructure:

Netball is just like a central government structure, with the three tiers of federal, state and local government. We have a national approach to a range of things: overall branding, elite player development, sponsored national and international competitions, playing rules, coaching and umpiring accreditation, and curricula. Activities more specific to the states include coaching and development, scouting and regional competitions. And then the local associations and clubs are the final level of operation – they are the grass-roots of the netball community.

The central organization strives for close liaison between all facets of netball administration, from national down to club level, with a balance between being entrepreneurial and working for the common good. Despite the potential for conflicting interests to be reflected in the activities of the board and the national office, the organization has created a powerful community that is marked by inclusion. Netball Australia is the only organization that insisted on beginning its interview schedule with us as a team, before spinning off into individual meetings. During the group meeting, seven members of the board, national office and the state associations gave commentary on every aspect of the organization. According to Pam Smith, unity in the face of considerable diversity depends on a passion for the sport and a steely determination to employ a wide range of skills in the most effective manner possible. These elements, she argues, provide for automatic commitment.

Pam Smith herself is a key inspirational player who is responsible for effective co-ordination at the 'center'. A no-nonsense person, she relies heavily on her ability to create leverage through an extensive network of relationships. People know very well that conflict and disagreements are not going to unhinge her:

> In the overall scheme of things, everybody works together. Our organization is about a team sport, and the philosophy of being in a team extends off the court as well. So, we're all committed to a philosophy of collaboration. Nor are we backward in coming forward in telling one another what we think. I separate personal issues from professional issues – I have people that I can work with and have fun with, as well as have a large disagreement with them. I don't have time for getting back at people – I think that stuff is rubbish.

On the more personal level, she describes her style:

> Most of the people who I work particularly well with on the board would say that my background in politics has been a bonus for the sport. Another strength is that I don't get overly concerned when people disagree. I certainly get frustrated at times, but I'm not the sort of person who goes home and tosses and turns, and worries about what's going to happen the next day. I believe that's just negative energy, and wasted time. If a decision's been made, I'm quite happy to live with it, even when it's the wrong decision,

because once you've made up your mind, you've gone ahead and done something, there's no point worrying about it. It's too late!

As the link between the national office and the board, Pam Smith has to tread a fine line between operational activities and issues of a broader strategic nature. One of the most important relationships that she nurtured is between herself and the President of Netball Australia and Board Chairperson, Sue Taylor. Pam Smith:

As a friend, I don't think I will ever lose track of Sue, probably because we think in a similar way. She's bloody stubborn. I know where I stand with her. We can totally disagree on an issue, but I feel very comfortable in putting my point of view forward without fear of being ridiculed. She's blunt, she forthright, she's intelligent, and she's not motivated by a desire for personal glory. She's on the board because she believes she can contribute to a sport that she's been involved in all her life, and she's got a passion for it.

Peak performance is about enduring inspirational relationships. Netball Australia has benefited from a succession of presidents who have provided both stability and direction, and sustained and energized the dream, from the grass-roots up. Pam Smith says that Netball Australia has a 'legacy of inspirational administrators such as Eunice Gill, Lorna McConchie, Gwen Benzie, Marg Pewtress and Joyce Brown'. Sponsorship, gate receipts and related marketing activity provide funds for the elite, but like all sports netball is largely dependent on a volunteer workforce at the grass-roots. This combination of volunteers and inspirational administrators, many of whom have themselves been elite netballers, make up the administration of the Australian netball community.

The headquarters of Netball Australia is based in a nineteenth-century character-house, nestled within the concrete high rises of Paramatta NSW. The outward calm of the building belies an energized, colorful interior, where a sense of enjoyment and fanatical enthusiasm prevails. Fun sustains and is sustained by a peak performance work ethic, which is in turn sustained by the power of community belonging, and a potent sense of purpose. Carley Baker, National Marketing Manager, encapsulates the spirit of the place. She explains that when selecting staff, 'We are looking for work ethics; we know the type of people who will fit into our working environment.' Somewhat diminutive alongside the elite squad, she more than makes up for this with an effervescent and dynamic presence which enables her to sustain a schedule of activity that would exhaust most. Conversation is frequently disrupted by the mobile phone, which cannot be switched off. She is the glue. A missed call cannot be contemplated:

> Some days I think to myself, I would love to go home to bed after we have been on tour for two weeks. We have missed two weekends, a public holiday and we are all back in the office ready to go again. You know we have got to get this thing done and you know it doesn't matter how many people say, 'Take your holidays, don't come back from your holidays, switch your mobile phone off.' You know that at the end of the day you are accountable for that, and your work habits are so strong that you don't want your reputation to go down at all.

As one of a small number of professional staff in the national office, Baker occupies the hot seat. It is her responsibility to deliver a viable product for public and media consumption. Much of her work is based externally, in particular she has to work closely with the states and their different marketing campaigns. For Baker, this is all about 'accountability in terms of picking up our numbers – from sponsors to game attendance to the television audience'. To achieve this she holds 'sit-down marketing meetings' with the states, where common national themes for marketing and events are established. At the same time, she works hand-in-glove with both media and sponsors to ensure maximum coverage of the sport. In a competitive industry, Baker wins plaudits all around. Telstra Executive Adam Jeffreys, who is responsible for Telstra's sponsorship agreement with the Women's

Hockey Association, recognizes that the netball marketing machine is one of the best in all of Australian sport. It is no surprise that Pam Smith characterizes her marketing guru as 'Ms million miles an hour!' Baker's work with the states, media and sponsors means that she also plays a key role with the national squad. She is the conduit through which much of the organization's activities are communicated to the team. Sponsors develop campaigns around key players: 'Our twelve elite players go out into schools and do information sessions; we have shopping center appearances; we use their faces on our marketing and on our cardboard cut-outs. We send them to business lunches and other celebrity events.'

She works so closely with the elite players that the boundaries between different areas of responsibility begin to blur. She is no longer simply in charge of marketing. She is respected by the players. She knows when and when not to approach them for media work, or the circumstances under which it is possible to co-ordinate the autographing of uniforms, match-balls and the like. More importantly, she monitors closely the mood and general condition of the players:

> On a recent tour we didn't get the chance to sit down to ask the players if they were happy with everything. A few days after the test matches were over I gave them an open book with some pens and said, 'Spit out whatever you want to spit out.' They are over the moon with this consultation process, because we take on board their concerns and address them.

Baker describes her activity within the organization as providing a 'mental link'. Pam Smith is more effusive about her role: 'She's brilliant. Sponsors love her.' Nowadays, Baker invariably travels with the team on tours abroad. Smith's greatest fear is that her marketing manager will be 'pinched from me.'

Current captain of the Australian Netball Team Vicki Wilson has been a key factor in Australia's supremacy for over fifteen years. She is a brilliant, ruthless shooter and a fast, articulate speaker. As one of the greatest players of all time she is well placed to define the qualities an effective sports administrator needs:

> Good administrators can understand a player and think like a player, but can then step out of that environment and know exactly where they are heading as an administrator. I believe that a good administrator can come in and mix with the players so that there is good communication, and then return to do the job they are supposed to do.

Organizational excellence creates and sustains the winning tradition. Chris Burton, National Director of Umpiring, explains that countries outside the top three, including England where the game began 100 years ago, are far behind in terms of their administrative infrastructure: 'New Zealand and Australia are miles ahead; South Africa is not far behind.' Although the UK has the largest number of school-age netball players, it lacks centralized playing areas, cohesive networks and well-co-ordinated local, regional and national competitions. As a consequence, interest in the game falls off beyond school level. Pam Smith:

> Other countries don't appear to have the same access to sports sciences or realize the importance of rest, recovery and diet. Their coaching fraternities do not appear to have the same commitment to best practices. Our coaches look at a whole range of innovations in other sports. For example, we have people who run ball skills and eye-handling co-ordination skills for rugby foot-ball. Our coaches work with soccer players to assist their co-ordination. We actually cross-pollinate with other sports and take their best bits and pieces. Its more about organization and knowledge than it is about money, although I would love to have the massive money that England get from their lottery.

The Netball Australia infrastructure 'works for the grass-roots, which eventually comes through and feeds into the Australia team', explains Liz Ellis, Australia netball team Goal Keeper. The infrastructure creates the future through tremendous depth. Children aged five to seven are taught motor-based skills and activities through the nationwide 'Fun Net' program, while 'Netta Netball', a modified version of the game with smaller goal posts and ball, provides friendly competition for ages eight to ten. Graded competition commences from age eleven. Club, regional and national competitions provide a staircase of graded challenges for junior athletes. This hones their skills, giving them ongoing opportunities to exceed their personal best. 'The 21 & Under development program for our younger players ensures that they have had world-class international exposure prior to making it into the national team,' says Sue Taylor. The elite players are closely involved in development. Vicki Wilson:

> One hundred percent of A grade players have coached; all of them have coached a team or can go in and take coaching clinics on their own. Through coaching and umpiring you can analyze games better. You can see where the game is breaking down and you can whisper in someone's ear, 'Hey why don't you try this or that?' You can analyze the opposition and work out where their strengths lie. And when you umpire you get a better knowledge of the rules and you can think quickly and know what the call is going to be.

Coaching in all walks of life develops the coach as much as the coached.

The shift in elite netball from sport to entertainment flowed from the 1997 Netball Australia partnership with the Commonwealth Bank of Australia. The domestic inter-state competition was redeveloped into the National Netball League (NNL), which competes for the Commonwealth Bank Trophy (CBT). This institutional change of focus was designed to increase media coverage and sponsorship opportunities for Netball Australia. Pam Smith:

The NNL gives us a netball elite season with a televised profile which starts in April and continues through until September. As a consequence we get requests to be part of other television magazine and sports shows, and the newspapers ring us for comment on sporting and social issues beyond netball.

The new league brought new sponsors, eight new teams, each with bird brand names – Firebirds, Kestrels, Phoenix, Orioles, Sandpipers, Swifts, Thunderbirds, Ravens – eye-catching new uniforms, and a format designed to maximize entertainment and fan appeal. Logos and team colors enable fans to identify easily their team. Pam Smith:

We have a centralized approach to our National Netball League for the Commonwealth Bank Trophy. We own all the logos and marks and we secure sponsors for the teams, pay their airfares and uniforms, and pay the teams to be in the competition.

This continuously competitive domestic environment for Australia's elite players provides them with probably the best domestic competition in the world,' says National President Sue Taylor. 'This makes sure our top players are exposed to tough on-court challenges on a regular basis. Carley Baker is now trying to build netball into our sponsors' advertising. Someone like Fisher and Paykel can buy so much space on television.' 'The administrators are doing a great job getting sponsorship then allowing the players to get out on court and show their wares internationally as well as at home,' confirms Lisa Beehag, Assistant National Coach.

The CBT is a high profile competition which gives young players the opportunity to worship and learn from their heroes, and it provides career pathways in coaching, playing, administration, umpiring, public relations and marketing. Women's team sports do not feature highly in the global market for sponsorship and media coverage; the NNL marks a significant breakthrough. Vicki Wilson dreams of seeing women's team sports offering top quality live entertainment on a par with men's sport, arguing that, 'It's even better in the flesh, like alive. Nothing better than coming out to a live game. It is fast, it is exciting, and we are skilful, and we are athletic, and we do sweat!'

Fisher and Paykel, the innovative domestic appliance manufacturers, have sponsored international competition with the other global top teams, New Zealand and South Africa. Carley Baker:

> If you weren't aware that Fisher and Paykel has been involved with Netball Australia, then all of a sudden this massive truck delivers your washing machine, and its got three elite netball players throwing a ball on the side of the truck; its going to hit you really, really quickly. Women have purchasing and buying power. Sponsors see netball as a prime medium to get their messages out, alongside our message encouraging women to get involved with netball. We give the sponsors a vehicle to get their brand and product into the market place. They use the profile of our players, our logo and our branding to align themselves with us.

John Bongard, White ware Manager for domestic appliance manufacturers Fisher & Paykel:

> Families are central to the Netball Australia brand. By associating with the highest levels of netball we install the Fisher & Paykel brand as standing for the families of Australia. Fisher & Paykel thereby gains connection to a huge following of netball fans and we are seen to be a company that supports women's sport. The relationship we have with Netball Australia is great. The officials are enthusiastic and co-operative and the players are great ambassadors for Australia, their sport and their sponsors.

The CBT and international competition together create a demanding annual schedule which builds to a crescendo in World Championship or Commonwealth Games years. In addition to the NNL there is a National Championship sponsored by Qantas in which the eight states and territories compete, which further intensifies domestic competition.

The Australian Institute of Sport (AIS) has done much to promote the success of Australian athletes. Netball has had a residential program at the AIS since 1981, which is aimed at assisting junior elite athletes to achieve their peak potential, with training based on the skills and tactics used by the national squads. The large majority of Australia's championship team members are graduates of the AIS. Wilson explains the importance of the AIS in the development of the netball community:

> I believe that the Institute program played a big part in making elite netball like being part of the family. You left home and you had to get on with the other players. You lived with these people for two years and so you got to know them really well, and you became close.

The AIS has recently decentralized and now provides youth training throughout Australia. In collaboration with Netball Australia it gives younger players the opportunity to participate in international competition. Pam Smith: 'For example, the South Australian AIS may come to New Zealand and play some regional matches. Or we may send a group to England made up of the Australia 21 Team and AIS scholarship holders.

Netball Australia has nurtured its infrastructure to develop an enduring sense of community which sustains the netball dream of providing a lifetime of opportunities for achievement and recognition, and satisfies the players' social needs. Vicki Wilson has a unique perspective on the Netball Australia community:

> You enjoy others' company, and there have been some wonderful friendships made over the years; there have been great times on tour, there have been funny times and sad times. We experienced the highs and the lows, and if you did that on your own I think you would be quite lonely. But when you can do it with a bunch of people who are out there and trying to achieve something, these memories stick with you for a long time. Going out to achieve

something that is common to us all unites us even closer, even though we come from very different backgrounds.

The unity of the elite squad is reflected in the organization as a whole, and in the teams and clubs throughout Netball Australia.

Like all elite sports, netball is intensely competitive. Ensuring that individual competition does not destroy community is essential to maintaining the magic. Player selection provides a good example. 'They used to announce team selection at the end of a training weekend,' explains Carley Baker:

On a Sunday they might finish training at 2 p.m. and go home or go into the changing room for a shower. They would be back at 3 p.m. and the list would be read in alphabetical order. If they weren't in the team and had been dropped after being in the sport for say nine years they would be devastated. So in the last two years they have felt that players would prefer to ring someone such as myself. This gives them a few hours to think it through, and then they ring the coach later on for a discussion about their career.

According to Vicki Wilson, 'All the players are given the opportunity to be involved in advising on the selection process. They run it by us and we have a vote as to how we want to do it.' It is a matter of trust, respect and dignity.

Lisa Beehag, Assistant National Coach, describes how fun and practical jokes relieve tension and foster community:

I played for New South Wales for ten years. We always had a lot of fun and practical jokes, but we also knew the time to get serious. You have got to have the skills, but there are plenty of athletes who have the skills. It is finding the extra that make the difference, and I think fun and enjoyment are two high priorities.

Community doesn't mean the players live in each other's pockets. Liz Ellis, National Team Goal Keeper:

> One comment made to us a few years ago was that we don't spend a lot of time together. We sometimes go out to different places and do different things, whereas you often saw the Kiwis doing a lot of things together. That was perceived to be the best way, but I think this team has got so many strong personalities that if we spent too much time together it could damage community.

Netball Australia shares the dream with participants and players, spectators and sponsors through community, combined with a passion to win and celebration of achievement. The 1995 World Championship earned the Australian Netball Team a ticker-tape parade through the center of Sydney, the first time an Australian women's sport had received such an accolade. Carley Baker experienced the magic 'over in Birmingham in 1995; after the match I went into the changing rooms; the celebrations were just amazing; it's something that will stay with me for the rest of my life'. PPOs celebrate peak performance whenever and wherever it occurs. Celebration and tradition help to create the magic, and success flows from success. Vicki Wilson describes the importance of tradition:

> Even when we have a change in the team experienced players remain who can teach a little bit of history of the game. I think it's important that we teach about the history, inject some traditions into the game, and value what's happened in the past. It's all about the magic and significance of wearing the green and gold uniform.

International competitions such as the Commonwealth Games, the World Championships and the Fisher and Paykel International Series create a global focus. Netball Australia co-operates with other countries to build the Netball industry. For example, Jill Mc[...] National Coach, regularly travels to Asian and the P[...] to share the netball dream, help identify ta[...]

clinics. This expands both the reach of the game and the commercial opportunities. Netball Australia then competes intensely within the larger arena it helped to create.

The expanded context provides new challenges for the athletes. Lisa Beehag, confirms the importance of renewed challenges in maintaining the focus necessary for peak performance: 'For the older players in particular the Commonwealth Games have given them a new focus, a new lease of life. It's a new carrot dangled in front of their eyes.' Netball Australia went on to win the Gold medal in the 1998 Commonwealth Games. Embedded in human nature is a desire for renewed purpose, and renewed reason for the sustained effort and concentration which lead to peak performance. Pam Smith:

> In 1999, when South Africa were soundly beaten in all three tests of their New Zealand tour, their coach came out with the statement that it was apparent that New Zealand are the team to beat. That comment was relayed back to our team, who said, 'Well, OK what was the biggest winning margin between New Zealand and South Africa?' Somebody says 45, and the next thing our team comes out with is a 62-goal win.

Peak performance requires focus.

Jill McIntosh notes that, 'The players leave problems off the court and focus on what they have to do.' It's vital to concentrate upon the actions necessary for peak performance, not upon the result require Carley Baker describes the absolute respect for focus that exis tch days:

> s have a focus on a match day that is so intense; blicity. There is lots of respect. Players don't rms – they go on the game court, train, go home and sleep, go to a team meeting h. That's pretty much the secret for

The same intensity exists throughout the organization.

Vicki Wilson describes how individual focus has to fuse into team focus:

> You have to focus on your own performance and you have to focus on the team as well; you have your own goals and you have team goals. You focus on the game at hand; or you can even break it up into each quarter of the game and then every five minutes. On the way to the game you are imagining what you want to do and how others will react when you first step onto the courts.

And so it is with all teams, on and off the court, both in sports and in business organizations. Individual performance lifts the team performance, and the team lifts the individual. Exceeding personal best and exceeding organizational best go hand in hand.

In netball a 'flow on' is one movement where you catch the ball, step and throw to make forward movement within the context of the 'less than three seconds' and 'no running with the ball' rules. It is a fundamental element of court craft and is the basis for a fast-paced, flowing game. The pass has to be almost intuitive, using peripheral vision. 'They work on peripheral vision a lot,' explains Team Manager Bronwyn Roberts. 'They will do a flow on and the coach will pull out a color and the player has to throw to that color coming down really fast.' 'We work on our skills, getting the flow pattern in the team,' says Jill McIntosh. The game is all about court craft, vision and intuition. The art is to create as many leads as possible. Vicki Wilson: 'Lots of things happen off the ball, because I created space for others. On the court the game is so fast I can't control what's going on.' Intuition does not just happen – it comes through intensive and creative training. Intuitive team flow substitutes for set plays and formal structure, and is predicated on focus.

We observed this intuitive flow first hand during two international matches between Australia and New Zealand. Bronwyn Roberts helped us to understand what we saw:

If you look at Vicki Wilson, as soon as she gets the ball she doesn't even look and quite often her passes are gone; she has a vision of what is happening on the court. Some of those passes they give each other, like the ones Vicki sends someone under the post, part player' hair. She wouldn't do that if she didn't think the players was going to get it. They do miss occasionally, but there is no way she would do it if she didn't think they were going to catch it. It involves a huge respect for each other's ability, not as a person, but as a netballer. It wouldn't flow if I thought, 'My god I am not going to throw to her because she will drop it.' If team members respect each other as players, if they know that when they throw the ball it will be caught, and that it doesn't matter how hard or how difficult it is to catch, then you will have a great, free-flowing team. This is what our team has got.

As Team Manager, Roberts's task is to ensure that the team is able to concentrate exclusively on its court performance, thereby sustaining focus. She proudly boasts a unique heritage within netball. Her mother played on the very first Australian national side and Roberts was herself a member of the national team. In a career which has included stints as state coach in the South Australia league and marketing responsibilities in the national office she is well placed to reflect on how the organization pulls together. Relationships and respect are nurtured over time:

It's that word team, isn't it? But I believe the real word is actually respect. This is something that you can't create by trying to bond over a weekend of raft-building. I just don't believe that you can go out on a weekend and bond in a meaningful way. It doesn't work like that. Bonding happens when the team, and by that I mean organization, builds respect over time. You don't have to be someone's friend but you need to have confidence that if you throw them the ball, you know that the job is going to get done. Respect takes time.

This flow state between players enables them to exceed personal best. Liz Ellis says that, 'When you become confident it instills confidence in someone else. The mindset is that we are going to play a perfect game.' Another elite team member, Sharelle McMahon agreed: 'Being put on the team certainly lifted my performance one notch because I felt that I had to lift to another level to be on a par with them.' Jill McIntosh:

> There is a noticeable difference in the performance of some of them in the national league teams compared with when they put on the green and gold. Their performances lift. I think that is because there is a real respect and trust and belief among the players. They know they have done it before and that they will succeed. They have an overwhelming belief that, no matter what happens, even if they have a bad quarter and are down, that they are going to come through and win.

The same sense of mutually reinforced confidence and purpose pervades the organization, and enables organizational best to be exceeded. Former Australia 21 player and Netball Australia marketing team member Karen Miller provides a further illustration: 'You just got on the plane when you had to and you had the gear; we looked like the most professional team out there and that's probably what made us win in the end; all the fine details that went into creating the big picture. Carley Baker is responsible for much of the fine detail:

> My role with the team manager prior to a tour is to attend to every last detail, to ensure that it is all perfect. What size uniforms do you want? How many balls do you want? How many sports drinks do you want? Now I want every player wearing this shirt, this body suit and this bib. All interviews after the match must be done in bibs, with signage on them, no T-shirts, no hats. So much ordering and preparation are required to make an international event run. But it's informal, very informal, and the players like that.

Organizational flow is dependent on everyone in the team. Wilson explained that when selecting new team members she looks for confident, quick thinking players who are smart both on and off the court:

> We look for people who can contribute something special and fit into the team. Your off-court harmony has an effect on your on-court performance, and if you come to a point where you can't make up your mind you take the one that's happy go lucky.

She believes that peak performance depends on speed, agility, flair, intuition and creativity and affirms: 'We have got a well-educated team; take the creativity out of someone's play and the game no longer becomes open and fast flowing.' Jill McIntosh elaborated:

> If you train with someone often enough you know where they will go in certain situations. You don't know exactly where they will be at a given time, but you know how they think and therefore can judge where they are likely to go. And we can get the ball there ahead of them so they have time and space to react.

Creativity is founded in diversity. 'There is a high degree of diversity in coaching styles,' says Karen Miller,

> Australians like to play a fast, quick game and like a slope pass, whereas in Caribbean countries they have a big, loopy, jumpy sort of game. We don't want a systematic team, like, 'The ball has to go here; oh, my God the ball hasn't gone there, what do we do now!'

Intuition and communal thinking substitute for systems.

The Australian game is developed on creativity and flair and has 'changed heaps since 1985', according to Vicki Wilson:

It's a lot faster; it's a lot stronger. Even this year there is a lot more game sense; a lot more goals have been scored than last year because of the speed of the game. There is an intellectual component to the innovation. In fact there was a time when eight out of ten Australian players were teachers.

Creativity is assisted by 'The strong rivalry that exists between the state and institute coaches, who all have unique coaching styles – this adds to the strength of competition nationally,' explained Sue Taylor. The domestic experimentation engendered by this mixture of diversity and competition has strengthened the national elite squad. Many organizations fear that internal competition will be a waste of financial resources, but they should not. Internal competition strengthens skills, allows the best to come forward, and avoids the waste of the most valuable resource of all – human creativity.

Vicki Wilson believes that 'If you can improve the creativity of your own performance, you will lift the whole team's performance. Then you know when you have really got that rhythm happening that makes you go further.' Vicki remembered that to lift her overall game, 'One year in State training I decided I was going to shoot left handed the whole way through.' She advocates:

Have a go, take a risk, take a risk. I would be mad if you get pulled for a held ball; you have got to have a go . . . I took a risk, but it didn't pay off. If it had come off it would have been sensational, but I will learn from that. Take a risk; why not. It's OK if it doesn't work. You have so many leads coming at you. You have got to be court smart, switched on, with great vision – a thinking player. Creativity on the court is essential. Once you start taking that out of someone's play the game no longer is open and fast flowing. We all have different ideas, but we have a common goal of doing something well.

Game-breaking ideas within the team and within the organization flourish in an environment where, diversity, creativity, risk taking, and the freedom to fail and learn are the norm. A balance of experienced and new players needs to be maintained, both to prevent the repetition of prior failures and to ensure diversity.

In Netball Australia we found the essential elements of all great teamwork, founded in organizational flow:

- Respect for, and trust in, the abilities of other team members, built up over time
- Fast-paced, intuitive understanding of each other's needs
- Confidence and belief in success
- Passing the ball or information, so that team members have time and space to use it effectively
- Being there when needed
- Everyone contributes game-breaking ideas

Team flow, so evident on the netball court, is also manifest within the organization. Players undertake what needs to be done, when it needs to be done, based on an intuitive understanding which derives from community, empathy, respect for each others roles and abilities, close working relationships and a passionate commitment to a shared purpose. The concept of peripheral vision, derived from the netball court, can be applied to organization more generally, and it can be trained for. Organizational peripheral vision implies an awareness of events, actions and others' needs at the limits of the senses. Peak players notice details, from the visitor who looks lost or a torn carpet, to a step missing from a project game plan. And they attend to those issues there and then.

Conclusion

Highly focused teams that are passionate about what they do can consistently achieve peak performance. From Netball Australia we learned to understand the roles that focus, intuition, respect for other team members, intense awareness, harmony, rhythm, calm and poise, play in the achievement of peak performance. The complete involvement of all participants in challenging tasks for which they are fully prepared and confident are essential elements in peak performance, while trust, respect for other players and an intuitive understanding of each other's needs derived from a common focus and longevity of relationships lead to organizational flow experiences – commonly shared experiences of peak performance.

Australian Cricket Board: The Storytelling Game

"This is a storytelling game. That's why it appeals to corporate leaders. They may not go to a cricket game, every day, they may not watch every minute's play, but they follow it all the time. It's the cleverness of the game, the subtlety, the strategy and, in particular, the nuances of a Test match which provide intellectual satisfaction. Seeing the sheer majesty of a superb batsman at the crease, coping well with adversity – it's an ethos which is second to none in my view. The Australian Cricket Board is helping to tell the story of cricket. If we continue to do this well, we shall stand the test of time."

– DENIS ROGERS,
CHAIRMAN OF THE AUSTRALIAN CRICKET BOARD

'He's out!' So reads one of the most famous newspaper billboards in all of sporting history. Understanding the precise meaning of this exclamation is no problem for the last three generations born in the British Commonwealth. These two words can only refer to one man. It's Bradman. The mere mention of his name instantly conjures up a magical aura which compels cricket lovers of all nationalities to wonder why one man was blessed with natural talent and skill beyond reasonable comprehension. Each sporting code has its great players. Their performances, perhaps over a season of play and even over a lifetime, put them on a different plane from the journeymen and women on the pitch. Yet Bradman's feats do not even belong in this category. No sensible person would suggest that any future Test player could surpass Bradman's place in cricket history. Geoff Marsh, ex Test player and ex coach of the Australian Test and one-day international sides has no doubts about the importance of Bradman's contribution to the game of cricket:

The bottom line is that Sir Donald Bradman is the greatest cricketer who ever lived. When I was playing in the Test team, we were a young side and we'd never actually met the 'Don', and all we wanted to do was touch him. We wanted him to come into the dressing room, and just shake his hand and we'd have been very happy with that. However, Bob Simpson, our team coach, asked him to come and have a meal with us. It was the best of nights. I sat next to him. He was drinking red wine, just as I was. And we just talked and talked about the wonderful game of cricket. For him to pass on those experiences . . . it was like being in a dream world.

Non-cricket lovers puzzled by the brevity of the famous 1933 newspaper billboard may now surmise that the phrase, 'He's out,' is commentary on the utter improbability of the event. While batting, the possibility of his dismissal always seemed distant and highly unlikely. Without hesitation, it can be said that the well-worn phrase, 'We shall never see the likes of him again,' truly applies to Bradman. Geoff Marsh confirms that Bradman was not constrained by normal limits:

We had him down for a seminar in 1997. I asked him to come down and meet the players so that they could ask him a few questions. One of the questions I asked was, 'What sort of things did you do when you were out of form?' And he looked at me and he said, 'I can't answer that.' And I asked him why. He said, 'Well, when I played, I was never out of form.' You know, he's a really down-to-earth sort of guy.

In Australia, the Don's legendary playing feats of the thirties and forties, and the presence of inspirational players of the most extraordinary kind, fuelled a passion to both play and dominate the game of cricket.

The origins of the Australian game are firmly located at club level, and local cricket continues to this day to be the bedrock of international success. Rod Marsh, who currently heads the elite Commonwealth Bank Cricket Academy in Adelaide, first kept wicket for Australia in 1971, and went on to make ninety-seven Test appearances. He explained to us the pivotal role of the local club side in the Australian game:

> Club cricket, there's no doubt about it, is the major reason for the strength of Australian cricket. It must have been fantastic in the old days, in the Bradman era. He only played fifty-two Test matches, and those spanned twenty years. When he came home from an overseas Test series there wasn't a one-day international program to play in. In Australia, there might be a Test match series every two years, and only a few Sheffield Shield games, so the rest of the summer he'd be playing club cricket. A young player walks off the street into his local club, and all of a sudden he's playing with Bradman. On his first day, he's playing with Bradman! No wonder Australian cricket's going strong when that sort of thing used to happen.

Marsh also points out that in the modern game Test players still operate at the local club level. Even though the game is now professional, with million-dollar incomes earned by the top Test players, it is still feasible for the Australian captain to find himself at the community roots of the game. Patrick Keane, former ACB Media Manager, believes that the benefit of this type of playing structure is that it offers encouragement to aspire to greater heights in the game:

> When an Australian player comes back into his grade side and trains with his grade club, there are thirty or forty other young

players who watch what this guy does and want to be like him. They watch how he trains, and how he prepares. It's a small window on the highest level for them. He is a role model who shows them what the standard is like.

With a larrikin-like smile, Rod Marsh, a Test legend in his own right, revealed to us what the game really looks like from the inside:

> Club cricket is a reflection of life. Just because you're the Australian captain you can't sit on your arse in the dressing room and do nothing. On a Saturday afternoon, if it starts to rain, he helps the rest of the mob put on the canvas. Your team mates won't let you get away with it anyway. And you always want to be at club training, because that's where we all started, and you never miss a club game if you can help it. People from the local area play at the club, people who you went to school with. The strength of the ACB has to be club cricket, because ultimately, through the states, that is where the delegates come from.

These evocative descriptions of club cricket, although seemingly culled from another era, reveal the foundations of the ACB's sustained strength. Echoing similar sentiments, Sir Donald Bradman explained to us that Australia's long-term dominance of the game can be explained simply by, 'Our mental approach to the game, good climatic conditions and, perhaps most important of all, the opportunity to play.'

The ACB has controlled the development of the game of cricket since 1905, on behalf of the Australian nation. This responsibility includes all the technical and administrative aspects of the game, and fulfils Bradman's view that Australian cricketing superiority begins with maximizing the natural opportunities to play with a bat and ball.

The Acid 'Test'

Australia has the best record in Test-match cricket. The elite Test team has, since 1876, maintained a forty-two percent win record in all Test matches against England, South Africa, West Indies, New Zealand, India, Pakistan, Zimbabwe and Sri Lanka. In a game which offers a preponderance of draws, no other Test nation can match this win percentage. The Test side has been even more dominant in the last decade, winning forty-eight percent of their Tests. In the more recent one-day internationals, Australia has a leading fifty-six percent win record, including two World Cup victories. Their 1999 triumph was he culmination of six straight tournament wins and one draw. The womens' team, the Southern Stars are also World Champions in the one day game. Few Australians, however, have a sense of superiority about this, and fewer still would accept that the ACB has anything at all to do with global leadership. Cricket is the national game of a nation which lives and dies by its sporting prowess. Most Australians believe that they can pick the Test side much better than those currently empowered to do so. An obsessive media interest in all cricketing matters has long fuelled a national culture of criticism, sometimes constructive, at other times scornful, of those who control the game from Jolimont Street in Melbourne. To the outsider this might appear to be stress-inducing for the officials of the ACB, yet such behavior is symptomatic of national ownership. The ACB operates a fiduciary responsibility on behalf of all Australians, who are the ultimate shareholders of the game. Accordingly the ACB's status barely registers in the minds of cricket enthusiasts. Rather than being a peak performing organization, most Australians, if polled, according to David Fouvy, General Manager, Marketing, might score the ACB 'three out of ten'. The superiority of the Australian cricket side is likely to be explained only by way of reference to Bradman's bat or Dennis Lillee's arm. Unquestionably, world-class batting and bowling are the most obvious manifestations of cricketing peak performance, but they are also the product of organization. Denis Rogers, Chairman of the ACB, is entirely untroubled by the lack of popular recognition. He notes simply that the ACB has mastered the art of 'appearing to be losing while we are in fact winning'.

Perhaps not surprisingly, the national office of the ACB is a mixture of cricketing tradition and modern marketing. Suitably close to the world-famous Melbourne Cricket Ground (MCG) – perhaps equivalent to a few hefty throws from the boundary rope to the wicket-keeper – the entrance way leads immediately to the right and a small flight of stairs, at the top of which is a set of doors which cannot be opened without permission given via an intercom. Once allowed through the doors, directly ahead, visitors are greeted with a portrait of Bradman in his later years. You are unmistakably entering a place of legends. Wooden panelling, which instantly communicates tradition, quickly gives way to open-plan office space, decorated with generous splashes of color, dominated by various shades of green and gold. Marketing posters, signed portraits, bats, jerseys, brochures and fliers spill out of every available space. Some work-stations have been successfully organized so that computers and desk tops can be clearly identified, but for the most part, the national office bristles with cricketing artefacts which prevent any attempts to compartmentalize one area from another.

The formal division of labor in the organization is structured along classic functional lines. General managers in commercial, operations, marketing and public affairs, all report to CEO Malcolm Speed, who was appointed by the Board in 1997. There are some thirty full-time employees who share the national office with the state-elected, fourteen-member Board of Directors. This meets in a separate boardroom which retains the wood panels and historical elegance of another cricketing era. At one end of the boardroom, embedded in the center of the wooden paneling, is the Australian cricket coat of arms. Along each of the other walls are various Test-match bats, signed by the legends of yesteryear.

The Directors of the ACB meet monthly and stand at the pinnacle of the organization and of Australian cricket. Formally constituted in 1905, its structure mirrors the federalism of the country – representatives from local club cricket constitute the state bodies, which in turn elect the national Board. As custodian of the game, the ACB sees itself as responsible for ensuring that the spirit of the game is both protected and developed. A key element of this is the preservation of the relationship between the ACB and the states. In terms of governance this relationship is hierarchical, but Malcolm Speed has opted to take a different approach:

> In an effort to make the federal system work, we bring together the states and the chief executives in regular meetings. Since most of the money comes in at the top, and cricket, particularly at the state level, isn't terribly wealthy, they rely on money coming down from international cricket, which is where the money is generated. So in theory the national body generates income, formulates policy and then assists the states, who implement the policy. The states then have much the same role in co-ordinating the clubs who implement the policy locally, whether in coaching development or marketing.

Despite considerable potential for the message to be diluted, as it filters through this somewhat fragmented structure, two key ingredients maintain co-operation within the cricketing community. The first is simply the powerfully uniting nature of the game. For Denis Rogers cricket brings with it much more than Test series victories:

> It's to do with culture. During a game of cricket we spend six hours a day together, over lunch and afternoon tea, and, yes, with the obligatory scones, which should not be dismissed too lightly. As we watch every over of six balls, which takes about four or five minutes to bowl, the rhythm of the game allows for plenty of time to share in other activities and conversation. I wouldn't change that for anything. It builds genuine friendships, not just between players, but between spectators, television audiences and even between administrators of the game. We all love to hear the latest story that comes from the game of cricket.

While the ambience and spiritual qualities of the game are to be commended, Rogers is quick to point out the second ingredient: 'Australian cricket never loses sight of the fact that the prime purpose of its existence, its primary challenge, is to win every international cricket match.' To this end, Rogers argues that, 'Even in the face of fierce inter-state competition the state sides will rest their best players to make them available to represent their country.' Not surprisingly, the whole organization is geared to producing Test players who can perform victoriously in the international arena. Keane explains how this affects the ACB and its affiliates:

> Although the states want to win the Sheffield Shield competition, a much more important focus is that they all want to produce the most Test players. The focus is on the national side. Moreover, it's major prestige for a grade side to produce a Test player. Anyone who looks vaguely talented, will have a lot of work and effort directed towards him. The real focus is on how many Test players you can get, which means that there's a real sense of ownership of a successful Test side at all levels. A disproportionate number of our greatest players are actually from the country rather than the city, so the sense of ownership of the Australian team is spread across the entire nation.

To ensure the continued supremacy of Australian cricket by producing a steady flow of players of Test-match quality, the ACB has, over the last ten years or so, sought to create the future by putting together a comprehensive development program that begins in primary schools and finishes on the most famous cricket pitches around the world. The infrastructure which is now firmly in place more than confirms Sir Donald Bradman's belief that the simple 'opportunity to play' is the basic reason for the continuing success of Australian cricket.

Gerard Clarke, Manager, Development, sees the development of club-level cricket alongside school-based programs as the fundamental prerequisite for long-term success. Clarke inspires belief in the value of junior development. Formerly a state player with Victoria, Clarke quickly found an interest in cricket administration and, in particular, in creating a strong future for the game. With 5,500 clubs and 13,000 primary and secondary schools throughout the country, it is Clarke's responsibility to oversee the game at the grass-roots. This is a challenge he is more than willing to accept. With enormous conviction, he explains, 'This is *my* story – it is about changing and restructuring people's thinking about cricket.' Clarke takes full charge of this critical aspect of the ACB's work: 'In 1983, the first year of the fully sponsored development program, we had just one development officer in each state. Now we have about a hundred full-time development officers and about the same number of part-timers.'

At first the ACB used to wheel out high-profile players from past Test sides, but Clarke quickly discovered that, to be effective, a much more professional approach had to be taken:

> Quite often those guys can't deal with the kids in the way that we feel is best for the game's development. They are vital in the promotion of the game, but to actually develop the game from a skill point of view, we found that cricket clinics were best run by people with teaching backgrounds. Even now, to cover all the schools and clubs, we could quite reasonably use another hundred development officers.

The ACB's strategic aim is to build up a huge participation base by exposing children to cricket at an early age. Clarke believes this is the only way that 'we are going to have more good players coming through to be picked up by the elite programs'. Geoff Marsh, while coaching the national side, is also acutely aware that the quality of the elite squad rests squarely on a good junior structure:

> I believe that the ACB has structured cricket very well. We put a lot of emphasis on having a very strong first eleven and a very strong junior structure, which the ACB now see as their core busi-

ness. We are competing against every other sport, so we have got to go out there and make kids feel as though they're enjoying the game of cricket. We do that by giving them all an opportunity to play.

Under Clarke's stewardship the ACB has developed a staircase approach which has a clear line of sight, from the backyard to the Baggy Green cap. (The 'Baggy Green' is the cap awarded to and worn by Australian Test players.) This enables the dream of cricket to be shared with those who aspire to play the game and, perhaps, represent their country one day. The long journey to the Test side begins with Milo Kanga cricket in primary schools. Over a third of a million girls and boys are visited in primary and secondary schools by development officers. 30,000 children aged 5–10 years formally register for the Milo Have-a-Go program which is an introduction to the club cricket environment. Clarke has broad ambitions for this program.

> From my point of view, the customer is every boy and girl out there in Australia. The Have-a-Go program is something I'm very passionate about. At the start it was a battle to get nine clubs to run this program because it was different to traditional cricket, which could be characterized as the 'Saturday morning turn-up,' when sometimes only a few kids got to bat or bowl.

The Have-a-Go program is deliberately flexible about playing times, encouraging women in particular to choose cricket as a way to employ their children usefully in the after-school hours. According to Clarke, this 'is also a great way to recruit parents back into the game'. In recognition of their achievements, each child who participates is presented with his or her own Milo which is honored by the kids in the same way as elite cricketers honour the Baggy Green cap: 'I've seen the enjoyment that the kids get out of it. When we give them the green and gold Milo cap, the impact is amazing. The kids feel so proud when they get home.'

Finding out what type of program can be soundly implemented involves basic research – one of Clarke's four 'Rs'. Recruitment is an obvious necessity, but the problem of erosion of interest, as other sports or attractions detract from a pure cricketing focus, becomes evident during the teenage years. Retention thus becomes a prime objective along with the final 'R' – restructuring. Game-breaking ideas in the form of the Milo Super 8s create sufficient attraction to see participation from over 160,000 teenagers. The ACB has found it necessary to rethink and, in some cases, quite dramatically, restructure 'the product' in order to be at the head of the queue for the 'first-choice athlete'. Clarke explains the origins and intention of the Super 8s initiative:

> There are eleven kids in the traditional game, but Super 8s is a shorter, modified version of the game. It has been a huge success with kids, parents and teachers, since changes in school times have created a need for some form of cricket that can be played in less than two hours. Sections of the community are saying that they want a faster game, because they haven't got that much time to spend – they want to be able to get in, have a game and get out within two hours, and they also want to bat, bowl and field in that time!

Super 8s has in turn forced the ACB to adopt such developments at a more senior level so that the initiative attracts broader support. Super 8s contests at an international level have recently been staged in Kuala Lumpur. Cathay Pacific has also mounted the Hong Kong Sixes. Both these tournaments saw participation from elite Australian players. Clarke believes that taking these new ideas about the game to essentially non-cricketing nations is part of a process which 'is looking to restructure or change people's thinking'. The purpose of the Super 8s initiative at the secondary-school level is to ensure the retention of a broad cricketing base that can then be channeled into the local club structure. To achieve this, Clarke sees the need to sell the right product. 'We've got to play when *they* want to play, not when *we* think they should play and, more importantly, we have to take into account *what* they want to play.'

These development programs are designed to act as bridges between schools, the community and the club structure of the game. Further along, national coaching programs identify the talented players who are able to perform in the national schools' cup and the Under 17 and Under 19 Championships. Both statewide and international youth teams are given the opportunity to compete at a level that mirrors the stresses and pressures of the professional game. Specialist programs in fast bowling and spin bowling serve to underscore the massive commitment that ACB makes to developing the best players. Many of the specialist programs rely heavily on great players of the past who bring with them skills and stories that are both informative and inspirational.

The final element in the ACB development portfolio is the Commonwealth Bank Cricket Academy, founded in the 1988–9 season. Following the retirement, in the mid-eighties, of a number of Australian Test stars, the national team suffered several defeats at the hands of the English. Ever mindful of its stewardship of the game, the ACB approached the Australian Institute of Sport in 1987, and suggested that they jointly establish an academy which would draw on the technical resources of the Institute, while the association with the number-one sport in Australia would provide a high profile for the Institute.

The best youth players with elite potential in the state coaching programs are tagged for entry into the Academy using a nationwide database. Although most of these youth players are already well known to Rod Marsh, Academy Director, each year, twenty or thirty hopefuls will apply direct. Along with the under-eighteen and under-nineteen championship players, these applicants are judged on their suitability. Finally, fifteen or so will be chosen and provided with full-time scholarships. The intent is simple. Rod Marsh:

> We try to accelerate their progress from where they are currently, say the under-nineteen level, to elite status, and along the way give

them the knowledge and skills they need to actually go and play first-class cricket. In fact, we overload them with experience – our competition program is fairly intense – it includes an international and a domestic tour.

Even though the amount of funds available from the AIS is small in comparison to the Aus $60 million revenue generated annually by the ACB, the technical advantage, according to Marsh, is quite significant: 'Cricket has access to all their departments, including all the experts we can find. We have a swimming coach, a running coach, sports psychologists, nutritionists and a bio-mechanist. The Academy now has the best that cricket can offer.'

Additionally, many of the Test greats, past and present, spend time at the Academy, passing on 'the good oil'. 'Work-load diaries' record to the last detail the activities of the players on a season-by-season basis. This means that pace bowlers such as Glenn McGrath are followed by the Academy beyond their scholarship days. Marsh's reach is comprehensive: 'We know exactly how many balls he's bowled at training and in matches. In fact, through the national pace bowling program we have these statistics on all our pacemen. It's driven from here.' The Academy has been so successful that the Board has sanctioned its activities to include 'remedial' work for Test players who need extra help in certain areas of their game. This includes sending individual players overseas to experience specific playing conditions.

Finally, the work of the Academy has become so renowned that players from overseas have applied and been accepted. In a three-year period over seventy players from New Zealand, Zimbabwe, Malaysia, India, Sri Lanka, New Guinea, Bangladesh and Hong Kong have been through the overseas program. Although this might appear to be potentially self-defeating – assisting the competition to improve themselves – the ACB takes the high ground. Rod Marsh defends this policy with a combination of business acumen and a belief in the overarching importance of the game:

From a commercial point of view it's been worthwhile, but more importantly we believe we've got something to offer. We're happy to share the Academy with overseas countries because the important thing is that the game of cricket progresses. Because Australia is one of the leading cricketing nations, it's part of our duty to help the game of cricket develop in emerging countries.

Creating the future also involves putting in place alliances and networks between institutions, from schools to cricketing authorities overseas, and commercial sponsors. Inspired administrators such as Rod Marsh and Gerard Clarke are only the most obvious elements of Australian cricket's drive for global success. One of the results of looking after the infrastructure of the game is the concurrent growth of administration that this requires. Malcolm Speed joined the organization from a different professional sports background. Coming from the less-well patronized code of basketball, he is well placed to reflect on the organizational strengths of the ACB:

> Cricket historically throws up some good solid administrators who are well and truly tested through the club and state structures before they get to the national stage. These administrators are very thoughtful, diverse, intelligent, dedicated and experienced. By the time they get through to the national body they have earned their stripes, for sure.

Speed's appointment itself appears to be something of an enigma. The ACB seems to represent, at least to the public, a tradition of conservatism that would eschew an external person in the key role of CEO. Although Speed was 'quite surprised' at his own appointment, he very quickly realized that the image of tradition was not, by any means, the complete story. Indeed, in the years following the Kerry Packer inspired World Series Cricket (WSC), innovation and experimentation with game-breaking ideas became the norm for the ACB. The appointment of Speed was, in fact, typical of an organization which had long realized that constant change would have to be addressed by re-energizing the traditions of cricket, and that that would have to include new managerial talent.

Unquestionably, WSC was the catalyst which set in motion the modern game which now includes, at the international level, an integrated menu of Test matches and one-day games. Bob Parish, who was on the Board for thirty-six years, and is now the honorary ACB historian, played a leading role during the WSC era, and in the changes to the game that ensued. His tenure on the Board, which included stints as chairman, spanned the period 1977–9, when the media tycoon Kerry Packer contracted many of the world's top Test players to play a special brand of international one-day, limited overs cricket. Parish was the man who, in 1976, negotiated a television contract with Australian Broadcasting Corporation (ABC) for Aus $71,000 each year for three years. That year Kerry Packer offered Aus $1.5 million for sole television rights over the same period. Parish's hands were tied, as Packer's approach occurred after the ABC agreement had been finalized. In frustration, Packer started his own team, thus splitting the cricketing world.

World Series Cricket created a remarkable interregnum in the ACB's overarching control and promotion of the sport. The one-day game, or pyjama cricket as it is sometimes called, which was heavily promoted by WSC, reignited mass interest in a game which had not changed significantly since the turn of the century. However, in the long run, WSC could not be sustained without strong grass-roots development, which was the preserve of the ACB. At the same time, the ACB was well aware that revenue streams from the state-based Sheffield Shield competition and Test matches simply could not support the professional game. Bradman in particular, according to Parish, had long argued that a shorter game would have to be embraced in order to maintain cricket's pre-eminent position in the culture and psyche of the nation. Bradman's leadership on this question is of no surprise to Parish, who has long held that the Don's playing feats, while clearly inspirational on a global scale, over shadowed his supreme contribution to the ACB's administration of the game. Importantly, Parish and Bradman were at the center of the negotiations in late 1978 which saw a 'peace treaty', enabling total control of cricket to return to the ACB. In May 1979, when WSC proposed to the ACB the continuation of one-day internationals alongside Test matches, Bradman grasped the initiative. Bob Parish:

> In a small sub-committee this was unequivocally accepted by Bradman, without any argument. So we then went to the full Board, and it went through unanimously. No one argued with Bradman's support of the WSC proposal, he just turned over the page and said 'It's a good result.' That's the way it's recorded in the minutes. I think everybody was tremendously surprised at Bradman's reaction, but nevertheless that's the way he ran it. He influenced a lot of people to go along with his thoughts and the net result of it is that the ACB now controls and promotes the game.

Twenty years later, Bradman's views have not changed. Defending his position, with characteristic purpose, he told us that, 'It was time to make the game appeal to the public. The game had to change. People wanted a more exciting game than what was being played at the time.' Bradman's key role in returning control of the game to the ACB proved to be a watershed. It marked the moment when innovation came to dominate the Board's activities – never again would it be caught out. Parish believes that in the aftermath of WSC, 'It is the ACB which is now the initiator of new ideas.'

On The Front Foot

The legacy of WSC is now apparent in the current activities, structures and policies of the ACB. Ex Coach Geoff Marsh was the all-important conduit through which the ACB's work contributed directly to the players' on-field performance:

> In taking cricket into the year 2000 and beyond, the ACB is very, very positive. It is run by a good mixture of business people who all have a huge passion for the game. They are very flexible and

very good listeners – if there is a problem, you can go to them and they will sort it out in a very positive way. They are an extremely professional unit.

From a technical point of view, the ACB, through the national office, assists the team directly by overseeing the *Players' Handbook* which is issued to all Test-match players. It contains detailed information on fitness regimes, dietary habits, training schedules for tours and motivational mantras which demonstrate how players can focus on 'taking control of the 1% things'. Recently retired captain of the Australian Test side, Mark Taylor, said of the handbook that, 'It does certainly have its uses,' but players are presumed to be capable of making their own judgement regarding the details. Steve Waugh, current captain, told us:

It's important to a lot of the players, but I've never used it. I have my own personal diary which I've been using for years. Either way, it's important to have one. People who aren't on schedule or who don't look after themselves or don't do the right thing are generally pretty sloppy in their cricket. It's an overall attitude you have to have these days.

Waugh's comments are in part a response to the amount of professional cricket played at the elite level, and the necessity for players to pace themselves and look after logistics of playing and travelling. It is not unknown for the players to be on the road for well over 300 days each year, including overseas tours. Such a schedule is symptomatic of decisions made by the ACB, regarding the development of the professional game. As a forward-thinking organization that is prepared to break with long-held traditions, the ACB makes no distinction between Test cricket and the one-day game at the international level. The revenues generated from the shorter version of cricket need to be distributed to the states and, ultimately, to the club sides. Denis Rogers explains:

We should not be concerned about the delineation between Test cricket and one-day cricket, other than to say that they're different. In Test cricket you have to get twenty wickets to win, in one-day cricket you score more runs, but for us, they cohabit happily. They are both important to Australian cricket. When we do our promotions we show players with colored uniforms and players dressed in whites side by side. We don't discriminate by saying that one-day cricket is more important than Test cricket. What we say about Test cricket is that it's full of drama, it's serious, it's six hours a day for five days. There are nuances and subtleties which can also be strategic. We say that one-day cricket is colorful, entertaining and explosive, and it makes commercial sense. Even though its origins can be traced back to conflict with WSC we don't carry any baggage about that at all.

Rogers drives the Board by holding one-on-one meetings with each member, to establish, 'a level of intellectual rigour second to none, in order to resolve today's contemporary sporting challenges'. Vigorously embracing the one-day game has proved to be one of those challenges. Rogers also aims to get the best out of the Board through his establishment of a forum for debate where 'progress is made through disagreement'. This high level of engagement is also expected in the national office. Rogers insists that operational issues are kept away from Board meetings so that only the larger strategic concerns are dealt with at that level, which, he argues, means that policy issues can be addressed 'with fresh minds and fresh vigour'. In turn, this allows the national office to manage and implement Board policy. This 'clear dichotomy', Rogers explains, can only work if the people employed are outstanding: 'All my life, I've only recruited the best, and this was the same brief given to the CEO, Malcolm Speed.' The unmistakable focus of this approach is, according to Rogers, to 'generate revenue that enables Australia to keep focused on winning. The administration in Australian cricket will leave no stone unturned to create an environment where players are given every opportunity to win.'

For players to be paid a professional sportsperson's salary, more one-day international cricket has to be played, since this form of cricket produces the necessary revenues. Malcolm Speed astutely recognizes that the marketplace changes rapidly and continues to confront challenge after challenge, beyond the playing of one-day cricket. Moreover, he acknowledges that in order to maintain the position of cricket as the number-one playing and spectator sport in terms of gate attendance and, even more importantly, television viewing, the ACB has to develop 'well-thought out strategies' which will effectively lead to healthy revenue streams. These income streams are split into television rights, match attendance, sponsorships and licensing. The need to maximize these revenue-generating possibilities has led to the intensive marketing of cricket. Indeed, if there is one area that the ACB has developed unswervingly, it is the sponsorship and selling of the game. Malcolm Speed:

> When you look at old photos of Test matches, there is not a corporate sign to be seen. Now, if you go to a cricket ground, the perimeter is covered in corporate signs. I think if you compare the progress that has been made in marketing, over the last twenty years, compared with most other sports, cricket has really picked up in providing better entertainment.

This is a far cry from the first days of television coverage, which Bob Parish sold to the ABC network 'for the magnificent sum of £25'. Sponsorship money was also less than spectacular, prior to WSC. Parish recollects that 'The first Benson & Hedges contract I signed in 1973 was for Aus $50,000, and I thought we were made.' Sharing the dream of Australian cricket through sponsorship alone, now brings in close to Aus $12m, with television rights more than double this figure. Gate money and licensing net close to Aus $15m. These activities are now the preserve of the marketing group, headed by David Fouvy, who joined the ACB in November 1993. The ACB only stopped contracting out its marketing in 1994.

Fouvy has the dual responsibility to build revenue and a brand image for cricket. This has led to the development of separate, yet mutually reinforcing, brand wheels for Test cricket and one-day Internationals. Each wheel contains different brand attributes, benefits, values, personalities and core essence. Prior to 1993, the selling of the game was usually based around the next game to be played by the elite squad. The new initiative from Fouvy's group takes a brand focus rather than a gate focus for the first time in two decades of Australian cricket. David Fouvy:

> There are a number of brand drivers. First, how the elite teams perform on the field. Australians adore winners, and this is something we have been able to tap into with respect to the Australian team performance since the late 1980s. Another driver is how well we do the job of promoting cricket at the grass-roots level, how accessible it is. Finally there is the cohesion between all the programs.

In keeping with the aim of making cricket available to all those who want to play, Fouvy has been careful to position the game as one that is very portable, and can be played for fun almost everywhere. Advertising campaigns on television emphasize that the very spirit of the game resides in the schoolyard, on the beach and in the backyard, as children and adults enjoy trying to emulate their heroes. These evocative images, which lie at the heart of the 'Go Aussie Go' campaign, are specifically designed to be both inspirational *and* aspirational, so that each image of backyard cricket is mirrored by one of an elite player carrying out the same action. The sharing of the dream is powerful and clear. Additionally, key inspirational players such as Sir Donald Bradman, Dennis Lillee, Ian and Greg Chappell, Allan Border and many other legends of the game, form a marketing tool of unrivalled potency to assist in the building of the brand. They help to establish cricket as the game to both watch and play.

Some of these marketing and promotional initiatives aim to recast the core traditions of the game. Chairman Rogers confirms that loving the traditional game can also include 'freshness that challenges sacred cows in an educated way'. Fouvy's team has challenged several sacred cows along the way. In the spirit of entertainment that is more evident in one-day internationals, Fouvy's division came up with the notion of musical interludes which could be used to introduce incoming batsmen or bid them farewell when they were dismissed. A dropped catch would be followed by the famous Homer Simpson exclamation, 'Doh!' The Press, who took an immediate dislike to this Board-sponsored initiative, raised the issue to that of a national crisis. Under siege, Fouvy was forced into making an astute observation:

> Here was this bastard child, hated by everyone, even though it was simply light entertainment. But all of a sudden people were saying that's against the *tradition* of the one-day game, 'You can't do that.' I was left thinking, how many years do you have to have before you get a tradition? Apparently less than twenty is the answer. It was an interesting experiment. It showed me that you have got to harness this passion for the game, but in such a way that you don't kill it.

Despite the occasional setback, the ACB is still receptive to game-breaking ideas which challenge traditional ways of thinking. Fouvy was instrumental in one of the most startling innovations in one-day cricket – the impetus behind the initiative came purely from a marketing perspective. During the 1994–5 season Zimbabwe, a relative newcomer to international cricket and a team with little profile in Australia, was scheduled as one of the three teams playing in the one-day international series, then known as the World Series. Fouvy's concern from a marketing perspective was that the proposed line up of teams might lead to a reduced level of consumer interest in the annual World Series. His solution, which was duly submitted to a subcommittee and then the full Board, was to introduce a fourth team which was a second Australian team. This team was simply called Australia 'A'. This would generate increased public interest and be a further opportunity to showcase the depth of Australian cricket. Moreover, it would also provide a stimulus for those cricketers on the verge of international honors, by creating a new arena in which their skills and ability would be exposed to competition. To Fouvy's amazement the Board approved the idea:

> 'Australia 'A' was a brave move. I was pushing hard, and was frankly surprised when they went for it. They haven't got many decisions wrong. This decision added a new dimension to Australian cricket.

The search for new ways to promote, sell and share the dream of Australian cricket flourishes in the ACB. Fouvy and other senior figures give great credit to Malcolm Speed for embracing and driving new ideas and direction. He is the important link between the Board and management. David Fouvy:

> He's very open and is prepared to consult in the development of a joint vision. More importantly, he is not biased in any way. Although new to cricket administration, he has worked in other sports. This, together with a legal background and a logical approach to issues, makes for excellent leadership.

Denis Rogers also acknowledges the impact that Speed has had on Australian cricket, noting that, 'In the last two years I've no doubt that he's been vital to what we've been able to achieve and will achieve.' Malcolm Gray, past Chairman of the Board and President-elect of the International Cricket Council, taking a global view, pays the ACB CEO the highest accolade of all: 'Speed, in my judgement, is excellent. He is the best cricket administrator I have seen around the world. He is a thinker who is resilient, unshakeable, hard working and energetic.'

Malcolm Speed is now keeper and holder of the dream. This might be remarkable, given his relatively short tenure with the organization, yet his pivotal role reflects a strong community that quickly enables inspirational players to establish their credentials. Denis Rogers calls it the 'cricketing family', which comes together to support and assist any and all contributions to the wider aim. The concept of the cricketing family is frowned upon by the media, but Rogers is unwilling to back off: 'I still think it's key, and I won't step back from that point of view.' Even though the national office is relatively new, in terms of many of its employees, it has considerable continuity with little turnover. Fouvy's team, for example, which has a 'real camaraderie', has all been appointed within the past few years, while veterans such as Parish and other long-serving staff and Board members help to preserve identity, continuity and trust. Those who, for whatever reason, step outside the stated purpose and focus of the ACB, are unlikely to remain.

The elite squad has its own long-held and powerful identity. It is a sanctum that only the privileged few can enter. Geoff Marsh: 'There is a huge spirit amongst past and present Australian cricketers. It has a real family thing about it. One of the reasons is the passage of different eras. Ian Chappell, Allan Border and Mark Taylor – there is a huge spirit about each of them.' A strong integrating factor is the team's method of celebration, which has stayed the same across the years. At the conclusion of a Test match victory and, particularly, a series win, the dressing-room door is locked and the players (and players alone) sing, 'Beneath the Southern Cross'. Geoff Marsh explains that, 'You're only allowed to sing it once, and it's got to be a very special moment if it's sung twice.' Much of the energy in the Australian team revolves around symbols and artifacts. Steve Waugh, known for his passion for tradition, takes his rituals seriously. Geoff Marsh marvels at the ceremony that Waugh engages in when it comes to the Baggy Green:

> Steve wears the same Baggy Green that they gave him back in '86'
> – it's been through all the parties. The next day in the dressing
> room, Steve will be sitting at the basin washing out his Australian
> cap because someone has poured beer all over it, but he washes it,
> hangs it up, dries it and then next day he'll go out and bat with it
> and field with it. Steve's a traditionalist – he loves the game with a
> passion and all those little traditional things about cricket.

After a recent Ashes series victory against the English, there was a bet within the team as to how long the players could wear their caps. Marsh remembers that, 'Some of them wore their caps for more than four days. Justin Langer went to bed with his cap on.' Marsh believes that this is in stark contrast to the England side, who 'wear faded caps which look terrible – we just couldn't believe it, pride is a big word in our side.'

Perhaps understandably, this level of commitment leads to considerable mental anguish and disappointment when a batsman is dismissed. David Fouvy has learned not to request promotional duties from such players, even if they appear to have time on their hands due to early dismissal. In a 'story-telling game' there are, inevitably, some 'real corkers' which communicate what is at stake at the international level:

> With David Boon I don't know what was worse, seeing him out for a duck or seeing him out for 50. In short, when he came into the dressing room, you needed to get out and give him some privacy. Allan Border was similar – no matter how many runs he got, he was always unhappy to get out. One time, Michael Slater was so affected that he tried to flush all his gear down the toilet, his pads, box, gloves, everything.

Although difficult to confirm, there are strong rumors that many players, when selected for the Test side, have their allocated number tattooed on their posterior. Colorful though these stories are, they represent a community determined to excel. As a past captain of the side, Mark Taylor believes that they are part and parcel of an organization that 'just keeps beating itself'.

Conclusion

The ACB has a clear idea of what it wants to achieve and how it will do it. Sharing the dream of cricket and providing opportunities for everyone to play the game easily translates into a passion for winning at the international level. Moreover, the Board recognizes what it has to do to produce the elite players who can sustain peak performance. Inspirational players and past legends of the game promote cricket through myriad activities. Sponsorship revenues and the continuing pre-eminence of the game in a sports-crazy country enable the ACB to maintain a constant stream of talented players who have access to highly developed programs, from junior cricket to the elite level. The pervasive feeling of family and community encourages risk, innovation and game-breaking initiatives. Players, both on and off the field, are constantly provided with challenges which spur them to better themselves. The organization is at its best when it has earned the right to tell yet another story which adds a new ring to the contours of the cricketing soul.

12

Women's Hockey Australia: The Color is Gold

"The night we won the gold medal in Atlanta, we came off the dais and because of all the security problems they wouldn't let us go up to our parents. Mum and Dad fought their way down from the grandstand, where they could stand right on the edge of the barrier. My sister Katrina (who is also on the team), and I had to get plastic chairs to stand up on so that we could just reach them with our outstretched arms. I have never seen my Dad cry and Mum was hysterical. It was a big thank you for everything, for both of them, for everything they had done for us throughout our lives. Buying hockey sticks, paying for fees, paying for trips, taking us to trains, waiting in cars, driving us home from training – it was a huge moment for them and us. I will never forget that night, on Friday 1 July 1996"

– LISA POWELL,
HOCKEYROOS, DEFENDER

The driving rain on a late June evening in Perth forces a handful of spectators to seek protection under the canopy of an otherwise empty Bentley hockey stadium. The heart of the game resides here. Night and day the facility hosts a whirl of bustling activity, with games, drills, practice and meetings. School children, national athletes and veterans alike constantly come and go, interacting, playing and learning. The stadium complex is hockey heaven, and exudes a friendly communal warmth.

For the few remaining observers who are not accustomed to dealing with inclement weather, bone-chilling conditions such as these are a substantial shock to the system. Shoulders are drawn closer to ears, and arms and hands are either thrust deeply into pockets or pulled ever tighter around waistlines. A veterans' game has long since been completed, leaving just a handful of players, who, seemingly oblivious to the unrelenting rain, continue to practice what appear to be set plays involving rapid passing across the field, ending with a shot on goal. The crack of stick on ball, which echoes loudly around the floodlit stadium, is interspersed with the odd shout or mock whoop of triumph, as the ball crashes into the back of the goal from time to time. By some measure, meaningless to others or not, these goals still seem to count to those on the pitch. One of the players who is apparently unaware of the marked deterioration in the weather, continues to pound the synthetic turf inexorably. She is Rechelle Hawkes, Co-captain of the Australian team.

It is literally only a few days since she returned with the rest of the Hockeyroos from yet another gold-medal-winning performance at the World Championships in Utrecht, Holland. For Hawkes, winning gold is something of a habit. In 1998 she added a Commonwealth gold medal to four Champions Cup gold medals, two World Cup gold medals and, finally and most precious of all, three Olympic gold medals from Seoul in 1988 and Atlanta in 1996 and Sydney in 2000. With this astonishing record of achievement, Hawkes takes her rightful place on the world stage, as one of the greatest female athletes of her generation. In the last decade, Hawkes and Hockeyroos have utterly dominated the game of women's field hockey. Since the appointment of coach Richard Charlesworth they have achieved an astonishing win record of eighty percent in over 200 games.

But for Hawkes there is no let up. Not yet satisfied with her cache of gold, the opportunity for self-improvement, and to exceed personal best, appears to offer her a far greater sustained challenge than the quest for gold:

Training is enjoyable when you push yourself to the limit. You see the rewards afterwards. I've always loved training, being able to see how hard I can push myself and feel the improvement. If I am not improving every time or getting something out of it, I get *really* annoyed. I guess that is something within my personality. I can't go through the motions of training without getting something out of it. This is self-imposed pressure.

Playing for the Australian team that she loves and is 'totally wrapped up in,' presented opportunities that are in stark contrast to what might have been. Thinking back on her very first selection to the national team, Hawkes reflected on the divergent paths that lay before her:

The defining moment for me was at eighteen years of age. I was studying at the time, baby-sitting two kids when I got a phone call from Women's Hockey Australia. It was the secretary from the Hockey Association, who had tracked me down at someone's house and he said, 'Rechelle Hawkes, you have been chosen for the Australian women's hockey team,' and I said, 'What!?' and he said, 'Yes, you have been selected to play a series against Germany.' I was in total disbelief, because I hadn't even made the state team at this stage, and I was selected straight into the Australian team. I took some convincing. I remember thinking at that time that this was a new direction, a turning point for me. I could have ended up having kids of my own in the next year or so. Equally, without the hockey path, I could have also ended up baby-sitting five days a week.

Hawkes, along with 160,000 women in Australia who play hockey at various levels, is living the dream that began in 1910, when the All Australia Women's Hockey Association was formed. Membership was set annually at one guinea, and the ruling committee was made up of three members from each state who elected the president annually. So began the strong tradition of state involvement in the grass-roots development of hockey. The initial rules of the Association set out in 1910 ran to all of fifteen points printed on five pages measuring two inches square. The Women's Hockey Australia (WHA) has always guided the growth and popularity of the game and, as this is an amateur sport, the professional Sydney national office now in existence co-ordinates a huge volunteer force responsible for administration of the game at state level.

One of the WHA's objectives ever since its foundation has been to provide women with the opportunity to participate in a structured competitive sport, and its annual report states that it currently seeks to 'raise the profile of women's hockey nationwide as a healthy, recreational and social team sport.' In the early 1980s an additional element was added – that of preserving the WHA's high profile in world hockey. The aim is global domination of field hockey. Finally, the success of the organization means that it has made a major contribution to developing the leadership role of women in society. Nowhere is this more apparent than in the national office.

Upon entering the Sydney premises it is immediately clear that activity flows smoothly around any objects, human or otherwise, that might impede progress. Full-time employees, board members and volunteers constantly cycle through the office. Stick and ball might be absent, but there is a strong sense of shared purpose. A sudden collective cheer, signifying the equivalent of scoring an 'office goal', would not seem out of place. Although the tempo is high, it is not frenetic. Calm, co-ordinated activity with no obvious locus of control creates an impression of flow.

Perhaps with an eye on sponsorship priorities, at first take the national office appears to be focused on the Hockeyroos. Trophies and symbols of international success are never far from the eye, yet they are not ostentatiously displayed. Even a brief conversation with the women in action reveals a commitment to the game of hockey itself above the more limited considerations of elite success. Their passion is evident, almost contagious, especially when the subject of being the best in the world is raised.

Unquestionably, the managerial ambience is one of friendly informality, yet with sponsors and government money involved, formal accountability, not to mention democratic rationale, necessitates a degree of formality and procedure that we failed to encounter in any of the other case studies. Even though the WHA gets by on a slender budget of less than Aus$3 million, the yearly business plan runs to some forty pages. Each committee is held accountable to measurable objectives, with cost estimates of expected activities, the source of revenue and finally an explanation of variance if so required. With annual performance monitoring of office staff, the operation is run as tightly as the Hockeyroos defence. Pam Tye, the current WHA president, is well aware of the formalities that are demanded of the WHA by external bodies, and deliberately spends time in the office helping to establish informality, heaping plenty of praise on deserving staff, and demonstrating passion and interest in the tasks undertaken. It might also include 'sitting down and having a Scotch with the president'.

'Brenda Cawood, our general manager, who works very well at keeping lines of communication open, is key to what happens in the office,' Tye observes. Cawood is the crucial conduit who ensures that trust and loyalty exist between the board, the states, and the elite programs in Perth. Her inspirational contribution to the WHA is not as a fixer or deal-maker between the constituent parts of the organization, but as a constructive catalyst who opens up channels between potentially partisan interests. Cawood believes that risk and gamebreaking ideas developed between herself and the board are the result of dialogue and policy debate which has a positive, constructive flavor. A significant example of this is the formation of the Telstra STIX National Hockey League, an initiative primarily stewarded by herself and last incumbent president, Meg Wilson.

Within the office, Cawood holds informal weekly management meetings with a view to keeping the organization 'happy and harmonious'. This creates a flow of information which ensures that each area is able to work through to resolve the inevitable task interdependencies. Another value of this process is that it constantly reinvigorates the dual focus between development and the elite. Tracey Edmundson, Media Manager, knows that the best opportunities for increasing media coverage come from having a successful national team. This inevitably provides the organization with a wider turning circle in terms of delivering good value for existing sponsors, and attracting new ones. Success is all the more critical given that hockey has to compete for coverage and sponsorship with several other high-profile sports in Australia, such as Australian Rules, cricket, tennis and rugby league. While Edmundson needs to extract every possible advantage from the Hockeyroos' success, Marg Ryan, Coaching and Technical Manager, has to focus on the development and technical accreditation of officials at the grass-roots. Coaching and umpiring are the sinews of the game. Securing board support for an umpire development officer is as important to Ryan as celebrating the latest Hockeyroos gold medal. Even though Ryan was manager of the Australian team in the early eighties, she strongly believes that, 'The WHA mission is to provide sport and recreation for women and girls in Australia. That's what I'm interested in, to be able to have them exercise and enjoy recreation. I don't care whether they're elite, I just want them to play the game.' To this end she runs the National championships, reviews the Intensive Training Center Coaches in the states and develops the national officiating program. She is literally responsible for how the game is played.

Another equally vital element of the developmental focus of the WHA, is getting young girls into the game of hockey. This responsibility belongs to the development manager. Fortuitously, when the position was advertised in 1995, one of the applications came from an occupational health and safety officer working with Australia Post. Sharon Buchanan was an inspirational choice, not least because she happened to have captained the Hockeyroos to gold in the 1988 Seoul Olympics. Buchanan is the player who was rightfully associated with the emergence of Australian Field hockey supremacy. In a stunning performance, her two goals in the Olympic semi-final, against a hitherto dominant Dutch side, are widely held to be the turning point in the fortunes of WHA. While other players have since sustained WHA supremacy Buchanan's performance that day made such dreams possible. Describing the first goal she scored, Buchanan's memory of the occasion, to this day, remains vividly clear:

> I knew Tracy was going to pass to me and so I instinctively got into position to receive the ball. When it came I had the opportunity to pass or shoot. Passing was the easier option but there was no question in my mind about what I was going to do. All through training we had practiced this shooting position, so I had all the confidence and focus I needed to make the shot. There was never any doubt in my mind that I was going to score. This was the chance I had always wanted.

Returning to the hockey family, Buchanan also brought with her a natural love of the game, outstanding professional abilities and a passionate commitment to the developmental side of hockey. Additionally, as Australia's first women's hockey celebrity, who is often called upon to do hockey commentary for television, Buchanan's public profile is a powerful vehicle for sharing the dream with young players. To this end, and as part of the WHA's extensive developmental program, the secondary-school based Telstra Buchanan Cup was established, enabling both the organization and chief sponsor to take advantage of her fame.

Her past glory as a player and her role as Development Manager, allow Buchanan to bridge different WHA activities. In particular, she keeps a close personal contact with many former team mates. This provides an extra perspective for the national office, without distracting from Buchanan's main role, which is to create the future by building hockey from the ground up. Sharon Buchanan:

> We have a number of different competitions. Even at the minky, primary-school level, we have a state-based competition, run through either schools or clubs for the youngsters. We also try to link the schools and the clubs through extensive coaching visits. Then we have three under-sixteen tournaments for ages twelve

through to sixteen. A state competition and two invitational tournaments attract about twenty, ten and eight teams respectively. Then we go into under-eighteen, over twenty-one, junior and senior squad competitions and then finally the Telstra STIX National Hockey League. We've also got what we call the 'Let's play Hockey' program which has been put out by our sponsor, Telstra. That program goes to the schools of Australia, where certificates and stickers are presented to the participants.

Buchanan's poise and grace lift those around her. In a very real sense she stands at the heart of the hockey community. She is able to access a respectful, perhaps even deferential, audience when pushing for support for her development agenda, but she does not expect resources to be forthcoming simply because she is an Australian icon. Support for the development program occurs for exactly the same reason as for the other portfolios.

Daphne Pirie, a member of the board of directors, described to us the ties that unite the organization:

Respect of each other, love of the game, plus a determination to succeed. It's not much different from being a player. In an organization such as this, either on the board or in the national office, you still attack the job in the same manner, you set yourself goals just as you did as a player. It makes no difference if we are talking strategic plans, budgets or whatever, you still have to see the bigger picture, which is what we had to do when we were playing. If we could have our time over again we would all still rather be out on the paddock than in the boardroom or office. Our collective memory keeps it together.

Sharon Buchanan, the most recent person to make the transition from playing to managing, expresses similar sentiments:

I know my developmental perspective for the organization is very different from a lot of others, but even so, the first thing that really comes to mind for me is our overall success, so we need to do all these other things too. If we don't do them well, we will no longer be successful. Now, we just have to keep improving all the time.

The national office is where partisan interests and tensions are distilled. Each portfolio pushes its own agenda to the limit, but never to the point of losing sight of the broader dream. The duality of development and the elite is also one of the distinctive dilemmas that Dr Richard Charlesworth, National Coach, has to face.

Why would an organization dedicated to the development of opportunities for women have absolutely no qualms about turning to a man to ensure that it remained successful? In the first instance, after several years as national coach, Brian Glencross had already successfully taken the Hockeyroos to their first Olympic gold medal in 1988. When the position was advertised in 1993, the WHA was a very different organization from the time of his appointment in 1980. It had become a much larger professional outfit with pretensions to global leadership, and women had been deliberately deployed, mentored, resourced and placed in positions of responsibility and authority. Even so, the new national coach would be appointed to help achieve the overarching dream of the Association, and as having the top national team in the world was an essential part of that dream, the best coach available would be employed, regardless of gender.

As the national coach, Dr Richard Charlesworth has yet to see any color in tournament play other than gold. Brian Glencross, now high performance manager at the Australian Institute of Sport (AIS), argues that, 'He is unique, he is probably the best coach in the world'. Charlesworth's background is eclectic to say the least. A stand-out hockey player with 227 caps for the Australian men's team, he won a gold medal in the World Championships in London in 1986, but despite four attempts Olympic gold eluded him, silver being his best result in Montreal, 1976. He is a medical practitioner and was, for several years, a Member of Parliament. In the eyes of the WHA he is peerless. He commands complete respect. Sharon Buchanan, who was coached by Charlesworth in her last year as a player, has such a belief in him, that she feels,

> He could coach just about any sport and be successful. He demands so much of himself and you know he will demand the same of you. He's just got that competitiveness which is fantastic. You would lie down and die for him if that enabled someone to score a goal for us.

When Charlesworth accepted the appointment as women's national coach, the WHA knew that they had snared the best coach in Australia. Charlesworth:

> I sort of fell into this you know. I never thought I would be doing this job if you had asked seven years ago when I was in Parliament. I made a decision in about July of 1992 to get out of politics, because although it was a very interesting job, it was a terrible life. About two or three months later a couple of players on the national team rang me and asked if I was interested. I hadn't been involved in hockey since I finished playing in 1988, and indeed that was probably a very good thing, because I had had nothing to do with it and I was quite fresh. I thought about it and thought, oh yes, that might be an interesting thing to do, so I got involved. I was accepted and given an opportunity.

Charlesworth's philosophy clearly matched that of the WHA, who were looking for someone who could take the Hockeyroos to the next level.

> I suppose I had an abiding belief that we had never really developed a team as a sports team could be developed. Our state teams and our club teams developed in a unified way, and I felt that that should be possible with the national team. It is extraordinary how poorly prepared teams are in terms of team work and integration in tournaments like the soccer World Cup. What you have is a

complex integrated team which requires all sorts of judgements and decisions to be made by people in a split second. It is a very hard thing to tie together. In hockey we need the sort of understanding and unity that you can only develop by really working at it. I believed that we could go a lot further in terms of that in our national team. I don't think we have ever done very well at this in the past.

There were other reasons why the new national coach felt that the Hockeyroos were a good bet to succeed. First, Charlesworth saw that women who were good enough for consideration for the national side were generally younger than the corresponding men, and were in a different stage of their lives, usually without large financial commitments and firm career expectations. In consequence, he argues, 'Their focus was much more performance orientated – they were simply better athletes, faster and much more willing to train hard.' Second, it was possible for women's hockey to recruit more 'first-choice athletes' since the number of team sports open to women was significantly smaller than those available to men. Men could choose to concentrate on rugby, cricket, Australian Rules or soccer, while women had a choice of two codes – hockey or netball.

The WHA head hunted Charlesworth primarily because, by reputation, they knew he was a supreme inspirational player and an innovator who would maintain and amplify the team's natural instinct for flair and attack. His well-known quest to challenge and improve both himself and others also sat well with the WHA's never-ending search for both administrative and technical advantage. Put simply, the WHA wanted game-breaking ideas from Charlesworth to ensure their global dominance of the code – the Hockeyroos' record since 1993 obviously speaks for itself. In explaining to us how this remarkable record was achieved, Charlesworth shared much more than a coaching manual. His philosophy of team performance is a compelling example of managerial style. It begins, however, with the individual player exceeding personal best:

Everybody gets carried away with the score. I like to develop different attitudes in the players. One of the most critical things that you have to do is develop an attitude which is analytical and clinical. We keep a lot of statistics to help us look closely at everything that happens. Each person gets an efficiency rating for every game they play, so we know that if they got the ball forty-five times and they turned it over fifty times, that is not good – or if they only turned it over twice and they were penetrating on fifteen occasions then that's very good and their efficiency is ninety-five percent or whatever. Although somewhat an arbitrary figure, it means something.

This enables players to look behind the result. They can be honest in a way that is not threatening. It is all about improving. If you improve yourself, you will beat the opposition. We actually don't go out there to win, we go out to play well, and winning is the byproduct of that. The focus is on how we play, rather than the outcome.

For Rechelle Hawkes, the training regimes which accompany this style of coaching are heaven-sent. Fitness, skill levels, detailed analysis and constant execution of plays are taken to a higher plane than in other teams: 'factors which separate us from other countries who are simply not as intensely prepared as we are'.

Personal responsibility for performance is strongly reinforced by Charlesworth's insistence on playing the game using all available resources. Unlike every other hockey team and almost every other sporting code, the Hockeyroos do not employ, and will not countenance, the notion of a bench. This means that there is no 'first eleven', plus others who substitute with lesser skills and ability. Charlesworth explains the reasons behind this:

That was a conscious decision that I made six years ago. Every time I had a bench, implicitly or explicitly I was saying, 'You are not good enough to start.' Players start to believe that. If I say to them, you are all going to play, then those people believe that they are good enough *and* they surprise you *and* they play with more skill *and* better than they did before. This is important for a number of reasons that are very practical. The game can be very hot and difficult anyway, so using all our players allows us to play at a higher tempo which other teams simply can't sustain. It also lifted those people and made them believe that they were good enough. It unified the group.

Although this perspective is very much in line with the overall development of people within WHA, we suggested that the notion of 'bench strength', particularly as it applies to basketball, was a sound concept. 'It's all bullshit in my opinion,' was the swift and non-debatable response. If we had any further concerns about the validity of Charlesworth's approach, they were more than dispelled by Jenny Morris, fullback for the Hockeyroos:

> Everyone knows that when they go to a tournament they will play. It creates heaps of team spirit because everyone knows they are going on to the field. We don't even use the word bench. It took us ages to get used to that. There is no such thing as a bench, or substitutes or reserves – as much as the media still like to talk that way.

Charlesworth means what he says. Alyson Annan, arguably the best hockey player in the world, had less time on the field during the 1998 World Cup than several other players. The constant interchange of players has other benefits too. With European teams dedicated to marking each player, their game plan is severely disrupted if the best player in the world isn't there to mark. Changing positions also allows the coach to interact with the team as the game progresses.

Many of Charlesworth's innovations and game-breaking ideas, based around flair and flexibility, have simply left the opposition floundering. It even includes completely changing a player's game. Lisa Powell turned out for many years as an attacker, but after losing her place, Charlesworth suggested that she should re-establish herself in the side as a defender, thus adding some pace to the team where it was least expected. In less than six months Powell fought her way back into the team. When these initiatives fit together the players experience a heightened state of flow. Rechelle Hawkes:

> There is intensity. There is the running off the ball, helping each other, communication, confidence, and everyone wants to get involved. All eleven on the field want that ball, or are helping someone to get it. It feels as if we are on a roll. We feel like we have got this invincibility. Everyone is so confident in the team and in themselves, we believe that we can really overrun a team.

Sentiments such as these are also indicative of the strong community that has been built around the team. For the 1996 Olympic Games in Atlanta, the WHA was able to obtain the necessary finances to bring the team together in Perth for several months. This helped to create significant bonds, as the squad was able to knit together socially. Ann Konrath, who works in administration for the national coach, described to us how, in the lead-up to a major tournament, rigorous training schedules are balanced with more recreational activities:

> Sometimes, after training, the whole team will come over to my house for a meal, or we might all go out to lunch. In the very hot weather some of the players who live here offer their homes because they have a pool. They are a fun, committed, hard-working group.

The self-confidence that travels with this team, wherever it goes, has its origins in Charlesworth's ability to develop the whole person. Peak performance requires a fundamental merging of both conception and execution of task. Success on the hockey field provides a powerful metaphor for organizational life. Richard Charlesworth:

> Once the ball is in play, the opposition rarely do what you expect them to do. In every situation, something else happens. In prepa-

ration for this, we have to make the players better decision makers, and give them the authority to do it. Give them the opportunity. Help them to make that critical decision for themselves and the team. Increase their capacity to decide. In the end, they have to play, you cannot do it for them.

Shirley Davies explains that the emphasis on maintaining individuality runs through the entire coaching system:

> Under our elite system, there is an intensive training scheme whereby a coach is appointed in every state so that the national coach at the top can feed into the elite coaches in every state. This structure ensures that people are being coached along the same lines, but without pushing away their flair. And there will be other coaches watching players in the states. They will gather information from their elite coach so that anyone who has the talent in the states is automatically picked up. The Intensive Training Center (ITC) coach is responsible for developing these elite players, whether they're the talented under-sixteens, or the talented under-eighteens.
>
> Our three national coaches will develop a pattern of play, but although there is a common thread they're all encouraged to do it their way, so that the flair comes through. We don't want to have the national coach saying 'Everyone does it this way, or that way.' You've got to give people the opportunity to develop their own style. Otherwise you'd have a system where people wouldn't be able to use their own creative talent on the field. If you want people to react in particular ways then you've got to give them the ability to be able to do it.

In the organization as a whole, everyone has their own 'Rick' story. Veronica Newman, whose board jurisdiction includes finance, spent her first two years in the position of being constantly challenged with requests from the national coach. According to Newman some of these experiences were 'intense' to say the least, yet she credits

Charlesworth with developing a financially sustainable elite structure around the team, with excellent administration, assistant coaches and support activities which, crucially, include a stress psychologist. She is also mindful of the way in which his proposal to use 'Direct Athlete Support' money, 'enticed the players to go to Perth to prepare months ahead, as full-time athletes for the 1996 Atlanta Olympics'; Newman praises the results: 'I don't think that I've ever seen a hockey team so well-prepared for a competition, both mentally and physically. It would have to be one of the best teams that I have ever seen. In the end we put it down to the creativity of the coach.'

Charlesworth sought out Newman after the gold-medal-winning game in Atlanta, to thank her for her work. This was seen as something 'quite special'. In similar vein, the unexpected photograph of the Olympic team on the dais in Atlanta, signed with thanks and sent by Charlesworth, to Tracey Edmundson, Media Manager, 'keeps the dream alive' for her. Jenny Morris remembers well a game in England where she got 'whacked in the face' with a stick. She endured blood, injections and stitches, and 'Rick helped me get through the pain, without allowing me to wallow in self-pity.' The stories of respect and admiration go on and on. Charlesworth is unquestionably a mighty inspirational player who stands at the center of WHA's current sustained period of peak performance. Pam Tye: 'He's such a perfectionist. He's a very questioning person, whereas perhaps other coaches are not, or not to the same degree. We want him to continue challenging us. I like that.'

Indeed, in order to keep the Hockeyroos at the pinnacle of performance Charlesworth generates a constant stream of organizational challenges from Perth, which are processed by the board and the Sydney national office.

Despite fielding competitive teams for many years, in the past the amateur nature of the game precluded the development of a truly elite squad. Moreover, with the game firmly anchored in Europe, both cost and absence of opportunity served to undermine active consideration of an aggressive program of international competition. Beating England on their home turf, in 1959, was the catalyst which first prompted a growing passion and intensity for top-flight success. Organizationally the WHA was less than prepared for an expansion of its role. Shirley Davies, a former player for Australia and current board member, recalls vividly that back in the seventies, at her first council meeting some two days were spent dealing with matters arising from correspondence, but there was a growing thirst for more. Although creating the future took time, the WHA had inspirational players prepared to chart the necessary course. Shirley Davies:

> Within the Association there was a growing number of teachers and lecturers who brought administrative skills from their own careers into our board structure. More important was the ability to look at the sport and know what we had to do to change. By the early eighties we had an excellent group of people with a deep feeling for the sport who were committed to advancing the cause of women and Australian hockey. Over about a decade, we went from a completely amateur group to a professional entity. The big vision was to see women's hockey established as a very well managed business that could achieve success at a national and international level.

A further catalyst was the disappointment of not being able to attend the boycotted Moscow Olympics in 1980. This fuelled a desire to be competitive in Los Angeles in 1984. Participation in the Olympic tournament enabled women's hockey to access funds and elite programs developed in conjunction with the Australian Institute of Sport (AIS), which was established in Perth at the Bentley Stadium at that time. Key administrators were acutely aware of the opportunities that had been created by the Australian government's commitment to sport, channeled through the Australian Sports Commission. As Shirley Davies explains, 'You get recognition by being the best in the world,' something which now appeared to be within grasp, but this dream could not be achieved without clear planning.

Meg Wilson, who took over the presidency of the WHA in 1986, was the key inspirational player during this period. A member of the

Australian team during her own playing days, her presidency lasted a decade, coinciding, not by chance, with Australia's rise to dominance in world hockey. On the field of play, the Australian penchant for attacking flair in the face of the dour defenses of the European teams had already shown fruit with a fourth place in the 1984 Los Angeles Olympics. National Coach Brian Glencross was starting to manufacture a winning formula, and Wilson's organizational agenda straddled both the elite squad and the grass-roots programs located within the states. 'You've got to have a strong base so that many players get their basic skills right, from minky to junior and even social levels of play. From this base, talented players can be developed and fed into the elite system.'

Developing the game during the eighties was as much an organizational issue as it was one for the coaches charged with the responsibility of lifting the game on the field. Meg Wilson knew what was needed and, more importantly, what had to be done to make it happen. Of measured character, she is a reflective thinker who prevails through relentless determination, born out of a combination of passion and astute analytical ability, together with an uncanny knack for being able to coax others into doing things for which they would not normally consider themselves eligible. We were immediately made aware of Wilson's penchant for influencing events when she 'suggested' that rather than use the convivial Bentley Stadium offices under the stand, for her discussion with us, she would prefer to use one of the external observation booths, where she could keep track of the fiercely contested hockey game below.

Exposure to international competition, according to Wilson, is the key to maintaining an elite squad that can compete on an ongoing basis. With limited funds available to travel overseas, the women's game needed to develop a strong profile which would make Australia an attractive place for other teams to tour. As a past player and Australian selector, Wilson was well placed to develop a network of international contacts which were 'activated' the moment she was elected president of the WHA. Soon after her domestic elevation she became the first Australian woman ever to represent her country on the Federation of International Hockey (FIH). Wilson then set about getting Australian officials placed on FIH committees:

> I was the logical person to use the power of the FIH. That involved getting Australian women on to the development committees, umpiring committees, and on the jury for appeal, as well as getting an Australian umpire appointed at the Olympic Games. I also got an Australian person on to the technical bench – where the power resides. So Australian women were being recognized all the time. Once you've done all this, you can plan for your next bid.

Wilson's agenda was to bid for, and successfully host, the 1990 World Cup in Sydney. For this she needed money and an administrator with the consummate skills necessary to pull off such a major event. It was a bold initiative, but not out of place, as by the late eighties the Australian team was beginning to challenge the Dutch for world supremacy.

Against the expectations of many, the Hockeyroos won Olympic gold medal at the 1988 games in Seoul. The dream was well under way and, fortuitously, an opportunity to share it was about to present itself. Watching the magic-making gold medal celebrations in the Olympic stadium was an executive from the Telstra Corporation, who immediately saw the potential of a long-term association with a winning hockey team. Meg Wilson was not about to let slip a chance to share the dream with a major sponsor who would be able to provide funds for long-term development, which would in turn enable the WHA to bid successfully for major international tournaments. Using an uncharacteristically forceful voice, Wilson sought to impress upon us the significance of the Telstra initiative:

> In the end, when you get to a final, it's national success gets you a sponsor, and there's no doubt that success breeds success. You have to seize that success and make the best of it. Seize it. Go with it, or you will have lost the chance, you'll lose the momentum. That's what it's all about.

The momentum created by the gold medal, and the extra cash injections, came to a head when the FIH duly awarded Australia, and Sydney, the 1990 World Cup. The WHA then needed to demonstrate that they could be 'very good at managing'. A well-run World Cup would pave the way for teams to visit Australia on a more regular basis. This was a central feature of Wilson's determination to build a lasting dynasty.

Since the early eighties, the infrastructure of the WHA had grown alongside the programmes and operations associated with AIS in Perth. As new council members from each of the states are elected onto the federal body, Wilson ensured that each was given extensive responsibilities and portfolios. One of the emerging council members was Pam Tye, from Sydney. As early at 1986, Tye had put together a budget for hosting an international tournament. This kind of initiative ignited Wilson's belief in seeking out and mentoring women who had the passion and drive to elevate the profile of the WHA. Her long-term development of inspirational players as an essential element in creating the future is heavily underscored by Pam Tye's career path. Her personal growth and development as an outstanding administrator were clearly not accidental – her organizational exposure was meticulously planned. Within a very short time of her initial election to council, she was given enormous responsibility in the form of running the 1990 World Cup, which in turn gave her the necessary skills and profile to become a member of the board of directors, and finally to be elected as president of the WHA in 1996. The final piece in the jigsaw was securing her position in FIH upon Wilson's departure. Meg Wilson:

We went through a deliberate process. In the business of getting our people known, we deliberately made Pam the chairperson of the organizing committee. You don't get people into top positions in a federation in international hockey unless they already have some kind of profile. As a result of running the World Cup, Pam was well known, and when I wanted her to replace me on the FIH Board, I was able to do it because the ground had been prepared already. You absolutely must ensure that you are well recognized in areas such as federations, international sports commissions and the Australian Olympic Committee. You establish the kudos of the people in your organization so that your association can progress.

Pam Tye who readily recognizes Wilson's key role in driving the organization forwards over the year:

> Meg, in her leadership style, targets key people within the community she feels can assist in driving where she is perhaps incapable of doing it. She will focus on people and get their support – she has done that consistently over the years. In fact, I wouldn't be on the international scene if Meg hadn't had the foresight to realize that she would have to have a woman come through the ranks to replace her. In her development of people in the right places within the managerial structures of WHA she has made an enormous contribution. And I don't think many people realize how strong and clear thinking she was for the future.

The growth of the WHA necessitated a more formal review of its structures. The Bradley report, written in early 1991, reflected the expansion of the sport and the growing need to address the developmental side of women's hockey at state level, while ensuring that the elite program could deliver a world-beating national side. Rather than rely on infrequent general council meetings and a small cadre of executive officers to run the WHA, Bradley devised a five-member board of directors and president, nominated and elected by the states. The board is ultimately answerable to the council of sixteen state representatives. Several policy and operational committees were also established, with each of the board members allocated responsibility for their overall management. On the policy side, portfolios were created in development, international, marketing and promotions, finance, coaching and umpiring. Operational committees were established for selection, umpiring, indoor hockey, technical and coaching.

At the start of the eighties the WHA was an amateur body staffed almost entirely by volunteers. By the end of the decade the transformation to a thoroughly peak performing professional association was almost complete. Pam Tye saw the last vestiges of the old regime before Meg Wilson began moving the organization forward in the mid-eighties, and by the nineties she was at the center of activity designed to extend the supremacy of Australian women's field hockey on the world stage. As a school principal, authority comes easily to Tye. She is never lost for a controversial word or three, and positively delights in 'close-to-the-bone' remarks that will guarantee her close attention. Typically not pulling any punches, Tye tells how it used to be and what she wants to see now:

> In the early days it was a very amateurish organization, with the national body not as strong and developed as it is now, and the relationship with the states was not very well defined. Although I see my role as president is to provide an opportunity for the continued development of our elite players, the development of the game at the grass-roots level is equally important. We need a very strong, broad base from which we can operate, and I believe we are not doing our job if we fail to consider the development of younger players through to elite players. Our core business is our players.

From a public-relations point of view, Tye, with tongue in cheek, argues that, 'If we are not seen in the media and on television as successful, then they are all going to play netball and we can't have that.' The constant balancing act between development of the game at state level the need to drive the achievements of the elite program and the Hockeyroos, calls for a double focus. This is Tye's greatest challenge:

> I don't want to 'lose' representatives from the states because, from our perspective, we must always consider what's happening at this important level. We must provide them with the resources and the information that they require, but we've also got to develop a

greater understanding within our states of what the national body is doing, its relationship with international people and the importance of elite success, particularly with the Sydney Olympics in 2000.

Overall Tye believes that 'after "Bradley" we have developed further and become a lot stronger'. Confirmation of this comes from Rechelle Hawkes:

> My observation of the organization is that there is constant development in their professionalism. They are all passionate about hockey and they love the game and always try to do their very best to promote hockey. I have seen improvement in the last three or four years which I hadn't noticed before. It is important that they all have a real passion for the game. The administrative push for hockey to be at the top, together with the developments in the junior game all speak highly for WHA.

Unquestionably, by the time of the 1996 Olympics in Atlanta, a combination of sponsorship money, greater exposure and experience in tournament logistics, and the continued professionalism of the elite programs was clearly evident in the superior support systems and preparation of the national team. Planning and attention to the last detail set the Australian team apart from their international competitors. Hawkes's reference to the concept of 'improvement' carries with it a subtle nuance that is extremely perceptive. The WHA, without question, is the most self-critical organization in this study. Members of WHA rarely express satisfaction with current performance. Invariably, descriptions of processes, procedures or activities are couched in terms of how the next iteration will improve on current, sub-optimum results. The push to exceed personal best is utterly relentless.

Seeking to better one's own performance frequently leads to game-breaking ideas. Pam Tye, ever mindful of the continued strength of the European Federation, which is reflected in the prestigious and hard-fought European Cup competition, feels that the WHA is now strong enough to widen its field of influence by establishing an Asia-wide competition that would include teams from New Zealand, Korea and China. Sharing the dream of women's hockey encompasses building and developing the game elsewhere.

Conclusion

The national team is based in Perth. The national office is located in Sydney. The state associations are voluntary. In a moderate sized corporation the revenue streams would barely pass for expenses. The sporting culture in Australia is, for the most part, male dominated. In most circumstances, these would not be attractive odds to pick a winner. But it has happened. The Hockeyroos have sustained peak performance for more than a decade, displacing along the way the powerhouse sides from the European Federation.

Key inspirational players such as Shirley Davies and Meg Wilson initially began to lay the foundations for international success. This is an organization that has targeted and developed its people like no other we have seen. Opportunities have been carefully maximized by finding those talents who are willing and able to maintain the momentum for success. In a very deliberate fashion, those with a flair for administration have been plucked from the state associations, given resources, charged with responsibilities and then promoted to positions of authority – Pam Tye is the most obvious example of this process. Shirley Davies moved from player to council, to the board, to handling the critical portfolio of the elite program. Almost every senior administrator in the organization has been 'pulled' through on a calculated line of career progression. The organization creates its future by putting its people at the right time in the right place. This system of mentoring has enabled the WHA to sustain peak performance.

It is no surprise then, that the organization boasts a continual influx of inspirational players, none of whom put themselves above the dream. The tension and balance between elite success and grass-roots development continues to be handled astutely by all those who face the dilemma daily. Some personnel have two decades of tenure, but this continuity has not served to slow down the rate of change. Administrators and players alike constantly strive for improvement, better ways to do things and game-breaking ideas that others simply cannot match. In this, Coach Richard Charlesworth occupies a special place next to greatness.

There is, however, one development on the horizon which will sorely test the ability of the WHA to maintain its pre-eminence. From 2001, women's hockey will be merged with its male counterpart, to become Hockey Australia. Pressure from FIH affiliates and the Australian government have combined to alter the field of play irrevocably. Typically, almost all senior administrators in the organization support the move, arguing that they will be able to maintain the focus which the WHA has unswervingly served. Pam Tye:

> We have the ability to open our eyes and look down the track, to ensure the provision of opportunities for women to have highly successful careers in sport, to experience the exhilaration of an organization that is well run. Amalgamation will not alter the dream. It will add to it. What more can I say?

13

Peak Performing Organization Theory

Introduction

Peak Performing Organization Theory explains how to organize for sustained peak performance. Peak performance is defined as continuously exceeding organizational best in pursuit of the organization's purpose. A consistent pattern of success is evident from the different dreams of the sports organization stories. This chapter is a synthesis of those stories, highlighting the key ideas and attitudes that run through the hearts of these exceptional organizations. This synthesis has produced PPO Theory, a set of principles and concepts that can be applied to any organization—sporting or business—to enable it to become the best that it can be.

An organization is based on people and, in particular, inspirational players who are the driving force in putting PPO principles into action. They are the organizers. The combination of inspirational players and PPO principles and concepts constitutes PPO Theory.

There are four PPO principles: purpose, practice, potency, and performance. Purpose provides intent, meaning, and direction for people within organizations. Practice puts in place the organizational context, environment, and practices that provide the foundations for sustained success. Potency relates to the processes that occur in consciousness—thoughts, emotions, intuition, desire, will, and memory—that provide the energy for sustained peak performance. Performance explains the actions necessary for sustained success.

Each principle embraces three mutually reinforcing concepts:

Purpose: the greatest imaginable challenge, the inspirational dream and the focus

Practice: creating the future, sharing the dream and family

Potency: harmony, passion, and flow

Performance: the last detail, game-breaking ideas, and exceeding organizational best.

Inspirational Players

PPO Theory commences with "inspirational players." We use this term to denote agents within a PPO who are instrumental in effecting the PPO concepts. We have avoided the traditional terminology of leadership because of the huge number of different theoretical perspectives that have been put forward over the years as to what constitutes effective leadership. In addition, "leadership" necessarily implies "followership," and there was no evidence of following in our PPO case studies; indeed, the idea is antithetical to the PPO concept of flow.

Inspirational players are central to establishing an organization's purpose. They start the play. Subsequent generations of inspirational players live the dream, make it happen, and inspire others to own the organizational dream in their own right, to exceed their personal best and to become peak performers. In every case they are powerful people with powerful ideas. PPOs have several inspirational players positioned throughout their organizations.

The dream to make the Atlanta Braves the best ball club in baseball originated with Ted Turner, but the key inspirational players who made it happen, both strategically and operationally, were its president, Stan Kasten, and general manager, John Schuerholz. The dream to win and retain the America's Cup for New Zealand originated with Michael Fay, but the inspirational players who made it happen were Peter Blake, Alan Sefton, Russell Coutts, Tom Schnackenberg, Brad Butterworth, and others. We found no evidence to support the idea of a charismatic leader single-handedly transforming the fortunes of the organization. Inspirational players from previous eras are honored and remain essential members of the PPO family. For example, the usher at the San Francisco 49ers who retired at age ninety-five was a legend, while inspirational soccer players from Bayern Munich's past are positioned throughout the organization.

Inspirational players are role models in that they provide a benchmark for others to emulate and exceed. They also recruit, mentor, and develop people, providing for succession within the organization. The success of the Chicago Bulls owes much to Steve Schanwald in nurturing people in the right places throughout the management structure. Simultaneously, inspirational players are the catalysts for creating the key sense of community or familylike environment. They inspire trust in themselves, in others, and in the organization.

Inspirational players are also actively involved, and make their own direct contributions, exemplifying perfection. Technical Director Patrick Head can name and explain the precise purpose of any part in the Williams factory. Their enthusiasm is infectious. They are accessible, energetic, and passionate.

Some inspirational players become icons of the sport and of society as a whole. Franz Beckenbauer is German soccer. Michael Jordan personifies basketball; there may never be another athlete who can exceed his skill and charisma. But PPOs successfully ensure that their sports icons do not overshadow their brand. The powerful Bulls brand, arguably the most evocative in all of pro sports, was built separately from that of Michael Jordan, while Franz Beckenbauer features only lightly in the marketing of his organization. They extend, rather than transcend, the inspirational dream.

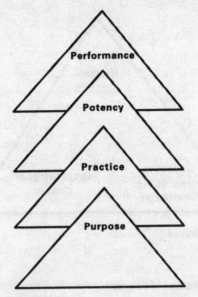

FIGURE 1—Principles

PPO Principles

Figure 1 depicts the relationship among the four PPO principles. The principles must be implemented sequentially and cumulatively, and they are mutually reinforcing. Inspirational players are instrumental in implementation.[19]

Purpose

Purpose provides intent, meaning, and direction for people within organizations. It comprises three PPO concepts: the inspirational dream, the greatest imaginable challenge, and the focus. These concepts are mutually reinforcing and, in combination, they provide the all-important clarity of purpose that is essential for success. They are illustrated in the purpose triangle (Figure 2). Inspirational players are instrumental in establishing the organization's purpose.

[19] Ideas about how to organize are incommensurable with ideas about who organizes insofar as illustration in a one-dimensional model is concerned. Each PPO principle and concept presumes human agency. PPO theory is empirically dependent on inspirational players who are instrumental to the achievement of peak performance.

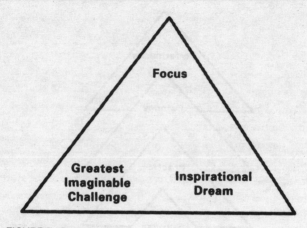

FIGURE 2—Purpose

The Inspirational Dream

The inspirational dream derives from deep conversations within the organization and emerges from its histories and traditions. It is a mental image of an ideal state or destiny for the organization that provides meaning and recognition for the individuals who work there. It relates to why activities are undertaken rather than to what must be achieved by those activities. As a consequence, it is not measurable.

The dream makes people want to belong, because it provides a sense of recognition and collective importance. For Williams the dream derives from the joy of racing faster than everyone else, and members of the Williams family achieve global recognition for the speed of their cars on the racetrack. FC Bayern Munich wants to win championships, but the dream that gives this meaning is "More than 1–0": soccer working for the greater good of society. There is intrinsic value in the dream beyond winning championships. But by winning championships attractively, Bayern Munich raises its status and that of soccer, thereby creating more influence for the club to do "good things" for society and create meaning for the fans.

The inspirational dream is akin to the Greek philosopher Plato's notion of Thymos,[20] "spiritedness" or "recognition." People wish to be acknowledged as having worth or dignity; this enhances their self-esteem and increases their pride in themselves. People extend this desire for recognition to the ideas, principles, or activities that they invest with value. They are prepared to make great financial and physical sacrifices for recognition, including long hours of work, physical discomfort, pain, and, in extreme cases, even death. The need for Thymos lies at the heart of political and religious conflict and many wars. It urges people to enter sailing races in the stormiest waters of the world or risk death in Formula One racing cars. Thymos underpins the inspirational dream that lies at the heart of great endeavor and Peak Performing Organizations.

The Greatest Imaginable Challenge

Peak performance is defined in terms of the greatest imaginable challenge that an organization sets itself—being the best that the organization can be. The challenge is the dream in action. It is the most demanding and rewarding tangible achievement that can be imagined for the organization. It must be imaginable and feasible, as well as important, stretching, and exciting. It must also be measurable, so that achievement is clear. The U.S. Women's Soccer Team has set out to win all the major international soccer tournaments—World Cups and Olympics—for years to come, while the Chicago Bulls want to be back in contention for NBA championships. Each challenge set is related to the organization's unique context, circumstances, and aspirations. In both sport and business it can be defined in relation to regional, national, or international competition. By working toward a great challenge, people achieve recognition and self-esteem through being part of the best, and from individual opportunities for peak performance. The greatest imaginable challenge provides the basis for

---

[20] In *The Republic*, Plato explained there are three parts to the soul that explain much of human behavior: desire, reason, and Thymos. Desire makes people seek things beyond themselves, while reason shows how to get them.

focus and direction for organizational participants, and once attained, it must be reimagined to sustain success.

The inspirational dream and the greatest imaginable challenge must be in harmony with each other, but on their own they do not provide a basis for action. Many people dream of doing outstanding things, but few succeed. They do nothing to turn the dream into a reality. By contrast, a PPO defines its greatest imaginable challenge and then moves on to focusing systematically on achieving it. Beyond the dream and the challenge, the third essential concept of purpose is the focus.

Renewing the Challenge

PPOs provide an organizational context in which players are able to achieve intrinsic and extrinsic rewards to the maximum of their potential as they aim to meet the challenge set. But once achieved, the challenge is no longer a challenge. PPOs know that to sustain purpose, the challenge must evolve once it has been achieved. They also understand that external forces will change the nature of the game, but equally such change can be leveraged to enhance success. Nothing stays the same for long in any industry. Renewing the challenge and retaining focus as the game changes is the essence of a PPO.

There are four ways in which the challenge can be renewed.

1. Changing the rules of the game. When the America's Cup Association agreed to change the rules of the game to replace 12-meter class yachts with a new international America's Cup class, all design syndicates had to return to the drawing board, and prior competitiveness in 12-meters meant little. The new America's Cup class is bigger, faster, and more exciting, creating new sponsorship opportunities and media spectacles. Every Formula One season is marked by technical changes to the specifications of the car, which the designers and testers have to understand and work with in order to find a new edge over their rivals. In rugby union there have been numerous rule changes to the tackle, scrum, and line-outs, which the All Black players and coaches have had to master to be able to retain their supremacy in the sport. Equivalent rule changes exist in business, such as tariffs, stock exchange requirements, exchange rates, antitrust laws, trade agreements, and environmental legislation. All these and many more are capable of changing overnight the rules of the corporate game. PPOs create value for themselves by being instrumental in changing the rules of the game. For example, Michael Fay was instrumental in changing the rules of the America's Cup through the big boat challenge.

2. *Changing the league.* A European super soccer league has been proposed involving all the leading clubs, which as a consequence would mean that they would not be available to participate in their national leagues (i.e., if the plans for this league are implemented, Bayern Munich would no longer play in the German Bundesliga but would instead line up against the leading teams from other European countries such as Real Madrid from Spain, Juventus from Italy, and Manchester United from England). The revenue to the national leagues would change dramatically as the emphasis moves to the super league and its constituent clubs. The equivalent to changing the league in business is competing in a different market, expanding from local to national to global. PPOs seek to be in continuous championship contention in the leagues in which they play, and then move on to ever more challenging leagues once dominance is achieved in the existing league. If a more challenging league does not exist, they will create one.

3. *Changing participants.*
   • Public: enlarging or shifting the fan or customer base changes the game. The FC Bayern Munich fan club network extends globally. It even has a new fan club in China. PPOs reletentlessly look for opportunities to expand their customer base.
   • Partners: WilliamsF1 dropped their Renault engine in 1998 because Renault no longer had a strong enough commitment to development. Their new association with BMW will be dramatic, as BMW and Mercedes (through McLaren) race each other vicariously. This

association has created new technical challenges and opportunities as well as the need to redefine relationships.

• Players: As team members move on to different challenges, the opportunity is created for new people to live the inspirational dream and to become inspirational in their own right.

4. *Changing the game itself.* This may involve changing the dream, which cannot be undertaken lightly. For example, the U.S. women's indoor soccer league provided enhanced revenue for leading players and participating clubs, but took the emphasis away from the traditional outdoor game. There was an increased risk of injury to key players and dissipation in focus. Saatchi & Saatchi (one of the authors is worldwide chief executive), the global advertising agency, provides an example of changing the game in business. They are repositioning themselves away from advertising toward becoming an ideas organization. This has necessitated profound rethinking of all aspects of the way they do business. The merger and acquisition activity in the corporate sector, so prevalent in the past ten years, is a clear example of how many businesses have suddenly been faced with an entirely new game to play.

Change renews the challenge (or provides a challenge for new people), and provides new opportunities (or opportunities for new people). PPOs use change relentlessly to enhance individual and organizational renewal and reward and to leverage additional financial resources with which to create the future. PPOs nurture and sustain their purpose in the face of external turbulence, altering the challenge to reflect or create the external environment.

Focus

Establishing the inspirational dream and the greatest imaginable challenge are prerequisites for focus. The focus of an organization is the concentration of energy on actions necessary to achieve the organization's purpose. It provides clear direction and interest for participants. Focus involves identifying specific actions to be undertaken, rather than targeting the end result required. The fewer the actions in focus, the better. The focus for WilliamsF1 is to push back technological barriers to make the car go faster; the whole organization is aligned behind this. The focus for the San Francisco 49ers organization is to look after the team; they do so in any and all ways possible so that the players can focus on peak performance.

Focus clarifies priorities and aligns everyday tasks. People focus their attention and energies on meaningful, challenging goals as an essential ingredient in achieving peak performance. Rolling game plans or short-term action goals provide direction and the basis for real-time feedback and assessment of performance. Action goals must be demanding yet feasible, and are set by the individuals responsible for action. The goals require the active use of skills and lead to discovery, exploration, and problem-solving, which in turn provides the basis for participant satisfaction. The activities themselves become intrinsically rewarding. Ever more challenging goals are always being developed. PPOs measure themselves continuously against these goals to ensure that they are improving. Short-term action goals aligned to Williams's focus might include:

- Redesign the wheel nut to be multisided to increase the torque potential and reduce time for wheel changes.
- Redesign the nose cone to reduce drag.
- Redesign the exhaust system to increase brake horsepower.

Effective game plans will be action-based, challenging, worded in the affirmative, and include a time frame. Goals derive from focus and break it into smaller units, while focus is ultimately derived from the challenge set by the organization.

Players must receive commensurate intrinsic or extrinsic rewards to feel valued and to increase their ability or willingness to focus on the achievement of peak performance. As Peter Blake explained, PPOs "pay the very best they are able, and expect the very best."

The following table sets out the relationship among the inspirational dream, the greatest imaginable challenge, and the focus for each of our PPO case studies. Note that the dreams provide a sense of meaning and importance, the challenges are measurable and stretching, and the focus relates to actions rather than outcomes.

Organization	Inspirational Dream	Greatest Imaginable Challenge	Focus
Atlanta Braves	Live the American dream through sustained baseball supremacy	To win the World Series	Recruit and develop the very best players through coaching and scouting
Bayern Munich FC	More than 1–0: soccer for the greater good of society	To be the world's greatest soccer club	Recruit and develop the very best players through coaching and scouting
Chicago Bulls	Winning for Chicago	To be in contention for NBA championships	Create magical sports entertainment theater
New York Yankees	Live the American dream through sustained baseball supremacy	To continue to be the world's most successful baseball team	Recruit and develop the very best players through coaching and scouting
New Zealand Rugby Union	Inspire the New Zealand nation with their rugby achievements	To win all international matches	Build a portfolio of world-beating brands
San Francisco 49ers	The quintessential football family	To win the next Super Bowl	Look after the team
Team New Zealand	Sailing and technological supremacy for New Zealand	Beat the billionaires!	Increase the speed and maneuverability of the boat
U.S. Women's Soccer	Recognition and respect for women's soccer	To win all international games	Development of infrastructure
WilliamsF1	The joy of speed and technological excellence	To win all Formula One championships	Technological innovation to make the car go faster

Multiple Challenges

Single-product organizations such as Team New Zealand and WilliamsF1 can create shared purpose more easily than those with multiple products or brands such as U.S. Soccer or the New Zealand Rugby Union. Challenges must be feasible yet stretching. It follows that in a complex organization with multiple products or brands it may be necessary to imagine multiple challenges, because what is feasible for one product or brand may be infeasible or inappropriate for another. If the challenges vary, in all probability so will the focus.

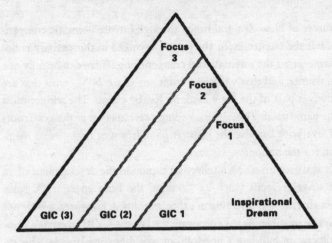

FIGURE 3—Mulltiple Challenges

However, the inspirational dream must be common to all areas of an organization. In the absence of a common dream, there is nothing to share internally or externally. If a shared dream cannot be found, the organization can never become a peak performer. In this case it would be better to create multiple enterprises in which the people can then be inspired by their own dreams and challenges.

Tensions arose in the past between U.S. Women's Soccer and the National Federation of Soccer because of the lack of a shared inspirational dream and a feeling among women soccer players and officials that there was insufficient respect and recognition for the women's game. This has changed in recent years and the sustained international success of the U.S. Women's National Team has brought respect and recognition for U.S. soccer generally, such that a shared inspirational dream becomes possible.

The New Zealand Rugby Union has multiple brands. The All Blacks, the Super 12s, the Black Ferns, and the Maori All Blacks can all share the common challenge of winning all international matches. But the NPC, or National Provincial Championship, provides domestic competition. It is grassroots rugby, rugged and raw, where local and regional passions come to the fore, and it is essential for creating the future of New Zealand rugby through intense domestic competition. But the challenge for the people involved in this activity is not the same as for the international competitions. There can be only one NPC winner, and that will come from one of the NPC teams that are themselves part of the New Zealand Rugby Union. The winner must be the game itself. Through exceeding previous best at the grassroots level, everyone can live the inspirational dream of rugby as an inspiration for the nation.

It is worth investing intellectual capital in the development of an ideal singular focus (such as "making the boat go faster"), since dream-sharing and direction are then simplified. However, it may not always be possible. At the corporate level of the NZRU there is a common focus on building a portfolio of world-beating brands. This relates directly to the dream and challenge. But it is too remote a call to action to engage all functional areas of the organization. Area-specific focus may be appropriate in complex organizations, but they must all harmonize with the dream and challenge and the top-level focus.

Passionate commitment to purpose is a prerequisite for peak performance. Business units should be based on a shared dream, challenge, and focus in such a way that flow becomes possible. Flow is not possible across multiple challenges and focuses (and business units), but peak performing parts of an organization can be integrated into a peak performing whole if there is a shared dream. This is illustrated in Figure 3 above.

Practice

Practice will proceed in different ways dependent on the organization's purpose. In particular, the focus will establish direction and priorities. For example, if "developing the required infrastructure" is the focus, the organizational context will be designed on this basis. Practice defines the characteristics of PPOs, creates the environment, and puts in place the organizational actions that provide the foundation for sustained success. It comprises three concepts: sharing the dream, creating the future, and family. The concepts are closely interrelated and should be viewed in combination, as each one plays to and draws from the others. In particular, creating the future through the appointment and development of excellent people, and sharing the dream among all organizational participants, leads to a sense of family and mutual commitment to the shared purpose. Inspirational players again hold the pivotal role—they share the dream primarily through telling stories; they create the future through appointing, coaching, and developing only the very best people; and they foster family by acting as role models for relationships.

Sharing the Dream

Sharing the dream is achieved through a process of internal and external communication. The dream provides meaning and it sustains involvement. It is built on historic performances and reinforced by legends, histories, and traditions, creating a legacy of dreams. Sharing the dream is achieved through storytelling, constant celebration of success, and the display of compelling tangible symbols of success. Stories are told and retold, orally and through the media, and new stories are constantly created. Inspirational players are first and foremost storytellers.

The dream is made real by the compelling symbols of achievement and success that are displayed throughout the organization, and beyond it through marketing and media relations. World Series base-

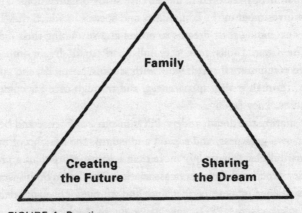

FIGURE 4—Practice

ball caps, Super Bowl pennants, and models of Grand Prix winning cars carry the dream to the fans. These symbols emotionally connect everyone to the dream and create an organization in which people feel that anything is possible, that something amazing is going to happen. For Williams, the dream is manifested in the Formula One cars, center stage in the atrium and the museum.

The inspirational dream is widely shared with:

principals (shareholders or owners)
players (organization participants)
purchasers (people who do business with the organization)
partners (alliance partners and sponsors)
philanthropy recipients
public
press

We call these the 7Ps. Each of these groups is made to feel valued. Relationship building and dream sharing is imaginative and sustained. The organization's infrastructure is designed to nurture relationships among each of the 7Ps. Sharing the dream widely sustains it within the organization, and extends magical experiences to others. They are enchanted with the special nature of their relationships with PPOs.

Philanthropy featured in all the case study organizations. There was an investment in the community and society in which they live, thereby extending their dreams to others and sustaining their meaning. The CharitaBulls take the Bulls basketball dream into the Chicago community through work with schools, hospitals, and youth centers, through player appearances, and through care for community causes. They belong.

By sharing the dream widely, PPOs inspire confidence and belief in their own greatness, and sustain and enlarge the horizon of business possibilities. Clients buy more than a game, more than a product. They experience the aura of association. The dream both sustains and is sustained by peak performance and winning. Through celebration of achievements, PPOs make magic for all involved.

Creating the Future

Creating the future is based on programs of investment in long-term development. PPOs create the future through people, infrastructure, and financial systems. They live and die on their organizational infrastructure. Without exception our case study organizations have carefully constructed physical and financial infrastructures. Federal structures, alliances, and information networks all serve this end. The precise form and the degree of formality is of little consequence as it is personal relationships rather than formal organizational structures that make the difference. Hence the importance of the continuity of inspirational players.

PPOs align their infrastructure to their focus. In Williams and Team New Zealand the infrastructure revolves around making the car or the boat go faster. In the Atlanta Braves and FC Bayern Munich the farm team[21] infrastructure provides for relentless recruitment and development of first-choice athletes. The infrastructure allows for complete, open, and rapid accessibility to and sharing of information inside the organization, but the secrets of success are closely guarded from those outside.

The future of PPOs is grounded in tradition. They have all built excellent processes for scouting, selecting, attracting, and promoting the very best elite players, both on the field and in the organization. They invest in peak performing depth throughout the organization. PPOs make an enormous commitment to mentoring and development. Bill Walsh of the San Francisco 49ers explained that mentoring and development lay at the heart of their success.

There is a clear preference across all the PPOs for promoting internally and growing people within the organization, but this is balanced by careful recruitment to sustain the organization's energy and capacity. For example, as we have already seen, FC Bayern Munich has inspirational players from previous eras positioned throughout the organization, but they also recruit externally both within Germany and beyond to complement existing skills. Continuity is of para-

[21] A team associated with the PPO from which they recruit, develop, and nurture the next generation of players.

mount importance, but this is balanced with the acceptance that there can come a time when further growth can occur only beyond the organization. The NFL is positioned throughout with people who developed their skills in the 49ers way. Recruitment, development, and continuity create depth. Depth is the investment for the future, and enables careful succession planning. PPOs seldom advertise for positions—inspirational players are selectively invited in to sustain and amplify the dream. A PPO's phenomenal record of success is built on employing the very best. Many inspirational players in the San Francisco 49ers have moved on to take up important roles elsewhere, but the 49ers have developed an uncanny ability to replace departed icons of the sport with others of equal or even greater ability.

Each organization has built long-term financial equity and is financially secure, but it is not money that made them into PPOs. Financial security is achieved through peak performance, but it is not necessarily a prerequisite for PPO progress. We learned from several cases that the availability of excessive funding reduces the ability to find focus, as it shifts the perspective from "How do we make best use of our funds to realize the dream?" to "What do we do with the money?" Team New Zealand retained America's Cup 2000 on less than a third of the budget of some of the challengers.

Family

Close, long-lived relationships provide a secure environment that:

- enables mental calm and confidence
- dispels entropy, and
- facilitates exceeding personal best.

Creating the future ensures that excellent people are recruited and developed. Sharing the dream ensures that there is widespread commitment to the shared purpose. In combination, this leads to a sense of family in which rituals and relationships create a calm, relaxed, and informal environment that facilitates the mental clarity necessary for peak performance.

An infectious sense of humor and fun pervades PPOs. For the Women's U.S. Soccer Team, humor among the players is constantly evident, and their children become part of their training sessions. This strengthens the family and builds relationships. PPO members live the dream and belong to the PPO family. The family looks after its own. For example, the night before San Francisco 49ers home games, players, coaches, and administrators and their families assemble and mingle at the San Francisco Marriott Hotel, exemplifying the comfortable relationships that provide the peace of mind necessary for peak performance. The New York Yankees picture the Yankees "family" in their 2000 yearbook.

We have used the term "family" to describe this concept because when we interviewed organization participants it was mostly "family" that we heard when they were describing the relationships within the organization. However some organizations used the term "community" to mean the same thing. It is an extended family to which people come and go, but never really leave. For example, in 1999 Bill Walsh returned as general manager of the San Francisco 49ers, eleven years after departing the coach's bench as the most successful coach of his era. April Heinrichs, a former player with the U.S. Women's Soccer Team, is now their head coach. The family satisfies members' basic needs for security. They share joys and sorrows, successes and failures; and together they overcome adversity, celebrate achievements, and enjoy financial rewards. Everyone benefits from success, as bonuses are based on the success of the organization as a whole. Everyone at WilliamsF1 receives a bonus when the team wins a Formula One race. PPO players are paid well, but their deep rewards are intrinsic—being part of the best. Relationships are built on mutual trust, respect, pride, tradition, loyalty, and a sense of belonging. In sport this pride in belonging is made visually apparent through pulling on the jersey, the symbolic representation of the best. The championship rings given to all family members in our North American PPOs symbolize this elite involvement.

The longevity in relationships within PPOs can lead to sacrificial plays—sacrificing personal glory for the benefit of other team members,

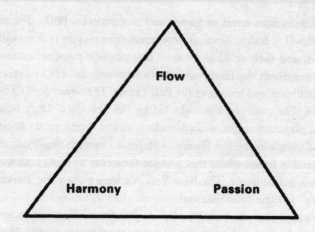

FIGURE 5—Potency

or the organization. For example, Russell Coutts gave up the opportunity for taking the world record for the number of straight America's Cup victories when he handed over the helm of NZ 60 to Dean Barker for the last race of America's Cup 2000. By sacrificing personal glory he helped to create the future, because Dean Barker will be the skipper for the next defense.

Potency

Potency relates to the processes that occur in consciousness—thoughts, emotions, intuition, desire, will, and memory. This principle explains how organization participant develop the shared mental models that provide the necessary energy[22] for sustained peak performance. Potency defines the capacity, ability, latent talent, hopes, and attitudes of a PPO. The departure point for potency is the feeling of calm, confidence, and well-being that derives from the family environment that has been created. The three concepts of potency are harmony, passion, and flow. Harmony with self and others combined

[22] For further consideration of energistic approaches to consciousness, see Carl Jung, "On Psychic Energy," in C. G. Jung, Collected Works, vol 8, Princeton, N.J.: Princeton University Press, 1960, and M. Csikszentmihalyi, *Flow: The Psychology of Optimal Experience*, New York: HarperCollins, 1991, p.30.

with passionate commitment to the organization's purpose facilitates flow. Flow is a state of optimal experience, readiness, or preparedness for peak performance. Inspirational players are instrumental in creating an organizational climate that focuses mental energy on sustained success.

Passion

People are emotionally connected with, and committed to, the organization and its purpose. Passion derives from the focus and the family environment that has been created, and from a deep commitment to the dream that provides the meaning. In a PPO there is an insatiable passion to win and an unrelenting, intense belief in being the best, which creates an expectation of success. Greatness is deeply entrenched in the psyche of the organization—it is built on historic performances, legends, histories, and traditions, and is reinforced by the constant, collective celebration of success. There is a shared atmosphere of excitement, a mystique of belonging, and a love of the game and the industry. In each of the case studies people are clearly passionate about what they do. This is because they feel that they are able to make a difference, and that they are contributing to a purpose that is both meaningful and important.

The New York Yankees display their passion for the pinstripes in a remarkable way. Throughout Yankee Stadium and alongside the celebration of their feted baseball legends are plaques and portraits of staff who have served the organization as administrators. In the front office, longtime receptionist Doris Walden earns the right to be placed next to Ruth, DeMaggio, and Mantle. Pete Sheehy, Yankee equipment manager, "Keeper of the Pinstripes," and Jimmy Esposito, Yankee Stadium superintendent, have their plaques right in the Yankee dugout.

People invest personal energy in the organization's purpose because it provides meaning and direction in their lives beyond the material rewards of the job. Tom Schnackenberg joined Team New Zealand for the 1995 America's Cup campaign before ascertaining the reward package because he believed that he could make the greatest difference with Team New Zealand. Because people choose to invest personal energy and emotion beyond that which is necessary to earn their paycheck, they feel in control of their own destiny. They feel in harmony with themselves and others who have made a similar choice. Work, pleasure, and leisure merge.

Harmony

Harmony is a dynamic clarity of thought and sense of emotional well-being deriving from shared purpose and based on intuitive, instinctive, long-lived relationships. Having a focus and a sense of being able to participate in creating the future within a family environment leads to harmony. Harmony with self and others leads to balanced, natural relationships achieved through mutual respect rather than through rules, policies, or procedures. It removes clutter from the mind and allows meaningful thought or action.

The opposite of harmony is mental entropy, a state in which consciousness is jumbled with a multiplicity of anxieties, problems, and uncontrolled thoughts. Most of us will experience this at times when our minds wander aimlessly, or family, health, or work-related stresses and strains create such anxiety that little useful activity is possible. If, by contrast, we feel safe in our relationships, healthy, financially secure, and at one with our inner selves, this enables mental clarity, which is essential for focus and peak performance.

PPOs create a mutually supportive, familylike environment to sustain harmony and minimize the risk of organization-induced entropy. PPO people take a personal interest in each other to assist in minimizing the effect of personal issues creating individual disorder. Tim Hallam of the Chicago Bulls explained how Bulls' people had over the years supported each through all manner of personal problems, crises, joys, and sadness.

If there are too many challenges, or if the challenge is too great, we feel anxious. Alternatively, if the challenges are too few or insufficiently meaningful, we become bored. We appear to need ever-increasing challenges to sustain our interest and commitment, yet through ever-increasing complexity we run the risk of becoming overwhelmed and less effective. A PPO sustains harmony through focusing on the "just right" challenge.

Deep understanding of the minds of others leads to a special rhythm in relationships, which in time translates into effective performance. Heinz Harold Frenzen described the flow of activity in the Williams pit-lane garage as having a special rhythm. This leads to a calm, mutually supportive environment in which there is anticipation of others' actions and perception of others' needs. Similarly, on the field of play the U.S. Women's Soccer Team seem to know instinctively what each other will do. A clear focus on what needs to be done, long-lived relationships, and a familylike environment enable real-time improvisation and a sense of peripheral vision or "360-degree radar." Over time, PPO people develop a sixth sense. Actions in harmony can take place based on the merest glance, change in expression, or body movement, such as we witnessed on NZ 38 or in the Williams pit-lane garage. As a consequence, PPO people pick up problems and opportunities to which ordinary organizations would be oblivious. Actions are based on doing what needs to be done before it needs to be done rather than in response to specified job descriptions.

Flow

Flow, or optimal experience, describes the calm and effortless flow of mind and body in synchronization with surroundings in the focused completion of complex tasks or actions toward the achievement of an important challenge. The concept of flow has been developed and popularized by Mihaly Csikszentmihalyi[23] during more than two decades of research. He explains that "the most basic requirement (to achieve flow) is to provide a clear set of challenges," leading to "discovery, exploration, and problem solving."[24] The individual must

[23] Csikszentmihalyi M., *Flow: The Psychology of Optimal Experience,* New York, Harper & Row, 1990; *Creativity: Flow and the Psychology of Discovery and Invention,* New York, HarperCollins, 1996; *Finding Flow: The Psychology of Engagement with Everyday Life,* New York, Basic Books, 1997.

[24] Csikszentmihalyi M., *Beyond Boredom and Anxiety: The Experience of Play in Work and Games,* San Francisco, Jossey-Bass, 1975.

perceive the challenges to be demanding yet attainable. To achieve flow the activity must be engaged in out of choice, be intrinsically rewarding, and provide clear and immediate feedback, and necessitate the active use of skills, which may be physical, cerebral, or both.

Flow is best understood on a continuum varying in intensity, with peak flow at one end and low-level flow at the other. Flow experiences also vary according to the individual and across cultures—activities capable of providing flow experiences to one person may be intensely boring to another. Clarity of focus is critical to enable PPOs to develop an environment in which peak flow can occur.

Many of us will have experienced peak flow momentarily during our working or social lives. It can be experienced in any challenging activity for which you are well prepared, whether rock climbing, ocean sailing, or work. It can occur when we have tackled a task that we feel exceptionally well prepared for, and undertaken it beyond our best expectations. People experiencing peak flow achieve extraordinary awareness, confidence, and power. They are totally focused and totally absorbed. They expect to succeed, and feel intense pleasure when experiencing this state. They feel at one with surroundings, friends, teammates, colleagues, and themselves. Time is transformed, with hours of focused time appearing to fly by in minutes. They feel unbeatable, and have an extraordinary joy in life. To sustain peak flow, goals that extend skills and abilities must be developed and redeveloped continually.

It is possible to create a state of intense awareness and readiness for peak flow that is critical if sustained peak performance is to be achieved. The players must find themselves in an environment in which they have the best possible chance of achieving peak flow. They require a state of calmness facilitated through the development of a familylike environment out of which they have the possibility of being able to concentrate the mind on the team's clear and tangible focus. Csikszentmihalyi developed his theory of flow in relation to the psychology of individual performance and experience, and we have chosen to extend the theory to the domain of organizations. We observed that teams and organizations could share flow experiences in circumstances when common goals are pursued and the team feels well prepared and mutually supportive. In PPOs the collective thoughts and actions of individual participants combine to achieve sustainable organizational peak performance. Peak organizational flow describes the apparently effortless achievement of demanding organizational tasks in harmony to the intense satisfaction of participants. Peak flow develops among PPO members as they learn how each other thinks and acts and can anticipate each other's needs intuitively. They interact in ways that enable the organization to be greater than the sum of its players.

Information flows easily before it is needed and forms the play. Flexibility, sacrificial plays, and making space for others are the accepted norms, while players are committed to their own and others' intellectual and technical development. Preparing for a home game at the United Center, the Chicago Bulls coordinate a raft of interlocking activities. Without obvious urgency or frenetic activity, stadium operations, ticketing, sponsorship programs, pregame entertainment, media, and the basketball team all merge into a coherent package. Year in and year out, organizational flow delivers a unique experience to the sold-out United Center. Organizational flow can also be critical at a time of potential crisis. When the New York Yankees were faced with the prospect of having a weather-related cancellation of their year-2000 opening-day game, CEO Lonn Trost was able to swiftly establish an impromptu decision-making process that required each department to assess the impact of a cancellation decision on their own area and, more important, upon other functions directly associated with their operations. Intuitive recognition of what cancellation meant to others, rather than simply one's own domain, enabled the Yankees to avoid a messy process of discordant indecision.

Flow and peak performance are often used interchangeably in sports psychology, but we distinguish between them. Flow is the experience; peak performance is the achievement. The existence of organizational flow minimizes the usefulness of formal organization charts, policy manuals, or job descriptions. Relationships take their

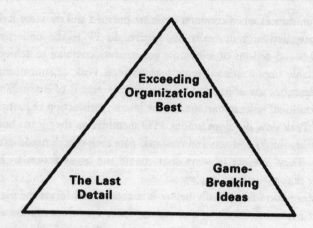

FIGURE 6—Performance

place. Flow eliminates the need for management-inspired cross-functional teams. Instead, we found traditional teams of functional specialists, each expert in its own domain. The easy flow of information and assistance between members integrates activity across the PPO, focused on the dream in action.

A PPO workplace flows. Rituals and routines create a calm environment in which action and complete awareness can merge, leading to intense pleasure. Practices provide the organizational context in which flow can occur. Few people can sustain flow permanently, but in a PPO people spend more time in flow than in ordinary organizations. Peak performance is imagined, not managed. As a consequence, the need for motivation is not an issue. It is replaced by passionate commitment to the organization's purpose.

Performance

Performance explains how the organization's purpose is achieved. Catching the last detail and imagining and implementing game-breaking ideas enable the continuous exceeding of organizational best. A clear purpose, careful practice, and developing potency are all prerequisites for performance. In particular, potency is based on the achievement of individual and organizational flow during a high proportion of work time. Inspirational players are role models as well as being central to the action. Performance is illustrated in Figure 6.

Game-Breaking Ideas

PPOs achieve peak performance through a combination of radical change and nonstop incremental improvements. They bring about radical changes to the rules, the league, the players, and the game itself to enhance their ability to live the dream and renew the challenge. In addition, game-breaking ideas change the way the organization's game is played to create winning opportunities. Intellectual pressure is constantly applied to all aspects of the organization's activities, and there is continuous experimentation derived from looking to exceed one's personal best. Focus provides direction.

New ideas flow naturally, and there is an enthusiasm for risk-taking because innovation gains recognition and credit. PPO people are not penalized for failure—the emphasis is upon putting things right, not allocating blame when things go wrong. Innovation often goes through considerable periods of failure before success is arrived at, and ideas that do not work are regarded as opportunities for further learning, while a powerful institutional memory prevents the repetition of earlier mistakes. Innovation and game-breaking ideas flourish in this atmosphere because there is no fear of failure. Progress is achieved through experimentation and, as a consequence, anything is regarded as possible—there is always a better way. However, experimentation is undertaken in such a way as to minimize risk to product or service quality and client relationships.

Everyone contributes, and people with ideas are able to make them happen, regardless of whether or not the issue in question falls within their area of responsibility. To assist in this process, information is freely shared within the organization but carefully protected from outsiders, while frequent informal communication crosses functions and structures. Mental space is created for individual and group creativity, and the calm environment and easy relationships fostered by the familylike structure encourage clarity. As a consequence, there is a cross-fertilization of ideas, which enables new ways of seeing. Imagination drives innovation, fueled by the purpose.

The Last Detail

PPO people are committed to catching each and every last detail. A PPO strives for perfection in all aspects of its relationships with clients and the delivery of its products and services. All activities are constantly reviewed. Catching the last detail can win the game and is the essence of PPOs—a single point or 1/500th of a second can make the winning difference. Contracts can be won or lost on small details, and customer satisfaction can be undermined by seemingly trivial product defects or negative service experiences. People exhibit personal discipline in the use of their professional judgment because they care for the organization and its people. Individual responsibilities rather than organizational rules guide action. Each organizational process, no matter how small, is vital, since it can make the difference between winning and losing. The family environment is critical to this approach.

Information flows freely throughout PPOs, enabling players to anticipate tasks rather than wait for instructions. People are aware of the tasks of others, and because all actions are aligned through the organization's clear focus, they help others when their own tasks are complete or when others are seen to need assistance. As a consequence, problems are fixed rather than talked about and anticipated rather than reacted to.

The last detail is directly related to peak performance. In preparation for the World Cup, the U.S. Soccer Federation ensured that the team reviewed a presentation on refereeing made by Esse Baharmast, their director of officials. By providing them with discreet knowledge of how top games are officiated, the team was able to avoid the potentially crippling impact of cautions and sending-off decisions. Baharmast called this "the one-percent contribution." Likewise, the 49ers leave no stone unturned to ensure that their players are not distracted from their game focus. All possible disturbances are removed from the players. From travel to training, every detail is calculated and taken care of by administrative staff. None of this is achieved by way of formal job descriptions. Catching the last detail is an attitude and mind-set that transcends any particular department or organizational function.

Exceeding Organizational Best

Exceeding organizational best is based on continually resetting higher challenges and beating them. The emphasis is on beating one's own best performance and the actions necessary to achieve that, rather than on results and beating the competition. PPO players exceed their personal best through a combination of hard work, creativity, commitment, and discipline. They have a deep commitment to improving their own knowledge, skills, and personal performance and are never satisfied. Creativity, risk taking, flair, and intuition are regarded as vital to finding the edge. Failure is acknowledged openly and learned from. People hold themselves supremely accountable for the impact that their particular job has on the final product and take responsibility for themselves and the organization. There is a commitment to "making the plays," and to deeds rather than words. The passion for improvement is relentless and never-ending—PPOs continually set more challenging, focused, and previous-best benchmarks—and beat them. Pride in accomplishment and a commitment to improving on prior performance have intrinsic value for participants.

Because the organization's focus is aligned to meeting the challenge it has set itself, when individuals exceed their personal best, peak flow is facilitated, which will then lead to exceeding organizational best. In the Atlanta Braves organization, exceeding organizational best is a way of life that means as much in the office as it does on the baseball diamond. In the early days of his tenure, General Manager John Schuerholz would look outside to other preeminent baseball franchises to get a fix on what individuals should do to try to be the best. When the Braves became a winning team, that focus shifted decisively toward internal assessment. "The spotlight is brighter here. The heat is turned up a notch more. Your expectations grow higher. We have high internal expectations; the external expectations are high too, but more important to us are our internal expectations."

Responsibility for personal performance extends to responsibility for others. People master their own areas of responsibility and research and experiment on an ongoing basis in order to learn more. They continuously discover new ways of performing their daily responsibilities. They learn about the responsibilities of others in order to interact better with them and educate others about their own area. Exceeding personal best extends to exceeding organizational best, which effectively renders performance management obsolete. Command and control and traditional leadership are redundant features in PPOs.

Can Any Organization Be a PPO?

The answer to this question is an unequivocal yes. Because each organization chooses its own greatest imaginable challenge and inspirational dream, it chooses the league in which it wishes to play. PPO Theory can assist any organization to be a peak performer in the context that it chooses—to be the best that it can be.

An organizational health warning: PPO Theory is not organizational steroids, not a quick fix. To become a PPO takes time. From the start of the Atlanta Braves' PPO development, almost ten years passed until their first winning season and World Series appearance. Michael Jordan joined the Chicago Bulls in 1984; their first NBA Championship did not come until 1991.

We recommend taking time out as an organization to reflect on current practice. The time out should involve everyone, as PPO Theory cannot be imposed from above—it has to be embraced from within. But inspirational players start the play. How each of the concepts should be implemented will be contingent on the existing organizational relationships and practices. A game plan should be developed through deep conversations among all participants and by applying intellectual pressure to aspects of organizational practice that are seen to be deficient. PPO Theory is more a state of organizational mind than a series of actions or activities. If the organization believes it can be a peak performer, it is well on the way to becoming one—the process of collective thinking about how to become a PPO will be instrumental in achieving sustainable success.

Organizations that adopt PPO Theory will be capable of developing sustainable peak performance. It offers a long-term development plan for organizations seeking to achieve and sustain their maximum potential. It can also provide a benchmark against which organizational achievements can be assessed. The practices have to be carefully constructed, usually over several years. How they are implemented and which ones are emphasized will vary from organization to organization. We are not suggesting one best way. There are an infinite variety of PPO progressions depending on the resources available and the inspirational players, but all the principles and concepts of PPO Theory must be developed to achieve sustained peak performance.

Sustaining Peak Performance

Achieving peak performance is easier than sustaining it. PPO progression is evolutionary, but regression can be rapid and dramatic. The loss of inspirational players, the destruction of the dream, the undermining or destabilization of the infrastructure can lead to PPO regression. Achievement of peak performance requires high levels of organizational fitness and skill development, and these must be maintained, but the key factor that enables sustainable winning lies in the requisite mental state. This can be achieved through the sustained application of all the concepts of PPO Theory to the organization. Yet it is not quite as simple as this.

The psychology of flow experience tells us that a challenge once met is no longer a challenge and consequently loses its status as an energizing driver. To sustain peak performance, the three concepts that make up the organization's purpose—the greatest imaginable challenge, the inspirational dream, and the focus—must remain in a strong relationship, while the challenge itself must be enriched or renewed periodically.

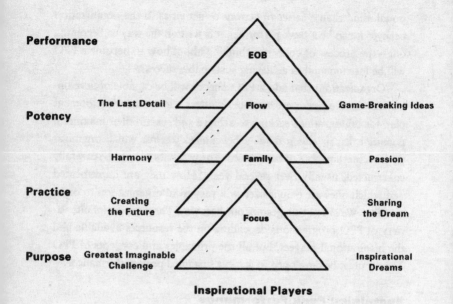

Performance

EOB

Potency

The Last Detail   Flow   Game-Breaking Ideas

Harmony   Family   Passion

Practice

Creating
the Future   Sharing
the Dream

Focus

Purpose   Greatest Imaginable
Challenge   Inspirational
Dreams

Inspirational Players

FIGURE 7—PPO Theory

Conclusion

The four PPO principles develop from each other and flow together
toward peak performance, as illustrated in Figure 7. The two base
concepts of each triangle support each peak or apex concept. All the
concepts develop from and relate to each other in a seamless manner,
summarized below.

> *Inspirational players provide a meaningful challenge for an orga-*
> *nization and its players that is both important and stretching and*
> *that becomes the focus of the organization's actions that are*
> *undertaken to live the dream, and in so doing a purpose to the or-*
> *ganization is established that must be nurtured for the future*
> *through the careful recruitment and development of the individu-*
> *als that make up the organization, together with a long-term*
> *commitment to an effective infrastructure that allows the dream*

to be shared, which builds an aura of association and sense of be-
longing and a feeling of family based on trusting relationships,
leading the participants to a sense of harmony with self and
others, and allowing a passionate commitment to the purpose of
the organization that establishes an environment with the potency
for peak flow or optimal organizational experiences, leading to
catching the last detail and imagining game-breaking ideas that
enable the continuous exceeding of organizational best in the end-
less pursuit of the organization's shared purpose and ultimately to
sustaining peak performance.

For a PPO implementation project to be successful, it must be
embraced by everyone within the organization and extended to the
7Ps (principals, players, purchasers, partners, philanthropy recipients, public, press). We believe that the PPO stories and theory are
accessible at all levels within potential PPOs, and as such we see this
book as important equipment for making it happen. We have also
developed a series of videos that take viewers on a unique tour behind the scenes of high-profile international sports organizations.
Through these images you will be able to envisage peak performance, thereby facilitating the PPO progression of your own organization.

In PPO theory, purpose replaces vision and mission, focus replaces strategy, flow replaces motivation, and inspiration replaces
leadership. Storytelling, not change management, provides the path-
way to peak performance. What is the purpose of your organization?
Why does it matter? How does it provide meaning to organizational
participants? PPO Theory can help you to make it happen.

The Teams

Soccer is the world's most popular sport. We were interested in studying the highly competitive European football scene. With its outstanding record in the World Cup we chose Germany as the domain for inquiry. At the time of our research in 1998 Germany was the reigning European champion, as it has been twice before in 1972 and 1980. At the time of writing,[25] no other European nation had won more than once, although France's success in the 2000 European Championship has now brought their total to two victories. FC Bayern Munich has dominated the German Bundesliga throughout its history, with fifteen Fussball–Meister titles, a further seven second-placings, and three third-placings, together with ten victories in the Deutscher Fussball–Bund (DFB) cup. In 1999, FCB were crowned Fussball–Meister, winning by a fifteen-point margin, the largest in the history of the league. In 2000, FC Bayern Munich secured victory in both the cup and the league. No other team comes remotely close to this record of continuous cup and league contention in Europe's most consistently competitive soccer nation.

Since 1972, up to and including the 1999 season, WilliamsF1 has won nine Formula One Constructors' Championships and seven World Drivers' Championships, compared with next-placed Ferrari and McLaren, which have won nine and eight Constructors' Championships respectively. During the 1990s, Williams won five Con-

[25] Team records were calculated as of 2 July 2000.

structors' Championships, McLaren three, and Ferrari one. The percentage win records related to all Grand Prix starts as of the end of 1999 were Ferrari nine percent, McLaren twelve percent, and Williams fourteen percent.

The New Zealand All Blacks rugby team has a relentless win record in excess of seventy-two percent sustained over a period of more than 100 years. During the 1990s the All Blacks won 73.9 percent of all international matches (next-placed Australia won 73.7 percent), and since turning professional during 1996–99 won 75.6 percent (Australia 72.9 percent). The All Blacks won the Rugby World Cup in 1987, but failed to win any of the three Cups during the 1990s. The Black Ferns won the inaugural Women's Rugby World Cup in 1998.

In 1998, the Chicago Bulls won their sixth National Basketball Association Championship in a fourteenth-straight NBA Championship play-off appearance. The Bulls' championship run began in 1990, and the team secured six championship rings in the next eight years. In the strike-shortened 1999 season, the Bulls dropped from first to bottom of the division after the retirement of Michael Jordan and Coach Jackson and the departure of Dennis Rodman, Luc Longley, and Scottie Pippen. There can be no question that the Bulls were the team of the 1990s. But can it rebuild? Will the Bulls be back? We believe they will.

Since their turnaround season in 1991 when the team went from worst to first, the Atlanta Braves have won nine consecutive divisional titles, five National League titles, and the World Series in 1995. No other team in the history of baseball has matched this level of sustained peak performance in a decade.

Since 1980, the San Francisco 49ers have amassed an amazing fourteen National Division championships, sixteen play-off appearances, and sixteen consecutive winning seasons. Along the way they converted NFC championships into five Super Bowl titles in 1981, 1984, 1988, 1989, and 1995. They have never lost a Super Bowl contest. The 49ers were the most successful NFL team of the 1980s and the 1990s. The record of 109–35 (76.4 percent) in the 1990s is the highest achievement in history, surpassing the previous record of 105 wins set by the Dallas Cowboys in the 1970s.

New Zealand, a country with a population roughly the size of San Diego, has been a dominant influence on the international yachting scene for the last decade. New Zealand reached the finals of the Louis Vuitton Challengers' Cup in 1987 and 1992. In 1995 Team New Zealand sailed away from heavily bankrolled international competitors to seize the America's Cup by the first 5–0 grand slam in the cup's illustrious 150-year history. In 2000, they repeated this score in the first-ever successful defense of the cup outside the United States.

The New York Yankees won 25 World Series and 36 American League championships during the twentieth century. With a World Series win in 1999, they became the unchallenged team of the century.

The U.S. Women's Soccer team won the World Cup in 1991, placed third in 1995, won Olympic gold in 1996, and recaptured the World Cup in 1999. They have won the U.S. Women's Cup playing against some of the world's preeminent national women's soccer teams in every year from inauguration to the time of writing.

The Australian Netball team has won eight out of ten World Championships in thirty-five years, and been placed second in the remaining two. In 1998 it won the inaugural Commonwealth Games gold medal for netball. It has remained dominant over a longer period than any other national team in our study. Netball is one of the most popular participant team sports in the world with seven million players in more than forty-five countries.

Cricket, the archetypal British game, is dominated by Britain's former colony Australia. Under the auspices of the *Australian Cricket Board*, the Test team has, since 1876, maintained a forty-two percent win record in all Test matches.* The West Indies, England and Australia have each secured three places in the finals of the seven cricket World Cups played since 1975. Although the West Indies has won twice, its last appearance in a final was in 1983, when it lost to

---

*In a game with a high preponderance of draws no other nation approaches this achievement.

India. England has never won. Australia has won twice, in 1987 and 1999, and was placed second to Sri Lanka in 1996.

Since 1988, the *Australian Women's Field Hockey* team has won three Olympic gold medals, in 1988, 1996 and 2000, the 1998 Commonwealth Games gold medal, two gold medals at the World Championships in 1994 and 1998, and gold medal for the last five Champions Trophy tournaments since 1991. The team has achieved an eighty percent win record in over 200 international games over the last decade.

Bibliography

Bennis, W., and P. Biederman, *Organizing Genius*, London: Nicholas Brealey, 1997.

Bethanis, S. J, "Language as Action: Metaphors with Organization Transformation," In S. Chawla and J. Renesch, eds, *Learning Organizations: Developing Cultures for Tomorrow's Workplace*, Portland, OR: Productivity Press, 1995.

Brandenberg, A. M., and B. J. Nalebuff, *Co-opetition*, London: HarperCollins, 1998.

Burns, T., and G. M. Stalker, *The Management of Innovation*, London: Tavistock, 1961.

Collins, J. C., and J. I. Porras, *Built to Last*, New York: HarperBusiness, 1994.

Csikszentmihalyi, M., *Beyond Boredom and Anxiety*, San Francisco: Jossey Bass, 1975.

————*Flow: The Psychology of Optimal Experience*, New York: Harper & Row, 1990.

————*Creativity: Flow and the Psychology of Discovery and Invention*, New York: HarperCollins, 1996.

————*Finding Flow: The Psychology of Engagement with Everyday Life*, New York: Basic Books, 1997.

Daft, R. L., *Organization Theory and Design*, New York: South Western, 1998.

Dyer, W. G., Jr., and A. L. Wilkins, "Better Stories, Not Better

Constructs to Generate Better Theory," Academy of Management Review, 16 (3), 1991.

Eisenhardt, K. M., "Building Theories from Case Study Research," *Academy of Management Review*, 14 (4), 1989.

Fowler, H. W., and Fowler, F. G., *The Concise Oxford Dictionary of Current English*, Oxford, Oxford University Press, 1964.

Greenleaf, Robert K. *Servant Leadership*, New York: Paulist Press, 1977.

Hodge, K., G. Sleivert, and A. McKenzie, eds., *Smart Training for Peak Performance*, Aukland: Reed Books, 1996.

Hofstede, G. H., *Cultures and Organizations* (rev. ed.), New York: McGraw-Hill, 1997.

Kouzes, J. and B. Posner, *The Leadership Challenge*, San Francisco: Jossey Bass, 1987.

Kushel, G., *Reaching the Peak Performance Zone: How to Motivate Yourself and Others to Excel*, New York: Amacom, 1994.

Peters, T. J., and R. H. Waterman, *In Search of Excellence: Lessons from America's Best-Run Companies*, New York: Harper & Row, 1982.

Schon, D., "Generative Metaphor: A Perspective on Problem Setting in Public Policy," in A. Otttony, ed., *Metaphor and Thought*, Cambridge: Cambridge University Press, 1993.

Senge, P. M. *The Fifth Discipline: The Art and Practice of the Learning Organization*, Milsons Point: Random House, 1993.

Slack, T., *Understanding Sports Organizations: The Application of Organziation Theory*, Champaign, IL: Human Kinetics, 1997.

Tichy, N. M., and R. Charan, "The CEO as Coach: An Interview with Allied Signal's Lawrence A. Bossidy," *Harvard Business Review*, 73 (2), 1995.

Wheatley, M. J., *Leadership and the New Science: Learning about Organization from an Orderly Universe*, San Francisco: Berrett-Koehler, 1994.

Index